An Introduction to
Jain Philosophy

It is well-known that the Jain tradition has been extremely influential in the development of Indian thought and culture. The Jain tradition teaches that there is an interdependence of perception, knowledge, and conduct unified by an axiomatic principle of non-violence in thought, speech, and action. In this way, non-violence defines the core of the Jain tradition, which has had a profound effect on other dharmic traditions originating in India. Jain Dharma is so significant that in some ways it may be incomplete to attempt to understand other Indian traditions (such as Buddhism or Hinduism) without knowing the basics of the Jain tradition, since these other traditions developed in an ongoing dialogue with the insights and wisdom of Jain respondents and visionaries.

This book enables the reader to enjoy a comprehensive journey into the intricate world of Jain thought and culture in a way that is philosophical in its compelling rationality, deeply spiritual in its revelations, yet accessible in its language. The organization of this book allows the reader to engage in an overview of the central teachings of the Jain tradition, but also to ascertain the profundity of its depths. It can be read with equal efficacy in succession from beginning to end, or pursued by individual topics of interest to the reader. Either strategy will have the same effect: a systematic understanding of what the timeless teachings of Jain thinkers have to say about the universal issues of the human condition - and how we might understand our harmonious relationship with other living entities as a powerful and effective spiritual journey.

An Introduction to Jain Philosophy

Based on Writings and Discourses by
Ācārya Sushil Kumar

Parveen Jain

Foreword by Rita Sherma
Prologue by Jeffery D. Long
Edited by Cogen Bohanec

DK PRINTWORLD
Publishers of Indian Traditions

ISBN: 978-1-7332236-2-1 (paperback)

The Parveen and Neeraj Jain Endowment
2636 Gayley Place
San Jose, California 95135
PNJEndowment@gmail.com
www.parveenjain.com

D.K. Printworld (P) Ltd. (hardcover only)
Vedaśrī, F-395, Sudarshan Park
ESI Hospital Metro Station, New Delhi - 110015
www.dkprintworld.com
indology@dkprintworld.com

Hardcover originally published in India in 2019
Paperback published in 2021

First edition
9 8 7 6 5 4 3 2 1

To

Ācārya Sushil Kumar

— my Gurujī and beacon of light —
whose inspiration and spiritual guidance
awakened me to connect with my inner-self

and

Neeraj Jain

— my wife and soulmate —
for everything

Contents

Ācārya Sushil Kumar

Ācārya Sushil Kumar (1926-94) is one of the most revered Jain monks of the twentieth century. He was a pioneer Jain monk who traveled outside of India to globally promote Jain philosophy and its message of peace and brotherhood. He was the architect of a systematic endeavor to establish the Jain tradition outside of India – especially in North America. In doing so, he worked with religious and non-religious leaders from around the world to educate them of the rich heritage of Jain Dharma.

Fondly addressed as Gurujī by his followers, Ācārya Sushil Kumar was born on 15 June 1926 in a small village called Shikhopur (now known as Sushil Garh) in Haryana, India. His parents, Pandit Sunehara Singh and Bharati Devi, who were Hindu brahmins, named him Sardar Singh. From the age of seven, he started living with his father's sister and her husband. From there, he eventually traveled to Jagraon – a small town in Punjab – to visit and seek blessings from a Jain monk, Muni Chhote Lal. Young Sardar Singh was so mesmerized by the inspirational discourses on Jain Dharma by Muni Chhote Lal that he decided, and got his uncle's consent, to remain with the monk.

Before his eighth birthday, Sardar Singh started living like an ascetic under the guidance of his *guru*, Muni Chhote Lal. He immersed himself in the study of Jain Dharma, mastering Ardhamāgadhī, Prākr̥t, and Sanskrit – the languages in which Jain scriptures are written – and began memorizing all the major Jain scriptures with astounding comprehension. Sardar Singh studied and developed a thorough understanding of the *namokāra mahāmantra* at an early age. He learned the science and spirituality behind the *mantra*'s formulation and the immense powers associated with its chanting. He mastered the art of awakening those powers and continued to have an uncompromising faith in *namokāra mahāmantra*. Gurujī practiced it till his last breath.

Once, during meditation Sardar Singh envisioned another Jain monk, Muni Roop Chand – a profoundly spiritual mendicant who had lived several decades earlier and whose memorial (*samādhi*) was located in Jagraon, the town where Gurujī had the first inspiration to become an ascetic. Thereafter, he started experiencing frequent appearances of Muni Roop Chand and would receive exquisite teachings and expositions on Jain philosophy. Soon, Sardar Singh began to venerate Muni Roop Chand as his spiritual *guru*. In one such appearance, Muni Roop Chand prompted him to get ordained as a Jain monk and Sardar Singh decided to pursue the suggested path of austerity. He sought and obtained consent from his parents for the same. With the blessings of his worldly *guru*, Muni Chhote Lal, young Sardar Singh was formally initiated as a Jain monk on 20 April 1942, at the age of fifteen years. For this auspicious event, he chose Jagraon, the very city where Muni Roop Chand had first appeared to him. From now on, Sardar Singh would be known as Muni Sushil Kumar.

As a monk, Gurujī started spending all of his time in personal spiritual growth. In addition to learning Jain scriptures, he underwent intense yogic training and self-practices to master meditation, *yoga*, and *samādhi* (deep state of meditation). He mastered the science of astrology, *mantra*s, breathing (*prāṇāyāma*), and chanting. In conjunction with this rigorous practice, he earned various advanced Indian academic degrees in religion, literature, and history. Along with all this, he developed extraordinary oratory skills to eloquently deliver Lord Mahāvīra's message.

By the mid-1950s, well before the age of thirty years, Gurujī had become one of the foremost religious figures of India and was recognized as an effective purveyor of the fundamental truth (*tattva*) and wisdom. He traveled all across India on foot, as required by the vows of Jain monkhood. It is estimated that he walked over sixty thousand miles before starting to use mechanized vehicles in 1975. Gurujī's discourses were routinely attended by thousands of people from all walks of life. In particular, the young and educated people were attracted to him because of his rational and highly logical explanations. He was rapidly becoming a force of progressive change for wider proliferation of Jain Dharma, especially among the young Jains. He undertook several initiatives for the benefit of the Jain community, which included promoting the use of harmless technologies (such as microphones and electric lights) by the ascetics, engaging youth in spiritual activities, promoting the Jain way of life, women's education, and facilitating the unification of the tradition-splintered monk groups.

Gurujī's charismatic personality and spiritual acumen were winning admiration from all the religious, cultural, and social circles, including the prime minister, Pt. Jawaharlal Nehru, and president, Dr. Rajendra Prasad of India. His influence had extended beyond the borders of India. In November 1957, at the age of just thirty-one years, he organized the first World Religions Conference in New Delhi, where people of all faiths from around the world participated. Over 100,000 people attended the opening session. Gurujī organized six more successful World Religions Conferences in the subsequent twenty years.

Gurujī firmly believed in the profound impact of spirituality on the cultural, social, and political fabric of the society. He had unwavering belief that only genuine *ahiṁsā* (non-violence) and peaceful means could provide lasting solutions for human disputes. He emphasized *ahiṁsā* in all walks of life and worked tirelessly to foster the sense of universal brotherhood. Gurujī was revered by the followers of all faiths. They trusted his objective and impartial judgments and regularly sought his guidance in amicably resolving their inter-faith conflicts.

Gurujī's global reach and popularity were rising but he was continually distressed by the escalating violence and conflicts around the world. He was convinced that the world needed to hear Lord Mahāvīra's message of *ahiṁsā* more than ever before. One day, during meditation, Manidhāri Jinchandra Suri Dādā Guru, a legendary twelfth-century Jain monk reverently called Dādā Guru by his devotees, appeared and implored him to travel outside of India to bring Lord Mahāvīra's teachings to the world stage. This was Guruji's calling. He decided to travel abroad as a messenger of peace to stimulate Jains residing in foreign lands to organize and raise the awareness of Jain teachings. But before that, he had to make a significant decision – to travel using mechanized means forbidden for Jain monks (despite the growing evidence that Jain monks had used means such as boats during Lord Pārśvanātha and Lord Mahāvīra's times). He made this bold decision, keeping in mind the larger good of humanity.

Gurujī received blessings and tacit support from Jain and non-Jain monks and *ācārya*s for success in this remarkable endeavor. He picked the second day after his forty-ninth birthday as the day to embark on this mission.

On the historic day of 17 June 1975, Muni Sushil Kumar boarded an airplane bound for the United States. He was about to go on the mission of his lifetime – to promote Lord Mahāvīra's message where it was needed the most – for which he had become a monk in the first place. This was such a momentous day that a special session of India's parliament was convened to give him a warm send-off. At the time of his departure, large crowds had gathered on the route and at the airport to show their admiration and enthusiasm for the mission he was undertaking.

Thereafter, Gurujī embarked upon non-stop travel to all the large and small cities, towns, and villages around the world. He motivated Jain communities to practice Jain Dharma and educate people around them to promote the philosophy. Very soon, with his inspiration, there were over fifty Jain institutions and temples in North America, and more in other parts of the world. In doing so, he steadfastly remained focused on the fundamentals of Jain doctrine without indulging in any sectarian or ritualistic nuances. Education was always in the forefront of Gurujī's thinking, and to that end, he worked with several universities of the world to start offering courses on Jain philosophy. In addition, he helped secure a permanent representation of Jains on the global platform at the United Nations.

All along, Gurujī maintained vigilance to the furtherance of his efforts in India as well. Over the years, with his inspiration, several institutions had been established in India. He regularly visited India and stayed connected with those institutions. In 1980, with the blessings from the supreme Jain Ācārya, Gurujī was conferred the esteemed religious title of Jain Ācārya by the revered Ācārya Amar Muni (Kavijī) in a function attended by several renowned religious dignitaries. Thereafter, Gurujī founded Arhat Jain Sangha, an order of ascetics from all Jain traditions and sects, which was honorably felicitated in March 1987 by the president of India, Giani Zail Singh, in a gathering of many prominent Jain and other scholars and religious leaders.

Gurujī had always envisaged the creation of a profound and everlasting center of pilgrimage (*tīrtha*) outside of India, where all Jains and like-minded people would visit to spiritually reinvigorate themselves and stay connected with the Jain heritage. The historic moment came in 1983 when Gurujī inspired the founding of Siddhachalam in New Jersey (United States). He had pictured Siddhachalam to be the center of spirituality, education, and culture to promote the rich heritage of Jain Dharma. Over the years, Siddhachalam has flourished into a true spiritual abode. With over 121 acres of wooded land, sprinkled with temples and chambers for spiritual, religious, meditation, and *yoga* practices, Siddhachalam provides a perfectly natural environment of peace and tranquility.

Ācārya Sushil Kumar's influence was soaring along with his continuing success in his mission. His followers believed he would continue on this path for many more years, but destiny had something different in store. On 22 April 1994, while at his ashram in New Delhi, Gurujī delivered his normal discourse and chanted in the morning. Thereafter, in the afternoon, to everyone's overwhelming shock, his soul left his body for its next heavenly journey. Gurujī bid his final farewell blissfully at the age of sixty-seven years in a meditative state sitting in a lotus posture – considered to be a truly auspicious state.

Interestingly, the week of 20 April was of great significance in Gurujī's life: 20 April 1942 was the day of his initiation into monkhood, and 22 April 1994 was the day his soul departed for its heavenly abode.

To summarize, Ācārya Sushil Kumar comprehended Jain Dharma and genuinely personified it at the most fundamental level. As the young Sardar Singh, he immersed himself in the profound teachings of Lord Mahāvīra. He persevered to learn all aspects of monastic life and modeled his life to be a true Jain. As Muni Sushil Kumar, he reached the summit of his popularity at a very young age but did not allow it to affect his reverence and stalwart commitment to Jain Dharma, its originators, and the *gurus* from whom he learnt it. The highest-ranking individuals from all walks of life regularly visited and bowed in front of him, but he remained humble without letting his ego get in the way. He was revered by hundreds of thousands of people in India, but happily gave all that up and came to America so he could propound the values of *ahiṁsā* and peace in a global forum – sometimes to only a handful of people at a time. As a monk, and then as an *ācārya*, he inspired the founding of a multitude of great spiritual institutions, but never let his name precede the institutions. He had no attachments to, or personal expectations from, those institutions. He never put himself ahead of Jain Dharma, the *tīrthaṅkara*s, or his *guru*s. Ācārya Sushil Kumar possessed profound wisdom and the clearest understanding of the fundamental truth (*tattva*), yet he considered himself to be a dutiful disciple of the great teachers. He considered his life to be a journey of learning and self-improvement, and he lived it exactly that way.

The writings and discourses by a profoundly wise thinker, spiritual practitioner, and apostle of peace like Gurujī serve as a great source for learning about Jain Dharma. This perception became the motivating force behind the creation of this book. It has been prepared with inspiration from his lifelong work and the thoughtful interpretation of his teachings.

Foreword

WHILE there are several excellent books on the topic of Jain Dharma, until the production of the current work there has been a scarcity of published voices from *within* the Jain tradition represented in both popular and academic presentations of this important tradition. However, the reader will be pleased to find that this is not only a work that articulates the broad vision of the Jain tradition in an approachable and profound way, but it represents two very important voices from within the tradition: the teachings of the venerable Jain saint, Ācārya Sushil Kumar, and Dr. Parveen Jain, who has been a stalwart leader in the North American Jain community for decades.

As it stands, this important work is of immense value to anyone who has an interest in learning about the Jain tradition, from those whose knowledge of the tradition is sparse, to academics who are experts in the tradition and who will benefit from a systematic exploration of Jain teachings – and especially for those who belong to this powerful dhārmic tradition that has been so influential on Indian thought and culture. It is a rare quality for a book on a specific religious tradition to be simultaneously comprehensive in its scope and nuanced in delivering easy-to-apprehend profundity. This is a great achievement on the part of Dr. Jain, and an important contribution to the proliferation of this jewel amongst humanity's aggregate wisdom.

Jai Jinendra!

Dr. Rita Sherma
Director of Mira and Ajay Shingal Center for Dharma Studies
Associate Professor of Dharma Studies and Core Doctoral Faculty
Graduate Theological Union (GTU)
Berkeley, California, and
Editor of the *Journal of Dharma Studies*

Prologue

I WAS delighted when my friend Dr. Parveen Jain invited me to write a prologue to his very important and timely book, based on the teachings of Ācārya Sushil Kumar in English and making them available to a global audience. My own interest in Jainism, like my interest in Indian spiritual paths and philosophies in general, emerged early in life, the result of a convergence of an innate interest in the "big questions" of human existence, and a series of tragedies that befell my family in my childhood. Concepts such as *karma* and rebirth have always made a great deal of sense to me, evoking in me a desire to understand the cultures and traditions in which these concepts emerged. Similarly, non-violence has always seemed to me, intuitively, to be preferable to violence, and long ago I began to feel that we live in a society and in a world where cruelty is all too common, and that there must be a better way to live.

One idea, in particular, that I have long found to be compelling, is captured in Sri Ramakrishna's teaching, *yato mat, tato path*: The world's religions are so many paths to the highest realization. When, early in my graduate studies, I came upon the Jain teachings of Anekāntavāda, Nayavāda, and Syādvāda, I was immediately drawn in by the vision of a logical system for articulating how it is that diverse systems of thought, each making claims that appear, on the surface, to contradict one another, could actually exhibit a deeper harmony, when properly contextualized and viewed in a non-absolutist light. I dedicated my doctoral studies to elucidating this profound Jain wisdom and showing its relevance to contemporary conversations around truth and the diversity of worldviews. This eventually led to a deeper study of Jainism as a whole, and to my authoring a textbook, *Jainism: An Introduction*, which gives a broad overview of this ancient tradition.

Dr. Parveen Jain has done a great service to the Jain tradition, as well as to humanity as a whole, by making the teachings of his revered Gurujī available to the English-speaking world. Our world is very much in need of Jain wisdom.

While the Jain teachings of *ahiṁsā*, *anekānta*, and *aparigraha* have always been deeply relevant to human existence, there is a particular urgency today in getting these teachings to the wider world. Our environmental crisis, brought on by heedless consumption of the earth's resources, and facilitated by our greed, and by our lack of regard for life forms other than ourselves, as well as our political crisis, in which there is an ever-growing lack of respect for the other – whether that be another nation, another ethnic group, another religion, or another party – make the Jain message an especially important and timely one.

Ācārya Sushil Kumar had the foresight to perceive the crisis into which humanity was, even in his time, plunging headlong, and in which we find ourselves today. He knew that something radical was needed in order to address our current situation. Rather than abiding by the traditional Jain strictures forbidding a monk from traveling abroad – rooted though these are in the wisdom of non-violence towards all living things – he brought the wisdom of his tradition to a – for him – foreign shore and established the *āśrama* at Siddhachalam, providing a beacon in North America for those who would be drawn to the Jain path. Dr. Parveen Jain, having written this volume, is carrying forward his *guru*'s vision and spreading knowledge of Jain thought to an audience that might not otherwise become aware of its profundity and its importance.

I have myself had the privilege of staying and speaking at Siddhachalam several times. Gurujī's spirit of *ahiṁsā* – of complete non-violence – pervades this place. During my first visit, my wife and I got up one morning and left the guesthouse where we were staying to walk to the main building where a conference was being held, and where I was to present a lecture. When we left the guesthouse, on the front sidewalk there was a small bird, looking up at us and showing absolutely no fear whatsoever. We thought at first that he must be injured, because he did not fly away as we walked towards him to make our way to the main building. We looked at him closely, and he looked up at us, and then, eventually, flew away. His odd behavior was not due to any injury. He was simply completely unafraid of human beings. It was as if he knew that he was in a place of non-violence, where no harm would come to him. On subsequent visits, we observed similar behavior by deer and other wild animals. Siddhachalam, due to the *ācārya*'s influence, has become a microcosm of what our entire world could be, if only we would all follow the path of *ahiṁsā*, *anekāntavāda*, and *aparigraha* (non-violence, non-absolutism, and non-attachment).

This book is a comprehensive overview of Jain philosophy and it makes the subtlest and most difficult Jain concepts understandable to the average educated reader. I believe this book will become important both for scholars of Jain and Indian philosophy as a whole, and for laypersons wishing to better understand these teachings. Thank you, Dr. Parveen Jain!

Dr. Jeffery D. Long
Professor of Religion and Asian Studies
Elizabethtown College

Preface

OVER the years, I have heard from many young Jains – especially those born outside of India – about the need for a book in English that provides an easy-to-understand overview of the Jain doctrine. There are numerous books, commentaries, and interpretations on this subject in most major languages, so one may ask why such a need exists. In my view, there are three important elements that need attention to speak to the modern audience. First, the discourse should have a Western context which resonates with global readers. Second, the content should focus on the philosophy of the Jain tradition without emphasizing sectarian or ritualistic practices. And third, the book should provide an overview rather than writings on specific research topics which appeal more to the academic community or advanced readers.

The above observations served as the key motivators for this project. Fortunately, there already exists a set of extraordinary writings and transcripts of discourses by Ācārya Sushil Kumar which eloquently describe the Jain philosophy. Ācārya Sushil Kumar (affectionately addressed as Gurujī by his followers) was a great Jain monk during the twentieth century. He was astoundingly knowledgeable and was unmatched as a Jain philosopher. With unwavering belief in the teachings of Lord Mahāvīra, Gurujī lived a truly fulfilling life of a Jain mendicant. His deep and unblemished understanding of the doctrine was instrumental in enabling him to succinctly discern and articulate the intricacies of Jain teachings in easy-to-follow terms. Gurujī was a tremendous orator who captivated large audiences in his frequent sermons. Using the same acumen, he explained the doctrine in his writings and discourses while staying on the philosophical plane, avoiding ritualistic and sectarian aspects. With all these inimitable attributes, I found Gurujī's work to be a uniquely qualified source of learning for all those who are hungry to study a doctrine that is so important and critically relevant for humanity today.

Most of Gurujī's original works are in Hindi and to thoroughly and truthfully interpret them was a monumental task. I have earnestly tried to accurately and comprehensively present his elucidation of the Jain philosophy. Much of my understanding of the doctrine comes from listening to Gurujī's discourses and studying the literature written by him, my own self-studies as a lifelong practitioner, and conversations with other Jain scholars. Although I was fortunate to spend a lot of time with Gurujī, only a small fraction of that was devoted to discussions on Jain philosophy. However, contact with exalted individuals like him can be edifying and transformative in very subtle ways just by being in their proximity and observing them.

I consider myself a common Jain householder and have endeavored to use that as a strength in this undertaking. It has enabled me to describe Jain Dharma in a language which is not overly academic yet is an accurate representation of Gurujī's work. This book, purposed to serve as a source for an overview of Jain doctrine for both academic and non-academic readers, is intended to generate spiritual curiosity and become a stimulant for deeper studies and research of the Jain doctrine, tradition, and the Jain way of life.

This project commenced more than twenty years after Gurujī left his body. Thus, a lot of diligence was needed to understand and convey his thoughts as expressed in his work. To this end, I have herein supplemented his work with my recollections of private conversations with him, his public discourses, and my conversations with other scholars. The strength of the resulting work does not speak to my spiritual or writing abilities but to Gurujī's extraordinary ability to explain the highly intricate subject in simple language. I hope to have accurately captured and presented his thoughts. My sincere apologies for any and all oversights because they are reflective of my shortcomings and are not of his doing.

Finally, Jain tradition provides a comprehensive rational road map for a righteous and structured lifestyle that is highly beneficial for humanity, both at individual and societal levels. The doctrine addresses the integrated and interdependent coexistence of all human and non-human living beings with the ecology and environment. Lord Mahāvīra framed and elucidated the Jain doctrine more than 2,500 years ago. Over the centuries, although some deviations have occurred in the way it is practiced, its fundamental tenets have remained unchanged and are as applicable today as they were centuries ago, if not more so. This speaks to the strength and comprehensiveness of the Jain philosophy. This book is an attempt to introduce the Jain doctrine to those who desire greater awareness of this great tradition, and I hope to have succeeded in that endeavor.

Jai Jinendra!

Parveen Jain

Acknowledgments

I AM indebted to some esteemed individuals who provided significant help during the course of this project. Dr. Rita D. Sherma is foremost among them. She provided invaluable guidance and advice throughout the project in transforming the original idea into a reality. Dr. Sherma is Director of the Mira and Ajay Shingal Center for Dharma Studies at the Graduate Theological Union (GTU) in Berkeley, California. She is Associate Professor of Dharma Studies, GTU Core Doctoral Faculty, and Editor of the *Journal of Dharma Studies*.

I would like to express my special thanks to Cogen Bohanec for his editorial assistance during the course of this project. At the time of this writing, he was a graduate student pursuing a PhD in Religious Studies at GTU, a world-renowned university for theological studies; he had acquired his MA degree in Buddhist Studies from the same school in 2015. Cogen dexterously reviewed and edited my manuscript and provided invaluable feedback for it to become an effective source for learning the fundamentals of Jain philosophy. I was fortunate to have him as a partner in this project and truly appreciate his precious contributions to this endeavor.

We have on many occasions referred to *The A to Z of Jainism* by Kristi L. Wiley (2009), and I would like to make a special mention of her work. It is difficult to translate the philosophical terms from one language to another while preserving their intent and true meaning. It becomes even harder when the language being translated is not in common use. Such is the case with the original scriptures of Jain Dharma, most of which are in the Ardhamāgadhī language, which prevailed 2,500 years ago in Lord Mahāvīra's time. Through her extensive research efforts, Dr. Wiley compiled and described in the abovementioned book many of the terms used in Jain scriptures. Her work has become valuable reference material for this project and would be such for any scholars or others who are interested in Jain studies.

As noted in the preface, sources of material for this book include the writings of Ācārya Sushil Kumar (Gurujī), his public discourses, the author's notes of personal conversations with him, and the author's personal research and his conversations with other Jain scholars. In particular, the book *Jain Dharma* (written in Hindi), authored by Gurujī in 1958, was used as a major source. Recently, two organizations of his followers have published separate Hindi-language versions of the original book. The two organizations, which have copyrights to their respective Hindi versions, are Vishwa Ahimsa Sangh (Acharya Sushil Ashram, Ahimsa Bhawan, Shanker Road, New Delhi) and Acharya Sushil Muni Memorial Trust (Acharya Sushil Ashram, C-599, Chetna Marg, Defence Colony, New Delhi).

Many other individuals helped me during the course of this project. In particular, I would like to thank Carrie Picket for proofreading the manuscript very diligently, Sharon Donovan for sharing with me the nuances of publishing, and Susheel Mittal, the publisher, for working patiently with me and for producing a high-quality product.

Finally, I have been gifted with a very special family, and no words can describe my love and respect for my wife, Neeraj, and our children, Puneet, Rupali, Manu, and Navita. They have been the pillars of my strength, not only during this project, but through all of the endeavors in my life.

Editor's Note

THE current editor has made an effort to convert and translate many of the technical terms employed in this book into Sanskrit. Generally, the original terms and content of this book were acquired by Dr. Parveen Jain from Hindi sources of Ācārya Sushil Kumar's works. Dr. Jain has deftly translated the writings and discourses of Ācārya Sushil Kumar and, as needed, has applied his own knowledge of the Jain tradition.

It is not uncommon for technical terms that originate in a Jain text to be translated into their (approximate) Sanskrit equivalents in English works on Jain Dharma. This is done, in part, as a way to orient the material around a broader understanding of Indian thought for the benefit of English readers who tend to favor Sanskrit terms over other possible Indian linguistic sources. While most early Jain texts were written in a Prākr̥t language (such as Ardhamāgadhī, although there certainly are Sanskrit Jain works), and contemporary Jain thinkers often employ modern vernaculars (Hindi, etc.), it seems, to the current editor, that the best way to ground all of these linguist streams into a broader, (Indian) indigenous lexicon is to employ Sanskrit approximations of the terms that may originate from these other Indian languages (i.e., Hindi, Prākr̥t, etc.).

This choice isn't at all unconventional in terms of English works in the field of Jain Dharma. However, the reader who is familiar with such Sanskrit terms from the context of other dhārmic traditions (such as Buddhist and Hindu traditions) should employ caution since their use in the Jain context will no doubt have unique connotations that are befitting to the unique cosmology, philosophy, and other norms of the Jain tradition. A certain charitable semantic flexibility would be advised on the part of the reader – regarding both English and Sanskrit terms – so that connotations outside of the Jain tradition are not imported, thereby distorting the tradition. This will allow one to broaden one's connotative association with these (English and Sanskrit) words to include the unique worldview of Jain Dharma, and thereby broaden the reader's worldview in general. Such flexibility will go far to ensure that as little as is possible is "lost in translation," and that this important and insightful tradition can be understood *on its own terms*.

In short, regarding issues of language and otherwise, the reader is encouraged to *listen carefully* to what the tradition has to say about itself by allowing the reader's own interpretive lenses to be clear and open to the message of Jain Dharma – a message that, among a plethora of other merits, has broad potential in terms of addressing many urgent problems facing the current era of humanity.

Cogen Bohanec
Editor
Graduate Theological Union
Berkeley, California

Scheme of Transliteration

VOWELS

अ *a*	आ *ā*	इ *i*	ई *ī*	उ *u*	ऊ *ū*	ऋ *r̥*	ॠ *r̥̄*[1]
(Roman)	(palm)	(it)	(police)	(put)	(rule)	(rig)	
ऌ *ḷ*	ॡ *ḹ*[1]	ए *e*	ऐ *ai*	ओ *o*	औ *au*		
(able)		(there)	(aisle)	(no)	(loud)		

CONSONANTS

Guttural	क *ka*	ख *kha*[2]	ग *ga*	घ *gha*[2]	ङ *ṅa*
	(skate)	(blockhead)	(gate)	(ghost)	(sing)
Palatal	च *ca*	छ *cha*[2]	ज *ja*	झ *jha*[2]	ञ *ña*
	(chunk)	(catch him)	(john)	(hedgehog)	(bunch)
Cerebral	ट *ṭa*	ठ *ṭha*[2]	ड *ḍa*	ढ *ḍha*[2]	ण *ṇa*
	(start)	(anthill)	(dart)	(godhead)	(under)
Dental	त *ta*	थ *tha*[2]	द *da*	ध *dha*[2]	न *na*
	(path)	(thunder)	(that)	(this)	(numb)
Labial	प *pa*	फ *pha*[2]	ब *ba*	भ *bha*[2]	म *ma*
	(spin)	(philosophy)	(bin)	(abhor)	(much)
Semi-vowels	य *ya*	र *ra*	ल *la*[3]	व *va*[4]	
	(young)	(drama)	(luck)	(vile)	
Sibilants	श *śa*[5]	ष *ṣa*[5]	स *sa*	ह *ha*	
	(shove)	(bushel)	(so)	(hum)	
Others	क्ष *kṣa*	त्र *tra*	ज्ञ *jña*		
	(*kṣatriya*)	(*triśūla*)	(*jñānī*)		

अं (ं) *ṁ anusvāra* is a nasal off-glide that immediately follows the pronunciation of a vowel as in *saṁskr̥ti*.

अः *visarga* = *ḥ* consists in abrupt release of breath after a vowel as in *prātaḥ*.

ऽ *avagraha* shows non-pronunciation, that is, deletion of "a" after "e" or "o" as in *ime 'vasthitāḥ*. In Vedic Sanskrit, it can also show word division.

HINDI LETTERS (extras)

ँ = *m̐*	ं = *ṅ*	ड़ = *ṛa*	ढ़ = *ṛha*
(*candrabindu*)	(*anusvāra*)		

---

1 Longer form of the preceding vowel.

2 Aspirated forms of the preceding consonants. The compound words given as examples should be pronounced without a syllabic break at the underlined places. The combinations "tha" and "pha" should not be pronounced as fricatives.

3 Retroflexed and written "L"as "*ḷa*" in certain phonetic contexts.

4 Pronounced like "w," without aspiration.

5 The sound "*śa*" is palatal; "*ṣa*" cerebral or retroflex.

1

Characteristics of Jain Dharma (Jain Dharma kā Svarūpa)

FROM ancient times, philosophers and thinkers have had differing opinions about religion and its role in life and society. The result of these differences is that today hundreds of different sectarian groups have come into existence around the world, and new ones continue to be formed regularly. Right from the beginning, there have been many religious philosophies that have had positive impacts on society. At the same time, on many occasions, sectarian forces have controlled and manipulated religion and its disposition in society. In a way, this is similar to how political forces have biased the progression in science and technology for their own agendas.

Since time immemorial, human beings have utilized the platform of religion and science for the search of truth. Asia has been the world's source of many religious explorations and evolutions. The continent has been the birthplace of many of the world's foremost religious canons that have come to diffuse across the entire globe. Within Asia, India has been at the forefront of many of those religious and spiritual developments, especially those that promote communal living integrated with nature and ecology. Jain, Buddhist, and Vedic doctrines are some of India's monumental contributions to the world religions, while Christianity, Islam, and Judaism all originated in Palestine and Arabia. The Zoroastrian religion, which originated in Iran, thrived at one time but is all but extinct now, except for a small community in India, where they are known as Parsis. The religious philosophies of Confucianism and Taoism came from China, and Japan was the birthplace of the Shinto religion.

The originators and philosophical thinkers behind the religions of the world may have not necessarily intended to initiate a new religion, and often only sought to unravel and promulgate eternal religious truths that are beyond the limitations of time. For their followers, their work has illustrated ways to realize the Ultimate Truth.

Lord Mahāvīra,[1] the most recent great teacher of the Jain tradition, says, "All the *Jina Arhant*[2] divinities (*tīrthaṅkaras*[3]) of the past, present, and future, expound only one and the same eternally profound framework of doctrines."[4] This framework is defined by the principles of "non-violence against all living beings, non-persecution of all living beings, and never enslaving anyone nor allowing oneself to be enslaved by anyone."

Similar to the spirit of the Jain tradition, while addressing his disciples, Lord Buddha stated:

> My fellow monks, I have envisioned an ancient pathway that has been adopted by pre-historic *arihantas* (great teachers). By following the trails illustrated by them, I have been able to demystify many fundamental principles of nature and divinity.[5]

There is a *mantra* in the *Ṛgveda*[6] that states: "There is only real truth, but the scholars express their interpretations in many different ways."[7] By this, one can see a commonality whereby the true religions of the world are not just empty

---

1 Mahāvīra, the honorific title meaning "Great Hero," and prevalent name of Vardhamāna Jñātṛputra, is the twenty-fourth and last of the Jain *tīrthaṅkaras* of the current era, who lived in the sixth century BCE (599-527).

2 *Jina* or *jina arhant* or *arhant*, literally "spiritual victor," who has attained omniscience, is worthy of worship and is still in body form.

3 *Tīrthaṅkaras* are the preceptors, ford-makers, saviors, and spiritual teachers of the righteous path, who have absolutely and completely conquered all personal deficiencies such as attachment, hatred, anger, ego, deceit, and greed.

4 *Savve jīva na hantavva.* (All of the *jīvas* should be spared all types of hurt.)

5 In the Jain tradition, "divinity" refers to the auspicious attributes resulting from the attainment of right perception (*samyag-darśana*), right knowledge (*samyag-jñāna*), and right conduct (*samyag-cāritra*) – the terms to be defined in subsequent chapters. It refers to the qualities and auspiciousness of the enlightened *jinas* (*tīrthaṅkaras*) who have achieved perfection and have freed themselves from the shackles of rebirth cycles. Since Jain tradition does not believe in God as the creator, there is no single divine figure, and all the *jinas* or *tīrthaṅkaras* are considered to be the divine figures.

6 An ancient Indian collection of canonical, sacred Vedic Sanskrit hymns.

7 *Ekaṁ sad viprā bahudhā vadanti* – *Ṛgveda* 1.164.46

dogmas. Their tenets are defined by a set of teachings related to the cause, nature, purpose, and formation of the universe. By a common dialectic in Indian thought, the variegated teachings of each religion are not the exhaustive truth but are multiple pursuits of the one Ultimate Truth. Each of these religions constitutes a field of research for truth in itself, and collectively they may be seen to illustrate a direction to achieve the perception of the irrevocable truth of reality.

In Jain Dharma, this pursuit of the Ultimate Truth by different religions is described as the *dharma* (doctrine) of Anekāntavāda[8] – the tenet describing multiple manifestations of one Ultimate Truth. This is an encompassing and eternal doctrine because it ascribes that no single unilateral (partial) view of truth can be considered predominant (absolute truth) among the diversity of coexisting, multilateral expressions of truth that are found in the world's many traditions.

However, many religions have asserted their individual, unilateral expressions of truth. This has resulted in the development of several hundred diverse religious dogmas in India alone. They may claim to be unique based on their definitions and understandings of truth, and their followers may continue to diverge from other beliefs or even from the irrevocable truth itself. However, such unilateral belief systems that act outside of the dialogical relationship of a pluralistic religious environment may give rise to incomplete understanding that is devoid of a more inclusive perspective. If more religions were to recognize that there might be multiple interpretations of the Ultimate Truth, their differences would be based solely on the principles of reality and truth, and they would not differentiate on the basis of artificial variances and arguments designed for self-promotion. In fact, it could be argued that the essence and inherent nature of religions should be one and the same – the pursuit of the Ultimate Truth and acceptance of the right to live in peace and tranquility with all living beings.

Lord Mahāvīra discussed 363 different religious doctrines during his era.

---

[8] *Anekāntavāda*, meaning "non-absolutism," described later, is a unique principle, and one of the basic principles, of Jain Dharma that encourages acceptance of relativism and pluralism. According to this doctrine, truth and reality are perceived differently from different points of view, and no single point of view is the absolute and complete truth.

Some of those were doctrines driven by ritualistic practices (*kriyāvādī*), others were based on ethical codes (*vinayavādī*), and even others were put forth by sceptics or agnostics (*ajñānavādī*). There was no coordination between them. The glaring mistake has been that while following the practices of one religion one often ignores or disputes other teachings or practices of the same religion, or teachings or practices of other religions. For example, the practitioners of ritualistic acts, who expect to achieve spiritual advancement, may dispute non-ritualistic practices which emphasize spiritual advancement by learning and practicing religious principles though studies, contemplation, and meditation to conquer anger, ego, deceit, and greed. This results in an unwarranted, one-sided insistence on a single point of view, while another seemingly opposing viewpoint could be equally imperative or impactful.

Wisdom and Ethics Described in the Sthānāṅgasūtra

In the Jain scripture *Sthānāṅgasūtra*, Lord Mahāvīra taught two aspects of religion (*dharmas*) – *śruta* and *cāritra*. *Śruta*, which literally means "revelation," refers to right knowledge (*samyag-jñāna*), while *cāritra,* which literally means "behavior," refers to ethical conduct (*sadācāra*). In the religious context, truthful revelation occurs through the achievement of knowledge that is acquired by seeking it through the means of studies, thoughtful meditation, and personal experiences. The studies could be through institutional academic training or such education accompanied by self-studies. The sense of the term *cāritra* indicates the right path (*samyag-mārga*) to achieve personal goals of rectitude and self-improvement. Right knowledge (*samyag-jñāna*) is instrumental in personal growth and self-improvement. When someone advances in acquisition of right knowledge and development of wisdom, that person's conduct starts molding their character towards righteousness as well. Right conduct entails following the principled path of living based on ethical and moral behavior. This path requires concerted personal effort guided by a divine light (*prakāśa*) that is illuminated by right knowledge. Such right conduct (*sadācāra*) leads to *nirvāṇa*, the ultimate salvation and enlightenment, and is considered as an adjunct to *śruta dharma*. It is described in the *Sthānāṅgasūtra* as a composite of ten associated conduct tenets or faiths such as village conduct, city conduct, and dweller conduct, each addressing a specific and well-defined application of the doctrine of right behavior.

One of the key purposes of religion is to help followers transform from being outwardly focused to inwardly focused. This entails continuous engagement in introspection and self-improvement – along with the removal of personal deficiencies – instead of constantly looking for faults in others or in one's surroundings. It is believed in the Jain tradition that the true-self is not the physical body, but the soul. The physical self is continuously hankering for bodily comforts and is indulged in *karma* (acts) to fulfill the sensory desires. However, such acts can never provide true comfort for the soul, i.e., the inner being or true-self. Sense-driven acts are harmful in the long run and lead to destruction of the individual's righteous qualities and obstruction of the soul's inherently blissful characteristics. Also, according to Jain doctrine, religions of the world that condone or promote acts of violence or sacrifice of life for attainment of eternal salvation or heavenly blessings are not religions in the truest sense of the term. Such a religious path is not meant for devout spiritual seekers who are looking for divine bliss and ultimate spiritual delight. Rather, the true religious praxis is directed towards realizing the ultimate delight of the seeker's spiritual essence. Herein lies the difference between exterior sensory pleasures and divine bliss – the former is fulfilling the sensory desires, while the other is nurturing spiritual attainment.

The result of spiritual attainment is a pervasive, ever-present, and eternally resplendent wisdom. But the biggest obstacles to achieving such a state are actions that work against the realization of one's inherent nature, which is the nature of the soul. These can take the form of predominant negative thoughts and actions. In addition, Lord Mahāvīra taught that a lack of right knowledge or a gain of false knowledge results in spurious behavior that is contradictory to one's own spiritual nature and results in harmful conduct or beliefs, which in turn leads to inadvertent and negligent actions riddled with mistakes and false pretentions. This results in harming others either physically or in one's thoughts. And any harmful action inhibits the realization of the soul's all-pervasive, right knowledge and hinders one's efforts in achieving one's full spiritual potential.

Until that time when the soul realizes its true nature, it will have to endure the world's negativities and onerous surroundings. The soul will have to endure the vicissitudes of elation and abjection while transmigrating through birth and rebirth via multiple reincarnations. Until its spiritual potential is fully realized, the soul will remain transitory while repeatedly sojourning through the universe.

Lord Mahāvīra, while wandering as a *śramaṇa*[9] pursuing *kevala-jñāna,*[10] stated that:

> *Dharma,*[11] in the form of the quest for impeccable truth, is the inherent characteristic of any entity (*vatthusāhavo*).[12]

Attainment of this innate characteristic personifies *dharma* (faith), which is the ever-pleasing harmony of the soul. The practices and efforts to uplift consciousness and to impel it on the path of spiritual growth is the practice of *dharma*. *Dharma* can only be felt or expressed through experience and not in any language or sound. It is the wisdom, or "comprehensive consideration" (*viveka*[13]), and consciousness (*cetanā*) of the soul (*ātmā*) that motivates one's progress towards immortality, which is distinctly different from the pursuit of other material objects that are devoid of consciousness. The wisdom and consciousness attributes of soul define an individual's duties, obligations, and morals. They guide one to define one's ultimate goals, such as the removal of grief and attainment of *nirvāṇa*[14] (enlightenment), and helps one to make

---

9 *Śramaṇa*: One who practices religious exertions while observing a set of ethical principles; practices a detached life with a view to liberating oneself from the worldly life by living a life of renunciation.

10 *Jñāna*: Knowledge – it is the quality (*guṇa*) of the soul (*jīva*) that ascertains the details of an object. *Kevala-jñāna* is absolute knowledge, or omniscience. It is knowledge of all substances (*dravyas*) in all of their temporal modes (past, present, and future).

11 *Dharma* can often be used as the Indic equivalent of the Western term *religion*. In Jain philosophy, it is commonly used in expressions like *ahiṁsā paramo dharmaḥ* (non-violence is the supreme religion). The term is also used to refer to inherent characteristics of an entity, and to convey a sense of duty; for example, it is mendicants' *dharma* to teach.

12 *Vatthusāhavo dhammo.*

13 *Viveka* is the ability of rational thinking while differentiating between what is right and what is wrong.

14 *Nirvāṇa* and *mokṣa* are commonly used interchangeably. In Jain tradition, *mokṣa* is the state which a spiritually enlightened *jīva* (soul) attains subsequent to achieving perfection in all respects – perfect perception, unbounded perfect wisdom and perfect conduct after discarding all eight *karmas* (see chapter 11). Instantly thereafter, the

progress on the spiritual path. The true nature and inherent characteristics of the soul are obstructed by the layers of virtual particles created by one's *karma* and actions, resulting in kārmic bondages.

One must understand the negative effects of kārmic bondage so that one might liberate oneself. To that end, one needs the proper knowledge to understand these bondages and the proper conduct to break free of them. While describing the such proper knowledge and conduct, Lord Mahāvīra said:

> Non-violence, self-control or moderation, and penance or austerities are the characteristics of *dharma*. They are wonderful and auspicious activities.

When it comes to non-violence (*ahiṁsā*), one has to be vigilant because *ahiṁsā* has two forms: (1) prohibition of violence (as a restriction, *niṣedhaka*), and (2) injunctions or implementation of non-violence (as a prescription). The prohibitory aspect suppresses the effects of impending and/or manifested harmful kārmic results before their effects contaminate the soul. The injunctions regulate the activities and protect individuals from inauthenticity and deceptiveness, such as wrong perception (*mithyātva*), while encouraging and leading them towards righteousness comprising of enlightenment (*samyaktva*), right conduct (*samyag cāritra*), spiritual alertness (*apramāda*), dispassion (*akaṣāya*), and auspicious activities (*śubha-yoga*). Jain Dharma is uniquely disposed to guide one to accomplish this mission because its objective is to take humans from an inauspicious state (*aśubha*) to an auspicious one (*śubha*), and finally lead them towards the state of ultimate purity (*śuddha*). Non-violence is the path for the fulfillment of this mission. All living beings want to live in peace and a widespread practice of non-violence gives them that opportunity.

In a Jain scripture, the *Praśna Vyākaraṇasūtra* (The Sūtra of Questions and Answers), Lord Mahāvīra states:

> Non-violence (*ahiṁsā*) is the exhibitor and illuminating light for the spiritual passage that one should pursue. It is an island of relief for human beings who are drowning in the ocean of material existence. It is the salvation,

soul discards the body and attains *nirvāṇa* – the ultimate and eternal liberation – and settles in *siddha-loka*, considered to be at the top of the universe in Jain cosmology. In the Buddhist tradition, *nirvāṇa* is defined as the state where *jīva* (soul) is free of birth–death cycles.

> shelter, and remedial state. It is the foundation on which the building of spiritual achievements rests. Non-violence is a comfort for those who fear any unwanted acts that might be inflicted against them. It is as beneficial as a flight in the open sky is for birds. It is quenching for the thirsty, and nutritious for the hungry. It is medicine to cure the sick and is akin to a ship of salvation upon the ocean of recurring life cycles. These are just a few instances, but non-violence is vastly more healing. It brings a surplus of welfare for all, auspicious for the earth, water, wind, fire, vegetation, seeds, and water-bound, earth-bound, air-bound, insects, and all other livings beings. Undoubtedly non-violence is like a mother who bestows life while protecting all living beings from vexatious elements. Non-violence is like an elixir of life with an endless supply, whereas violence is like a venom and a repository of toxic elements.

An individual, a society, and even a nation experience enhanced calmness, peace, comfort, and well-being with an increasing adoption of non-violence in lifestyle and culture. One's fortunes will continue to grow while achieving more stability. On the other hand, the increase of violence in one's life, society, or nation causes commensurate restlessness, agitation, distress, and frustration.

So, the question is: How does one impliment non-violence in day-to-day life? The answer lies in self-control (*saṁyama*) and modesty. That is why self-control is considered the second-most important principle of *dharma* – right after non-violence (*ahiṁsā*). If non-violence is a vast tree, then self-control or restraint is like the trunk of that tree. It entails restraining one's senses (seeing, hearing, tasting, touching, and smelling) and sensory desires, and diverting the senses and mind from any activity or thought that involves violence of any kind. Non-violence is the objective, and self-control provides the means to achieve that goal. In life, practicing non-violence becomes possible only by establishing self-control. A person who is not compassionate towards other living beings, whose senses become uninhibited, and whose mind wanders without any tether, is uncontrolled and cannot practice non-violence.

Jain scriptures have described seventeen different types of self-control, but all of these can be categorized in two major types – sense control and life control. Sense control involves stopping the senses and mind from instinctive, negative conduct. It involves diverting them towards positive behavior that is in line with true nature of the soul. Life control is giving up violence against all kinds of living beings.

The third key tenet or aspect of *dharma* is the combination of penance and austerity (*tapasyā*). It is necessary to practice austerity in order to observe and exercise self-control (*saṁyama*) in life. Penance involves the control of desires, which otherwise can run limitlessly if left unchecked. In day-to-day life, individuals work futilely to fulfill their endless desires, and this cycle will continue on an escalating scale if they do not curb their insatiable longings. In order to fulfill desires, one relinquishes self-control and loosens behavioral restraints. The result is that acts of violence and inappropriate behavior increase – acts that are contrary to the soul's inherent nature. Hence, penance and austerity are needed to bring a sense of restraint and control back into one's life. This is essential to continue on the path of self-improvement.

While encountering thorns on a pathway, in order to protect one's feet from thorns one does not try to cover the entire pathway with leather. Rather, one wears shoes (preferably not leather) on the feet. Similarly, one should not try to fulfill each and every desire simply because one has the means to fulfill them. It is important to restrain one's longings to maintain internal peace and satisfaction. The restraint of longings or desires is penance. This empowers one to exercise self-control, which in turn increasingly establishes non-violence in daily life.

Those who unceasingly practice penance, self-control, and non-violence in life percieve their unblemished, immaculate, and dispassionate[15] soul. Then even the heavenly beings bow to them with the deepest respect and admiration.

While rendering a description of Jain Dharma, one of the Jain *ācārya*s (head of monastery) has stated that Jain Dharma exists where:

1. A principle or fact has been fully critiqued and investigated to find the Ultimate Truth, while keeping in mind the multiplicity of views and true aspects of that principle.

---

15 It is to be noted that the term "passion" may have a positive connotation in English (for example, to "be passionate" about something), but it is seen as a psychological encumbrance in Jain doctrine, where, whether positive or negative in appearance, passions are believed to inhibit the soul from achieving perfection.

2. Facets of truth have been assembled in a unified manner to attain the complete and ultimately irrevocable truth.
3. Favoritism to a particular viewpoint has no place and objectivity prevails.
4. Hurting any living being is considered a sin.
5. Non-violence persists in thought, speech, and conduct.

In other words, the irrevocable truth combined with purity in thought, speech, and conduct defines Jain Dharma. It is the "faith of conquerors" (literal translation of *jina*, who were the founders and great teachers of Jain Dharma) because it is the religion articulated by those who have attained victory over attachment, jealousy, and malice. It is also known as the religion of *nirgrantha*s (those who have no tangible or intangible possessions) because it is preached by *arihanta*s who have destroyed all kārmic enemies (attachment, aversion, anger, ego, deceit, and greed) that indulge in creating or committing impure *karma*s and activities. It is called *paramahaṁsa-dharma* (saintly *dharma*) in the *Śrīmad Bhagavadgītā*, and *yati dharma* in the *Kevalya Śruti*.

During the current era, spanning several thousand years, Lord Ādinātha was Jain Dharma's first expounder (*tīrthaṅkara*), and Lord Mahāvīra Swāmī, who was born in 599 BCE, was the last one. In every era, whenever human beings forget or drift away from their true being, *arihanta*s and their inspirational teachings bring the message of non-violence, self-control, penance, and oneness with nature to reunite them with their own pure self. It will be great day when – with the help of right perception, right knowledge, and right conduct – one can awaken from the inner slumber to experience ultimate delight (unobstructed happiness) and limitless understanding (wisdom).

In a Jain scripture, the *Uttarādhyayanasūtra* (chapter 12, verse 44), Lord Mahāvīra summarizes the process of self-improvement while exercising non-violence through *karma* (deeds), self-control, and penance.[16] He explains the process by drawing parallels to the then prevailing acts of *yajña* (sacrifice)

---

[16] *Saccā yajña: tavo joi jīvo joi-ṭhāṇaṁ, jogā suyā sarīraṁkārisaṁgaṁ, kammehā sañjam jog-santī, homaṁ huṇāmi isiṇaṁ pasatthaṁ.*

performed by many religious leaders, who believed in a ritualistic form of religion which often involved animal sacrifices. The *yajña* involved burning a special incensed fuel poured over a fire in a vessel called *homa*, and was accompanied by the chanting of verses by the religious leaders. In this verse, which is a part of a sermon to his chief disciple Gautama Svāmī, Lord Mahāvīra says:

> Hey Gautama, in performing a religious *yajña* (ritual) in truly spiritual settings, penance is like fire and living beings are like sources of light. The unification (*yoga*) of mind, body, and speech is like a stirrer, and our body is like a vast vessel (*homa*). Our *karma* or deeds are like fuel, and self-control is like chanting a peace sermon. Using all these, we perform this spiritual *yajña*, which the learned ones have termed as the clearest and most admirable religious act.

Mapping Lord Mahāvīra's sermon onto the act of aforementioned *yajña*, one can analogize that one's body is a vessel (*homa*) in which to perform this spiritual *yajña* using penance (likened to the fire) to burn *karma* (likened to the fuel) while controlling it with right unification of mind, body, and speech (stirrer), and where the fire is started by borrowing it from a lamp (spiritual inspiration – the source of penance fire). As such, the process of *yajña* is understood to be an internal process of self-discipline rather than an external performative routine.

This sermon by Lord Mahāvīra is the essence of Jain Dharma, where the effort is focused on progressing towards the intrinsic pure state of the soul through penance, deep meditation, and righteous conduct motivated by non-violence and other honorable acts. The following chapters describe the unique characteristics of Jain Dharma starting with the venerable history of the tradition.

2

A Glimpse into the Past (Atīta kī Jhalaka)

THE doctrine of Jain Dharma has existed since time immemorial. It is the religion espoused by the *jina*s, the enlightened ones who attain self-purification by conquering maladies such as attachment, malice, and jealousy. According to the tradition, *jina*s have wandered the earth through eternity; hence, it is impossible to pinpoint the origination of Jain Dharma. No single individual, book, or canonical work can be accredited with its origination.

From time to time *jina*s have appeared to roam the earth and have given discourses on Jain doctrine. They present fresh perspectives of Jain principles relevant to contemporary times. From that viewpoint, Jain Dharma can be seen as a teaching that is relevant to any age. Innumerable living beings in the past have practiced Jain Dharma to attain salvation and continue to do so in this current age. The tradition's auspicious doors are always open for those who seek. However, impacted by the prevailing conditions of the contemporary societies, the teachings have been obstructed to some degree at various times and places. Historically, *jina*s have appeared at such difficult times to clear the obstructions to the practice of Jain Dharma in a cycle of spiritual vicissitudes that has existed forever and will continue to exist into the indefinite future.

In Jain doctrine, a cycle of time (*kāla-cakra*) is split into two main phases – *utsarpiṇī* and *avasarpiṇī* – which are somewhat related to the four phases known as Satya, Dvāpara, Tretā, and Kali *yuga*s of Vedic religious philosophy. The *utsarpiṇī* is the phase of progress and positive developments marked by progressive health, age, strength, and other positive qualities, and similar improvements in the surrounding material and physical world. The *avasarpiṇī* phase is the opposite for both living and non-living beings and is marked by the continuous decline in the quality and value of life. In other words, *utsarpiṇī* is the phase of a progressive transition from misery to happiness and well-being, whereas *avasarpiṇī* is the phase of regressive transition from happiness to increasing misery.

Each of these two phases is divided into six periods termed *ārā*s, analogous to how the wheel of a vehicle has multiple sectors. The six *ārā*s are called:

1. *Sukhmā-sukhmā*: the period of immense happiness and welfare.
2. *Sukhmā*: the period of moderate but declining happiness and welfare.
3. *Sukhmā-dukhmā*: the period of decline in happiness and initiation of misery.
4. *Dukhmā-sukhmā*: the period of increasing misery and declining happiness.
5. *Dukhmā*: the period of moderate but increasing misery.
6. *Dukhmā-dukhmā*: the period of intense misery.

The above cycle illustrates the regressive periods of *avasarpiṇī*, while progressive periods of *utsarpiṇī* would appear in opposite order. Twenty-four *jina tīrthaṅkara*s appear in each *utsarpiṇī* and *avasarpiṇī* phase. The first *jina* revives the *dharma* that has been lost over time, and the following twenty-three continue to propagate it.

Currently, we are in the fifth period (*dukhmā*) of the *avasarpiṇī* phase where misery is expected to increase to reach the intense levels in the sixth period (*dukhmā-dukhmā*). The *tīrthaṅkara*s started appearing during the third period (*sukhmā-dukhmā*) of the current *avasarpiṇī* (regressive goodness) phase. Lord Ādinātha was the first *jina* to appear, and he attained *nirvāṇa* thirty years and eight and a half months before the end of the third period (*sukhmā-dukhmā*) of the current *avasarpiṇī* phase.

In Vedic doctrine, according to the *Śrīmad Bhāgavata Purāṇa* and the *Manusmṛti*, Lord Ṛṣabhadeva (also known as Lord Ādinātha) took birth in the fifth generation of Manu, which turns out to be towards the end of the first Sat Yuga (also Satya Yuga). Currently, it is the twenty-ninth Sat Yuga. These references in Vedic scriptures serve as historical evidence in support of the timing of Lord Ṛṣabhadeva's appearance. After him, twenty-three *tīrthaṅkara*s appeared in the *dukhmā-sukhmā ārā*, the fourth period of the current *avasarpiṇī* phase. Lord Mahāvīra was the last *tīrthaṅkara*. In Jain scriptures, the time difference between the first and last *tīrthaṅkara* is measured in numerous *sāgaras*, where a *sāgara* measures several thousand years. In the current *avasarpiṇī* phase, Lord Ṛṣabhadeva is considered to be the creator of social, political, and economic infrastructure with appropriate laws, rules, and policies.

Lord Ṛṣabhadeva

Long ago, at a time that precedes historical reference, there was no religion in the land where humans lived, known in Jain scriptures as Bharat-Kṣetra. There was no family or social structure, no political or civic establishment, no rule of law, no infrastructure for art or any education system. In other words, humans were living in a completely unstructured way, although they were ruled by a king. They were dependent on the fruits and vegetables discarded by the trees called *kalpavṛkṣas*. In Jain scriptures, this period is known as the Yugala Kāla.

This is the period in which Lord Ṛṣabhadeva took birth. His father was King Nābhi, the last clan leader of that period, and his mother was Marudevī. Lord Ṛṣabhadeva spent his childhood in this civilization when times were changing rapidly. Greed and selfishness had started to impinge on human behavior. Nature itself was going through a revolutionary change and its fecundity was in decline. Driven by this, peaceful living was being jeopardized. The trees that were the lone source of livelihood for the population started to yield decreasing amounts of crops. At that stage, agricultural processes had not been established and people were not aware of any means to improve crops. These occurrences resulted in heretofore unseen life-threatening conditions. In order to overcome these difficulties, a new system of living needed to be devised to organize this materialistic and consumption-based chaos into a structured, task-oriented, and functional society.

Lord Ṛṣabhadeva established an infrastructure based on individual qualities and physical abilities to create a self-sufficient and self-dependent society. For the benefit and uplift of the common people, he introduced one hundred twenty art forms such as language, reading, writing, mathematics, economics, music, and sculpture. Seventy-two of these were for men and forty-eight for women, reflecting their respective general interests and responsibilities in those days. He first trained his daughter Brāhmī with a written script, which came to be known as the Brāhmī Script, after her. In addition, the arrangements and facilities for workload, production, and distribution of products from agriculture, cow and animal welfare, storage facilities, etc., were all the creations of Lord Ṛṣabhadeva.

Lord Ṛṣabhadeva had two wives, Sunandā and Sumaṅgalā, who gave birth to two daughters and one hundred sons. Two of his sons, Bharata and Bāhubalī, were especially famous historical figures. After implementing all arrangements for structured living, Lord Ṛṣabhadeva wanted to renounce the world and free himself from attachments. With that in mind, he handed over the kingdom and welfare of its people to his sons.

Lord Ṛṣabhadeva acquired absolute and unbounded wisdom (*kevala-jñāna* – omniscience, supreme enlightenment) after exercising strict austerity and rigorous penance accompanied by one thousand years of the highest level of meditation. After that, similar to how he had previously established the socio-economic infrastructure, he created an organized system for spiritual and religious activities to present the populace with an elated and noble objective of living. He propagated major vows for renunciant monks and nuns, and minor vows for householders. To this day, his teachings continue to guide humanity when it endures escalating difficulties, and they will continue to do so indefinitely.

It is noteworthy that Lord Ṛṣabhadeva has been respectfully mentioned and praised with the highest spiritual regard at various places in Vedic scriptures where he is likewise recognized as the apostle of structured *dharma* (religion) who possesses absolute unbounded knowledge. He has been cited at various places with deep reverence along with descriptions of his structured doctrine promoting a lifestyle which is inspired by austerity and righteous vows. In a similar way, references to Lord Ṛṣabhadeva are found in the *Śrīmad Bhāgavatam*, where he has been cited as an accomplished soul and referred to as the Supreme Master of this universe, heavenly beings, learned ones, and the animals, and whose character and teachings destroy all the sins of human beings.

The *Śrīmad Bhāgavatam* has presented a detailed description of Lord

Ṛṣabhadeva and includes a collection of his discourses. Lord Ṛṣabhadeva has been referred as *arhat* and the religion expounded by him is called *paramahaṁsa-dharma*. Regarding the appearance of Ṛṣabhadeva in the *Śrīmad Bhāgavatam*, it is said that King Nābhi wished for a son to enhance religion in the world and to show path to ultimate salvation. Upon hearing the king's desire, the sages and learned ones said: "Your Honor (*arhat-tama*), your wish will definitely be fulfilled."[1] Then they prayed to the Almighty God who granted the wish and sent an *arhat* to take birth as the king's son.[2] *Arhat*s are those who are unattached to the temptations of material existence (*asaṁspṛṣṭa*), and teach the path to deliverance and liberation of the soul. Lord Ṛṣabhadeva's self-nature was completely harmonious with the inherent characteristics of soul. He was completely devoid of violent, evil, and sinful behavior in thought and action. He was perpetually immersed in pure and joyful thoughts as the very personification of the Almighty. He showed compassion and charity towards all living beings and friendship for all humans irrespective of their background and status. In addition, the *Śrīmad Bhāgavatam* clearly states that Lord Ṛṣabhadeva's eldest son, Bharata, was a renowned king of ancient India who ruled the subcontinent and helped usher in an era of profound happiness and prosperity. For that reason, the country was named after him as "Bhārata" (the traditional name of India).

Lord Ṛṣabhadeva's eldest son, Bharata, received the entire kingdom, and the remaining ninety-eight sons, excluding Bharata and Bāhubalī, did not inherit anything. They all became very perturbed and met with Lord Ṛṣabhadeva to express their frustration about this arrangement. On noticing his sons' anxiety, Lord Ṛṣabhadeva delivered a very compassionate sermon for their welfare. The following twenty-one units provide the essence of that sermon:

1. Dear sons, progeny of humanity, our physical body is the home to all

---

[1] *Athāyam eva varo hy arhat-tama yarhi barhiṣi rājarṣer varadarṣabho bhavān nija-puruṣekṣaṇa-viṣaya āsīt.* (O Supreme Arhat, now that wish will indeed manifest for everyone to behold.)

[2] *Kiñcāyaṁrājarṣir apatya-kāmaḥ prajāṁ bhavādṛśīm āśāsāna īśvaram āśiṣāmsvargāpavargayor api bhavantam upadhāvati.* (Morever, this pious king, desiring an offspring, approaches You, indeed the Lord of benedictions, with respect to heaven and liberation.)

the miseries of this world. It is not worth the price of indulgence, but rather is to be employed as a vehicle for conducting austere penance. Penance helps in achieving internal and ultimate purification of soul, which leads to a supreme and comprehensive spiritual ecstasy.

2. Dear sons, devotion to the conduct of noble and ascetic individuals leads to the primary entrance to the world of enlightenment. The one who has duty-bound attachments only to faithfully fulfill the needs for honorable conduct in this world and universe, is an impartial, a content, and a peaceful holy person.
3. The one who labors for the fulfillment of carnal delights of the senses and life is not considered an exemplary individual. This is because attachment to the body creates impediments for soul's purification.
4. Until a monk grasps the splendor of the real self, he does not understand much. He is oblivious and in the dark. So long as he is involved in external activities such as ritualistic *yajña*, the bondage between the body and the soul remains unbroken, the causal and physical bodies remain attached, and the accumulation of *karma* continues.
5. Even the learned individuals who do not have wholesome and pure conduct, even after achieving the right wisdom (*samyag-jñāna*[3]), may become indulgers in physical pleasures. An individual may be drawn to the life of physical pleasures instead of asceticism due to incomplete and incorrect knowledge. This leads to endless miseries.
6. The sensual attraction of a man towards a woman is the foundation of sensory desires. It leads to an individual's attachment towards family and children, wealth, business, and other physical possessions. This enhances the feelings of attachments.
7. When the feelings of attachments that bolster the heart's desires are brought under control, such attachments start weakening. Under such conditions, the individual starts to disconnect from worldly affairs and moves towards ultimate liberation, and eventually achieves *nirvāṇa*.

---

[3] *Samyag-jñāna* is right wisdom for consistency and perfect understanding of what is right and what is wrong, what is worth practicing and what is not for the purification of soul.

8. An individual who understands the difference between wholesome and adulterated knowledge starts revering the *tīrthaṅkara*, the possessor-purveyors of the ultimate wisdom, and becomes devoid of all attachments (*rāga*). Pure reverence results in destruction of corrupted knowledge. In that state, the individual relinquishes sensory desires and outlooks of misery and pleasure, and starts yearning to understand the real essence and fundamental truth. With penance, one conquers attachments and continuously destroys the kārmic particles attached to the soul, and finally reaches the pinnacle of ultimate tranquility.
9. The attachments to worldly affairs and physical desires of the body, like a misguided spearhead, drag the soul towards the abyss or hell.[4]
10. Dear sons, the one who lacks advancement and is negligent in the cultivation of a serene perspective, and is burdened by physical desires, cannot understand the essential path to worldly salvation.
11. An individual who dilutes their wisdom with attachments and treads the path as an unscholarly individual, will never be guided to the path of salvation by the gentle, learned ones.
12. Dear sons, the one who treats all creation, immovable and movable beings, the same way as he treats myself, and who understands the reasons behind the shedding of *karma* particles attached to the soul, attains the true *dharma*. The essence of *dharma* is exemplified by an accurate and noble perception.
13. The ascetic who adopts the principles and tenets of austere living, and achieves the understanding of the true-self through discreet and secluded penance and learning, and lives the life of devotion and principled living, that vigilant individual reaches the doorstep of ultimate liberation.
14. The one who goes through life with prophetic wisdom, knowledge, science, *yoga*, calmness, alertness, and solitude achieves contentment. He is my true disciple.

---

[4] The idea of "hell" (*naraka*) in Jain Dharma is not to be confused with that in Abrahamic traditions. In Jain Dharma, souls are not sent to "hell" (*naraka*) as a punishment or result of divine judgment. In addition, like the dhārmic traditions in general, hell is not eternal, but can last a long time depending on previous *karma*. Once the duration of kārmic fructification is complete, one can be reborn in a higher realm.

15. Destroy the heart's desires in order to conquer the dependence on kārmic actions that serve as blockages to the advancement on the spiritual path. Corrupt and untrue knowledge creates these blockages that are further supported by negligence and distractions.
16. Covered by kārmic particles, the soul's insight has been clouded and overwhelmed by selfish desires. Dear children, be selfless and dispassionate while ignoring worldly desires and pleasures, and destroy accumulating kārmic particles to stop the acquisition of misery.
17. Just as a blind person may proceed on a wrong path because they are not able to see, the individual who is blinded by their deeds and desires may continue to tread upon an undesirable path. Because of incorrect knowledge one might not have sufficient devotion to the true path of *dharma*.
18. Dear sons, my body is not the real me. My body is an undesired result of my own deficiencies. My true-self is my soul and its characteristics are spiritual. That is my real *dharma*. I have overcome those deficiencies in this life and have destroyed my unholy traits. That is why I am known as a supreme achiever (*śreṣṭha ārya*).
19. Ritual praxis (like Agnihotra) does not provide contentment and bliss (*sukha*) comparable to that which is achieved from spiritual refinement gained through penance and austerity.
20. I value the type of *yajña* and *dharma* that comprise seven noble capabilities – tranquility, restraint, truthfulness, kindness, penance, forgiveness, and understanding. Numerous souls have achieved salvation by following this path. This is the enlightened path.
21. Always maintain fearlessness towards immovable and movable beings. This is the enlightened way to salvation that destroys detrimental attachments and infatuations. One must work hard to achieve salvation; the supreme objective that results in eternal peace and liberation.

Lord R̥ṣabhadeva's sons were captivated by the sermon and all of them decided to forego worldly lifestyle to adopt that of ascetics. They moved away from a life consumed by worldly deeds and progressed towards the path of purification of the soul.

The *Śrīmad Bhāgavata Purāṇa* contains a very passionate description of Bhagavān Ṛṣabhadeva's life and the austerities that he performed. The Bhagavān surmounted multiple difficulties and trials while crossing all the impediments that came his way. He lived in the forests, practicing penance and meditation, and faced multiple calamities. Finally, he peregrinated into the towns and cities to spread the message of peace and non-violence. He was insulted as idle, blind, dumb, deaf, ghost-like, mad, etc. He was threatened and beaten and insulted and assaulted by the hurling of urine, spit, stones, stool, and even by flatulence. Despite all this, he remained unmoved, indifferent to the insults or praises hurled upon him by people. He had a special aura about him that radiated an exquisite energy that mesmerized everybody around him. After completing his pre-destined duration of life that marked the complete destruction of all of his *karma*, he accomplished ultimate and unbounded wisdom (*kevala-jñāna*), attained *nirvāṇa*, and became liberated forever.

Lord Ṛṣabhadeva's life is presented very respectfully in the *Śrīmad Bhāgavatam* and the description is very similar to that in Jain scriptures. In Vedic religion, Lord Ṛṣabhadeva is considered one of the twenty-four incarnations of God. In fact, although the *Śrīmad Bhāgavatam* characterized him as being respectful to the Vedic scriptures, he was never associated with the then prevalent *yajña* practices.

Jain Dharma in the Ancient Hindu Upaniṣads

Two religious and spiritual ideologies had become prevalent during Lord Ṛṣabhadeva's time. As stated, one ideology was dominated by ritual praxis (*yajña*), which could involve the sacrifices of living beings. The other involved penance, self-control, meditation, and learning. Nowadays these ideologies are known as Brāhmanism (the former) and the *śramaṇa* tradition (the latter). Lord Ṛṣabhadeva was the original promoter of the *śramaṇa* philosophy, and any mention of the *śramaṇa* movement in the Upaniṣads is interpreted as a reference to the Jain tradition.

Ten non-violence (*ahiṁsā*)–based tenets are described by the great sage, His Holiness Dattātreya, in the *Jābāla Upaniṣad*, which are subsequent to the four Vedas (also Veda Saṁhitās). These are the same ten Jain tenets propounded by Lord Ṛṣabhadeva. In addition, aspects of Jain doctrine are present in the Vedas, so the Jain Dharma promulgated by Lord Ṛṣabhadeva may arguably be older than Vedas. This is perhaps the reason for its strong influence on Dattātreya in the *Jābāla Upaniṣad.*

While criticizing the ritualistic and outwardly focused religious practices, Dattātreya states that "indulging in such practices, instead of knowledge and penance-based practices, is like considering a pound of dirt to be more valuable than gold." Here, Dattātreya's thoughts are strikingly similar to those found in the Jain philosophy.

In another place, Dattātreya states that a soul reaches the immortal, spiritual summit by gaining ultimate knowledge while practicing non-violence and other related *śramaṇa* tenets. He presents and supports ten tenets, which were similar to those in Jain Dharma. Regarding penance, he mentions *kṛcchra-cāndrāyaṇa* practiced by Vedic followers that involves fasting synchronized with the cycles of the moon. However, Jains accept only penance as the act that assists soul in removing all attachments and motivates one towards the path of salvation.

Dattātreya separated himself from the mainstream Vedic philosophy. Undoubtedly, he is an *ācārya* of *śramaṇa* philosophy even though Vedic followers have a deep respect for him. Although from early times, many monks have associated themselves with the *śramaṇa* philosophy, no reference can be found to any innovator of these practices other than Lord Ṛṣabhadeva and the philosophy promulgated by him. Dattātreya has historically served as an important bridge between brāhmaṇic and *śramaṇa* practices, although he never accepted or indulged in the brāhmaṇic ritualistic practices.

Jain Dharma in the Medieval Hindu Purāṇas

Some consider the Purāṇas as contemporary to the Upaniṣads. These texts describe aspects of Jain philosophy at great length. Whenever the Jain philosophy is presented with praise in Vedic literature, it is called *vrātya dharma*, *paramahaṁsa-dharma*, or *yati dharma*, but never Jain Dharma. However, wherever it is criticized, it is called out as Jain Dharma or a hypocritical *dharma*.

A lot of references can be found in the Purāṇas regarding the attire of Jain monks – or rather, the lack thereof. The *Padma Purāṇa* has descriptions of naked Jain saints (known as Digambaras[5]). References to Jain saints with a piece of cloth over their mouths (Sthānakavāsī Jain saints) can be found in the *Śiva Purāṇa* in sentences such as, "bearers of cloth on the mouth."[6] In the *Mahābhārata*, there are references to the white-cloth-clad Jain saints (Śvetāmbara Jain saints). It is evident that all three types of Jain monks have been cited in Vedic scriptures and literature of ancient times.

Although the *Padma Purāṇa* is critical of Jain Dharma, its intrinsic characteristics are quite evidently related to Jain philosophy. The description of King Veṇu is worth a close inspection in this regard. The sages ask:

> "Hey Sūta, if King Veṇu was born of a sage, why did he relinquish the Vedic religion?" To that Sūta replies, "let me tell you the whole story. A naked and charismatic saint with a well-built body and a white glow on the forehead visited King Veṇu's royal court." This "saint" fits the description of a Jain ascetic.
>
> Upon seeing one such saint, King Veṇu respectfully asked him, "Who are you?"
>
> The saint replied, "I am a soul with ultimate and unbounded wisdom, absolute truth, and boundless powers. Truth and *dharma* are my virtues. I am the conqueror of all *karmas*."
>
> Veṇu asked him, "who are your *guru* and God and what is your religion?" The saint replied:
>
> "*Arihantas* are our gods, renunciate saints are our *gurus*, and compassion is our religion. My religion does not embody rituals such as *yajña* and study

[5] Today's Jain community is divided into four mainstream sectarian traditions. Originally, there were two major traditions, both worshipping *jinas* in iconic (image or idol) form – Digambaras, who are unclothed or "sky-clad" monks, and Śvetāmbaras, who are "white-clad" monks and nuns. Their differences are primarily related to the practice and ritualistic procedures. In fifteenth century, some Śvetāmbara followers left the tradition to start Sthānakavāsī tradition, which does not believe in iconic worship. The Sthānakavāsī tradition was further divided in seventeenth century when a new non-iconic tradition called Terāpantha was formed based on thirteen (*terā*) core tenets (*pantha*). The remaining Śvetāmbaras, not belonging to Sthānakavāsī or Terāpantha traditions, are known as Mūrtipūjakas, and are the largest of the three Śvetāmbara groups.

[6] *Tuṇḍe vastrasya dhārakāḥ.*

of Vedas. We have forever given up animal cruelty and sacrifices. Our religion considers the meditation on liberated souls as the most auspicious act. Influenced by attachments, people perform rituals such as *śrāddha* – the act of feeding brāhmaṇas on behalf of departed souls with the expectation of providing them with peace in the hereafter. However, after leaving a body, the soul does not need any food and food eaten by brāhmaṇa does not reach the departed soul. Rather, compassion and charity are most auspicious. Hey King, forego the deceptive practices and work to protect living beings and promote non-violence. A person who does such, whether previously a criminal, or from a low caste, or even a hangman, is the real brāhmaṇa in our *dharma*. The path shown by the *jina*s is the most benevolent one. With peaceful and kind heart, show compassion to all living beings."

The king further asked the saint: "The brāhmaṇa claim the rivers such as Gaṅgā are the complete grounds for salvation. Is this true?"

The saint replied: "Hey King, the clouds in the sky rain the same water all over the earth. The water from the mountains and plains collects and flows in streams to form rivers. Rivers are just the channels for flowing water so how can they be the salvation grounds (*tīrtha*)? If taking baths in rivers would lead to salvation, all water-borne living beings, such as fish, would be liberated. Hey King, only *jina*s are the real source of enlightenment. Just pray to them."

Thereafter King Veṇu developed his conviction in Arhat Dharma – the religion of *jina*s – and adopted Jain Dharma.

Veṇu's conversion resulted in much anxiety among Vedic saints. This legend is well-known and the purpose of its citation here is to illustrate that even in ancient times the principles of Jain Dharma were so well respected that individuals such as highly acclaimed King Veṇu were its adherents. His story is a testament to the fact that Jain Dharma is about uplifting the state of a soul and not about the external behavior of the body that it resides in at any point of time.

In the *Skanda Purāṇa*'s Āvantya-Rekhā section, certain hypocritical people denounced the practices of renunciation and austerity. They instead proclaimed the Vedic practices and ritual bathing in the Narmadā River as the path to salvation. In other Purāṇas and the *Bṛhadāraṇyaka Upaniṣad*, the description of the self and question–answers of Ajātaśatru also seem to indicate the philosophy of Jain Dharma.

In the area of devotion and penance, Arhat (Jain) Dharma is considered to be both the most difficult and the most beneficial. It represents a comprehensive set of devotional practices for self-improvement that are fundamental resources for achieving an ultimately pure state. Jain devotional practices emphasize the improvement in the true spiritual self rather than the illusory materialistic self.

In the *Atharvaveda*, the descriptions of meditation, devotional practices, and difficult penances performed by Lord Ṛṣabhadeva and by monks who were bound to vows, indicate the prevalence of Jain Dharma. Even in such ancient scriptures Jain devotional practices are designed to destroy attachments to the body while eliminating egotistical behavior and one's self-centered nature. Such practices do not promise dreams of paradise but illuminate the righteous path of salvation.

In the *Viṣṇudharmottara Purāṇa*, section 2, chapter 131 is exclusively devoted to *yati dharma* under the name of *Haṁsa-Gītā*. This is a collection of practices and teachings on Jain Dharma, such as limited (once a day) food intake, observance of silence, control of senses, and elimination of attachments and envies. The key practices of *yati dharma* mentioned in this canonical work are the ten religious practices described in Jain Āgamas as commonly discussed among the followers of Digambara tradition.

The *Śiva Purāṇa* calls Lord Ṛṣabhadeva the "benevolent purveyor of the universe." In addition, in the *Yoga-Vāsiṣṭha*, Rāmacandra expresses his aspirations:

> I am not Rāma and I have no desires, and my mind (*manaḥ*) is not within my emotions (*bhāvas*). My wish is to be established in peace, verily in the same way that Lord Jina is within his own soul (*svātmani*).[7]

The above-mentioned accounts in various scriptures lead to a consistent conclusion. Although the religious canon established by Lord Ṛṣabhadeva is the foundation of *śramaṇa* practices or Jain Dharma, it has made important

---

[7] *nāhaṁ rāmo na me vācchā, bhāveṣu ca na me manaḥ, śāntim āsthātum icchāmi, svātmanyeva jino yathā.*

contributions to Brāhmanical traditions. Viewed as the first religious preceptor or the first great sage of this era, Lord Ṛṣabhadeva's teachings are directly or indirectly present in all these religious scriptures, including Vedas, Vedic Purāṇas, and, of course, the Jain scriptures. He was an incomparable religious personality, not only in India, but also around the world.

Tīrthaṅkaras of Jain Dharma

Table 2.1 presents the names and birthplaces of the twenty-four *tīrthaṅkara*s mentioned earlier. Of the twenty-four *tīrthaṅkara*s, Lord Dharmanātha, Lord Arahanātha, and Lord Kunthunātha were born in Kuru-vaṁśa lineage; Lord Munisuvrata was born in Hari-vaṁśa lineage, and all others were born in the Ikṣvāku-vaṁśa lineage. All *tīrthaṅkara*s led a life of intense austerity; they embraced asceticism, conducted extreme penance while practicing the highest level of meditation (*sādhanā*[8]), and attained ultimate unbounded and complete wisdom. Even after achieving the ultimate state, they taught the path to salvation inspired by compassion towards all living beings, established vows and spiritual practices, and illuminated the genuine nature of fundamental truth. At the end, they attained *nirvāṇa* (spiritual liberation), to become enlightened souls or *siddha*s or *buddha*s with pure, untainted qualities. The life cycles of the last three *tīrthaṅkara*s are particularly important and are presented next.

Lord Ariṣṭanemi (Lord Neminātha)

Lord Neminātha was the son of the immensely influential King Samudravijaya and Queen Śivā of the Yadu-vaṁśa lineage. He was a cousin of Lord Kṛṣṇa, who was the son of Lord Neminātha's father's younger brother. He is praised in the Vedic *Sandhyopāsanā* couplet entitled *ariṣṭanemiḥ śāntir bhavatu*. He has also been mentioned in numerous places in the Vedas.

In one of the most well-known and inspirational episodes from Lord Neminātha's life, his marriage was arranged with King Ugrasena's daughter Rājamatī. On the wedding day, his wedding procession was near the palace of his father-in-law when Lord Neminātha heard painful screeches from

---

[8] *Sādhanā* comprises of penance and austerity including the highest level of meditation, contemplations, control of senses and mind, self-restraint, equanimity, self-efforts and self-initiatives, and the like.

Table 2.1: Names and Birthplaces of the Tīrthaṅkaras

	Name of Tīrthaṅkara	*Place of Birth*
1	Lord Ṛṣabhadeva	Ayodhyā
2	Lord Ajitanātha	Ayodhyā
3	Lord Śaṁbhavanātha	Śrāvastī
4	Lord Abhinandananātha	Ayodhyā
5	Lord Sumatinātha	Ayodhyā
6	Lord Padmaprabhu	Kauśāmbī
7	Lord Supārśvanātha	Kāśī
8	Lord Candraprabha	Candrapurī
9	Lord Suvidhinātha (Lord Puṣpadanta)	Kākāndī
10	Lord Śītalanātha	Bhaddalapura
11	Lord Śreyāṁsanātha	Siṁhapurī (Sāranātha)
12	Lord Vāsupūjya	Campāpurī
13	Lord Vimalanātha	Kampilā
14	Lord Anantanātha	Ayodhyā
15	Lord Dharmanātha	Ratnapurī
16	Lord Śāntinātha	Hastināpura
17	Lord Kunthunātha	Hastināpura
18	Lord Arahanātha	Hastināpura
19	Lord Mallinātha	Mithilāpurī
20	Lord Munisuvrata	Rājagṛha
21	Lord Naminātha	Mithilā
22	Lord Ariṣṭanemi (Lord Neminātha)	Śaurīpura
23	Lord Pārśvanātha	Kāśī
24	Lord Mahāvīra Svāmī	Kuṇḍagrāma (Vaiśālī)

some animals. He came to know from the chauffeur of his chariot that the cries were from the animals who had been assembled to be killed to serve his wedding attendees. Upon hearing this, he had unbearable emotional agony and was filled with compassion for the animals. He immediately ordered the chauffeur to release all the animals unharmed. This incident left an everlasting impression on his life. He decided to cancel his wedding and left the luxurious princely life to live as an ascetic in forest and immerse himself in intense penance and deep meditation (*sādhanā*).

Lord Neminātha's animal-welfare movement started from a place near Jūnāgaḍha and soon extended to the entire state of Saurāṣṭra and ultimately to the rest of India. This mission opened the community's eyes to the plight of animals. Through this act, the message of compassion spread all around and left an impression for posterity. Even today, Saurāṣṭra has much less animal violence than any other place in the world.

Lord Neminātha retreated to the hills of Giri after renouncing worldly life. He became omniscient after destroying all his soul-defiling[9] *karma* and ultimately attained *nirvāṇa*, the ultimate salvation. This was an immensely revolutionary step in the Yādava lineage.

Lord Pārśvanātha

Lord Pārśvanātha was born in the intellectual center of Kāśī as a prince in 872 BCE, to King Aśvasena and Queen Vāmā Devī. One of the most famous tales cited from Lord Pārśvanātha's life concerns his early age. Once, on the banks of River Gaṅgā, a ritual practitioner was burning some wood pieces while engrossed in religious practice. Prince Pārśvanātha was passing by and pointed out that the practitioner was inadvertently burning a pair of serpents who were inside one of the hollowed wood pieces. Upon hearing this, the practitioner became angry. But when Prince Pārśvanātha insisted, to prove him wrong the practitioner cut open the wood and found the serpents. The bystanders were impressed and questioned the practitioner's intellect; he thereupon became embarrassed and angry. Although the practitioner

[9] As described later, soul-defiling *karmas* are knowledge-inhibiting, perception-inhibiting, hindrance-causing, and delusion-causing *karmas*. Other *karmas* are non-soul-defiling, which are eradicated at the time of *nirvāṇa*.

couldn't do much at that time he carried vindictive thoughts. After death, he was reborn as a god. On the other hand, Lord Pārśvanātha renounced his princely life and became an ascetic. That revengeful ritual practitioner, who had become a god, proceeded to inflict hardships upon Lord Pārśvanātha. In one instance, he tried submerging Lord Pārśvanātha under water, but the serpent pair – who were now born as the God Dharaṇendra and the Goddess Padmāvatī – came to his rescue.

Lord Pārśvanātha was born into the country's most illustrious family lineage of Nāga-vaṁśa. Eminent scholars of history have described his life in the following manner:

> Lord Pārśvanātha's *dharma* addressed behavioral aspects of human nature in its entirety. His four-pronged message of *dharma* centered on relinquishing violence, untruthfulness, stealing, and possessiveness. He carried this message all over India. This was the first instance of such a structured and succinct message of non-violence (*ahiṁsā*) in ancient India. He unified teachings of non-violence with truthfulness, non-stealing, and non-possessiveness. Until then, non-violence was limited to monks and saints living in seclusion in forests, as it was not a part of general behavior. With Lord Pārśvanātha's teachings, it began to be an important aspect of social behavior patterns.

Lord Pārśvanātha spread his teachings of non-violence for over seventy years. At the age of one hundred years, He attained *nirvāṇa* on the hills of Samveda Śikhara (also known as Sammeta Śikhara). The ubiquitous acceptance of non-violence all over India and in the world can be largely attributed to Lord Pārśvanātha. He was instrumental in converting numerous individuals, clans, and groups such as the forest-dwelling tribes to non-violent ways of living. In order to forever memorialize him and his powerful humane messages, many national mountains have been named after him. For instance, Sammeta Śikhara is also known as Pārśvanātha Hills.

An episode highlighting the power of his message of peace and love involves pacifying a group of local rulers involved in violent infighting. When one of the rulers, Prasenajita, was under a cruel attack, Lord Pārśvanātha was the only one from the Kāśī–Kauśala kingdoms to offer him help. With Lord Pārśvanātha's kindly worded inspirational message, all the infighting kings became calm and friendly. This was a great example of his unmatched spiritual purity and oratory. He preached that love is immensely powerful and peace prevails only where love exists. Lord Pārśvanātha taught that wars never truly solve problems because they emanate from violence and are devoid of love.

Lord Mahāvīra

King Ceṭaka was the dominant ruler approximately around 600 BCE. He had a sister by the name Triśalā who was married to a kṣatriya king by the name of Siddhārtha of the Jñātṛ lineage. In Jain scriptures, King Siddhārtha has been mentioned as "*siddhathhey khattiye* (Siddhārtha, the Warrior)" and "*siddhathhey raya* (King Siddhārtha)," and he and Triśalā Devī were the honored parents of Lord Mahāvīra.

In the year 599 BCE, the beautiful spring season was at its exquisite peak, nature's untouched beauty was blossoming, and its ecology was blissfully invigorating all humans and other living beings with joy and excitement. During that heavenly period, on thirteenth day of Caitra-śuklā,[10] Lord Mahāvīra took birth to sanctify the planet Earth. Because King Siddhārtha had witnessed immense economic and spiritual growth and contentment in his kingdom just prior to Lord Mahāvīra's birth, he decided to name his

10 A month in the Jain calendar. For Jains, the day of Lord Mahāvīra's ultimate liberation or *mokṣa* (new moon, or Amāvasyā, in the month of Kārttika of Jain calendar) is the most important day (15 October 527 BCE according to the Gregorian calendar). They have marked the day after the *mokṣa* as the beginning of the Jain calendar known as Vīra Nirvāṇa Saṁvat calendar, marking a new Jain Era. The Jain calendar, like many other Eastern calendars, is a lunisolar calendar, whereas the commonly used Western (Gregorian) calendar is purely a solar calendar. In the lunisolar system, a regular year has twelve months with 353 or 354 or 355 days in the year, and a leap year has thirteen months with 383 or 384 or 385 days. The months are based on the position of the moon with respect to the earth and begins on the day of the new moon. The day or date, which is known as *tithi*, indicates the moon phase. To coincide with the sun to bring the month in phase with the season, the calendar is adjusted by adding an extra month (*adhika māsa*) once every three years. The months of the Jain calendar and corresponding Gregorian months are: Caitra (March–April), Vaiśākha (April–May), Jyeṣṭha (May–June), Āṣāḍha (June–July), Śrāvaṇa (July–August), Bhādrapada (August–September), Āśvina (September–October), Kārttika (October–November), Mārgaśīrṣa (November–December), Pauṣa (December–January), Māgha (January–February), and Phālguna (February–March). As a reference, year 2015 of the Western calendar corresponds to 2541-2542 of Vīra Nirvāṇa Saṁvat calendar.

newborn child Vardhamāna, which literally means "purveyor of fulfillment, prosperity, progress, and happiness."

Jain scriptures are filled with the childhood tales of Lord Mahāvīra which all validate the famous saying in Hindi, "Healthy and shiny leaves of a plant are indicative of a healthy tree in future."[11] Consistent with this, as a child Lord Mahāvīra possessed unsurpassed wisdom, and he was extremely calm, generous, and brave. His parents were followers of Lord Pārśvanātha, and as such he was raised in an environment of non-violence, kindness, compassion, and restraint. He displayed the traits of non-attachment and non-possessiveness right from childhood. For instance, while living in palaces, he was surrounded by all kinds of materialistic possessions like clothes and jewels, yet he was neither attracted to nor interested in any of his possessions. His inner-self was glowing with a special divine light that illuminated his unique spiritual path.

Vardhamāna was intensely solemn and righteous by nature. He was extremely handsome with a tall, powerful stature, a thickset chest, and healthy skin with a natural shine. He appeared as if he had been forged as a one-of-a-kind masculine idol of unmatched attractiveness. But even with all this physical allure, his inner-self was not even the least bit interested in worldly pleasures. He often appeared very serious and solemn as if he were more concerned with freeing himself from the ongoing life–death cycle that was filled with miseries. Even his splendorous youth and the countless worldly distractions presented to him would not dissuade his soul's pursuit on the path of salvation. It was clear that his intentions were all focused on spiritual growth and ultimate salvation.

According to the Digambara canon, he remained unmarried. However, the Śvetāmbara tradition believes that he got married although he never indulged in marital distractions. When he was twenty-eight years old, his parents passed away. His inclinations towards non-attachment and renunciation, with which he was born, now became irresistible. He sought permission of his older brother, Nandivardhana, to renounce the world to live an ascetic life. Nandivardhana was already distraught over their parents' demise. Upon hearing Vardhamāna's plea, he became even more so. He said to Vardhamāna,

---

[11] *Honhāra viravān ke, hota cīkane pāt.*

> Please do not sprinkle salt on my wounds. The parents' departure is already unbearable and now you are suggesting that you will leave me alone. Please do not bring up the thought of leaving me at this stage. I will not be able to bear this all by myself.

Vardhamāna possessed limitless compassion, composure, modesty, and simplicity. He wouldn't do anything to deprive anyone of a smile, leave aside causing another pain. He agreed with Nandivardhana to postpone his decision for two years, without altering his resolve to renounce worldly life. He spent the next two years as a family-bound ascetic while continually progressing on his path of penance and renunciation.

Ultimately, at the age of thirty, Vardhamāna relinquished his worldly life and left home to live and wander in forests while undertaking intense penance and deep meditation (*sādhanā*). He left home only after seeking permission and blessings from his relatives and did not quietly abscond in the night when everyone was in deep sleep.

This marked the beginning of the ascetic (*śramaṇa*) life of Lord Mahāvīra. He undertook intense penance for twelve years, five months, and fifteen days (4,545 days) to attain unbound wisdom (*kevala-jñāna*). At the time of his attainment of *kevala-jñāna*, Lord Mahāvīra was in deep meditation on the banks of R̥jubālā Stream.

Jain literature and scriptures are full of detailed descriptions of Lord Mahāvīra's intense penance during this long duration. From these accounts, it appears that Lord Mahāvīra's penance was exceptional and glorious. It is astounding to read about his self-mortification. Countless eminent individuals have reached extreme heights of spiritual achievements and attained liberation, yet no one comes close to the level of devout austerity and the highest level of meditation that Lord Mahāvīra undertook. He showed exemplary courage and remained equanimous (*samatā*) while exercising complete restraint under the harshest kind of tortures. His unrelenting restrained demeanor during the mental and bodily torment inflicted on him by other beings, including Gopāla, Śūlapāṇi Yakṣa, Saṅgama Deva, the serpent Caṇḍakauśika, Gauśālaka, and the tribal people of Lāḍha Deśa, illustrates his great equanimous ability for self-control and endurance. Throughout many tribulations, Lord Mahāvīra remained steadfast, unmoved and unwavering like the Himālaya, during even rousing and passionate inflictions. With this extraordinary courage and restraint during his penance and highest level of meditation, he became the very personification of the moniker "Mahāvīra," the bravest of all. Usually a brave person earns such a reputation by displaying resolute courage and the ability to fearlessly face all calamities and pains. Lord Mahāvīra actually invited these hardships to test his ability to self-purify and eradicate soul-defiling *karmas*. He fought these difficulties with peace and self-restraint, and ultimately he won for perpetuity. That is why he came to be known as Mahāvīra.[12]

Lord Mahāvīra's penance and deep meditation (*sādhanā*) were marked by many immaculate practices. During his 4,545 days of *sādhanā*, he ate only on 349 days and fasted the remaining days. He spent as much as six months at a time without food and water. It is fascinating to note that, other than just one exception, Lord Mahāvīra did not sleep at all during his penance and fought to always stay awake. Whenever he felt sleepy, he would slightly change his posture to get rid of sleep. This demonstrates that with practice one can win control even over sleep, which is a pretty severe penance in itself.

Lord Mahāvīra attained the quintessential spiritual achievement as a result of his exalted *sādhanā*. He became omniscient and achieved ubiquitous and unbounded knowledge and wisdom (*kevala-jñāna*). After that, he followed the path of Ultimate Truth while progressing towards final salvation. He spent thirty years moving from one place to another spreading his message of supreme non-violence, restraint, and wisdom. He ultimately reached Pāvāpurī. The moment of his salvation approached while he continued to offer the message of righteousness, benevolence, and sacredness in his pure and loving voice. In the end, at the age of seventy-two, on the night of the new moon (*amāvasyā*) in the month of Kārttika,[13] Lord Mahāvīra freed himself from all *karmas* and the physical body for the last time. He attained the ultimate spiritual liberation (*mokṣa*).

---

[12] For a more detailed account, refer to the *Ācārāṅgasūtra*, the first and second Śrutaskandha; the *Kalpasūtra*: the *Āvaśyakaniryukti*; the *Āvaśyakacūrṇi*; and other Jain scriptures.

[13] Kārttika is a month in the Jain calendar, and usually falls in October or November of the commonly used Western or Gregorian calendar. Year 2015 of the Western calendar corresponds to 2541-2542 of Vīra Nirvāṇa Saṁvat calendar.

Lord Mahāvīra is an unmatched personality of eminence in the world. His multifaceted spiritual revolution was not limited to one place or one nation. His contributions are invaluable and widespread, encompassing spirituality, academics, socio-economic order, language, and many other aspects of life. For instance:

1. He showed the ascetics of his era to focus on internal and conscientious *sādhanā* (penance and deep meditation) rather than outwardly ritualistic practices such as *yajña*.
2. He demonstrated the widespread benefits possible through the proper performance of penance, meditation, and austerity.
3. He taught the acceptance of a multiplicity of diverse views to those who were indulging in fights and arguments dominated by self-aggrandizing, singular views.
4. He refuted the birth-based, socio-economic caste system that ignored personal achievements, and promoted a system that valued one's quality and ability over status of birth.
5. He established a female system of nuns, denouncing the male-dominant system that had engulfed the nation and had largely ignored the immense contributions women make to the society.
6. He showed the true spiritual path to those ritualistic practitioners who were blindly engaged in animal sacrifices and other cruel practices supposedly for their own selfish advancement.
7. He denounced any religious basis for self-immolation (often known as *satī* practice), the striving for heaven simply by bathing in rivers and ponds, collecting wealth in the name of religion, and other such immoral activities done in the name of religious precepts.
8. He employed the language of common person (Ardha-Māgadhī or Ardhamāgadhī) to convey his messages rather than elite language such as Sanskrit, used by priests, which very few people understood. This ended the claims of academic superiority merely on the basis of language usage.

In summation, Lord Mahāvīra sought to convert all of the egotistic, violent, and selfish ways in which society measured and looked at itself into practices that were spiritually motivated and promoted a wholesome lifestyle.

LORD MAHĀVĪRA'S BENEVOLENT COMMUNITY

Lord Mahāvīra had 14,000 male disciples who were monks and 36,000 female disciples who were nuns. Out of these, eleven were prominent and they became famous chief disciples, known as the *gaṇadharas* ("those who uphold virtue") in Jain tradition. All of them had formerly been followers of Vedic Hindu doctrine. They were highly respected authorities on the Hindu scriptures (Vedāṅga). Among them, Indrabhūti Gautama was considered the most accomplished sage. He came to Lord Mahāvīra to challenge and debate him based on his prior knowledge of scriptures and essence of spirituality. In the process, he was so mesmerized by Lord Mahāvīra's reasoning and logical explanations that he requested to be adopted as a disciple. Similarly, the other ten *gaṇadharas* also followed Indrabhūti Gautama to be adopted by Lord Mahāvīra as disciples. They embraced the sainthood in the Arhat Saṅgha (association of saints) of Lord Mahāvīra and became the main pillars of Mahāvīra's Jain tradition.

Upon witnessing Lord Mahāvīra's consummate penance, sacrifices, discipline, and self-control, eight predominant kings of that time also embraced asceticism under Lord Mahāvīra's tutelage. These kings were: Vīrāṁgaka, Vīrayakṣa, Sañjaya, Eṇeyaka, Seya, Śiva, Udayana, and Śaṅkha. In addition, many princes including Abhaya Kumāra and Megha Kumāra became disciples. Many ascetics also joined Lord Mahāvīra's congregation upon understanding the true purpose of asceticism and renunciation. Similarly, princesses Candanabālā (who became the chief female disciple) and Devānandā and many other women joined Lord Mahāvīra's entourage of nuns and female ascetics.

Lord Mahāvīra had accrued a large number of followers from among both regular and high-class householders. This included notable aristocrats such as Śreṇika, Kuṇika (also known as Ajātaśatru), Vaiśālīpati Ceṭaka (Mahāvīra's maternal uncle), and Caṇḍapradyota of Avantī. The tens of thousands of followers also included Ānanda, Kāmadeva, and Śakaṭāla. Individuals such as Harikeśī and Metārya were granted sainthood although they belonged to the so-called lower class (śūdra). This represented a major revolutionary step under the prevalent circumstances. In the known history of

India, Lord Mahāvīra was the first eminent person who openly spoke against untouchability in strong words and followed that by granting them prominent positions in his own communion and organization.

LORD MAHĀVĪRA'S CONTRIBUTIONS

Lord Mahāvīra made immense contributions towards not only the religious and spiritual awakening of the populace, but also to their social and cultural lifestyle.

1. Lord Mahāvīra established equally accessible religious and spiritual ordination that was not based on the prevailing caste system that promoted divisiveness of the society among the brāhmin, kṣatriya, vaiśya, and śūdra castes. At the same time, he motivated them all towards a unified path to progress based on human values rather than the parochial creed one was born into.
2. He inspired the entire world to honor the fundamental desire of all movable and immovable living beings that are simply striving to achieve eternal happiness, reach greatness, and endeavor to obtain everlasting peace and joy. With that in mind, one must neither hurt any living being nor encourage anyone else to cause harm to others.
3. He taught that one should endeavor to enrich one's behavior with non-violence, cultivate harmony in one's thoughts, and practice non-possessiveness and non-attachment in one's conduct.
4. He taught that the *dharma* of righteousness is the inherent nature of every soul whereas wickedness is not. This is the reason that Lord Mahāvīra advocated for equal freedom for men and women to pursue their individual paths to salvation.
5. Lord Mahāvīra adopted the widely used vernacular of Ardhamāgadhī for his sermons and other communications instead of Sanskrit, which was used primarily by *paṇḍits* and scholars at that time. Language can be an obstacle in bringing people together, and his use of a common vernacular was an attempt to unite people from all backgrounds and regions.
6. Lord Mahāvīra condemned the ongoing violence against animals, and their sacrifices and torture by individuals in rituals and during religious celebrations. He spoke against the problematic notions of purportedly achieving heavenly pleasures by such demeaning and violent acts, while

promoting the importance of penance, renunciation, non-violence, discipline, and controlled conduct.

7. His sermons addressed and promoted the virtues of contentment, non-attachment, suppression of materialistic desires, spiritual progression, non-stealing, forgiveness, non-egotistic living, carefulness, benevolence, and non-possessiveness. He inspired everyone to continually enrich their lives with these virtues.
8. Lord Mahāvīra preached that one's destiny is not crafted by an external God-like force, but one's own internal divinity.[14] He emphasized the importance of the combination of honorable and honest efforts in one's deeds, innate nature, and fruition of *karma* that has the power to define the repercussions of actions and activities in one's life.
9. Some of the unique contributions of Lord Mahāvīra's teachings consist of: theories of soul as the real self (Ātmavāda), ecological integration with environment (Lokavāda), the relationship between one's acts and future outcome (Karmavāda), one's tendencies while enacting deeds (Kriyāvāda), the doctrine of Fundamental Principles (Nayavāda), the doctrine of Non-Absolutism (Anekāntavāda), and the doctrine of Qualified Assertion (Syādvāda), among others.
10. He preached that every soul could achieve eternal greatness, and that a human devoid of animosity, jealousy, and attachments is the true brāhmin, not simply the one who is born in a certain lineage. He sermonized that controlling or foregoing one's desires is the true *yajña*, and that purification of the soul is not accomplished through physical wealth but through spiritual exertion, and to that end, renunciation is the only way to attain spiritual benefit. He preached that true courage consists in the victory over one's ego and in the preservation and protection of one's innate virtues.

The practice of the true *dharma* of righteousness is in the friendly behavior towards all living beings, the cordiality towards virtuous individuals, the practice of compassion towards all disadvantaged individuals, and being accommodating of individuals with contrary views. Lord Mahāvīra preached that one must be truly helpful to others, and self-correcting and self-improving towards oneself.

---

[14] See "Glossary of Terms" for the definition of the term "divinity" in the Jain tradition.

RELIGIOUS LEADERS DURING THE TIME OF LORD MAHĀVĪRA

Many religious leaders were trying to establish their own religious traditions that they founded during the same time period as Lord Mahāvīra. This included Jamālī, Maṅkhalī Putta, Gośāla, Pūraṇakaśyapa, Prakruddhakātyāyana, Ajitakeśa, Kambali, Sañjaya, Velaṭṭhiputta, and even Gautama Buddha. Jamālī was Lord Mahāvīra's son-in-law (according to Śvetāmbara tradition), and he eventually became Mahāvīra's opponent approximately fifteen years after Lord Mahāvīra's attainment of *kevala-jñāna*.

One of Lord Mahāvīra's disciples, Gośālaka, initiated a separate religious sect known as Ājīvaka Mata, references to which can still be found in several religious scriptures, including some Buddhist texts. Gośālaka's life was quite remarkable. But as remarkable as it was, his life was equally undisciplined. He was born in a brāhmin clan, and acquired his knowledge under Lord Mahāvīra's guidance. Initially he was successful while establishing the Ājīvaka sect but eventually he lost a debate with Mahāvīra, who was his preceptor. To his credit, he pleaded for the lord's forgiveness and ultimately left his body.

According to Jain scriptures, whatever spiritual knowledge Gośālaka had, he received it from Lord Mahāvīra. Through his spiritual acumen, he was able to perform *tejo leśyā* (stealing one's luster or essence), which can be a destructive power and is considered to be very rare. However, his pernicious beliefs and obstinate behavior led him to establish Ājīvaka as a separate sect based on the doctrine of pre-destiny and not self-conduct. After receiving all the knowledge and skills, he became very egotistical and aggressive in nature, obviously contrary to his preceptor Lord Mahāvīra's philosophy. He was able to build some momentum with a few followers, but soon after his death the sect dispersed and ceased to exist.

In spite of having made certain advancements, Gośālaka lacked humility and grace. That is why Lord Mahāvīra considered him an unscrupulous disciple and not an honorable one. The interactions between Lord Mahāvīra and Gośālaka, and references to how Gośālaka killed two saints using his *tejo leśyā* skill, are described in the *Bhagavatīsūtra*, a Jain scripture.

Lord Mahāvīra's spiritual philosophy and demeanor differed significantly from the other religious leaders of his time. He emphasized conduct based on non-absolutism and respect for diverse perspectives through reconciliation of multiple viewpoints and incomplete or partial truths – the doctrine of Anekāntavāda. He considered the insistence on unilateral viewpoints to be impropriate and shortsighted. Thus, the doctrine of Anekāntavāda is Lord Mahāvīra's eternal gift to the world.

LORD MAHĀVĪRA AND LORD BUDDHA

Lord Mahāvīra and Lord Buddha were contemporaries and have some interesting similarities. The Buddha was born into the Śākya lineage as the son of King Śuddhodhana. Eventually, he became a great ascetic in the *śramaṇa* tradition and was even referred to as an *arihanta* who eventually achieved ultimate knowledge. Some aspects of the lives of these two great souls are shown in Table 2.2.

MAHĀVĪRA AND BUDDHA: SIMILARITIES AND DISSIMILARITIES

While there were some differences between the doctrines of Lord Mahāvīra and Lord Buddha, the similarities heavily outweigh the differences. Like Lord Mahāvīra, the Buddha held the vows of non-violence, truthfulness, non-stealing, non-possession, and right conduct (celibacy) in great esteem. Both of them promoted ascetic beliefs at a time when brāhmaṇic culture was widely practiced. They propagated the message of compassion and empathy all over India and Asia, and also around the world. They disseminated the path of spiritual progress through right knowledge and self-realization to scores of living and future humans. They had very similar approaches towards improvement of human life based on non-violence for contemporary and future generations. Both of them despised over-indulgence, attachment, jealousy, animosity, and malice, and they both inspired practices of self-purification and non-violent living.

SIMILAR INSPIRATION BETWEEN BUDDHIST AND JAIN DOCTRINES

Jain and Buddhist ideologies and cultures seem to be quite similar. A well-known Buddhist ascetic, Dharmānanda Kauśāmbī, states that the Buddha adopted the four principles/disciplines (*cāra-yāma*) of Lord Pārśvanātha to develop his own five principles (*pañca-śīla*) and eight limbs (*aṣṭāṅga*). Some scholars believe that Lord Buddha spent his early years with a monk from the lineage of Lord Pārśvanātha. He developed a strong disinclination towards

Table 2.2: Profiles of Lord Mahāvīra and Lord Buddha

	Lord Mahāvīra	*Lord Buddha*
Father	Siddhārtha	Śuddhodhana
Mother	Triśalā	Mahāmāyā
Clan (*gotra*)	Kaśyapa	Kaśyapa
Village (*grāma*)	Kuṇḍagrāma	Kapilavastu
Caste (*jāti*)	Kṣatriya Jñāta	Śākya
Year of Birth	599 BCE	600 BCE
Wife	Yaśodā (Śvetāmbara belief)	Yaśodharā
Offspring	Priyadarśanā (Śvetāmbara belief)	Rāhula
Year of renunciation	569 BCE (age 30)	571 BCE (age 29)
Years of penance	12	6
Place of *kevala-jñāna*	Banks of Ṛjubālukā	Gayā
Year of *nirvāṇa*	527 BCE	520 BCE
Place of *nirvāṇa*	Madhyama Apāpā (Pāvāpurī)	Kuśīnagara
Life	72 years	80 years
Grand vows	*Pañca-mahāvrata* (five great vows)	*Pañca-śīla* (five behaviors)
Fundamental principle	Anekāntavāda	Kṣaṇikavāda (Vibhujyavāda)

hard penance and departed to start his own "middle path" (*madhyama-mārga*), an offshoot spiritual method. Over time, it blossomed into a separate stand-alone religion. In his scripture, *Bhāratīya Saṁskṛti aur Ahiṁsā*, Dharmānanda Kauśāmbī has vividly compared Lord Pārśvanātha's *cāra-yāma* and Lord Buddha's *madhyama-mārga*, as shown in Table 2.3.

In this fashion, Lord Pārśvanātha's four principles were merged to create these three segments of *aṣṭāṅga-mārga* (eightfold path). The remaining five – right perception, right resolve, right application, right memory, and right trance – all foster the principle of non-violence.

Jain and Buddhist practitioners and their organizations have continually undertaken the immense task of spreading the message of peace and non-

Table 2.3: Precepts of Lord Buddha and Lord Pārśvanātha

Buddhist Precept	*Pārśvanātha's Cāra-Yāma*
Samyag-karma (right deed)	*Ahiṁsā, asteya* (non-harming, non-stealing)
Samyag-vāc (right speech)	*Asatya* (falsehood)
Samyag-ājīva (right livelihood)	*Aparigraha* (non-covetousness)

violence in the world. Both religions are based on the doctrines of asceticism, and even today both have a deep respect and conviviality towards each other.

THE SEVEN NINHAVAS AND OTHER OPPONENTS OF LORD MAHĀVĪRA

In the beginning, a small number of sects emerged to oppose Lord Mahāvīra's preaching. However, all of these became irrelevant and non-existent very soon after their inception.

1. Fourteen years after Lord Mahāvīra attained *kevala-jñāna*, Jamālī Ninhava established the Bahurata sect to oppose Mahāvīra. Presently, the sect has no following and its name remains only in Jain history books.
2. Sixteen years later, close to the time of Lord Mahāvīra's *nirvāṇa* (end of bodily living and liberation of soul), Tiṣyagupta, the disciple of Ācārya Basu, attempted to create a major controversy by inflaming regional differences.
3. Approximately 214 years after Lord Mahāvīra's *nirvāṇa* in 527 BCE, Āṣāḍācārya, a believer in unseen godly powers as opposed to self-realization, attempted to create a rift in the Jain organization by creating controversies around minor disagreements.
4. Similarly, approximately 220 years after Lord Mahāvīra's *nirvāṇa*, Aśvamitra tried to create another schism. He was a disciple of Kauṇḍinya, who in turn was a disciple of a non-believing sage, Mahāgiri.
5. Again, approximately 228 years after Lord Mahāvīra's *nirvāṇa*, another ascetic, Gaṅgācārya, attempted to create dissension in the organization. He was a disciple of Dhanagupta, who was another disciple of Mahāgiri.
6. Approximately 544 years after Lord Mahāvīra's *nirvāṇa*, Rohagupta,

a disciple of another non-believer by the name of Śrī Gupta, made yet another attempt to create discord.

7. Finally, approximately 584 years after Lord Mahāvīra's *nirvāṇa*, another skeptic and undignified saint, Goṣṭhā Māhila, attempted to create a rift, similar to that by Dhanagupta and Aśvamitra.

Lord Mahāvīra's followers and the organization remained intact and continued to flourish in spite of all the dubious attempts to break their unity. Each of the above seven dissenters failed in their efforts.

DIVISIVE ISSUES

Fundamental Vows: Four or Five?

Gautama Svāmī did not have a strong position on whether monks should be clothed or unclothed, but he expressed strong reasoning for adopting five principle vows (non-violence, truthfulness, non-stealing, non-possession, and celibacy) instead of only the first four espoused by Lord Pārśvanātha's followers. Similarly, he stressed *pratikramaṇa* (self-evaluation and correction), and proper arrangements for conduct during daytime and nighttime. He emphasized sincere effort in penance, meditation, knowledge, perception, and conduct for spiritual growth, and remained indifferent to the use or disuse of clothes by ascetics. He rendered the controversy around clothed or unclothed living by ascetics unimportant by calling it a worldly issue rather than one relevant to spiritual growth. That is why the Jain community has never been able to create a definitive, all-encompassing criterion in this matter.

Ascetics with or without Clothes

The single biggest point of discontent in Lord Mahāvīra's organization was the coexistence of monks who wore a sheet of cloth and those who were totally naked. The reason behind this was that Lord Pārśvanātha's followers wore a cloth whereas Lord Mahāvīra emphasized no clothes (sky clad), based on the injunction of owning no possessions. However, Lord Mahāvīra accepted both types of monks in his organization. This led to an amicable resolution for the coexistence of Lord Pārśvanātha's follower the ascetic Keśī Kumāra, and Lord Mahāvīra's first disciple (*gaṇadhara*), Gautama Svāmī.

Lord Mahāvīra stressed the need of observing five great vows and *pratikramaṇa* for self-cleansing and spiritual progress towards ultimate salvation. He did not stress in a similar definitive manner the wearing or disowning of clothes by ascetics. His highest expectation from the spiritual seekers was in their internal purification. That is why the dispute was resolved amicably during those times.

During his times, his own followers, who were naked, peacefully coexisted with those of Lord Pārśvanātha, who were clothed. However, the dispute continued to brew. After the death of the talented and magnanimous ascetics Jambū Svāmī and Bhadrabāhu Svāmī, the age-old dispute erupted into the formation of Śvetāmbara (clothed) and Digambara (unclothed) traditions as separate sects. However, both traditions agree that when Lord Mahāvīra left his home, he had a piece of cloth, but thereafter, gave up that last possession and became a possessionless unclothed ascetic.

Section (*śruta*) 1, chapter (*adhyāya*) 9 of the *Ācārāṅgasūtra*[15] (a Śvetāmbara scripture) contains a couplet which describes Lord Mahāvīra's position towards clothing. He had received a small piece of cloth from the God Indra at the time of his renunciation. However, he decided that he would give up that cloth and endure cold and hot weather.

Thereafter, he never took another piece of cloth during his life. He had accepted the piece of cloth as a ceremonial tradition of gifting and relinquished it thirteen months later. After that, he traveled all over without any clothes or any other possessions. Whenever he took food, he did so with his hands and not with any utensils owned by others. He did not care about respect or honor towards himself and he often went to the kitchen of householders and took only the food that was pure and cooked with minimum harm to the environment or airborne living entities.

This above-mentioned couplet shows that Lord Mahāvīra lived without clothes and all other worldly possessions, but the second chapter of the same scripture clearly shows that he allowed the use of cloth by monks. In addition,

[15] *ṇocevimeṇa vattheṇa, pihissāmi taṁsi hemaṁte* ।
se pārae āvakahāe, eyaṁ khu aṇudhammiyaṁ tassa ॥ – verse 2
saṁvaccaraṁ sāhiyaṁ māsaṁ, jaṁ ṇa rikkāsi vatthagaṁ bhagavaṁ ।
acelae tato cāī, taṁ vosajja vatthamaṇagāre ॥ – verse 4
ṇo sevatī ya para-vatthaṁ, para-pāe vi se ṇa bhuṁjitthā ।
parivajjiyāṇa omāṇaṁ, gacchati saṁkhaḍi asaraṇāe ॥ – verse 11

it is stated in fourteenth chapter of this scripture that monks can accept and wear clothes made of cotton or wool. All of this supports the Śvetāmbara position regarding clothing and monastics.

While not objecting to the clothed living of Jain ascetics (according to Śvetāmbaras only), Lord Mahāvīra did praise the clothesless living of Jain monks, according to the third directive (*uddeśe*) in sixth chapter (*adhyāya*) of the *Ācārāṅgasūtra*. He encouraged monks to give up clothes in the first of the three requirements of monkhood by saying "one should progress towards clothesless living."[16] In this manner, he justified clothed living of monks to those who believed only in clothesless living for monks. At the same time, he presented clothesless living as an honorable objective to strive for, with the objective of ending discriminatory behavior by beholders of one viewpoint towards the others. That is why no Jain scriptures indicate that the monks from Lord Pārśvanātha's lineage were required to forego clothes when they joined Lord Mahāvīra's ranks of monks. However, it is clearly indicated that they were all required to adopt five vows of conduct instead of the four vows they had previously followed while in Lord Pārśvanātha's lineage. In addition, they were required to conduct *pratikramaṇa* (confession) day and night. Clarification of this subject of use and disuse of clothes by monks was necessitated by the emphasis on distinctions between Śvetāmbara and Digambara traditions. But Lord Mahāvīra was neither the proponent of clothesless or clothed living, nor an opponent.

It is worth noting that due to emphasis on the requirement of clothesless living by monks in the Digambara tradition, female monks would not qualify to achieve *nirvāṇa* or attain *mokṣa* since they were not permitted to be in public without clothing. This could be considered by some to be at least one negative aspect of the requirement of clothesless living by the ascetics. The Śvetāmbara tradition has accepted that a soul in female body can achieve *nirvāṇa*. While renunciation is considered to be a genuine and honorable principle on the spiritual path, it may be more honorable to make progress on this path with principled living while acknowledging the importance of and not ignoring the conditions, actions, time, locality, and intentions behind one's renunciation.

---

16 *acel bhūyo āvaī.*

JAIN AND VEDIC PHILOSOPHIES SUPPLEMENT EACH OTHER FOR COMPLETENESS

Lord Mahāvīra has a unique position among proponents of ascetic beliefs and practices. He brought a revolution against the existing practices of dogmatic, insincere, and blind faith while spreading a spirituality that was purified of these encumbrances. Self-purification and destruction of attachments and jealousy were his major objectives. This deeply affected the prevalent religious traditions. India witnessed the emergence of the Jain and Buddhist philosophies, known as ascetic (*śramaṇa*) traditions, while those of Vedic and Vaiṣṇava societies were termed as Vedic or Brāhmanic traditions.

From the perspective of the contemporary lifestyle, Vedic philosophy would be effective for achieving excellence in execution for day-to-day operations, while Jain and Buddhist philosophies would be effective for excellence in vision and strategy for long-term spiritual progression. In that sense, the two philosophies supplement each other.

In life, certain aspects must be balanced carefully, such as cultural upbringing, devotion, actions, renunciation, salvation, abstinence, association, and attachment. To that end, if one were to critically analyze the relationship between Jain and Vedic beliefs, the conclusion would be that the provisions for ascetic institutions are not as succinctly defined anywhere as they are in Jain and Buddhist traditions. Such provisions in Vedic tradition seem to be a derivative of those in Jain scriptures. Similarly, provisions for the lifestyle of householders who follow Jain tradition seem to be an interpretation of those in Vedic scriptures. In the Jain *śramaṇa* (ascetic) tradition, abstinence and salvation are considered pre-eminent, and renunciation is considered the foremost practice to attain salvation.

The Jain, Buddhist, and Vedic philosophies taken together truly illustrate the strength of a diversity of views. They epitomize the glorious dhārmic traditions of India that mutually invigorate and validate each other.

Lord Mahāvīra promoted the idea that religious acts for divine appeasement (*yajña*) should be performed as internal thought processes, devoid of animal cruelty, rather than through physical acts involving animal sacrifices, in the spirit of his emphasis on *ahiṁsā* (non-violence). As a result, the violence-based practices among elite brāhmaṇas subsided. At the same time, political leaders and kings started giving up certain vicious practices while adopting the householder (*śrāvaka*) practices expounded by Lord Mahāvīra. His evangelization of non-violence has left everlasting impressions, to the extent that even after hundreds of years the practice of animal sacrifice in religious acts is almost non-existent today. Monks, saints, and spiritual seekers have continued with non-violent lifestyles, following Lord Mahāvīra's teachings on ascetic conduct. By studying and practicing his teachings, they have consequently established proper practices in societies. The impact of Jain beliefs is quite evident in the conduct and lifestyle of all the religious practitioners from dhārmic traditions.

INFLUENCE OF THE ŚRAMAṆA TRADITION ON OTHER RELIGIONS

There are many similarities in the principles related to conduct and behavior of monks of different sects and religions. Lord Mahāvīra's provisions in this matter were very well thought out, well organized, and progressive. Various religious traditions over time have adopted many characteristics from his guidance on monks' conduct. Even today, the world's scientific community continues to be impressed by the controlled demeanor and austerity of Jain monks. They wonder how Jain ascetics can go through such difficult austerities that help them in their quest for self-improvement and spiritual welfare. The respect bestowed on Jain monks to date is a boon resulting from the highly organized provisions of monks' conduct by Lord Mahāvīra.

The Jain ascetics are the ultimate travelers – they are walking itinerant dwellers who carry their entire belongings on their shoulders and are not dependent on anybody. Those who stayed for extended periods in villages or cities were termed "sinning ascetics" by Lord Mahāvīra because staying at one place could become a cause for declining self-restraint. Jain ascetics had to cover the entire journey by themselves across lands, through thick forests and dry deserts. That is why Jain scriptures have provided detailed descriptions of the calamities and atrocities suffered by Jain ascetics. At the same time, the scriptures provide instructions on how to choose an appropriate path when unpleasant situations arise. Lord Mahāvīra provided guidelines on the principled demeanor to be adopted by monks and nuns in the following situations:

1. During turmoil caused by thieves and robbers.

2. Regarding the use of vehicles to cross water channels.
3. Considering medicines and health care for disease outbreaks and stings by snakes and other poisonous animals.
4. At times when restrictions were imposed on Jain ascetics during political and social disorder.
5. During periods of the resolution of disorder caused by unjust and cruel kings and leaders.
6. When seeking solutions for scarcity of alms during famine and hunger conditions.
7. During periods of retribution enacted on the religion and community.

His prescriptions cover many more possible issues that the community of ascetics and householders could face.

HARDSHIPS ENDURED BY THE ŚRAMAṆA COMMUNITY

Guidelines for propriety based on conditions, actions, time, locality, and the intentions of monks and nuns provide a mechanism by which a community of Jain ascetics – in agreement, and with permission from the non-ascetic (householder) Jain community – can formulate legislation during changing times. The guidelines may need modifications to accommodate unexpected occurrences over time. Lord Mahāvīra, with his forward-thinking vision, incorporated such provisions in his guidelines for ascetic living.

From the viewpoint of historic research, one cannot even imagine the sufferings endured by the Jain *śramaṇa* organization in the prevailing conditions twenty-five hundred years ago. During those days, monks and nuns had to wander through thick and frightful forests. Inhabited localities were few. Those that existed were thinly populated, and well-formed pathways were scarce. People had to make their own trails through forests, deserts, hills, waterways and flat lands. But a mendicant lives to create his own path to traverse through the hardships of life and the turbulent ways of the world. Following the trodden and beaten path of others was not Lord Mahāvīra's way because invariably that would be the path under the influence of violence and excesses; that was the hallmark of a kṣatriya-run society.

During those times, tyrannical governance by unjust rulers was a source of ongoing hardships on the monks. On many occasions, the power struggles that followed the death of a king had a negative impact on ascetic organizations. Whenever a ruler was unfair and hostile to a particular religion, the monks and nuns of that religion were made to suffer immensely. In many cases, they were mistaken as spies and were punished with no justification at all.

In addition, dacoits had their own colonies, which were ruled by the dubious leaders of their own. If and when any monks and/or nuns entered such colonies by mistake, they were sure to be robbed, insulted, assaulted, and forced to endure other miseries.

While staying in the vicinity of townships, monks had to endure many difficulties as well. They had to patrol their living quarters (*upāśraya*s or *sthānaka*s) themselves. Thieves would hide their stolen goods nearby, or unruly individuals fleeing from the law would leave their evidence near the quarters inhabited by ascetics, which would alarm local authorities and implicate the ascetics. The monks and nuns also had to protect their colleagues from poisonous snakes and spiders, and so on, other animals such as wild dogs, and other dangerous elements.

Famine and other such calamities would have a severe impact on the livelihood of monks and nuns. The infamous impact of the Pāṭaliputra famine is very well documented. Countless ascetics had to leave the region during this drought, and as a result many Jain scriptures were destroyed during that period.

Because of the above-mentioned hardships, natural calamities, and acts of harassment, many monks and nuns felt compelled to sacrifice their bodies to protect their religion and their honor because they would rather die while living with their principles than bring dishonor to their asceticism.

In modern times, relatively orderly living conditions prevail under well-established and structured rules of law and governance. However, it is hard to imagine the amount of anguish that ascetics endured in days past while preserving their honor, duty, and religion. The rulers who made Jain ascetic predecessors endure such inhumane conditions are gone, along with those who persecuted Jain ascetics in ancient times. Nonetheless, Jain Dharma and Jain ascetics have endured, as evidence of the victory of *dharma*, justice, and truth over unlawful, violent, and deceitful treachery.

JAIN ŚRAMAṆA PROLIFERATION

Lord Mahāvīra's *dharma* is not under the ownership of any sect, creed, lineage, or society. It is a methodical philosophy that emphasizes internal self-purification. It guides one in a natural and unpretentious manner for systematic spiritual progression that ultimately leads to freedom from the cycle of birth and rebirth in hell, heaven, and earth. The perseverance and spiritual endeavors of the practitioner is the determinant factor of the efficaciousness of Jain Dharma, and the degree to which one partakes of this spiritual nectar.

The proliferation of a philosophy is contingent upon its optimum dissemination. Amazingly, Lord Mahāvīra's philosophy has been kept intact through the centuries, although philosophical proliferation is not an objective or a subject of devotion in itself.

As a righteous philosophy develops, its propagation naturally broadens, the knowledge about the philosophy increases, its following swells, and it creates a favorable environment for its further growth and sustenance. To this extent, it will propagate inter-personal amity, cooperation, and courage among practitioners. Lord Mahāvīra was the greatest propagator of the divine message. He called upon all of his disciples – monks, nuns, male and female householders, and even those who were not his disciples – to become engaged in this mission to their fullest extent. This would lead to their own self-emancipation and that of others as well.

Lord Mahāvīra always encouraged spiritual preceptors, social coordinators, and anyone who worked to further the cause of non-violence. In the Jain scripture *Upāsakadaśāṅgasūtra*, he praised Kuṇḍakoliyā after he triumphantly presented Mahāvīra's *arhat* philosophy to achieve victory over the Gośālaka sect. Lord Mahāvīra thanked him by saying, "Kuṇḍakoliyā, you are praiseworthy."[17]

The greatness of Lord Mahāvīra is illustrated by the following examples:

1. The detailed accounts of various householders including Śaṅkha Śrāvaka, Kāmadeva, and Ānandādi.
2. His acceptance of Gautama Svāmī's decision to send ascetics for facilitations and interactions with society at large.

---

[17] *dyanyo 'si kuṇḍakoliyā ṇaṁ tumaṁ.*

3. His allowing of the ascetic Skandhaka, who was Gautama Svāmī's childhood friend, to welcome Gautama Gaṇadhara; and other such events.

Similarly, dispatching Keśī Kumāra Śramaṇa to persuade King Paradeśī, and sending monks and nuns to various towns and villages, were all designed to effectively propagate Jain philosophy. The life of King Paradeśī, and Keśī Kumāra Śramaṇa's visit to Śvetāmbikā, are all prominent examples of the practice of spiritual evangelism.

Effective promotion is critical to the success of a *dharma* (religion). That is why Lord Mahāvīra considered religious influence a critical aspect of complete and ultimate spiritual truth. In the Jain scripture *Ācārāṅgasūtra*, in the prayers recited by the divine beings from nine heavens, their expectations for the welfare of masses are well expressed when they pray, "Please establish a *tīrtha* (ascetic abode) for the benefit of living beings and the universe."[18] The religion of non-violence was formed solely for the benefit of the world. Lord Mahāvīra designated those who serve to propagate his doctrine and the culture of non-violence, while facing all the untold difficulties, as the "honorable and blessed ones."

LORD MAHĀVĪRA AND HIS CONTEMPORARY SOCIETY

In order to properly organize the Jain *śramaṇa* (ascetic) tradition, a sort of "peace corps" was created around Lord Mahāvīra. This group was designed to bring about spiritual revolution in social and religious areas. This enabled Lord Mahāvīra to face and defeat the prevailing maladies of society. Although the key aspect of his philosophy was to move in the direction of salvation, the concepts of codifying the philosophy were no less important. The communities were seriously disturbed by the prevailing conditions of violent religious practices and accompanying inhumanity. However, because of the hegemony of Brāhmanic and upper classes, the common people did not have the courage to resist them. The masses could not defy the organizers of these inhumane practices, and society was like a prison where the lower strata of society were dependent on the pity and charity of the upper-class, rich individuals. The masses lacked freedom because they had no identity

---

[18] *Svva-jagga-jīva hiyaṁ titthaṁ, pavattehi.*

beyond that which was linked to their work, caste, and sect. During those dark days of that unjust era, Lord Mahāvīra shone like the rays of rising sun and people felt that a liberator had come for them. Not only humans felt this sentiment, but the animal world also had a collective sense of relief. The violent religious practices that reeked with the burning blood and flesh of animals were replaced by non-violent practices that glowed with the pleasant aura of burning *ghee* (clarified butter). Such changes brought peace, happiness, and progress in all areas of society.

Those who proclaimed that they possessed ultimate spiritual knowledge as ritualists and scholars bowed their heads in humility upon meeting Lord Mahāvīra. His was the victory of the heart over unjust knowledge, selfless sentiments over unruly deeds, and love over arrogant scholarship. He brought the elevated state of humanity that was instrumental in ending the prevailing inhumane behavior of human beings of the time. With the end of these incredibly violent ritualistic religious practices, the untimely killings of innocent animals and living beings met its own demise. An atmosphere of love, peace, devotion, and renunciation blossomed everywhere.

Moreover, Lord Mahāvīra offered elaborate solutions to various other prevailing social and cultural problems. He went to the extent of presenting the business community with vows for balanced, truthful, and awakened ways of conducting business. Further, he wanted his monks and nuns to conduct nationwide spiritual education by creating a force of civil servants who would bring every single human being to the path of spiritual awakening. He was acutely aware of the pernicious influence of money and economics and of the fact that, if not countered, mankind would become a slave to wealth, and would make others slaves in the pursuit of wealth. To counteract this, he not only presented values of contentment and indifference to material acquisition, but also proclaimed it to be a sin to hoard more than what one needs, a precept known as *aparigraha* – the doctrine of "non-possession" and "restrained acquisition." To this end, he established the practice of *anuvrata,* or committing to certain primary vows for the spiritual development of the individual and the benefit of society.

Lord Mahāvīra's provisions for *mahāvrata*s (supreme vows) for mendicants included the commitment to the quest for liberation from the life-and-death cycle, and revulsion towards over-indulgence or carelessness. Through these, he wanted to demonstrate the objective of transitioning from unjust or bad deeds (inauspicious *karmas*) to worthy deeds (auspicious *karmas*), and then finally, stopping the influx of *karma* and eradication of the acquired *karmas*. This results in absence of any unjust deeds and serves as the preliminary means in one's pursuit towards ultimate liberation.

Lord Mahāvīra's teachings condemned deliberate and premeditated forms of violence while enshrining peace and non-violence in day-to-day life within Indian society. Although many people do not realize it, violence does occur in the prosaic daily life of humans. But Lord Mahāvīra proclaimed that the highest ideal for householders should be to minimize daily violence, ranging from the more obvious, willful forms of violence to inadvertent occurrences, by adopting an increasing awareness and practice of non-violence in all aspects life. The life of such a practitioner becomes resplendent when one lives in this manner, and one progressively approaches salvation as a progression from inauspiciousness to auspiciousness – and then from auspiciousness to purity. His message was legitimated by the fact that he was himself a personification of his teachings, and these precepts were therefore more than just empty words; they were embedded in self-practice, proving that deeds can become a channel for uplifting and benefitting the masses.

Lord Mahāvīra wanted to transform humans to honorable and committed achievers by inspiring friendship through non-violence, trustworthiness through truthfulness, non-deception through non-stealing, charisma through supreme conduct, and contentment through non-possessiveness. In Indian history, Lord Rāma, Lord Kṛṣṇa, Lord Buddha, and Lord Mahāvīra are four of the most illustrious individuals who have contributed to the creation of a respectable civilization and fortified India's noble traditions. They all considered renunciation as a superior way of life to materialistic consumption and sensory enjoyment. One must commit deeds in the course of one's life, but the objective should always be pure in order to achieve ultimate knowledge. One must be vigilant to continuously study the world, and undertake only pure actions free of the maladies of materialistic consumption and violence. So long as one maintains a principled and noble attitude, the arduous commitment to performing only honorable deeds will come naturally to them.

Because of these reasons, during Lord Mahāvīra's time, Indian society and culture became infused with non-violence. Ethical conduct permeated the social realms of labor, academics, and spirituality, enabling countless individuals to pursue a lifestyle treading the path towards salvation.

SUPPORTING THE POPULAR LANGUAGE OF THE PEOPLE

Lord Mahāvīra's teachings had a profound influence on the life of people and helped end the trend towards unrestrained consumption and indulgence, and tyrannical governance. Increasingly, people vowed to behave and interact in a more humane fashion by adopting this honorable way of life.

In various fields of literature and academics, expressions and teachings of an unethical lifestyle lost the opportunity to take root, and the prevalence of spiritual literature witnessed unprecedented fecundity. People experienced their own intrinsic liberty while their mental landscapes became free of ill thoughts. Witnessing the effect of his teaching, Lord Mahāvīra wanted to see the creation of a corpus of spiritual literature that was imaginative, artistic, creative, and available to common people in their own language, unrestricted by the elite dialects of the literati. Thinking thus, he insisted upon the use of Ardhamāgadhī, the common vernacular of that time, to be used in religious scriptures.

Lord Mahāvīra's Message to the World

Lord Mahāvīra had ignited the fervor of a vast spiritual awakening against the prevailing immorality and wickedness of his time. However, his disciples, the individuals who were charged with the duty of ensuring its transmission to posterity, could not completely protect his teachings, and eventually they became fractured. The dogmatic orthodoxy of the caste system – social practices against which Lord Mahāvīra had resisted – slowly started to reassert themselves even among Jain householders. Jain Dharma is incompatible with those individuals who do not follow householder vows or do not reject immoral practices.

But now, the time has come to reinvigorate Lord Mahāvīra's genuine traditions against the deviation from the doctrine of love, non-violence, restrained consumption, and renunciation. Once again, spiritual practices are being dominated by empty ritualism and one must return to the path that was illuminated by the greatest *guru*. Only Lord Mahāvīra's teachings can help in the current time of spiritual need.

Lord Mahāvīra's message of love and non-violence has been inspiring humanity with peace for over twenty-five hundred years. Today, while the boundaries between nations are weakening with the inception of the information age, the dangers the planet Earth faces have reached a level of magnitude never seen before. The world is afflicted by some form of man-made or natural tragedy at any given moment. The number and influence of peace-loving communities like those of the spiritual traditions that one finds in India is dwindling at a shocking rate. It seems as though most of the inhabitants of nations believe that war and other violent means are the only way to somehow achieve a distorted sense of human welfare.

Despite the current situation, in the long run, humanity will ultimately achieve divine peace by following Lord Mahāvīra's teachings. Humankind will be empowered by non-violence, which will ultimately become the modus operandi of the entire world, guided by self-control in which humans will live for others and not for their own egotistical gratification. Lord Mahāvīra's teachings will become the concept and design of this integrated community, and create a legislative body that brings peacefulness to society. One can see evidence that humanity is increasingly ready to find solutions for its self-preservation against the horrors that the world faces today.

The Disciple Tradition

Gaṇadhara Indrabhūti (Śrī Gautama Svāmī) was Lord Mahāvīra's foremost disciple. He achieved *kevala-jñāna* at the time of Lord Mahāvīra's own *nirvāṇa,*[19] so he could not be made the *ācārya* (spiritual leader) of the community. Hence, the credit of being the very first *ācārya* of Lord Mahāvīra's tradition goes to Śrī Sudharma Svāmī, the fifth *gaṇadhara*. Śrī Sudharma Svāmī instituted the practice of transferring Lord Mahāvīra's teachings via the speaking-and-listening method. He eventually achieved *nirvāṇa* at the age of one hundred years.

After Śrī Sudharma Svāmī, Śrī Jambū Svāmī became the second *ācārya*

[19] *Nirvāṇa* is the eternally liberated state of an enlightened *jīva* (soul) when it attains bodiless form after achieving *mokṣa* – the state of perfection in all respects (with perfect perception, unbounded perfect wisdom, and perfect conduct), achieved after discarding all eight *karmas* (see chapter 11). The *jīva* then settles in *siddha-loka*, considered the top of the universe in Jain cosmology.

and has the distinction of being the last individual to attain *kevala-jñāna*. No other individual has achieved this level of wisdom after Śrī Jambū Svāmī.

After Śrī Jambū Svāmī, Ācārya Prabhava Svāmī was appointed as the third *ācārya* of the Jain community. In his pre-ascetic life, he was the ringleader of five hundred thieves. One early morning, he went to rob the home of Jambū Kumār (later known as Jambū Svāmī) before the latter's ordination. Jambū Kumār was getting ready to renounce the world to become an ascetic when Prabhava approached and was immediately inspired by Jambū Kumār's renunciation. He decided on the spot to become an ascetic as well, and ultimately became a successor to Śrī Jambū Svāmī.

Until Śrī Jambū Svāmī, the Digambara and Śvetāmbara traditions remained unified as a single Jain community. Thereafter, fissures became increasingly apparent. Those who identified with the Śvetāmbara tradition represented their lineage with illustrations of Śrī Prabhava Svāmī, Śrī Śayyambhava, Śrī Yaśobhadra Svāmī, Śrī Sambhūti Vijaya Svāmī, and Śrī Bhadrabāhu Svāmī. Those who identified with the Digambara tradition had illustrations of Śrī Viṣṇu Svāmī, Śrī Nandī Aparājita Svāmī, Śrī Govardhana Svāmī, and Śrī Bhadrabāhu Svāmī.

It seems the community's unified structure started to collapse right after Śrī Jambū Svāmī. However, the sectarian divisions did not take an aggressive and well-defined form for some time. That is why both traditions consider Śrī Bhadrabāhu Svāmī to be *śruta-kevalī* – one who is not completely omniscient but has complete spiritual knowledge acquired through speaking-and-listening methods.

Śrī (Ācārya) Bhadrabāhu Svāmī was the *guru* of the renowned Candragupta Maurya, the supreme ruler of India. At the age of fifty-three, Bhadrabāhu was ordained into ascetic life by Ācārya Yaśobhadra Svāmī – approximately 139 years after Lord Mahāvīra's *nirvāṇa* (527 BCE). He had attained a complete understanding of the fourteen sacred Jain scriptures (known as Pūrvas) and became an *ācārya* of the undivided Jain community for over thirteen years before leaving his body at the age of sixty-six years.

The most famous event during Ācārya Bhadrabāhu's time was the twelve years of famine that forced him to retreat to South India. This famine had a severe impact on the Jain community, with everlasting results. After his departure, the organization splintered into various groups, which were scattered over multiple regions. Propagation of Lord Mahāvīra's wisdom was diminished because until then it was being transferred via speaking-and-listening methods only. Many of the ascetics who had received the auspicious knowledge by listening to their teachers perished during this famine along with the knowledge they had acquired.

In the lineage of Jain ascetics, Śrī (Ācārya) Bhadrabāhu Svāmī is considered to be the last one with the comprehensive spiritual knowledge acquired through speaking-and-listening methods (*śruta-kevalī*). He transcribed his audible knowledge into ten Āgamas – the sacred Jain scriptures.

Both the Digambara and Śvetāmbara traditions have had many sages who were extremely influential, supremely spiritual achievers, and who were deeply knowledgeable of Lord Mahāvīra's teachings. They were all undoubtedly practitioners of complete self-control. Some abbreviated highlights of the lives of some of them are presented here to incite curiosity for further learning about these great sages. A tremendous amount of material is available from various sources for in-depth study, to learn from the lives of these venerable saints. For, it has been written that:

> *A righteous sage is symbolized by his virtuous qualities, whereas inauspicious qualities define a corrupt religious or spiritual practitioner.*
>
> *Adopt virtuous qualities and forsake inauspiciousness.*
>
> *One who learns about his soul from his own soul, and has no influence of attachments, animosity, and deceit, is worthy to be worshipped.*[20]

---

[20] From the Jain scripture *Daśaikaliksūtra: guṇehi sāhū aguṇehi a sāhū, giṇhāhi sāhū guṇa muñc 'sāhū; śramaṇadharmasūtra: viyāṇiyā appagamappaeṇaṁ, jo raga dosehiṁ samo sa pujjo.*

3

Path to Salvation – Right Perception (Mukti-Mārga – Samyag-Darśana)

JAIN Dharma places complete faith in the power of right spiritual knowledge. Right knowledge motivates the soul to forever break its bondages and achieve eternal salvation by fully developing its boundless and innate abilities (*śakti*). In this respect, Lord Mahāvīra said to Gautama:

> One who perceives, knows, and possesses the knowledge (*jñāna*) is the only one who can break the soul's bondages. The purpose of wisdom is to triumph over the spiritual darkness and attain a state of boundless bliss. The purpose of honorable (proper) conduct is to remove behavioral deficiencies to make the blissful state uncontaminated and solemn.

According to Jain Dharma, right perception (*samyag-darśana*) provides a genuine understanding of the real and Ultimate Truth. Right knowledge (*samyag-jñāna*)[1] develops an unshakable and uncompromising confidence in this Ultimate Truth. Right conduct (*samyag-cāritra*) rectifies deficiencies and enhances one's spiritual faculties by controlling one's innermost desires to create pure and perfect living – both internally and externally. The development of right knowledge (*samyag-jñāna*) becomes possible when it is concurrently accompanied by the development of right perception (*samyag-darśana*). They are followed by the growth of right conduct (*samyag-cāritra*). *Samyag-darśana* is steadfast belief in the existence of a soul, its inherent characteristics, and the true body-soul relationship. *Samyag-darśana* evolves with unwavering and faithful conviction in the teachings of the *tīrthaṅkara*s (the great teachers). *Samyag-darśana*, *samyag-jñāna*, and *samyag-cāritra* – the Three Jewels of Jain Dharma – are defined as a sort of confluence of three

---

[1] The words *samyak* and *samyag* have the same meaning of "right." They can be used interchangeably. However, when hyphenated with another word, like *samyag-darśana*, only *samyag* is used.

auspicious streams (*triveṇī*). The ascetic who bathes in this stream of virtues attains the unblemished state of compassion that is devoid of any deficiencies.

For the effective aspirant progressing on the path towards the ultimate liberation, conduct and day-to-day life are continuously and systematically inspired by the devotion to right knowledge, bliss, and fundamental truth. Whoever adopts the troika of right perception, right knowledge, and right conduct, and adheres to it, is the supreme spiritual traveler. Such spiritual seekers are the authentic devotees of the divine and they always prevail in their quest for transcendental development.

In nearly all religions, aspirants are seeking redemption. For Jains, such redemption takes the form of understanding the fundamental truth, or the realization of the ultimate courage or absolute fearlessness. It could also entail the receiving of divine grace. Jain Dharma unequivocally teaches that every soul possesses celestial qualities and that the natural expression of those qualities allows one to receive divine redemption in one form or the other – for instance, attaining the ultimate spiritual goal of divine enlightenment (salvation). In order to achieve salvation, the soul must accept the mandatory adoption of the troika of right knowledge, right perception, and right conduct. Jain texts unmistakably proclaim that without the right knowledge, no austere deeds – or other such actions like meditation, penance, and mind-body cleansing – can succeed in destroying the soul's impurities. Similarly, the knowledge that does not facilitate right conduct through the execution of proper actions and deeds will not help to accomplish the final goal of liberation. The only way to achieve the divine goal is to harmonize the three spokes of this troika in a coordinated manner. Sufficient motivation for salvation occurs with the proper cultivation of all three, and cannot occur when they remain separate and discordant.

In reality, right conduct – the most important characteristic of human life in general – is the essential outcome of right perception and right knowledge. One's status cannot be solely determined by the knowledge and perception of that individual. The true indicator of one's spiritual advancement is one's conduct. Similarly, one can see in daily interactions that until one's life is directed by right knowledge and perception, one's ability to succeed in worldly endeavors remains very limited.

The universe is in an uninterrupted continuous flow. Does it mean that living beings simply stumble and collide like lifeless stones? Will living beings always remain in a state of endless flux, or is there a restful foundation? Is there an ultimate destination? If the answers to these questions were "no" and there were simply no place or time for the end to the ephemeral passage of living entities, then there would be no end goal for one's penances and contemplative efforts. One's knowledge, perception, and conduct would all be squandered and would dissipate. But fortunately, that is not the case. Jain Dharma teaches that the soul can attain salvation from the clutches of kārmic bondages. This transitory life will find its way to an eternal existence, and the soul will reach ultimate, limitless salvation by rising above the illusory pleasures and sufferings. The achievement of self-realization and divine revelation is the noble result of the right conduct which one accomplishes through self-control and disciplined living.

The magnificence of the extraordinary nature of the Jain philosophy of fundamental truth is that it does not consider the life force or soul to ultimately destroy itself into non-existence. Neither does it consider the soul to merge into a larger force of nature and lose its independent existence like a lifeless stone or a drop of water merging into a pond. Jain Dharma teaches that soul continues its independent existence upon liberation. Its last stage of evolution – the state of salvation – is filled with immense pleasure, unlimited knowledge, and uninterrupted bliss. In this state, the soul's divine nature is fully awakened, and it enjoys eminent splendor.

The beautiful transition to this pleasurable state of liberation and uninterrupted bliss occurs with the coordinated development of right perception, right knowledge, and right conduct. These Three Jewels help to compose the beautiful symphony that elevates the practitioner and launches them into the everlasting state of liberation that has always been the desired aim of one's spiritual essence.

Right Perception (Samyag-Darśana)

Jain Dharma does not accept knowledge (*jñāna*) as merely a state of realization. The outcome of knowledge is science (*vijñāna*) – the understanding of acceptable insights into the nature of existence. Embracing science leads to adopting virtues and giving up wickedness. Knowledge plays a key role in purifying one's devotion or faith (*śraddhā*), and the role of that devotion is the sanctification of one's life. Consequently, Jain Dharma emphasizes pure devotion as much as genuine knowledge.

Steadfast belief in the existence of the soul and other related principles constitutes *samyag-darśana* – one of the most esteemed concepts in Jain Dharma. The individuals who lack right perception, even if they are the most knowledgeable with deepest levels of understanding, remain ignorant despite advancing in their knowledge. In such cases, even with the acquisition of knowledge, one's achievements might be based on some axiomatic falsehood. In one's pursuit of ultimate liberation, one cannot fully benefit from the accumulated knowledge (*jñāna*), even with pure devotion and firm commitment, unless the acquired knowledge is supported by an unwavering belief.

The primary reason for the deviation of the soul from its natural state of tranquility is the lack of *samyag-darśana* (right perception). Those who do not have the right faith cannot have a firm conviction in the soul's natural state, the limitations of its intrinsic entitlements, or a belief in the independent yet interconnected existence of countless other spiritual entities. Such a person becomes misguided and expects the world to submit to the dominance of one's will. This acrimonious view not only eclipses one's own soul, it destroys the peaceful existence of those who happen to coexist in one's surroundings. The main reason for this ill-advised behavior stems from a lack of understanding of the genuine fundamental truth – and not fully trusting in that truth.

In the universe, the fundamental truth cannot ever be changed or destroyed, and falsehood cannot actually be generated. Each entity retains its fundamental nature despite changes in external appearances. One type of matter does not suddenly transform into the other, but it continuously goes through changes while perpetually transitioning through life cycles. Thus, each entity changes but one entity does not ever transform into another and it always retains its independent existence.

As elucidated in the Jain scriptures the *Anuyoga-Dvārasūtra* and the *Sthānāṅgasūtra*, there are six essential elements (*dravya*s) and nine fundamental truths (*tattva*s) that are best understood alongside the system of multiplicity of views (*anekānta* – the Jain doctrine that one fundamental truth might have multiple facets). The canonical work assembled from the sermons of the *tīrthaṅkaras* is the best source for understanding these principles. The unrelenting belief in the *tīrthaṅkaras*' teachings results in a firm faith in the fundamental truth. This unshakable belief defines right perception.

Sometimes right perception is readily attained through internal purification, which is defined as the natural or innate method of attainment in Jain scriptures. Otherwise, it can be realized by being in the company of great souls or by listening to spiritual discourses, which is termed as an acquired means in Jain scriptures.

The opposite of right perception is holding a delusional view that is contrary to faith and truth. The delusional state occurs due to skeptical and unfaithful presumptions regarding divinity, *guru*, and *dharma*. The ignorant individual becomes incapable of comprehending that the venerated souls are pure, sacred, dispassionate, and enriched with unlimited knowledge. Because of such misgivings, the individual remains fastened in the world of spurious views.

Scriptural disillusionment ensues by not correctly interpreting righteous scriptures or by studying antagonistic literature. Also, much depends on the attitude of the aspirant. If one is kind-hearted and spiritually accepting, while following the principle of multiplicity of views (*anekānta*), they will be able to transform false doctrines, by abstracting partial truths from them, into right understanding. When the aspirant is adversely disposed, their negative tendencies will distort even the right messages into falsehoods.

Disillusionment may also occur by following an errant *guru*. Without understanding the real nature of the individual claiming to be a teacher, a spiritual seeker could easily be influenced by a specious outlook, saintly apparel, or beguiling oratory skills, or even some performance of optical illusions or magical tricks. Under the spell of such manipulation, the seeker may become swayed and eventually disillusioned by the pretentious *guru*.

Many times, certain individuals develop beliefs in non-religious or deceptive doctrines because they have never been exposed to, or do not understand, genuine doctrines. The misdirected individuals continue in this state of cynicism by terming even genuine beliefs as falsehoods. While Jain

Dharma teaches that one should guard oneself against false teachings and false teachers, one nonetheless must obtain sincere knowledge about right divinity, from the right *guru*, scriptures, and right *dharma*, and by renouncing corrupting practices.

A soul reaches the pinnacle of its own pure and wholesome self-nature through superior devotion and perseverance, and attains a limitless spiritual strength. Such a soul – by conclusively conquering negativities such as disillusionment, attachments, and ignorance – achieves omniscience and is known as an *arhanta*, and is therefore considered to be a divine soul. Any devotion that is cultivated towards an *arhanta* is the most pure and genuine devotion.

The ascetics who can be considered genuine *guru*s have their lives piously driven by non-violence (*ahiṁsā*), and they are in pursuit of the realization of the unblemished, natural state of their individual souls. They achieve this by steadily observing the five great vows of non-violence (*ahiṁsā*), truthfulness (*satya*), non-stealing (*asteya*), non-possessiveness (*aparigraha*), and celibacy (*brahmacarya*). Such individuals always desire and work for the welfare of all living beings.

A doctrine may be considered to be a true *dharma* when it guides the soul towards the above-mentioned wholesome state by enabling the adoption of the teachings of the liberated souls, and motivating a lifestyle based on the right conduct. This leads to the ultimate liberation. Compassion towards all living beings and unwavering belief in the multiplicity of views (*anekānta*) is genuine faith in essence, and complete non-violence (*ahiṁsā*) is a measure of righteous conduct. This conviction forms the core foundation of the concept of *samyag-darśana* (right perception).

A person with right perception has flawless thinking and does not possess any misbeliefs or egoistical traits. Such a person considers truth (*satya*) to be supreme, has unwavering faith in it, and courteously reveres it at all times. Any type or level of malevolent force cannot dissuade such an adherent from the committed path of confidence in the truth and in right *dharma*.

The person with right vision (*samyag-dr̥ṣṭi*) can visualize the soul in its pure, natural state, unadulterated by kārmic pollutants. Such individuals get acquainted with the unbounded ecstasy of such a condition, and consequently lose interest in physical and sense-driven materialistic desires. While living in the midst of such worldly pleasures, the adherents remain focused on spiritual goals and never allow themselves to be lost in – or be overwhelmed by – such pleasures.

In order to peacefully preserve the benefits of *samyag-darśana*, one must protect oneself from the following five deficiencies (*upāsaka daśāṅga*):

1. *Non-belief*: Not having full confidence and unwavering faith in discourses and sayings by the enlightened, supreme teachers.
2. *Desires*: Longing to adopt a lifestyle that appeals to physical senses and deviates from the true path of liberation.
3. *Suspicion*: Being skeptical towards the outcomes or benefits of true *dharma* and holding unkind thoughts towards ascetics or saying unkind words about them or to them.
4. *Misplaced praise*: To appreciate or glorify disillusioned individuals who have spurious beliefs.
5. *Ill-advised company*: To make acquaintance and become friends with disillusioned individuals.

Samyag-darśana (right perception) is the essence (foundation) of all spiritual practices (*sādhanā*) in pursuit of the ultimate liberation. Spiritual progress begins with it. Clearly, until the seekers have a pure end goal and their vision is unblemished, their entire knowledge – and the efforts based on that knowledge – will remain fruitless. The goal, the outlook, and the vision are defined by right perception. That is why it is considered to be the first step in the progression towards the ultimate liberation.

When right perception starts illuminating the inner spirituality of an individual, the inner darkness that has existed forever swiftly starts diminishing. All fundamental truths begin to emerge, one's interest in the realization of one's innate soul intensifies, and the desire for worldly pleasures wanes. This allows for an untainted vision of the door to ultimate liberation.

A life centered on *samyag-dr̥ṣṭi* (right vision) allows for the emergence of a fivefold sentiment consisting of pacification (calmness), impetus for spiritual enhancement, indifference towards worldly affairs, compassion, and the belief in supreme teachers. Such a person rises above all misbeliefs and recognizes the path to salvation.

Eight Elements of Samyag-Darśana

Just like a body is made up of multiple parts, right perception (*samyag-darśana*) is a collection of eight different elements described below. By fully grasping all of these, one can develop a comprehensive understanding of right perception.

1. *Niḥśaṅkita* (without doubt): The words of the enlightened teachers can never be false because spurious speech occurs only due to ignorance and inner deficiencies. The words of the enlightened beings are based on Ultimate Truth because they have conquered all types of weaknesses and insufficiencies, have no attachments, and have acquired unbounded pure wisdom. Keeping steadfast faith in their teachings is the *niḥśaṅkita* element of right perception.
2. *Niḥkāṅkṣita* (without desire): Certain desires can occur due to temptations for worldly comforts, or because of bad advice from ignorant individuals. Becoming completely devoid of such materially motivated desires defines the *niḥkāṅkṣita* element of right perception.
3. *Nirvicikitsā* (without uncertainty): Ascetics involved in deep penance, although still encaged in their bodies, have no passions regarding their bodies. They recognize their soul as their true-self and are always working for the welfare of the soul. That is why they do not care for their physical appearance. Having a positive impression of ascetics without any anxiety towards their appearance and not doubting the importance of *dharma* is the *nirvicikitsā* element of right perception.
4. *Amūḍha-dr̥ṣṭitva* (non-perplexed perceptiveness): Every aspect and directive of right perception is magnanimous (*vicāraṇā, viveka-pūraṇa*). Those who have chosen spirituality as the auspicious goal of their lives, adopt only the views and conduct supportive of that goal in their lives. They do not blindly follow others. They very carefully take every step only after close consideration, to be sure it will augment their progress towards enlightenment and be of benefit to society while setting an ideal example for people to follow. The process of staying on the spiritual path and not allowing unhealthy distractions is the *amūḍha-dr̥ṣṭitva* element of right perception.

5. *Upavṛṁhaṇa* (promoting): It is very noble to laud righteous individuals who have acquired great knowledge, have spotless religious demeanor, have self-control, appreciate and spread spirituality, and have the right perspective. The act of appreciating such traits and behavior, and to encourage and support it, is the *upavṛṁhaṇa* element of right perception.
6. *Sthirīkaraṇa* (reinforcing commitment): Sometimes a virtuous individual, who is on the path of right perception, loses direction due to some worldly difficulties, temptations, or some adverse influences. Such individuals could deprive themselves of the spiritual progress they have made towards right perception and right conduct. The act of helping such an individual to get back on track is the *sthirīkaraṇa* element of right perception.
7. *Vātsalya* (affection): Among the worldly relationships, those that are spiritually based are the most auspicious ones. In general, relationships give rise to a multitude of attachments. But spirituality-based relationships diminish inauspicious attachments while helping in mutual progress towards the divine goal. When one keeps this perspective in mind and platonically loves others like a mother loves her children, it is the *vātsalya* element of right perception.
8. *Prabhāvanā* (promulgation): The act of propagating the messages of the enlightened ones, eliminating misgivings about *dharma*, and highlighting the importance of *dharma* is the *prabhāvanā* element of right perception.

Every individual has one or more unique talents and powers. Some have academic prowess while others have special physical abilities. Some have exceptional conduct while others have the strength of penance. Still others may have exceptional self-control, the ability to renounce, extraordinary oratory skills, or unique writing skills. The act of enhancing the influence of *dharma* by effectively using whatever skills one may have is considered one of the main responsibilities of an individual progressing on the path towards right perception.

An individual who successfully fulfills all of the aforementioned eight elements is a genuine pursuer of right perception. It has been written:

> Dear brother, you are your own friend so why are you searching for another outward friend. Hey brother, bring your soul under your own control. By doing so, you will redeem yourself from all worldly miseries and unpleasantness.[2]

It is clear that acquiring *samyag-darśana* is essential for a spiritual seeker to progress on the *mukti-mārga*. That is why it is considered as one of the Three Jewels of the Jain doctrine, along with *samyag-jñāna* and *samyag-caritra*. *Samyag-darśana* defines the foundation of the practitioner's spiritual edifice. It unlocks and mitigates personal inhibitions of the seeker and transforms them into the receptors of the all-important auspicious knowledge. The process of acquiring right knowledge or understanding, *samyag-jñāna*, discussed next, begins with *samyag-darśana*.

---

[2] *purisā! tumameva tumaṁ-mitaṁ, kiṁ bahiyā, mittam icchasi?*
purisā! attāṇam eva abhinigijjha evaṁ dukkhā pamokkhasi.

4

Right Knowledge (Samyag-Jñāna)

According to Jain philosophy, knowledge (cognition, *jñāna*) is a manifestation of consciousness. It represents the innate nature of the soul and is therefore inseparable from the soul. Wisdom[1] and the soul are interrelated because the former is a virtue while the latter is virtuous, and therefore they cannot be differentiated. The soul possesses intellect and has a limitless power to develop knowledge. However, due to the emergence of *karma* that obstructs knowledge, the soul is blocked from developing its knowledge to the fullest extent. As kārmic obstructions subside, the soul progressively enriches itself with its greater concomitant knowledge. When the kārmic obstructions are completely eliminated, the soul achieves its perfect or impeccable state of fully manifested knowledge – the state of omniscience.

Knowledge cannot be acquired just by self-realization (*sva-prakāśya*), or by observing external factors (*para-prakāśya*) only. One develops knowledge by internalized efforts as well as by learning from external sources. Jain Dharma does not accept the mutual exclusivity of "knowledge" (*jñāna*), "knowledgeable" (*jñātā*), and "knowledge-seeker" (*jñeya*). They are intertwined. The soul is knowledgeable by nature, and by virtue of having wisdom (*jñāna*) as one of its intrinsic characteristics, it is a manifestation of wisdom (knowledge) itself. Finally, because of its own functional faculty, it is a knowledge-seeker. Similarly, when deeply philosophizing on the subject of knowledge, one can see that since know-how is critical to the understanding

[1] Generally, both "wisdom" and "knowledge" are considered to be the literal translations of *jñāna*, but in this work a distinction is made between "wisdom" and "knowledge." In this text, "knowledge" is generally used to mean *jñāna*, and "wisdom" is considered to be commonly understood knowledge plus virtuous qualities like non-attachment, compassion, and truthfulness. In other words, "wisdom of an individual" would mean knowledge coupled with the virtuous qualities of that individual.

matter (*vastu*), it is a form of knowledge in itself. Further, since knowledge is an enriched entity itself (*sva-prakāśya*), it is knowledgeable. Finally, being an implied agency of augmentation (*kartṛtva*), it is a knowledge-seeker.

Genuine versus Spurious Knowledge

Perfect or right knowledge results from acquiring genuine information, whereas imperfect knowledge results from acquisition of spurious information. But how does one differentiate between genuine and erroneous knowledge? First, one must know that true knowledge comes from two perspectives – philosophical and spiritual.

From the spiritual perspective, only the knowledge that is free of falsehood, misbeliefs, and pretentiousness can result in genuine knowledge. It becomes spurious when it is misdirected with impure objectives and impelled by belief in falsehoods and other negative views such as fanaticism and prejudice. Such knowledge does not lead to spiritual awakening.

From a philosophical perspective, any knowledge that is free of doubt (*saṁśaya*), perverseness (*viparyāsa*), and blind faith (*anadhyavasāya*) contributes to genuine knowledge. It is spurious when laden with doubts, contradictions, and perceptual errors such as mistaking a snake as rope.

A soul possesses perfect wisdom when it is enriched with genuine knowledge from both spiritual and philosophical perspectives, and has acquired a purified vision (*śuddha dṛṣṭi*).

Knowledge or Wisdom (Jñāna)

In general, knowledge is continuously evolving on its own. However, in order to understand the advancement of knowledge, the process is divided into steps based on the level, characteristics, nature, etc., of the state of knowledge. Fundamentally, there are five progressive states of knowledge:

1. *Mati-jñāna* (empirical knowledge)
2. *Śruta-jñāna* (scriptural knowledge)
3. *Avadhi-jñāna* (clairvoyant knowledge)
4. *Manaḥ-paryāya-jñāna* (mind-reading knowledge)
5. *Kevala-jñāna* (supreme or perfect or impeccable knowledge or wisdom)

DIRECT AND INDIRECT NATURE OF KNOWLEDGE (PAROKṢA- AND PRATYAKṢA-JÑĀNA)

Among the above-mentioned five states of knowledge, the first two, viz., *mati-jñāna* and *śruta-jñāna*, are considered acquired, mediative, or indirect states (*parokṣa*), while the other three are considered direct or innate (*pratyakṣa*). One could also say that the first two are imperceptible and the last three are perceptible or cognizable. In other religious philosophies of India, direct knowledge is considered to be that which is acquired through the five senses – seeing, hearing, tasting, touching, and smelling. However, Jain philosophy has a different viewpoint. Here, knowledge is considered direct, not when it is acquired with the help of senses, but by direct experience of the soul itself unmediated by the senses. Sense-based knowledge can be considered direct perhaps only in worldly affairs, but not in terms of the realization of one's spiritual essence.

Empirical Knowledge (Mati-Jñāna)

Mati-jñāna, the first of the two types of *parokṣa-jñāna*s, is of two fundamental types based on how it is acquired. As explained in the Jain scripture *Sthānāṅgasūtra*, *mati-jñāna* is acquired either by senses (such as sight, etc.) or by the mind. The development of knowledge by the mind is internalized and does not have physical form (*rūpa*) as an external object (*viṣaya*) like that which is usually associated with knowledge acquired through senses. Therefore, mind-based knowledge could be derived from, but is considered independent of, the senses. There are five types of *mati-jñāna* as listed below, and it gradually develops in progressive stages as discussed next.

1. *Mati* (mental): Knowledge acquired through the mind and senses that deals with the ongoing or present subject matter (*viṣayaka*).
2. *Smṛti* (remembrance): Knowledge based on the memory of past experiences (*pūrvānubhūta*). This includes knowledge gained in previous lives that becomes evident in the current life.
3. *Saṁjñā* (understanding): Knowledge that involves research, analysis, and synthesis of past experiences and present observations. This is also known as *pratyabhijñāna* (recognition).
4. *Cintā* (prognostication): Knowledge generated by pondering over the future.

5. *Abhinibodha* (consideration): Knowledge based on estimation and assessment.

STAGES OF MATI-JÑĀNA DEVELOPMENT

Consciousness (*cetanā*) is a manifestation of wisdom (*jñāna-rūpa*) characteristic (*guṇa*) of living beings. In essence, knowledge and consciousness are one, though they may be analyzed from different perspectives – sometimes on the basis of the subject matter, and other times on the basis of their causes. Knowledge acquisition starts at such a rudimentary stage that at first one cannot even understand the intrinsic spiritual properties of entities. One receives and absorbs only the features one can observe (size, shape, form, etc.) but is unable to grasp all of the entity's features (such as the specifics of origin, species, name, ethnicity, caste, and race) and characteristics (such as intelligence and spirituality). This initial stage is termed *darśana* (observance), perhaps more accurately described as "perception," or even literally, as "seeing." After *darśana*, the development of knowledge continues progressively over one's life cycles. However, its appearance may be hindered from time to time by the knowledge-obstructing *karmas*[2] that one acquires while on the journey through the cycles of life and death. Jain scriptures (e.g., the *Nandīsūtra* and the *Tattvārthasūtra*) have explained the progression in great detail, summarized herein in the following four general stages:

1. *Avagraha* (initial observation): The preliminary *mati-jñāna* stage of *avagraha* occurs when an understanding develops regarding the physical aspects of an entity and its extraneous elements. For instance, upon seeing a man or a woman, one ascertains that "this is a human being."
2. *Īhā* (curiosity): After *avagraha,* or the initial grasping of superficial properties, one may proceed to a deeper understanding of the nature and properties of the observed entity. This is the state of *īhā* ("curiosity," but also "exertion"), the process of thoughtfully analyzing what one has observed.
3. *Avāya* (confirmation): After *īhā*, one becomes capable of formulating conclusions about the observed entity based on the preceding *avagraha* and *īhā* stages. This is the state of *avāya* (confirmation), also known as *apāya* or "termination."

---

[2] Knowledge-obstructing *karma* is one of the eight types of *karmas*. It hinders one's ability to acquire knowledge.

4. Dhāraṇā (impression): Dhāraṇā is the acceptance of knowledge and its retention. It has three facets: *avicyuti* (not lost), *vāsanā* (imprinting), and *smṛti* (remembrance).

Once the *avāya* state transitions into the *dhāraṇā* state, in the state of *avicyuti* knowledge stays with the person and it is not reversed, diminished, or lost. When the subject matter that resulted in *avicyuti* has transitioned, but the knowledge is retained and leaves an impression, it is called *vāsanā*. At a later time, when *vāsanā* is awakened by some event or occurrence through a catalyst, it is called *smṛti*.

In this manner, the evolution of a single unit of *mati-jñāna* is marked by the progressive stages named above (*avagraha, īhā, avāya,* and *dhāraṇā*). These four are triggered by the five senses (sight, hearing, smell, taste, and touch) and the mind. Each of the four progressive stages has six further subtypes (not described in detail here, for brevity) for a total of twenty-four types of *mati-jñāna.*

It is worth clarifying that the six means (i.e., the five senses plus the mind) employed in the development of *mati-jñāna* knowledge are further divided into two methods. The first method, known as *paṭu-krama* (keen method), involves only sight and mind. The second method, known as *manda-krama* (dull method), is based on the use of four senses (hearing, smell, taste, and touch) that involve physical connection. For instance, the flow of air is felt when it touches the skin, taste occurs when a substance touches the tongue; one hears a sound when vibrations strike the ears, and one smells something only when the aroma carrying particles hits the nostrils.

The relationship between the senses and the objects is known as *vyañjana* (the act of distinguishing). Since it forms the means of knowledge acquisition in the above-mentioned *avagraha, īhā, avāya,* and *dhāraṇā*, *vyañjana* is also attributed with its own four additional types, which makes a total of twenty-eight types of *mati-jñāna* altogether. In summary:

1. There are twenty-four types of *mati-jñāna* because:
   i. There are four stages of knowledge (*avagraha, īhā, avāya,* and *dhāraṇā*).
   ii. Each stage has six acquiring channels consisting of five senses

(sight, hearing, smell, taste, and touch) and the mind.

2. Four additional types of *mati-jñāna* are attributed to four types of *vyañjana*, in which:
   i. A *vyañjana* is the relationship between the acquiring channels and the objects being observed, for each of the four general stages (*avagraha*, *īhā*, *avāya*, and *dhāraṇā*) of knowledge.

Scriptural Knowledge (Śruta-Jñāna)

The second stage of *samyag-jñāna* development is *śruta-jñāna*. The commonly used literal meaning of *śruta* is "what is heard." When words are spoken, a relationship is formed between the speaker and the listener. The knowledge gained by the listener through grasping spoken or written words is called *śruta-jñāna*, which is the second of the two types of *parokṣatā-jñāna*s (indirect knowledge).[3] From its definition, it is logical why *śruta-jñāna* succeeds *mati-jñāna*. As we have seen, the process of grasping words is an example of *mati-jñāna*. Understanding the essence of those words, extracting the knowledge associated with them, is *śruta-jñāna*.

DIFFERENCE BETWEEN MATI-JÑĀNA AND ŚRUTA-JÑĀNA

The relationship between *mati-jñāna* and *śruta-jñāna* is that of cause and effect. The former (*mati-jñāna*) is the cause and the latter (*śruta-jñāna*) is the effect, since *śruta-jñāna* cannot occur without the initial occurrence of *mati-jñāna*. Paradoxically, these two forms of knowledge are companions and are mutually indicative, but they are also distinct. In a sense, *mati-jñāna* is muted, whereas *śruta-jñāna* is explicit. Usually, *mati-jñāna* deals with the present, whereas *śruta-jñāna* is not bound by time and deals with past, present, and future. For instance, one could say *mati-jñāna* is milk (an ingredient) while *śruta-jñāna* is pudding, or *mati-jñāna* is fiber whereas *śruta-jñāna* is the rope woven from that. In other words, *mati-jñāna* can be considered as the beholder of the elements of raw knowledge acquired through senses and the mind in the ongoing (current) time. *Śruta-jñāna* would be those elements after they reach maturity through internalization, analysis, and prognostication.

---

[3] The first type of *parokṣatā-jñāna* is *mati-jñāna*. Both of these types of *samyag-jñāna* are *parokṣatā*; the other three *samyag-jñāna*s are considered *pratyakṣa* and include *avadhi-jñāna*, *manaḥ-paryāya-jñāna*, and *kevala-jñāna*.

One who reaches the stage of complete acquisition and full development of *śruta-jñāna* knowledge is known as *śruta-kevalī*.

Śruta-jñāna has two main states – *dravya-śruta* and *bhāva-śruta*. *Dravya-śruta* is word-oriented *śruta-jñāna* derived from the ancient Jain scriptures known as Āgamas. *Bhāva-śruta* is thought- and knowledge-oriented *śruta-jñāna* derived from contemplations over *dravya-śruta*.

AUTHENTICITY OF ŚRUTA

Scriptures are very important for any great religion. In many cases, a religion's activities revolve around, and are derived from, its scriptures. The civility, culture, and actions of a religious person originate from the teachings of the sacred texts of that religion. Like other philosophies, Jain Dharma also accepts the authenticity of a variety of religious scriptures. However, Jains have adopted a unique criterion to support the authenticity of its scriptures.

Jain scriptures do not seek to take refuge in divine, superhuman powers, or posit an unknown ancient time for their creation. Jains believe that it is unreal and unfeasible to link the creation of scriptures and their origination to unknown, mythical times. Instead, they believe that scriptures are trustworthy and verifiable when created by known, noble individuals who have conquered their passions and attachments. In the important Jain scripture known as the *Sthānāṅgasūtra*, two of the greatest Jain philosophers, Siddhasena and Samantabhadra have both stated:

> That which is spoken by a trusted individual who is dispassionate towards worldly attachments, which is defensible in debate and under cross-examination, and which is not obstructed by lack of evidence or assumptions, is the true religious scripture.

According to Jain Dharma, *jina*, the omniscient *tīrthaṅkara* – the promoter of non-absolutism (*anekānta*) who knows, lives with, and preaches the absolute and fundamental truth – has obliged mankind with a plethora of spiritual sermons out of his immense kindness. The *tīrthaṅkara*'s foremost disciples, the *gaṇadhara*s, captured, absorbed, and understood the sermons and recreated them in a transmittable form that eventually took the form of verifiable Jain scriptures.

For the spiritual aspirants, when reasoning and debates have ended – and yet one is still not clear or resolved about the end goal – and the mind starts wandering, at that time the scriptures created by the trusted and enlightened souls become the sole source of reprieve. Such scriptures are known as *dravya-śruta*. The knowledge generated with help from, and study of, *dravya-śruta* is known as *bhāva-śruta*.

JAIN SCRIPTURES AND THEIR SOURCES

Jain scriptures can be divided into two parts based on how they were created: *aṅga-praviṣṭa*[4] (original sources of Jain philosophy), and *aṅga-bāhya*[5] (interpreted Jain philosophy).

1. *Aṅga-praviṣṭa* are twelve-part scriptures created by transcribing interpretations of the original sermons of and teachings by Lord Mahāvīra as understood and interpreted by his great disciples (*gaṇadhara*s) and in turn communicated to their disciples. They are the essence of Jain philosophy, and are also known as *gaṇi-piṭaka* (collected baskets). As outlined in the *Nandīsūtra*, the twelve parts of *aṅga-praviṣṭa*, called Āgamas, are:
   - i. *Ācārāṅgasūtra*: Describes the conduct and behavior of ascetic life. It also describes the penance of Lord Mahāvīra. This is the oldest Āgama from a linguistic point of view.
   - ii. *Sūtrakr̥tāṅga*: Describes non-violence, Jain metaphysics, and the refutation of other religious theories such as Kriyāvāda,[6] Akriyāvāda,[7] Ajñānavāda,[8] and Vinayavāda.[9]
   - iii. *Sthānāṅga*: Defines and catalogues the main substances (*dravya*s) of Jain metaphysics.

---

[4] Literally, *aṅga-praviṣṭa* means "the limbs through which entry is made."

[5] Literally, *aṅga-bāhya* means "external limbs."

[6] Kriyāvāda: Doctrine which affirms the existence of soul (*jīva*), its impurities (miseries), and their annihilation through extroverted physical exercises such as *yajña*.

[7] Akriyāvāda: Doctrine which denies existence of the soul (*jīva*) and believes everything is of momentory existence.

[8] Ajñānavāda: Doctrine which denies the necessity and role of knowledge in attaining salvation.

[9] Vinayavāda: Doctrine which does not accept the scriptures but upholds the supremacy of reverence as a supreme virtue leading to perfection.

iv. *Samavāyāṅga*: Defines and catalogues the main substances of Jain doctrine from a different perspective than the *Sthānāṅgasūtra*.

v. *Vyākhyāprajñapti* or *Bhagavatīsūtra*: Explains the subtle knowledge of soul, matter, and other related subjects. The scripture includes 36,000 questions and answers to explain the basic concepts. It is the largest of the first eleven *aṅga-praviṣṭa* Āgamas.

vi. *Jñātr̥-dharma-kathā*: Explains Jain principles through examples and stories. This text is very useful in understanding the essence of Lord Mahāvīra's religious preaching.

vii. *Upāsaka-daśā*: Explains the code of conduct of the ten householder followers (*śrāvaka*s) of Lord Mahāvīra. This Āgama is very useful for understanding the Jain way of life of householders (*śrāvaka dharma*).

viii. *Anta-kr̥d-daśā*: Tells the stories of ten sacred monks who attained liberation (*mokṣa*) by destroying their *karma*s.

ix. *Anuttaraupapātika-daśā*: Contains stories of the ten additional revered monks who attained the topmost heaven, known as *anuttara* heaven.

x. *Praśna-vyākaraṇāni*: Describes the five great vows (*mahā vrata*s) and the five worst sins defined in Jain doctrine.

xi. *Vipāka-śruta*: Explains the results of good and bad *karma*s through several stories.

xii. *Dr̥ṣṭivāda* (now extinct): The twelfth *aṅga-praviṣṭa* Āgama, *Dr̥ṣṭivāda*, is presumed by all Jain followers to be lost. The scripture's description relating to Dr̥ṣṭivāda, which is found in the other Jain *sūtra*s, indicates that this *aṅga-praviṣṭa* Āgama was the largest of all Āgama *sūtra*s. It was classified in five parts: (a) *parikarma*, (b) *sūtra*, (c) *pūrvagata*, (d) *prathama-anuyoga*, and (e) *cūlikā*. The third part, *pūrvagata*, contained fourteen Pūrvas comprising the Jain doctrine's endless treasure of knowledge on every subject.

2. *Aṅga-bāhya* are the scriptures created by various monks and *ācārya*s over the centuries. These scriptures are consistent with the twelve-part *aṅga-praviṣṭa*. It is not possible to pinpoint the number of *aṅga-bāhya*

scriptures, but their origin and source of verification are definitely from the *aṅga-praviṣṭa* scriptures. Because they are derived from the interpretation of *aṅga-praviṣṭa* scriptures, they form the sources of *dravya-śruta* scriptures created by Jain spiritual leaders (*ācārya*s) over time. They consist of the following:

i. Twelve *upāṅgasūtra*s, which provide further explanation of *aṅga-praviṣṭa* Āgamas.

ii. Four *mūlasūtra*s, which are essential for monks and nuns to study in the early stages of their ascetic life.

iii. Four *chedasūtra*s, which provide the rule of conduct, reprimand, and repentance for ascetics. They also explain how the ascetics can repent for their sins and mistakes.

iv. *Āvaśyakasūtra*s, which describe daily rituals or routines of *sāmāyika,*[10] *caturviṁśatistava,*[11] *vandanaka,*[12] *pratikramaṇa,*[13] *kāyotsarga,*[14] and *pratyākhyāna*[15] – which are called *āvaśyaka*s (necessary) to perform during the day and night for the purification of soul.

---

10 *Samayika*: A form of meditation to facilitate unification with one's own soul and experiencing its purified state. It involves developing a state of undisturbed calmness while engaging in spiritual activities free of passions, desires, likes, and dislikes.

11 *Caturviṁśatistava*: Prayer (*stuti*) adoring the twenty-four *tīrthaṅkara*s who overcame their inner enemies like anger, ego, greed, and deceit, and praising their supreme characteristics while aspiring to become like them.

12 *Vandanaka*: Respecting and saluting ascetics (Jain *ācārya*s, *upādhyāya*s, and *sādhu*s), who, in the absence of *tīrthaṅkara*s, are the true teachers providing guidance to the path of liberation.

13 *Pratikramaṇa*: A daily, nightly, bi-weekly, quarterly, and yearly spiritual cleansing activity to reflect, review, confess, and repent own unrighteous deeds in thoughts, actions, and speech against all living beings by asking for their forgiveness. It also involves extending friendship to all and granting them forgiveness. This practice also involves a resolution to revert to the path of non-violence, truthfulness, non-stealing, celibacy, and non-attachment.

14 *Kāyotsarga*: Foregoing all attachments to the body, and connecting with one's own self (soul).

15 *Pratyākhyāna*: Renouncing certain activities for a duration for self-restraint and discipline, by taking vows according to one's own capabilities.

The above texts are supplemented with numerous interpretations, summations, reviews, and commentaries. All of these have had a major impact on Jain followers. In addition, Jain spiritual leaders, monks, philosophers, and researchers have independently composed innumerable spiritual, academic, and philosophical articles. Together they comprise heart-touching, thought-provoking, reasoning-based literary works that have contributed immensely to not only Indian literature, but also to world literature in general.

Jain spiritual leaders have extensively contributed to subject matters covering spirituality, academics, philosophy, and ethics. They have made immense contributions to grammar, poetry, composition, economics, science, medicine, politics, history, astrology, astronomy, art, and other subjects.

The art of presenting thoughtful and elegant literature in vernaculars is one of the most important contributions of Jain philosophers. They have made enormous contributions to ancient languages such as Sanskrit, Prākr̥t, and various regional dialects and languages of India, instantiated by the highly regarded early literary work of Jain scholars in Kannada, the language of Karnataka state in South India.

Clairvoyant Knowledge (Avadhi-Jñāna)

The *mati-jñāna* and *śruta-jñāna* – the indirect types (*parokṣa*) of knowledge acquired through the five senses and mind discussed above – are present to some extent in all living beings (*jīva*s), irrespective of the number of senses they possess. The level or type of knowledge may vary from one living being to another. The living beings may possess genuine spiritual knowledge if it is derived from right perception and is acquired through auspicious means. They may have imperfect knowledge if it is acquired by falsehood or inauspicious perception and attitude. Nonetheless, all living beings have some degree of *mati-jñāna* and *śruta-jñāna* types of knowledge.

Forms of knowledge (*jñāna*s) that are directly cognizable (*pratyakṣa*) according to Jain philosophy are discussed next. *Avadhi-jñāna* (clairvoyant knowledge) is the first of the *pratyakṣa-jñāna*s. Both common human beings as well as advanced mendicants and even prospective *jina*s acquire *avadhi-jñāna* only through penance and spiritual austerities. The *jina*s, in their last lives before attaining salvation, are born with fully developed *mati-jñāna*, *śruta-jñāna*, and *avadhi-jñāna*. For other practitioners, who have fully attained *mati-jñāna* and *śruta-jñāna* in their previous lives, the penance continues in their current lives, to start developing *avadhi-jñāna* or to further augment it from the level achieved in previous lives. A soul continuously goes through life-and-death cycles. When a soul takes a new life, it carries the repercussions of good and bad deeds (*karma*s) from the previous lives and possesses the corresponding traits – including the capability of knowledge acquisition in the current life. The soul that has experienced penance and austerity in previous lives may benefit from those in the current life, thereby enhancing the accumulation of *avadhi-jñāna*.

Literally, *avadhi* means "boundary," "restraint," or "focus." But its meaning in the context of the development of wisdom in Jain philosophy is clairvoyance. A soul is believed to enhance its *avadhi-jñāna* accumulation when it gets knowledge about other entities by means of its own spiritual strengths. This knowledge acquisition is beyond the help provided by the senses and mind. The souls dwelling in heaven and hell possess this knowledge during their time in those places, but they cannot do anything to further enhance their knowledge and progress in their spiritual journey – only human beings of the worldly realm have such ability. This could result in other beings having a certain degree of jealousy towards human beings. However, for the hell-bound[16] souls, the presence of *avadhi-jñāna* is usually a source of misery and discomfort because they understand the causes of their downward journey, but cannot do anything about it except to endure the suffering.

Avadhi-jñāna is considered beyond the range of mundane perception and must be acquired through intuition. From that perspective, it can also be defined as "extrasensory" knowledge. Both heavenly beings (*deva*s) and even hell-beings (*nārikī*s) are born with this knowledge. However, for human beings it may be attained through penance, various yogic practices, or spiritual disciplines.

Mind-Reading Knowledge (Manaḥ-Paryāya-Jñāna)

The *manaḥ-paryāya-jñāna*, which is the fourth stage of *samyag-jñāna*, is the second of the *pratyakṣa-jñāna*s. This form of knowledge is a telepathic

---

[16] Again, with the caveat that "hell" doesn't mean the same thing in dhārmic traditions as it does in Abrahamic traditions since in dhārmic traditions it is a temporary residence.

power that can be acquired only by accomplished and advanced ascetics. Such esteemed spiritual seekers have achieved outstanding self-control and are intrinsically peaceful and exceptionally unblemished. Through this knowledge, the possessor can read others' minds, their inner thoughts, and concealed traits.

Only human beings can practice advanced states of self-restraint, so only humans can obtain this form of knowledge. Both *manaḥ-paryāya-jñāna* and *avadhi-jñāna* are formless and boundless and cannot be sensed by others. From that perspective, acquisition of these forms of knowledge is unusual. The key characteristic of this achievement is that spiritual strength and self-awakening are the main sources of their appearance, and the senses and mind do not play any role in it. In modern terms, clairvoyance is similar to *avadhi-jñāna,* whereas telepathy or mind reading can be compared with *manaḥ-paryāya-jñāna.*

Supreme Knowledge (Kevala-Jñāna)

Jain Dharma considers the brilliance of knowledge (*jñāna*) to be boundless and ever pervasive. *Brahma-jñāna*, *ātma-jñāna*, or *kevala-jñāna* are all representations of this brilliance. *Kevala-jñāna*, which is the fifth stage of *samyag-jñāna*, is the third of the *pratyakṣa jñāna*s. It is the supreme wisdom with which the characteristics of all entities in the universe become known. With the acquisition of this knowledge, a soul becomes all-knowing (omniscient), all-seeing (omni-visionary), and attains supreme conscious. This is the final reward of extreme penance and self-restraint. After this, the soul is forever liberated from cycles of rebirth, and reaches the pinnacle of enlightenment.

Different stages of wisdom may have multiple levels due to context, subject, and reasons. But *kevala-jñāna* has no distinctions or levels because it is complete in itself. There is no ambiguity in its completeness. Of the five levels of knowledge discussed, *mati-jñāna*, *śruta-jñāna*, and *avadhi-jñāna* can be disingenuous when their appearance is in conjunction with the presence of spurious perception. However, *manaḥ-paryāya-jñāna* and *kevala-jñāna* may not be achieved by anyone who still has spurious perception. Hence, these are the impeccable forms of knowledge.

Discussion of Evidence Epistemology (Pramāṇa-Mīmāṁsā)

While describing the progression of knowledge in the five stages discussed above, Jain Dharma presents another aspect of investigating the validity of the right knowledge acquisition. This aspect is related to the process of *jñāna* development, and to that end Jain scriptures provide two methods of validation or critique. One is based on scriptures (Āgamas) and the other on logical reasoning (*tarka*). The two approaches are very similar, but their classifications are somewhat different. The scripture-based knowledge and the process for its development has been discussed earlier; a high-level discussion on *tarka*-based process is presented next.

Supreme or perfect knowledge is developed by eliminating doubt (*saṁśaya*), contrarian views (*viparyāsa*), and apprehension (*anadhyavasāya*). At the same time, its progression demands validation. From a logical point of view (*tarka*), the epistemological means or evidence (*pramāṇa*) are the methods of validation. There are four types of epistemological means to validate *jñāna*: (1) *pratyakṣa* (direct cognition), (2) *anumāna* (inference), (3) *āgama* (scripture-based testimony), and (4) *upamāna* (comparison), each of which is defined below:

1. *Pratyakṣa*: As described earlier in this chapter, *pratyakṣa-jñāna* is knowledge in which the characteristics of the entities under consideration are directly evident. It comprises three stages of knowledge development, viz., *avadhi-jñāna*, *manaḥ-paryāya-jñāna,* and *kevala-jñāna*. Of the three stages, *avadhi-jñāna* and *manaḥ-paryāya-jñāna* are only partially perceptible, whereas *kevala-jñāna*, being impeccable, complete wisdom, is fully perceptible.
2. *Anumāna*: *Anumāna* forms the foundation of logical analysis (*tarka*). Although *anumāna* is considered to be fundamentally a form of direct cognition (*pratyakṣa-mūlaka*), it has its own unique place in epistemological discussions.

   In the Jain theory of causality (*kārya-kāraṇa siddhānta*), *anumāna* is one way that evidential or correct knowledge (*pramāṇa*) emerges (*prādurbhāva*). For instance, when analyzing the causal relationship between smoke and fire, one infers that the smoke cannot occur in the absence of fire. This type of causal relationship is known as *vyāpti* (invariable concomitance) or *avinābhāva* (necessary connection), and is deduced on the basis of logical evidence (*tarka pramāṇa*). Once the necessary connection is established by observing causation the effect is invariable. Therefore, *anumāna* consists of deducing the effect based on causality.

As an illustration, upon hearing a sound, the listener tries to figure out the source; for instance, human or animal. Upon concluding that it is a human sound, the listener tries to determine if it is from a known, or unknown, person. If it is from a known person, the listener further conjectures whom it is. This inductive process is also *anumāna*.

Anumāna has two categories: inference for oneself (*svārthānumāna*) and inference for others (*parārthānumāna*). Inference for oneself is knowledge that is apparent to one's internal process and requires no proof. Inference for others is the logical proof for such knowledge that is required for presentation to others. Stated differently, *svārthānumāna* is the process whereby one acquires knowledge through one's own knowing and analysis. When one verbally conveys the knowledge to another person it is called *parārthānumāna*.

The scholars of logical reasoning (e.g., Nayavāda, chapter 7) have extensively reflected on the logical deduction necessary for *parārthānumāna* and have accepted a five-part deductive reasoning:

i. *Pratijñā* (hypothesis): for example, "There is a fire in the hills."

ii. *Hetu* (reason for the hypothesis): for example, "Because there is smoke."

iii. *Udāharaṇa* (citation of rule, based on invariable concomitance [*vyāpti*]): for example, "Wherever there is smoke, there is fire." One may know this because he observes smoke in a kitchen when there is a fire.

iv. *Upanaya* (application of the hypothesis as the premise based on observation and deduction): for example, "There is smoke in the hills, which are pervaded by fire." This includes the observation and the premise.

v. *Nigamana* (conclusion): for example, "Hence, there is fire in the hills."

Scholars of Jain logic do not consider it necessary to go through all five of these steps. The first two would be sufficient for expert logicians, but the remaining steps may be needed for those who are not experts.

3. *Āgama*: The value of the use of Āgama, or scripture-based evidence, has been presented earlier in this chapter under the description of *śruta-jñāna*.
4. *Upamāna*: With reference to the knowledge of the relationship between two different entities, when one establishes the identity or value of one entity based on experiencing or viewing the other, it is comparative evidence. For instance, yogurt is made from milk. So, if someone sees a type of yogurt somewhere, that person can establish that it was made from milk because one type of yogurt is comparable to any other type.

Alternate Classification of Pramāṇa

Some later logic scholars have used a *pramāṇa* classification approach which is different from that provided in the scriptures. They followed the divisions of *pratyakṣa* and *parokṣa* types of knowledge. As a result, their classification of *pratyakṣa-pramāṇa* (the epistemology of direct perception) is as follows:

1. *Sāṁvyāvahārika*: Everyday perceptions in the general dealings and experiences in the mundane world.
2. *Pārmārthika*: The ultimate, absolute state, which results from one's personal spiritual efforts.

According to this alternate classification, *parokṣa-pramāṇa* is of five types: (1) *smr̥ti* (memory), (2) *pratyabhijñāna* (recognition), (3) *tarka* (logic), (4) *anumāna* (inference), and (5) *āgama* (scriptures).

A detailed description of the alternate classification is beyond the scope of this book. The two classifications of *pramāṇa* described above may be different in their approaches, but both of them highlight the importance that Jain philosophy places on appropriate validation of the acquired knowledge.

5

Analysis of the Universe
(Viśva kā Viśleṣaṇa)

Arrangement of Substance (Dravya-Vyavasthā)

PURPOSE OF ANALYZING SUBSTANCE (DRAVYA MĪMĀṀSĀ KĀ UDDEŚYA)

UNDERSTANDING *dravya*s is essentially related to the understanding of the fundamental truth underpinning life. Literally, *dravya* means "substance." In Jain philosophy the purpose of understanding substance is not to just satisfy one's inquisitiveness; rather, it is instrumental to the refinement of human conduct. A spiritual seeker uses this knowledge for purifying the inner-self and conquering obstacles that are restrictive to spiritual growth. From that viewpoint, one needs to look at a substance in conjunction with its associated characteristics or qualities (*guṇa*s). Therefore, the term *dravya* serves as a substratum for different defining qualities or characteristics that have various aspects and modes. Also, one should not confuse *dravya* with the word "material" because the term "substance" (*dravya*) refers to irreducible entities, physical or metaphysical, in which *guṇa*s inhere. In this sense, the soul (*jīva*) can be a *dravya* despite it being non-material.

Jain philosophy is based on observable facts, so from that perspective, it is similar to modern science. Jain literature presents a profound analysis and critique of multiple topics and themes related to remarkable discoveries regarding the systematic arrangement of matter and substances. Some of these ancient discoveries have been validated in contemporary scientific research, to the surprise of even those in the scientific community. Despite many similarities, Jain doctrine and science serve different objectives. Jains developed their particular purview of understanding because it is critical for the spiritual progression of the individual soul to reach the ultimate salvation.

In science, the motivation is inquisitive pursuit of knowledge. It is astounding that self-trained ascetics, who gained knowledge through meditation and penance ages ago, were in some ways more knowledgeable than the scientists conducting research with the use of modern scientific apparatuses.

The path to liberation followed by seekers is shortened significantly when their thinking is influenced by the curiosity to learn the fundamental truth. With the increasing realization of nuances of the fundamental truth, they automatically progress in the path of non-violence and spirituality. As a result their actions evolve towards perfect conduct. This prerequisite for inquisitiveness is the reason that the knowledge of substances, as it relates to the fundamental spiritual truth, is essential for cultivating one's spiritual actions.

WHAT ARE SUBSTANCES? (DRAVYAS KĪ RŪPAREKHĀ)

In Indian languages the word *dravya* is related to the word *drava,* which means to "flow" or "dissolve." All substances of the world are formed and are subsequently destroyed. This ephemeral trend occurs at a speed that differs from substance to substance. Undoubtedly there are three stages of a substance: formation (creation), destruction, and stability (permanence). For instance, a sculptor creates a statue using clay. In the process the clay block is destroyed but a sculpture is created. However, in both manifestations (modes) of clay, the basic constituting ingredient of clay continues its existence.

It is important to emphasize that during the ongoing cycle of creation and destruction basic substances continue to exist. Lord Mahāvīra termed this knowledge of tripartite reality, consisting of creation, destruction, and permanence, as *mātr̥kā tripadī* (*tripadī sat*), meaning "three-legged truth." The harmonious coexistence of these three stages (creation, dissolution, permanence) is a characteristic of the fundamental truth. Every particle of this boundless and timeless universe follows this principle. No material entity can exist without adhering to this principle.

ESSENCE OF THE UNIVERSE (VIŚVA KĀ MŪLA)

Upon analysis, one finds that there are two fundamental types of *dravya* – animate (living) and inanimate (non-living). There are further subtypes, as discussed later. Philosophically, some doctrines posit the existence of only the entities that have consciousness, like the proposition of "absolute idealism," suggesting that somehow consciousness is fundamental to the universe and cannot be separated from the material universe any more than matter and energy can be separated. Others believe in only inanimate entities, a position thought of as materialism, physicalism, or related ideas, which see matter as being fundamental, and consciousness as being a characteristic of matter. However, Jain Dharma accepts a balanced and harmonious coexistence of both matter and consciousness.

Inanimate matter is so vast and multifaceted that Jain theorists saw that it was necessary to subdivide it into five categories. When combined with living or conscious entities, the entire universe consists of six eternal substances (*dravya*s):

1. *Jīvāsti-kāya*: The entity (*asti-kāya*[1]) which is living (*jīva*).
2. *Pudgalāsti-kāya*: The entity that is non-sentient matter (*pudgala*).
3. *Dharmāsti-kāya*: The entity that is the medium of motion (*dharma*). The principle of motion is sometimes labeled *dharma-dravya*.
4. *Adharmāsti-kāya*: The entity that is the medium of rest (*adharma*).
5. *Ākāśāsti-kāya*: The entity that is space (*ākāśa*).
6. *Kāla*: Time.

The entities in the above-mentioned categories of 3 through 6 can be grouped into a separate *dravya* group because they are all formless, non-visible, and non-sentient (*arūpī-ajīva*). The entities in category 2 are endowed with forms and are visible and non-sentient (*rūpī-ajīva*). The entities in category 1 (*jīva*) are formless, non-visible, and sentient (*arūpī-jīva*) because the soul (*jīva*) is an *arūpī* (non-visible) entity. However, the soul appears visible only because of its association with *pudgala* (non-sentient matter) in the form of a body, which is visible. In other words, only *pudgala* is a visible (*rūpī-dravya*) substance.

---

[1] The term *astikāya* is formed of two words: *asti* + *kāya*. *Asti* denotes *pradeśa* (the smallest part which is subtler than the atom) and *kāya* denotes *samūha* (group or collection). *Pradeśa* is the smallest possible form that is indivisible. Therefore, *astikāya* means aggregate of *pradeśa*s. *Kāla* is of only singular *pradeśa*, not in a group and not an *astikāya*.

The whole universe is an interconnected, intertwined, and interdependent network of these six types of eternal substances. According to Jain philosophy, no known force created these substances and there was no single moment of creation of this universe. Likewise, the soul (*jīva*) has always existed and will continue to exist forever. For many reasons, changes have always occurred and will continue to occur, causing each eternal substance of the universe to go through modifications uninterruptedly – creation in a shape or form and then destruction of the same. However, the underlying or basic substances associated with these manifestations (modes) are never destroyed and will never be created. Since Jain Dharma teaches that the universe has always existed, while supporting the doctrine of the existence of eternally liberated souls, it does not accept the theory that the eternally liberated souls are the creator(s) of the universe, since even the liberated souls themselves have at one time been bound by *karma*, just like everything else. Jain Dharma, like some forms of Buddhist doctrine, teaches that from beginningless time, all souls have been bound in the cycle of rebirth (*saṁsāra*) by *karma*. Thus, there is no God (*Īśvara*) or Superior Soul (*Brahman*) or Ultimate Reality that has never been bound by *karma*, although disembodied perfected souls that have attained liberation (*siddha*s) may be called (roughly) "God" (*deva*) or "Supreme Soul" (*paramātma*). But there is no supreme deity with the power to prevent *karma* from yielding its effects.

Since the sentient, living entities (*jīva*s) and the fundamental particles of non-sentient matter (*pudgala*) continuously go through changes and experience the resulting consequences, they are both considered a form of *dravya*. All *dravya*s continuously manifest into successive forms and all entities in this universe owe their existence to these *dravya*s.

Constituents of Substance (Dravya Pṛthakkaraṇa)

Three fundamental constituents (*aṁśa*s) are always present (*vidyamāna*) in an eternal entity – *dravya*, its properties (*guṇa*s), and its mode or migratory succession form (*paryāya*). An entity's (*vastu*'s) permanent characteristic (*nitya aṁśa*) is its *dravya*, to which its *guṇa*s inhere. The nature of an entity is defined by its associated (*sahabhāvī*) properties, and its modal (*paryāya*) form (*aṁśa*) is defined by its successive transformations (*kramabhāvī*). For instance, consider a living being – that is a substance in itself. It is always accompanied by knowledge (*jñāna*), which is associated with the *jīva*'s property of consciousness (*cetanā*). These are its *guṇa*s. Its successive modes (*paryāya*) could be human, cattle, insect, fish, etc. These three intertwined characteristics of substance, property, and modality (*dravya, guṇa,* and *paryāya*) coexist at all times, and they define the entity.

> Substance → property (adheres to substance) → mode (transformation of these)
>
> Example:
>
> Living entity (*jīva/dravya*) → consciousness (*cetanā-guṇa*) → type of being (*paryāya*)

In short, a *dravya* consists of *guṇa*s and *paryāya*. Despite going through the cycles of creation and destruction, it maintains its fundamental nature, which endures. Paradoxically – from that perspective – a *dravya* is permanent despite the transformation (*pariṇāma*) of its modalities (*paryāya*).

In one way, all entities have two distinctions based on the basic elements used in their creation – *anyatva-rūpa* (meaning "made from the same basic elements"), and *pr̥thaktva-rūpa* (meaning "made from different basic elements"). For instance, cream and yogurt are different entities but are made from the same basic ingredients (constituent of milk) and are therefore considered *anyatva-rūpa*. On the other hand, paper and pen are made from different basic ingredients and are *pr̥thaktva-rūpa*. In another example, one person is a child, the other a teenager, and the third an elderly person. The three entities are different, but they are all human beings. So, they are *anyatva-rūpa* and not *pr̥thaktva-rūpa*.

The *dravya*, its *guṇa*s, and its *paryāya* are truly not separable. The essential *guṇa*s of the *dravya*s are pervasive within it and have survived destruction from unknown times, despite their modal transformations. They remain associated with the *dravya* in its current form. The consequences of destruction from one cycle to reconstruction in the following define its form. The combination of the essential properties and the consequential modality define the substance.

Some of the characteristics of the aforementioned six categories of substances[2] are:

- Five of the six (except *kāla*) are called *asti-kāya* (literally, "a form that exists"), as described earlier, because they are manifestations of different physical forms.
- *Kāla*, on the other hand, has no physical form, so it is not *asti-kāya*.
- In addition, of the six *dravya*s the first (*jīva*) has consciousness (*cetanā*), whereas the other five do not.
- The second (*pudgala*, "matter") has a configuration (*mūrta*) of shape, form, taste, smell, and touch sensitivity, whereas the other five have none of these (*amūrta*).
- The living beings and matter (*jīva* and *pudgala*) are considered to be action-oriented (*sakriya*), whereas the remaining four are not (*kriyāhīna*). At first this may seem peculiar, particularly in the case of the third ("medium of motion" – *dharma*). However, since "medium of motion," "medium of rest," space, and time are what one might think of as universal abstractions (*samasta loka*), they may be considered inactive agents or non-specific forces. But they have their own functions. For instance, "medium of motion" enables *jīva* and *pudgala* to move; "medium of rest" enables *jīva* and *pudgala* to stop (rest); space gives abode to other five substances; and time "enables" or "changes" (*paryāya*) the other five substances uninterruptedly and determines what they will continuously undergo. These four forces (i.e., "medium of motion," "medium of rest," space, and time) are eternal and pervasive throughout the entire universe.
- Of the six categories of substances, "medium of motion" (*dharmāsti-kāya*), "medium of rest" (*adharmāsti-kāya*), and space (*ākāśāsti-kāya*) are pervasive and irrevocable, while the other three are not.

LIVING SUBSTANCE (JĪVA-DRAVYA)

The living substance is distinct from other substances because of its distinguishing property (*guṇa*) of *cetanā*. The additional distinguishing

---

[2] Six entites corresponding to the categories of substances are: (1) *jīva* (living-being/soul), (2) *pudgala* (matter), (3) *dharma* (medium of motion), (4) *adharma* (medium of rest), (5) *ākāśa* (space), and (6) *kāla* (time).

qualities of the living entity (*jīva* or "soul") are energy or vigor (*vīrya*) and bliss (*sukha*). A soul is never devoid of these qualities. There is an infinite number of consciousness-bearing entities, each in its own separate physical body. These entities have no shape or form of their own without being associated with a body, and they assume the same shape as that body.

A soul is a non-material, formless, and non-visible (*arūpī, amūrta*) entity. With the exception of liberated *jīva*s, a soul's associated *pudgala* body has a form and it occupies space. The soul itself is formless and does not occupy any space. The perception of the soul's occupation of space is like that of light whereby other *arūpī* substances can also occupy the same space. Each living entity has an infinite number of *pradeśa*s, which are infinitesimal and indivisible elements that are subtler than atoms, and are extensible, with the capacity to fill up the space allocated by the body – in the same way that light fills up the space. For instance, the *jīva* (soul) in an elephant can assume the body of an ant in its next life. Correspondingly, the life-giving elements, which were in the huge body of an elephant, will then fit into a tiny ant's body. The living entity also has modifiers (*viśeṣaṇa*) such as being a knower, viewer, user, consumer, teacher, master, doer, and one who is constrained, or is free.

Lord Mahāvīra said to his disciple Gautama: "The *jīva* cannot be perceived with the senses because it is formless and shapeless. And being abstract, it is eternal." As described in a Jain scripture, the *Ācārāṅgasūtra*, he continues:

> The *jīva* (soul) is neither tall nor short, nor long or round or rectangular. It is not spherical or black or red or blue or white. It is neither fragrant nor foul, neither sweet nor bitter or sour. It is not hard or soft. It cannot be destructed or created. It is not male or female or any other gender. Physically, it is neither beautiful nor ugly. It cannot be detected with the intellect but can be identified with direct experience. It cannot be explained with logic or reasoning but can be experienced spiritually. No words can fully describe its existence or form.
>
> Hey Gautama, knowledge (*jñāna*), perception (*darśana*), conduct (*carita*), penance (*tapas*), vigor (*vīrya*), fearlessness (*abhaya*), exhilaration (*sāmarthya-ullāsa*), and *upayoga*[3] (conscientious usefulness) are

[3] When translated literally, *upayoga* means "usefulness." But in the context of soul, *upayoga* involves its inclination towards knowledge (*jñāna*) and perception (*darśana*)

> characteristics of the *jīva*. The conviction of the realness of myself provides the most ascertaining cognizance of the *jīva*. There are numerous evidences of the existence of the *jīva*, but conviction of the "realness of myself" is paramount.

As mentioned before, the universe is filled with an infinite number of living entities. They all possess the same intrinsic properties discussed above (i.e., consciousness, strength or vigor, and bliss). However, because of the kārmic fruition of the individual's actions, each has developed its own unique set of kārmic layers that obscure these intrinsic properties. As a result of these personalized obscuring layers, each entity takes a unique *pudgala* body, state, and form – human or non-human. Based on this, the living substance (i.e., the *jīva*) can be split into two major categories – liberated (*mukta*) and bonded (*saṁsārī* or "worldly"). The living beings that have become pure (or "perfect," *śuddha*) after removing all the kārmic layers obscuring their intrinsic characteristics are the liberated souls (*mukta*). Those who still have these obscuring kārmic layers and continue to accumulate more *karma* through their impure (*aśuddha*) deeds are worldly and are therefore imperfect living beings (*saṁsārī*s).

Since the liberated souls (*mukta*s) are freed from all external influences, they are qualitatively alike. On the other hand, worldly beings have different shapes and forms depending on the degree of their *karma* burden. They have become physical entities due to the fructification of some kārmic residue. In spite of possessing infinite internal energy/vigor (*ananta vīrya*), because of their kārmic burden they are not independent from material existence – for example, they cannot see or hear without eyes or ears.

The bonded living beings (or worldly beings) can be further categorized into two major parts — *trasa* (moving) and *sthāvara* (non-moving or, literally, stable). *Trasa*s are endowed with more than one sense-capacity, while *sthāvara*s are endowed with only one sense, which is that of touch or contact (*sparśa*). Buddhist philosophy proposes twenty-two senses, while Sāṁkhya and some other philosophies propose eleven senses. Jain philosophy contends that there are only five senses. Based on this, worldly living entities are split into five categories corresponding to the number of senses they possess.

---

whereby the former (*jñāna*) provides the details and intricacies of the entity or object under consideration.

Living Beings with One Sense (Sthāvara Jīvas)

The unfortunate living beings that are endowed with only a sense of touch have the least capacity for consciousness. That is why they are often not fully understood either by common people or philosophers of other doctrines. Modern research regarding consciousness and its relationship to life itself has been incomplete and inconclusive. However, Jain philosophers have viewed the conscious living entity through a holistic perspective (*sampūrṇa*) and have provided very detailed descriptions. Accordingly, *sthāvara* beings are considered to possess all of the characteristics of worldly (*sāṁsārika*) beings, such as birth, death, consciousness, feelings of misery and pleasure, anger, deceit, and ego. This attests to their livingness. Such beings are categorized into five types:

1. *Pr̥thvī-kāya* (earth-bodied): These are living beings that have earth elements such as soil and minerals as their bodily forms. As long as the earth element remains rooted (*mūla*) to the *jīva*'s affliction (*piṇḍa*), that consciousness will be inseparable from the earth element.
2. *Ap-kāya* (water-bodied): These are the living beings that actually have water as their bodily form. They are different from the beings living in water, such as fish, who do not have water as their body.
3. *Tejas-kāya* (fire-bodied): A human body grows or shrinks depending on the nourishment it receives. In a similar manner, fire grows or shrinks depending on the fuel it receives. This helps in understanding the living nature of fire.
4. *Vāyu-kāya* (air-bodied): These are the living beings that actually have air as their bodily form, different from the livings beings such as birds, who live in the air. The air-bodied entities have the ability to navigate their movement without the influence or help of other entities. They have only one sense (touch) and form a category of *sthāvara* beings.
5. *Vanaspati-kāya* (vegetation-bodied): Trees, plants, vines, etc., are all living beings.

All *sthāvara* beings go through the birth–death cycle just like humans. All are believed to have traits like fear, shyness, sleep, and awakening, to become sick and healthy depending on food or environment, and can die from poison like humans. They are supposed to have an allocated lifespan as well.

Many contemporary scientists have been theorizing about the concept of *sthāvara* beings. However, it may be questionable to what degree the scientific community understands or might accept the concept in relation to the level of the Jain understanding. It is also a topic of modern philosophical discussion as to what the nature, status, and definition of life and of consciousness itself is, and it is far from clear if it is within the purview of the natural sciences to answer these types of questions. It may be that philosophical traditions, such as Jain Dharma, may be better equipped epistemologically to answer what has been called "the hard issue" of consciousness. But this is a longer discussion that is beyond the current scope of this work.

Mobile Living Beings with Multiple Senses (*Trasa Jīvas*)

These are the living beings with two to five senses:

1. *Dvīndriya-jīva*s (living beings with two senses): These are endowed with touch and taste senses – skin and tongue – respectively. Some examples may include certain types of mollusks such as mussels and clams.
2. *Trīndriya-jīva*s (living beings with three senses): These are endowed with touch, taste, and smell senses – skin, tongue, and nose – respectively. Some examples are ants, cockroaches, and other such insects.
3. *Caturindriya-jīva*s (living beings with four senses): These are endowed with touch, taste, smell, and sight senses – skin, tongue, nose, and eyes, respectively. Some examples are bees and mosquitos.
4. *Pañcendriya-jīva*s (living beings with five senses): These are endowed with touch, taste, smell, sight, and hearing senses – skin, tongue, nose, eyes, and ears, respectively. Humans, birds, animals, and hell-dwellings and heavenly beings are normally considered to have five senses. *Pañcendriya-jīva*s can be earth-bound, water-bound, or air-bound. Some move around on legs while others use both legs and arms. Some are mammals while others are reptiles or other non-mammals. Some are wise, while others could be unwise.

NON-LIVING SUBSTANCES (AJĪVA-DRAVYA)

Non-living types of substances are those which are devoid of consciousness and are formless and non-visible. As discussed earlier, in Jain doctrine *dravya* is not restricted to the sphere of the physical or material. It consists of both physical (*rūpī*) and non-physical (*arūpī*) entities in a contiguous, unified system. *Ajīva-dravya* entities go through continuous uninterrupted creation and destruction (*paryāya*) while maintaining their permanency of characteristics (not losing their inherent specific properties). They possess various common and specific characteristics. The *ajīva* substance is of five types: medium of motion (*dharmāsti-kāya*), medium of rest (*adharmāsti-kāya*), space (*ākāśāsti-kāya*), time (*kāla*), and matter (*pudgalāsti-kāya*).

THE SUBSTANCE THAT IS THE MEDIUM OF MOTION (DHARMA-DRAVYA)

In general, *dharma* has many meanings, including the innate nature of an entity. However, in the context of *dravya-vyavasthā* (the doctrine of the arrangement of substances), Jain philosophy defines *dharma* in a very unique way as a type of substance that enables the *pudgala* and *jīva* to move. *Dharma* does not actually make them move but acts as an enabler. For example, in the case of fish and water, the water is the *dharma* and it enables the fish to move, although the fish has to make its own effort for that movement. *Dharma* is a shapeless, formless, inactive, indivisible, non-visible, and all-pervasive substance. *Pudgala* and *jīva* cannot realize their potential in the absence of *dharma*. There is only one indivisible *dharma* in the *lokākāśa* (space) and it is termed *dharmāsti-kāya*.

THE SUBSTANCE THAT IS THE MEDIUM OF REST (ADHARMA-DRAVYA)

This substance is similar to *dharma-dravya* but differs in its characteristics. *Adharma* enables *pudgala* and *jīva* to stay at rest or be stable. It is an enabler but not a doer – it does not actually make anything stable or at rest. For instance, the shade of a tree can provide a place for resting but by itself it does not make anyone rest. Like *dharma*, *adharma* is also formless, inactive, invisible, indivisible, and eternal, but its characteristics are exactly opposite of those of *dharma*. There is only one indivisible *adharma* in *lokākāśa* (space), called *adharmāsti-kāya*. Its presence is instrumental for *pudgala* and the soul to remain steady.

THE SUBSTANCE THAT IS SPACE (ĀKĀŚA-DRAVYA)

This substance provides locality (or abode) to all other substances of the universe and can be considered akin to the concept of ether or vacuity. *Ākāśa* is the foundation for all entities, no other substance (*dravya*) supports it; and *ākāśa* is shapeless, formless, inactive, indivisible, non-visible, and eternal. In spite of being immobile (*akriya*) and indivisible (*akhaṇḍa*), it continuously goes through transformation (*pariṇāma*). The part of *ākāśa* that is pervaded (*vyāpta* or concomitance) by transformations of *dravya* (*dharma/adharma*), is called *lokākāśa* (worldly space), further divided into the three realms of the earth, heaven, and hell, where living beings dwell. The other portion of *ākāśa* is called *alokākāśa*, and is devoid of the potential for transformations (*dharma/adharma*), and therefore cannot sustain living beings. The *loka* portion of *ākāśa* is finite while the *aloka* portion is infinite. One could consider *lokākāśa* as that physically measurable universe which is observable objectively (*parimita* – to measure, observe, perceive, cast, throw, construct), and *alokākāśa* might be thought of as the opposite to this (*aparimita*).

THE SUBSTANCE THAT IS TIME (KĀLA-DRAVYA)

It is said above that the main trait of all *dravya*s is continuous transformation or change (*pariṇāma*) despite being constant and eternal (*nitya*). Although *dravya*s are foundational and axiomatic, they need an application or purpose as an impetus for their transformations. Time (*kāla-dravya*) provides that impetus. Just as *dharma* and *adharma* are instrumental for motion and rest, *kāla* is instrumental for the substances to undergo changes (*paryāya*). The rate of changes in living and non-living substances is measured in the units of *kāla* (time), but time is not the cause of the changes (*paryāya*). In one sense, it means continuity – the entire world is constantly changing on the basis of *kāla-dravya*. Entities go from being brand-new to old and worn-out, and finally to destruction. This is all linked to *kāla* as the dynamics of reality allowing for the relational comparison based on the temporality of older and younger. From traditional points of view, *kāla* is measured in units of time like hours and minutes. In Jain doctrine, the smallest unit of time is called *samaya*, which is indivisible and subtler than an atom. Combinations of *samaya*s are: moment, second, minute, hour, day, month, year, etc.

NON-SENTIENT, TINY MATERIAL SUBSTANCE (PUDGALA-DRAVYA)

The entire observable universe is made up of *pudgala*, including the bodily conglomerations of humans as well as non-human entities. It may not be possible to say for certain that whatever is *pudgala* is observable (there may be aspects of material reality that one simply will never be able to observe), but one can surely say that whatever is observable is made of *pudgala* (from an objectivist point of view). For instance, the *jīva* (soul) may not be independently observable by itself in that one can detect it by its association with a physical body. However, from a subjective observational perspective, one's soul can be perceived in a variety of ways, from a sense of consciousness to aspects of synchronic and diachronic unity of features of the consciousness. The formation or destruction, compilation or disbursement, etc., of observable reality are measurable by the different forms of *pudgala*. Of the six types of substances discussed, *pudgala* is the only one that has shape, form, color, odor, flavor, and touch sensitivity, which result in twenty unique qualities[4] (*guṇas*) of *pudgala*. These twenty unique qualities can be systematically combined to result in an innumerable number of shapes and types of matter, sound, smell, minuteness, vastness, shape, darkness, shade, moonlight, sunshine, etc. These are all instantiations of *pudgala*. Based on its state, *pudgala* has four classes: atoms (*paramāṇu*), aggregates (*skandhas*), position (*deśa*), and individuality (*skandha-pradeśa*, a particle). It should be emphasized that this *skandha-pradeśa* is a particle and not the same as the *pradeśa* of the other five substances. The *pradeśa* of those substances is the equivalent of *paramāṇu*, which is subtler than the current definition of an atom.

Skandha is the aggregation of matter (*pudgala*) which itself can be classified as having positioning (*deśa*) and individuality (*skandha-pradeśa*, a particle), further made up of individual units called *paramāṇus*. In general, some aggregates are gross (*bādara*) and may have the capacity for sense perceptions, while others are subtle (*sūkṣma*) and do not have such capacities.

---

4 Shape, form, and color are of five types: black, blue, yellow, red, and white. Odor is of two types: fragrant or pungent. Flavor is of five types: sweet, bitter, sour, salty, savory. Contact sensation has eight types: smooth, hard, soft, large, small, cold, hot, and fine or thin.

These two divisions can be combined in six ways:

1. Gross-gross (*bādara-bādara*): One that cannot be reassembled after breaks, like stone.
2. Gross (*bādara*): One that can be reassembled after it breaks.
3. Subtle-gross (*sūkṣma-bādara*): One that is massive and irrefutable, like sunshine or light.
4. Gross-subtle (*bādara-sūkṣma*): Although tiny, this allows for something to be sensed, such as through taste and smell.
5. Subtle (*sūkṣma*): Not perceptible by senses.
6. Subtle-subtle (*sūkṣma-sūkṣma*): Extremely minute, smaller than the previous level of subtlety. Example: the largest group of *karman-pudgala*s.

Paramāṇu is the smallest atomic form or part of *pudgala* that cannot be subdivided. In some literatures it is defined as being roughly equivalent to what in modern usage is called the atom. However, this is incorrect. A *paramāṇu* is the smallest conceivable part of matter that is not an individual unit (*skandha-pradeśa* particle), although it possesses perceptible properties of having a singular color, odor, and flavor, and two types of contact perceptibility.

Jain philosophy has defined the smallest indivisible unit of time or *kāla* as a *samaya* (moment). It is an infinitesimal part of the time it takes to blink an eye. By definition, it is similar to the smallest unit of *pudgala*, the *paramāṇu,* which itself has inconceivable speed and can go across the universe in one *samaya*. Likewise, time-moments (*samaya*) are distinct and irreducible. Jain scriptures state that *paramāṇu*s are not destroyed by fire, do not get spoiled, are not affected by wind, and are indestructible. However, when they merge with a *skandha* they suffer a qualified loss of independence by becoming part of the aggregate, but still retain their identity. After the *paramāṇu* separates from the *skandha*, it once again assumes its individual form and identity.

Jain Dharma has provided a vivid description of *paramāṇu* science in great detail, which surpasses other ancient literature. It is commonly said that today's world is a *paramāṇu* world (atomic-nuclear world). This is not true according to Jain philosophy. What today's science is grappling with is actually the *skandha* world. It would take many more years of research to reach the *paramāṇu* stage as defined in Jain philosophy.

In order to understand how one *paramāṇu* reacts to or combines with other *paramāṇu*s, one has to study the Jain scriptures which describe which properties of *paramāṇu*s can effectively unite with other *paramāṇu*s, and how their properties change before and after interactions. To find answers to these and many other issues, one should refer to Jain scriptures such as the *Bhagavatīsūtra,* the *Pannavaṇāsūtra,* the *Pañcāstikāya,* and the *Tattvārthasūtra.*

As an example, production of sound (*śabda*) results from interactions between *paramāṇu*s, although in a strict sense, it should be thought of as relating to *skandha*, not *paramāṇu*s. For instance, two *skandha*s strike to produce a word. In the past, many Indian philosophers thought that a sound is a property of formless and shapeless sky. However, a formless entity cannot have a well-formed and shaped property. According to Jain philosophy, a sound has definite form, a conclusion upheld by modern science.

This universe is the amalgamation and expansion of the six *dravya*s discussed above. There is no other *dravya*. It is astonishing that in the Jain understanding of matter (*pudgala*) is only one of the six substances of reality, while it seems that modern science has a difficult time seeing beyond only *pudgala*.

6

The Discussion of the Fundamental Truth (Tattva-Carcā)

In Jain doctrine, the discussion of fundamental truth (*tattva*) correlates with that of the nature of substance (*dravya*). Their classifications overlap as well; that is, *jīva* (which is animate or sentient) and *ajīva* (which is inanimate or non-sentient) are two basic types of *tattva*s, just as they are two fundamental types of *dravya*s. In essence, one could surmise that the discussion of *dravya* encompasses that of *tattva*, but Jain scriptures have presented separate discussion and analysis of *tattva* with a special purpose, which becomes evident in the discussion that follows.

The analysis of *dravya* is intended to accurately understand the nature of the universe (*sṛṣṭi*), and to address philosophical issues arising from the worldly existence (*laukika*). On the other hand, the study of the fundamental truth (*tattva*) is a spirituality driven pursuit to understand the pure soul – *ādhyātmika*.

It is important to understand the physical aspects of the universe and its constituents to resolve questions such as: "Is there a creator of the universe?" "What is its origin?" "What is it made of?" "Who am I?" "What are my inherent qualities?" "Who is like me and what is not like me?" etc. Such knowledge inspires seekers towards the path of spirituality. However, progress on that path is not possible without a thorough understanding of the principles of *tattva*. The doctrine of *tattva* is based on the soul (*ātmā*), its characteristics, and the interrelationship between the soul, *karma*, and kārmic matter (which are the subtlest type of *pudgala*). Even if one is not fully versant in physical and geographical conditions of the universe (*viśāla viśva*) or the constituent categories of matter (*padārtha*), they may still be able to progress towards spiritual salvation by thoroughly understanding *tattva*. But the reverse is not true. Therefore, there is no salvation without a thorough knowledge of the *tattva*. A structured evaluation and understanding of all elements of *tattva* is essential for spiritual progress. In the words of Jain's supreme teacher, Lord Mahāvīra:

> Spiritual seekers cannot advance towards ultimate liberation until they are fully capable of understanding their own fundamental and spiritual nature (*svarūpa*).

Such understanding of one's own spiritual nature is not different from comprehending the fundamental truth (*tattva*). According to Jain philosophy, acquiring knowledge serves two purposes: it enhances one's knowledge in a general sense and it augments the wisdom that is essential to spiritual progress. From that perspective, knowledge acquisition helps resolve two fundamental questions:

1. Why and how do different souls reach distinctly different states over time if they all started from the same perfect state?
2. If external forces created differences, what are those forces, how are they related to the soul, and how can one rid oneself of these afflictions?

To answer these and other such questions, one must first understand the path of the soul's journey towards salvation and its state after reaching the pinnacle of ultimate liberation. Jain philosophy addresses all such questions to the minutest detail through its unique doctrine of *tattva*, which elucidates the soul's journey towards salvation. An overview is presented here.

Many Jain scriptures (for example, the *Sthānāṅgasūtra*) have presented the doctrine of *tattva*, and have divided it into the following nine categories:

1. *Jīva* (soul, or living or sentient entity)
2. *Ajīva* (non-sentient entity)
3. *Puṇya* (righteousness or auspicious *karma*[1])
4. *Pāpa* (wickedness or inauspicious [sinful] *karma*)
5. *Āśrava* (influx of *karma* to the soul)
6. *Saṁvara* (cessation of the influx of *karma* to the soul)

[1] In general, *karma* refers to deed or action, but in context of the doctrine of *tattva*, *karma* (also called *karman*) refers to tiny particles of non-living substance (*ajīva-pudgalas*). These are the subtlest form of *pudgalas* and are non-visible, tasteless, odorless, and touchless particles.

7. *Nirjarā* (dissociation of the soul from adhered kārmic matter)
8. *Bandha* (bondage of *karma* with the soul)
9. *Mokṣa* (liberation of the soul from the kārmic bondage of *saṁsāra*)

It should be noted that some great Jain *ācārya*s have categorized *puṇya* and *pāpa* as subcategories of *āśrava* since they both refer to the influx of *karma* (both auspicious as well as inauspicious types).

The unique exposition of *tattva* in Jain Dharma is crafted with the specific purpose of highlighting the characteristics that either support or obstruct the path of spiritual growth. Based on the specific characteristics, Jain Dharma provides solutions to all sorts of important questions, such as those related to the progress, downfall, misery, pleasure, death, birth, and species type of an individual soul on its journey in *saṁsāra* (worldly existence). A brief description of the nine categories of *tattva* follows.

Soul: The Living and Sentient Entity (Jīva)

The characteristics of *jīva* in relation to the other types of *dravya*s have been discussed earlier. From the *tattva* perspective, one needs to understand why, despite being shapeless and formless, the *jīva* appears to be taking a shape due to the accumulation of *karma*. Every living being is affected by the kārmic accumulation that creates misery for the soul by allowing it to be enslaved by external forces that are not under its control. A soul has the freedom to accumulate different types of *karma*, but it has no control over the corresponding ramifications that it must bear. The only way to circumvent or minimize the manifestations of the repercussions may become possible when one exerts extraordinary efforts to discard the acquired *karma* (to be discussed in chapter 11). In that sense, a living entity (*jīva*) is responsible for its own progress or downfall and the resulting destiny necessitated by the fruition of one's acquired *karma*. The soul is not guaranteed to experience any specific changes to its state or to reach the pinnacle of liberation (*mokṣa*) without undertaking an extraordinary effort to shed its accumulated *karma*s. Rather than considering the soul as a solitary traveler in its journey, it might be better understood as an independent entity that is solely responsible for its own destiny. However, it is accountable for its actions and will inevitably receive the resultant repercussions.

The Non-Living and Non-Sentient Substance (Ajīva)

Ajīva-dravya (the non-living substance) has been discussed earlier in chapter 5. Beyond this, the subtlest non-sentient matter particles, called *ajīva-pudgala*, play a critical role in the doctrine of *tattva*. The *jīva* has deviated from its natural state because it has been accumulating *ajīva-pudgala*s, called *karma*s, over many lifetimes. The specifics of how and why *ajīva-pudgala*s (*karma*s), as material substances, form a relationship with the non-material soul is a topic of great interest to Jain Dharma.

The universe is full of *ajīva-pudgala*s (kārmic particles), but they do not affect or obstruct the inherent qualities of any *jīva* unless they become bonded to the soul. As discussed later in this chapter under *āśrava*, because of its delusions driven by attachments and aversions, and the activities of mind, body, and speech, a soul attracts *karma* particles, which hinder and obstruct the inherent qualities of the soul. The assemblage of all associated *karma* to the soul is called the "kārmic body" (kārmic *śarīra*). Every worldly living being has an associated kārmic body.

The Righteous and Auspicious Karma (Puṇya)

According to the doctrine of *tattva*, *puṇya* is an influx of auspicious *karma*s (*ajīva-pudgala*s) upon the soul, which upon manifestation may result in worldly and spiritual pleasures for the *jīva*. Such pleasures may include the emergence of a worthy destiny (such as a birth in human or heavenly body), prosperity, or the exposure to an honorable philosophy (such as Jain Dharma). Alternatively, from the viewpoint of one's actions, *puṇya* is that which purifies the soul by motivating it towards purification through the performance of meritorious acts that are instrumental in developing an inspiration to perform spiritual practices such as penance. Such meritorious spiritual practices may lead to the *jīva*'s progress towards the ultimate liberation when they are conducted respectfully without any worldly desires or unrighteous objectives. On the other hand, the same practices may result in gathering inauspicious *karma* when they are conducted with an expectation of worldly benefits or when they are accompanied by immoral expressions of emotions such as anger, or when they are driven by the motivations for gratifying one's ego through deceit and greed.

The attainment of wholesome spiritual qualities, devotional tendencies, general proficiencies, controlled living, and basic humanitarian traits are all the consequence of meritorious acts (*puṇya*) performed with a purity of mind, body, thoughts, and speech, and with no expectations of personal gain. Righteous behavior in part leads to even the achievement of the exalted state of becoming a *tīrthaṅkara*. *Puṇya* is the impelling force for those bound for liberation to follow the spiritual path, and it helps in achieving the quickest journey to salvation. In life, experiencing healthy and disease-free living, financial prosperity, and all other worldly benefits can be attributed to the results of *puṇya karma* (righteousness).

One of the most revered Jain saints, Ācārya Hemacandra, has expressed the softening effect of meritorious *karma* as righteousness in his verse: "The sign of the emergence of auspicious *karma* is the sign of *karma* driven by *puṇya*."

Examples of meritorious acts include:

1. *Anna-puṇya*: The offering of pure, guiltless, vegetarian food to others, and at the same time, minimizing the hoarding of food.
2. *Pāna-puṇya*: The offering of pure non-sentient water and other liquids to others, and reducing their usage and waste.
3. *Layana-puṇya*: The offering of shelter to the needy, and being satisfied with modest living place, e.g., housing for oneself.
4. *Śayana-puṇya*: The offering of a resting or sleeping place to others while being satisfied with a modest bed for oneself.
5. *Vastra-puṇya*: The offering of clothes to others while avoiding unnecessary accumulation for oneself.
6. *Mana-puṇya*: Maintaining pleasant, ethical, helpful, gentle, and auspicious thoughts of mind, and contemplating the elements of righteous *dharma*.
7. *Vacana-puṇya*: The use of dignified language, using kind, pleasant, moral, and respectful speech.
8. *Kāya-puṇya*: The use of the body to serve and assist others with ethical, moral, helpful, and honorable actions.
9. *Namaskāra-puṇya*: Maintaining and expressing reverence in front of

righteous people, including respectful, honorable, and learned worldly individuals as well as *pañca-parmeṣṭhī*[2] (the five-tiered supreme holiness).

There are two types of *puṇya*: *dravya-puṇya* and *bhava-puṇya*. *Dravya-puṇya* involves physical, outward and visible acts of charity and other virtuous actions, such as serving poor, needy, sick humans or animals, and donating for good causes. *Bhava-puṇya* involves noble thoughts and actions of service such as providing donations to those in need. It may involve internal thoughts that occur before the actual physical acts are carried out. Having such thoughts can themselves become the means of shedding accumulated *karma*.

Jain *ācāryas* teach that we should offer the above acts of *puṇya* to all "worthy people" (*supātras*) who are practicing self-restraint, pursuing the path of liberation, and need assistance. This includes Jain ascetics as well as honorable householders. They further suggest extending such offerings to all living beings out of compassion. All deeds of *puṇya* are advised to be performed privately without any publicity in order to fully experience the spiritual enrichment of these righteous actions.

The Wickedness Demerit That Causes Inauspicious Sinful Karma (Pāpa)

The doctrine of *tattva* defines *pāpa* as the influx of inauspicious *karma* that results from wicked and sinful acts of mind, body, and speech. Upon manifestation, such *karmas* may result in an unfortunate destiny (for instance, the attainment of a hellish or *tiryañca*[3] life), destitution, an unhealthy disease-ridden body, an inglorious public image, deprivation of exposure to righteous philosophy (Jain doctrine), and other such undesirable conditions.

The evil and harmful *pāpa* in thought, utterance, and behavior could result in observable and/or non-observable forms of sinful and wicked actions. It

---

[2] In Jain tradition, *pañca-parmeṣṭhī* is the supreme holiness worthy of worship, comprising of five categories – *arihantas* (enlightened supreme teachers in bodily form), *siddhas* (enlightened supreme teachers with liberated souls), *ācāryas* (mendicant leaders), *upādhyāyas* (mendicant preceptors), and *sādhus*/*sādhvīs* (male and female mendicants).

[3] *Tiryañca* is the term used for plants, animals, and insects in Jain philosophy.

is important to note that such acts may occur in one's thoughts, and are not restricted to just the physical actions. Such disgraceful acts (*pāpas*) create layers of impure kārmic accumulation over the soul that results in misery. Some of the sinful acts are:

1. Violence done to hurt and take life.
2. Disrespect and untruth in speech or dialogue.
3. Stealing and taking things without permission.
4. Acts of sexual harming arising from lust.[4]
5. Excessive consumption such as acts of unnecessary accumulation, attachment to worldly possessions, being inattentive to virtuous acts, unchecked craving for things, and hoarding.
6. Acts of anger and indignation.
7. Being egotistical, arrogant, and conceited.
8. Acts of deceit, fraud, trickery, and propagation of deceptive beliefs.
9. Acts of greed and the tendency to accumulate possessions beyond necessity.
10. Acts of attachment to, and being inappropriately enamored by, worldly possessions, people, and other living beings.
11. Acts of jealousy, envy, hatred, malice, and humiliation.
12. Acts of hostility, quarreling, anguish, and causing distress.
13. Acts of false accusation and blame.
14. Acts of slander, viciousness, and the spreading of rumors.
15. Acts of abuse, taunting, and disparagement.
16. Acts of inappropriate elation and sadness related to desire, sex, and eroticism.
17. Use of deceit and fraud to fabricate lies.
18. Acts of developing devotion based on false beliefs and deceptive, untruthful teachings. This could be the most harmful form of *pāpa*. It is considered to be the catalyst for the other seventeen sinful acts and is the root cause of a *jīva*'s wanderings from one life to another.

---

[4] *Maithuna-kāma-vikāra* (sexual desire that is injurious).

From the above discussion on *puṇya* and *pāpa*, one may surmise that the *puṇya* is preferred over *pāpa*, which is true when one is engaged in routine activities. However, spiritually speaking, both *puṇya* and *pāpa* result in the influx of *karma*. As much as *puṇya* is preferred over *pāpa* in the early stages of spiritual advancement, both kinds must ultimately be eliminated in advanced stages as one gets closer to liberation. In fact, in the upper echelon of spiritual advancement, the seekers automatically desist from committing even *puṇya* acts. This process is the transition of the seeker from *aśubha* (inauspiciousness) to *śubha* (auspicious) and, finally, to the *śuddha* (pure) stage.

The Influx of Karma upon the Soul (Āśrava)

As stated earlier, all actions in thoughts or physical behavior result in *karma* (*karma-pudgala*s or *karman* – which are non-sentient matter particles) acquisition and their accumulation in layers over the soul. *Āśrava* is the influx of *karma* towards the soul, and the means and reasons behind that inflow. This includes the tendencies and actions of living beings in thought, words, or physical acts that result in kārmic attraction to the soul. *Āśrava* is the first step in affecting the soul with impurities through acquisition of *karma*s. It is important, especially while in human life, to understand the reasons and tendencies that result in this *karma*-to-soul inundation. The human life is the phase when the *karma*-to-soul interconnection can be weakened or broken through deliberate corrective actions such as rigorous penance and meditation. It is difficult to name all the causes of kārmic influx, but Jain philosophy categorizes them in five areas:

1. *Mithyātva* (falsity or being delusional): Considered to be the opposite of religious devotion, falsity involves showing faith in spurious and harmful thoughts that are contrary to the teachings of the great *tīrthaṅkara*s.
2. *Avirati* (incontinence): Indulging in inauspicious activities such as violence, fraudulent actions, being untruthful, listening to and/or believing in spurious teachings, etc.
3. *Pramāda* (negligence): Adverse behavior such as showing disrespect to holy sermons by *tīrthaṅkara*s, being careless in activities of mind, body, and speech, and indulging in inauspicious acts.

4. *Kaṣāya* (passions): Not exercising control over interactions and behaving with anger, ego, arrogance, deceit, and greed.
5. *Yoga* (psycho-physical activities): Actions involving the mind, body, and speech that cause the influx of *karma* (*āśrava*). An important point to note here is that the literal meaning of the word *yoga* is "unification." In the context of the *tattva* discussion, *yoga* connotes the unified behavior of mind, body, and speech, which could be either positive or negative. Another notable point is that in contemporary times, *yoga* is commonly understood as a form of physical exercise. Even in that context, the learned practitioners consider it be a practice to unify oneself with the nature or true-self.

The Cessation of the Influx of Karma upon the Soul (Saṁvara)

Saṁvara (cessation) refers to the stopping of the *āśrava* of *karma-pudgala*s (non-sentient-matter particles) which collect in layers over the soul. When a spiritual seeker grasps the reasons and means by which an influx of *karma* occurs, and they develop the means to block it, the soul stops accumulating additional *karma*. This is the state of *saṁvara*. For instance, when one becomes devoted to veracious teachings, the *āśrava* of *karma-pudgala*s based on falsity (*mithyātva*) ceases (*saṁvara*). Similarly, influx of *karma*s ceases when one is involved in penance and meditation with positive and worthy thoughts. The cessation of hurtful inauspicious *karma* influx occurs when one replaces unrighteous (*pāpa*) activities with meritorious ones (*puṇya*), such as magnanimous behavior, exercising forgiveness, listening to and praising holy sermons, respectable conduct, and honorable business dealings. No spiritual seeker can adopt perfect blemish-free living while engaged in worldly affairs. However, Jain philosophy emphasizes the curbing of negative behavior as much as possible and replacing that with honorable conduct (*puṇya*). Whatever activities the spiritual seeker is involved in, it must be done with the right attitude, noble vision, respectful demeanor, and positive outlook. Such behavior will help in minimizing the influx of *karma* (*āśrava*) and will gradually allow for the *saṁvara* of kārmic accretion.

The Dissociation of the Soul from Adhered Kārmic Matter (Nirjarā)

As discussed above, *āśrava* signifies the causes and means of *karma* accumulation, and *saṁvara* signifies the ways and processes for stopping the *karma* influx. However, simply stopping the adherence of kārmic *pudgala*s to the soul is not enough; one has to get rid of *karma* that has already been collected. The process of eliminating accumulated *karma*s is known as *nirjarā*.

Consider a boat riding the waves on an ocean. If the water starts getting into the boat, the holes that allow the water to come in, and the causes of the holes' creation, might be likened to *āśrava* (the influx of *karma*). When the holes are all blocked and water stops entering the boat, that would be likened to *saṁvara* (the cessation of *karma* influx). In order to ensure safety, water inside the boat must be drained, which would then be figuratively akin to *nirjarā* (the riddance of unwanted substance). Thus, *nirjarā* can be taken to imply the shedding of the kārmic *pudgala*s that have accumulated in layers over the soul.

Nirjarā of the *karma-pudgala* layers accumulated over the soul may happen in two ways: involuntary or automatic shedding of *karma*s (*anaupakramika*), or the voluntary or deliberate shedding of *karma*s (*aupakramika*).

Anaupakramika nirjarā follows the natural path to fruition or maturation of *karma*s, and it takes place in its own due course (also known as *savipāka nirjarā*, implying "automated fruition" of *karma*s). In this case, the individuals do not make any special efforts to get rid of their accumulated *karma*s. The fruition or maturation of *karma*s that have been accumulating over the soul may happen in the same life or it may be delayed for multiple lives. Depending on the nature of the *karma*s, results of their fruition may be negative – which brings misery – or positive, which brings pleasure. The quality, intensity, duration, etc., of the repercussions resulting from the fruition depends on the type of acquired *karma*s (see chapter 11).

Aupakramika nirjarā involves sincere and deliberate efforts by individuals, which may result in the elimination of acquired *karma*s before their natural fruition. This might be understood as the fruition of *karma* at an accelerated pace. The process involves specific spiritual practices (*viśiṣṭa sādhanā*) consisting of rigorous penance, austerity, meditation, and other auspicious acts like charity, kindness, and devotion to virtuous teachings. The spiritual seekers who undertake the *aupakramika nirjarā* process are highly inspired individuals determined to work hard and accelerate their path to salvation. With continued special effort, they ultimately free themselves from all *karma*s and achieve the pinnacle of liberation. Clearly, their penance and meditation are the hardest, and their lifestyle is at the highest level of righteousness one can imagine. This involves supreme control, detachment from worldly affairs and materials, determination, and complete confidence. Jain philosophy describes the unmatched fortitude of such individuals as such that they not only leave aside the worldly materials and other living beings; the supreme ascetics go to the extent of foregoing sensory attachment to their own bodies. Not having sensory attachment to one's body does not mean one mistreats one's body. Rather, as explained in *samyag-darśana*, it means to spiritually and emotionally separate one's body from one's soul, and treat the soul as the true-self and the body as a source of soul's refuge in this life.

Such individuals are completely introverted. They immerse themselves internally and stay in meditative states at all the times. They achieve the ultimate goal of *nirjarā* by shedding the accumulated *karma* and rehabilitating the soul from the bondage of *karma*. They are filled with compassion but live in this world without any passions and sensory attachments, and are unaffected by the vicissitudes of life. Their powerful spiritual exertion forces their *karma*s to detach from the soul, which ultimately reaches its natural unblemished state of purity. The process is also called "intentional rehabilitation" (*sakāma nirjarā*) in Jain philosophy.

All living beings experience the involuntary (*anaupakramika*) process of kārmic dissolution, also known as "unintentional rehabilitation" (*akāma nirjarā*). Living beings may feel distraught upon the fruition of negative *karma*s or they may feel elated with the fruition of positive *karma*. However, while shedding accumulated *karma*s through the normal process, one continues to gather more. This cycle continues until one engages in the voluntary (*aupakramika*) intervention with hard penances and austerities. The normal, unchecked process will never lead to the ultimate salvation.

The Bondage of Karma to the Soul (Bandha)

How is it that the influx of *karma*s (*āśvara*) become bound (*bandha*) to the soul if the soul is a formless and shapeless entity? How can a formless entity (the soul) become entangled with one that has form (*karma*)?

Although inherently the soul is formless and shapeless, since beginningless time it has continued to gather *karma*s and has developed layers and layers of kārmic matter (*karman* or *karma-pudgala*s). This results in the soul acquiring a shape commensurate to its kārmic form. In the process, the living entity forgets the essential formlessness of its soul. Once a living being realizes this forgotten state and revitalizes the soul's essential purity through rigorous penance and meditation, it will never again gather any kārmic residue.

It is hard to determine exactly when any particular *karma*s initially collected in layers over the soul, just like it is hard to isolate the time when a particular mineral was formed within the earth. It has been an ongoing process since beginningless time (*anādikālīna*). The collection of *karma*s as layers on one's soul is analogous to the way dust particles accumulate on a smooth and sticky surface, and then calcify if not cleaned in a timely fashion.

Bandha (kārmic "bondage") has two forms: passion-bondage (*bhāva-bandha*) and substantial- or physical-bondage (*dravya-bandha*). Passion-bondage is the collection of *karma*s (*karma-pudgala*s) resulting from passionate or inauspicious emotions of attachment, deceit, jealousy, etc. When this kārmic matter collects due to material actions and coalesces in layers over the soul, it is known as *dravya-bandha*.

As discussed earlier, Jain philosophy asserts that kārmic matter (*karma-pudgala*) is ubiquitously present at all times in the universe. When one is involved in activities of mind, body, and speech, the kārmic material that is within the vicinity gets attached in layers over one's soul. At the time of this attachment, four characteristics get associated with the attached *karma*:

1. *Prakṛti-bandha* (nature of bondage): The acquired kārmic matter develops a specific temperament that results in a specific outcome depending on the nature of the act(s) that caused the *karma* acquisition. In general, *karma* can have innumerable qualities that can be divided into eight broad categories, described in chapter 11. *Prakṛti-bandha* defines the nature of the outcome depending on the *karma* that caused the *karma-pudgala*s' acquisition. For example, the type of *mohanīya* (delusional; see chapter 11) *karma* will determine whether it is a pleasant outcome or a suffering one, and *āyuṣya-karma* or *āyu-karma* will determine one's lifespan.

2. *Sthiti-bandha* (duration of bondage or predicament of fruition): This determines the timing, the state, or the predicament that would cause the repercussion from the collected *karma* to materialize. This includes the amount of time for which the *karma* will stay dormant, or the situation that would cause the fruition to occur. This could occur within a few seconds or it may take multiple lifetimes, and it depends on the intensity of passions that accompany the acts that resulted in the initial kārmic acquisition.
3. *Anubhāga-bandha* (type or quality of fruition): This determines the quality of the outcome depending on the degree and types of passions, and the extent of actions during kārmic acquisition. For example, this type of *karma* determines whether or not one would achieve success in a financial enterprise one founded, or whether or not one's well-meaning social endeavors would lead to prestige or indifference or even disgrace. Similarly, it would determine whether one's fortune (*anubhāga*) when seeking spiritual guidance will lead them to an illuminating *guru* or instead to a thug who takes one onto a path of destruction.
4. *Pradeśa-bandha* (magnitude of fruition): This determines the intensity or temperance of one's kārmic outcome, or its degree of impact, depending on the volume of the collected *karma* and the state of the soul's disillusionment. One might think of this as the difference between winning a lottery for $10 or $100 million, or the difference between a car accident that results in a small fracture or the loss of one's life.

To clarify the above four states of kārmic attachment, one might think of an analogy whereby a cow consumes grass and the food gets converted to milk through the biological processes of the cow. Depending on the individual characteristics of the cow and the types of grass she selects to eat, the nature of the milk may be sweet, thick, or thin. This is analogous to *prakṛti-bandha* (the nature of bondage). One may further consider the situation in which the milk stays unspoiled, or the state (or amount of time or predicament) that causes it to turn into curd or cheese, as *sthiti* (state). *Anubhāga-bandha* (quality of fruition) may be thought of as the quality of milk – it may be less sweet than buffalo milk or sweeter than goat milk. And the specific quantity of milk produced by the cow would be the *pradeśa* (magnitude).

Of these four types of *bandha*, *prakṛti-bandha* and *pradeśa-bandha* depend on the level of fickleness, wickedness, or generosity associated with the act that resulted in the kārmic acquisition. In other words, the repercussions of the kārmic bondage are directly related to the involvement and contributions by: (1) actions of body and speech, and (2) involvement of the thoughts of the individual, collectively called "kārmic acts." The nature or type of repercussions is determined by the *prakṛti-bandha*, which is dependent on the nature of kārmic acts. The timing and the events that cause the fruition of the *karma*s is *sthiti-bandha*, which depends on the magnitude and level of the kārmic acts. The quality of the fruition is *anubhāga-bandha*, which is dependent on the type and severity or temperance of the kārmic acts. The magnitude of repercussions is *pradeśa-bandha*, which is linked to the intensity of the kārmic acts.

The Ultimate Liberation (Mokṣa)

Jain scriptures such as the *Uttarādhyayanasūtra* provide vivid and detailed descriptions of how a *jīva* reaches a *karma*-free state after it has achieved complete cessation of the influx of *karma* towards the soul (*saṁvara*) and also has discarded all of the *karma-pudgala*s which had been collected in layers over the soul (*nirjarā*). At this stage, the soul is relieved of its previously acquired kārmic *bandha* and ceases the acquisition of new *karma*. Those *jīva*s who are devoid of all *karma*s, are freed from all of the repercussions that accompany *karma*-acquiring actions. They have reached the state of purity – the state of *mokṣa* according to Jain philosophy.

Upon achieving *mokṣa*, the soul reverts to a state of formlessness and shapelessness. It is no longer affected by the activities of the senses and mind. It has become omniscient (*sarvajña*) and omni-visionary (*sarva-darśī*). At this stage, it has acquired complete and unlimited consciousness (*ananta cetanā-ghana*) and it possesses endless vigor (*vīrya*) – the inherent and internal qualities (*guṇa*s) of the *jīva*. The soul has now been cleansed of all types of lowly and wicked traits and has achieved its sublime intrinsic nature, never to return to kārmic existence again. It is relieved from any cause of the influx of *karma* to the soul (*āśrava*) or the bondage of *karma* with the soul (*bandha*). At this exalted state, the soul's existence is eternal and free; it will never again reincarnate in the material universe.

The soul is an upwardly moving entity, ascending by its very nature. A piece of wood that is laden with sticky dirt sinks to the bottom of a pool. When the stickiness is dissolved in the water, the wood again floats to the top of water. A soul is similarly bound to rise spiritually when the kārmic material is removed. However, once it leaves the part of universe that is occupied (*lokākāśa*), there are no other entities and no further spiritual movement. It forever situates itself in the upper part of the universe (*siddha-loka*) above the heavenly realms.

While transient in the world, a soul collects a certain element of knowledge or experiences pleasantries and miseries that can eclipse the natural state of the soul. In the state of *mokṣa*, all impure traits are transformed to their pure state. That is why a liberated soul experiences complete, unrestricted, and untainted bliss and wisdom.

Thus, *mokṣa* is the achievement of freedom from reincarnating as various types of living forms. It is the complete and ultimate purity of consciousness, and is nothing less than the soul's transformation into a completely divine entity. This is the attainment of *jinatva* – the state of complete spiritual liberation. Reaching this pinnacle is the highest purpose of the soul (*parama puruṣārtha*) – the ultimate valor. It is simultaneously the essence and ultimate objective of all types of penance and austerities, and is the very purpose of the living entity.

7

Fundamental Doctrines:
Nayavāda, Anekāntavāda, and Syādvāda

The Doctrine of Fundamental Principles (Nayavāda)

THE ESSENCE OF VIEWPOINTS: NAYA-SVARŪPA

MOST philosophical systems of the world consider a singular vantage point based on evidence (*pramāṇa*) as a sufficient criterion for the proof of an entity's nature and existence. Jain philosophy approaches evidential knowledge differently. Jain philosophy posits that evidence produced from a single vantage point is not sufficient by itself. For accurate determination, in addition to the observable evidence one needs to acquire knowledge of fundamental or innate principles from different vantage points (*naya*s) and different frames of reference because reality itself is multifaceted. This doctrine is known as Nayavāda and is related to the doctrine of non-absolutism or non-one-sidedness (Anekāntavāda). This allows Jain doctrine to avoid the dogmatic adherence to a singular point of view. *Pramāṇa* is a critical component of knowledge acquisition and wisdom development, as discussed in chapter 4, but it may address only one aspect or one part of the entire complexity of a multifaceted entity. With Nayavāda, one can comprehensively address the core-constituting elements and components of an entity along with the characteristics of its existence.

According to Jain philosophy, knowledge is a highly complex entity composed of multidimensional, interrelated information from multiple facets such as constitution of substance (type, characteristics, and modal state); time of existence (past, present, and future); location of existence (over infinite space); and concurrently ongoing transmigratory nature (origination, destruction, and permanence). Therefore, in order to get a complete understanding of an entity, it is essential to conduct thorough research and analysis into its nature and existence from multiple vantage points. Without a variegated research methodology, it is impossible to get a thorough understanding. Such a process of research and analysis, and subsequent acts of comprehending the analyzed form, is an application of Nayavāda doctrine or methodology.

It is important to note that not only are there an unlimited number of entities, each of those may have multiple views according to the doctrine of Anekāntavāda (non-absolutism). Thus, there could be multiple viewpoints of the reality of anything. The endeavor to comprehend an entity from a particular viewpoint is called *naya*, and the system or doctrine of describing the reality of an entity from multiple viewpoints is called Nayavāda. Using this approach, one can investigate what seem to be mutually contradictory views and discover the valid sources of these contradictions. Empowered with this multifaceted knowledge, one can formulate a common ground out of the multiple different views without denouncing the validity of any one or multiple perspectives. On the one hand Nayavāda analyzes the causes and consequences of the specific views, while on the other hand it deciphers the root causes of the differences between the opposing views. Ultimately, it helps in discovering commonalities and establishing a unified solution.

There are always conflicting views on almost any subject matter – be it the nature of the soul, or whether certain beings are sentient or not. For example, one doctrine may believe there is only a singular soul of which all living beings are illusory fragmented components, whereas another one postulates an infinite number of completely individuated souls whose separate nature is not merely provisional. In such circumstances, the proponents of Nayavāda would conduct an investigation to determine what the reasoning is behind the perspective of innumerable souls and likewise to understand the arguments in support of a monistic view of an over-soul. In this manner, the practice of *naya* is designed to extract the basis of truth from scores of viewpoints by conducting research and analysis of those views with an a priori assumption of validity charitably extended to each one.

Nayavāda presents the means for reconciling the views of different philosophies of the world. Each entity under analysis could have countless properties, each of which in turn could have multiple characteristics in the context of the philosophy under which the entity is being observed. The intricate knowledge about each of its properties and corresponding philosophy-based perspectives conforms to *naya-jñāna*. A holistically observed knowledge about the same entity from a variety of philosophical perspectives leads to evidential knowledge (*pramāṇa-jñāna*). In simplistic terms, *naya-jñāna* deals with micro-level knowledge, whereas *pramāṇa-jñāna* deals with macro-level knowledge taken from an aggregation of perspectives.

THE TRUTH BEHIND NAYA (NAYA KĪ SATYATĀ)

One could argue that a singular perspective (*naya*) is by itself false knowledge (*mithyā-jñāna*) since it addresses just one of the multitude of properties of an entity. If so, the question arises as to how that particular *naya* perspective can be the basis for understanding the complete nature of an entity. The answer to this lies in the fact that the correctness of any particular viewpoint (*naya*) is dependent on it not being contradictory to any other correct perspective (*naya*). Take, for instance, the nature of the soul. According to one *naya*, it is eternal, while a different belief (*naya*) says it is not eternal. In support of the first *naya*, the soul's spiritual form is eternal, so it is indestructible. However, it continually reincarnates in different living forms – human in one life and an animal in another, and in hell in yet another life. Hence, it is not constant. The common ground would be that in spite of being eternal, a soul continues to go through transformations. Hence, Nayavāda allows for a dialectical compromise in what would be an otherwise polemical set of perspectives.

Using the above example, the "eternal" *naya* would be unflawed if (1) it does not completely disprove the "not eternal" *naya*, (2) if that eternal perspective always maintains a stance of indifference to the "not eternal" *naya*, and (3) if it limits itself to exposition of its own views rather than refutation of the other "not eternal" perspective. The same principles apply to the "not eternal" *naya*.

In simple words, if a *naya* challenges or disproves of another *naya* while exposing solely its own views, it falls under the "falsehood" category and is termed a deceptive *naya*. A *naya* is truthful only when it does not label the other as untruthful. If it does, it itself becomes untruthful.

THE CLASSIFICATION OF NAYA (NAYA-BHEDA)

As stated earlier, there are innumerable properties (*dharmas*) of an entity. Each property (*dharma*) has a corresponding, innumerable number of *nayas*. Jain doctrine states: "There are as many different types of *nayas* of an entity as there are words to describe the entity." In order to organize them from classical viewpoint, all of the *nayas* can be divided into seven different types as listed below:

1. *Naigama* (the teleological or commonly developed generic view)
2. *Saṁgraha* (the group, class, or collective view)
3. *Vyavahāra* (the practical or empirical view)
4. *R̥jusūtra* (the linear or momentary view)
5. *Śabda* (the literal or verbalistic view)
6. *Samābhirūḍha* (the etymological view)
7. *Evambhūta* (the actuality view)

Furthermore, fundamentally, an entity is a substance (*dravya*) and it takes different modes (*paryāya*) at different times, different lives, and different locations. From this perspective, the above seven types of *nayas* can be grouped into two categories:

1. *Dravyārthika-naya* (substance viewpoint): As discussed earlier, each entity has a fixed, fundamental property or nature (*dravya nitya*), such as, "the soul is eternal." The principle that deals with such a property is called *dravyārthika-naya.*
2. *Paryāyārthika-naya* (modal viewpoint): This viewpoint considers the modifications and conditions of an entity, and refers to how it continuously takes different forms and shapes through its transformational behavior. It indicates the infinite stances possible when an entity is analyzed in reference to the modes it possesses.

VIEWPOINTS THAT DEAL WITH THE NATURE OF SUBSTANCES (DRAVYĀRTHIKA-NAYAS)

1. *Naigama* (the teleological or commonly developed, generic view) consists of the perception of the basic characteristics of an entity from the viewpoint of worldly or prevalent beliefs or rituals. For instance,

consider a person is born on 16 January 1978. Generally speaking, every year 16 January is considered to be his birthday, although in reality, the birthday is just one – the day the person was born. Similarly, one commonly says, "This road goes to San Francisco." In reality, the road itself does not move.

2. *Saṁgraha* (the group, class, or collective view) looks at aggregate common properties of a group of entities. For instance, the properties (*guṇas*) of all living and inanimate (non-living) entities (substances) would be called the *saṁgraha-naya* of that substance (*dravya*). Similarly, all souls have common fundamental characteristics (*cetanā, vīrya,* and *sukha*) which constitute the *saṁgraha-naya* of the living substances. Keep in mind that different entities within a group may have their own distinctive characteristics. *Saṁgraha-naya* ignores those and focuses just on the commonalities.
3. *Vyavahāra* (the practical or empirical view) refers to the understanding of distinctive properties of entities as the converse position of *saṁgraha-naya*. For instance, the generic (*saṁgraha*) addresses the group called "humanity," while the "practical view" (*vyavahāra*) is the perspective that people come in different shapes, forms, demeanors, behaviors, cultures, etc.

VIEWPOINTS THAT DEAL WITH MODALITIES (PARYĀYĀRTHIKA-NAYAS)

4. *Ṛjusūtra* (the linear or momentary view) results when on certain occasions human understanding accepts only the present situation as the beneficial one while rendering the past and future occurrences as immaterial. Such a perspective accepts the endeavors of the present as the only real undertakings (*sattā*). The belief is that whatever happened in the past is gone, so it does not possess the status of being real. Similarly, the future is hard to predict, so its consideration is discounted as *asat* (unreal) as well. Therefore, neither past nor future considerations are important by this perspective, since only whatever is current can be perceived. For instance, whatever wealth one had in the past is devoid of any value today, and that which is coming in the future is just a dream. Neither of those has any bearing on today's life.

There is an alternate grouping of the *naya*s: (1) *artha-naya*s dealing with the essence or fundamental properties of entities, and (2) *śabda-naya*s dealing with the words or sounds associated with the entities (note that *śabda* can mean both "word" and "sound"). From the perspective of this grouping, the first four *naya*s (i.e., *naigama*, *saṁgraha*, and *vyavahāra* of the *dravyārthika* category, and *ṛjusūtra* of the *paryāyārthika* category) are considered *artha-naya*s. The next three are *śabda-naya*s.

5. *Śabda* (the literal or verbalistic view) accepts commonalities embedded within synonyms and considers their similar meanings. However, when the synonymous words are differentiated by time, gender, prefixes, or other such elements, they are not considered exact equivalents, but nonetheless have a similarity of meaning.

   For instance, when a writer writes, "New York City was ... ," it is a form of *śabda-naya*. In this case, New York City still exists, but the writer is referring to older time when the city might have been different. Hence, he uses "was" instead of "is." This is an example of the use of tense to connote a time-dependent difference. Similarly, different words are used to address differences in gender, food, travel, etc.

6. *Samābhirūḍha* (the etymological view) goes a step further from *śabda* and reflects on the subtleties of the specific applications of words and their differences based on etymologies. From this perspective there is only one exact meaning for every word. When it has multiple synonyms, each of those synonyms conveys a uniquely different meaning, and this form of *naya* seeks to highlight their distinctions. Even differences in gender and time can cause different meanings of the same word, and the different inflection of a word can represent different and unique meanings. It considers dictionaries or thesauruses to be inadequate by themselves because they include multiple words with the same meaning or interpretation without due attention to the context. For instance, the word "journal" could refer to "bulletin," "newsletter," "magazine," and "diary." However, one has to refer to the context to determine the true sense of the meaning. If one blindly follows the thesaurus, one could interpret confidential information in a personal diary (i.e., "journal") to be equivalent to public information in a magazine (also a "journal").

These differentiations in applied meanings of the same words caused by contextual differences are addressed by *samābhirūḍha-naya*.

7. *Evambhūta* (the actuality view) takes the discussion on the use and application of words even further. It addresses semantic distinctions at the subtlest level. When a derivation or a word-structure causes a change in its applied meaning, only that word-structure should be used that results in the appropriate applied meaning. When the interpretation of a word-structure results in an unintended action, it should not be used. *Evambhūta-naya* considers all words to be action-oriented because every word ultimately leads to an action. Therefore, when referring to an object that is involved in an act, the word one selects should refer to that object as it is in the state of action. For instance, when a man is teaching a class, he is called a "teacher." However, the same person could be called "father," "brother," etc., depending on the activities he is involved in or the roles he is playing. He should not be called "teacher" when he is not teaching. The same can be said of other professionals, such as a realtor or an actor. *Evambhūta-naya* assigns the word based on the activity and the object so that the word that is selected is an accurate descriptor entirely, and its meaning is precise in the strongest sense of the term.

By analyzing the above seven types of *naya*, it is clear that an entity, which is an indivisible conglomeration of a multitude of properties, can be described by properly highlighting one of its features. Potential descriptions of all other properties continue to exist but they assume a subservient role. The knowledge that accepts one perspective as only a single element of the absolute truth is known as Nayavāda. The elements of truth illuminated by different viewpoints (*naya*) and combined with other epistemological approaches define the fundamental and thorough knowledge of the existence of an entity. Jain scriptures have dedicated many sacred texts to the discussion of how to interpret various vantage points and the fundamental principles of apprehending a multifaceted, absolute truth.

The Doctrine of Non-Absolutism (Anekāntavāda)

As seen in chapter 2, along with his numerous spiritual gifts to mankind, Lord Mahāvīra was the source of inspiration for instituting the principles of conflict-free, harmonious living. To that end, he established the monastic order and a structured system for ascetic and householder lifestyles. He bestowed upon humanity a comprehensive system of living based on principles reflecting the fundamental truth (*tattva-vicāra*). In addition, he offered a specific language to describe the multifaceted characteristics of matter (*vastu*) in great detail. He elaborated:

> There are multiple thoughts (*aneka vicāra*), and many times, they appear to be contradicting (*viruddha*) each other. But in reality, they can have both harmony (*sāmañjasya*) and disharmony (*aviruddha*) at the same time. He who perceives this clearly is the real knower of the true reality (*vāstava tattvadarśī*).

Such an idea of coexisting perspectives in harmony and disharmony forms the basis of the doctrine of Anekāntavāda (Non-Absolutism). Anekāntavāda offers multifaceted views of reality that at times may seem to have mutually contradictory qualities. With the inspiration and teachings of Lord Mahāvīra, Jains have developed a system of formal argumentation for different philosophical standpoints (Naya or Nayavāda) that arises from the inherent limitations of human language when they attempt to describe a collection of complicated, multidimensional, and sometimes contradictory views with respect to an entity or a viewpoint. This system is the doctrine of Anekāntavāda.

The reason why there may be disharmonies in contradictory views on a given subject lies in the fact that any given object can be viewed from a multitude of perspectives. The form of an entity being observed by one person is not its only form. Being an object with unlimited properties, constituents, and powers, the entity may have innumerable observable characteristics. These are the inherent attributes of an entity. However, a person has only a limited capacity to comprehend. To add further, an observed entity, in addition to its perpetually inherent characteristics, also consists of ephemeral forms that are dependent on the collection of *karma*, among other things. These ever-changing attributes are countless as well.

Thus, equipped with innumerable qualities and ever-changing states, an entity is a collection of endless constituents. However, one can also understand that any given entity's apophatic qualities (*asattā aṁśa*) far surpass that entity's cataphatic qualities and states. So far, the characteristics that are used to define a specific entity have been discussed. But there is a parallel world of characteristics that are used to define how other entities are not this specific entity.

To illustrate, consider a smart phone. Clearly, it has many observable and non-observable properties, such as weight, material, size, glass top, color, software, in-built security, etc. In addition, it could have multiple modes of operation – it can be used to make or receive phone calls, send or receive email, watch movies, etc. These are the characteristics one generally knows as an entity's own characteristics. That is how an entity is defined – by what it is. Then, there are properties related to its own transformation or that of its components, such as after it breaks down and its components could be recycled into other products.

Now consider the parallel set of entities that all point to what the entity in question "is not." To use the above example, this would consist of anything that could not be defined as a smart phone. For instance, a computer is not a smart phone although it can be used to send or receive email, watch movies, etc. Neither is a car a smart phone, along with an infinite number of other entities. From the perspective of Jain Dharma, to comprehensively understand a smart phone, one must completely comprehend not only its own properties, but also all apophatic factors that are not possessed by that object in question. That is why Jain scriptures propose a comprehensive view of knowledge when they say:

> One who knows one entity, knows all entities, and one who fully comprehends all the entities, knows any specific one.[1]

As discussed earlier, there are two basic types of substances (entities) – living or sentient entities, and inanimate or non-sentient entities. However, each has an infinite number of permutations due to the observable and non-observable properties that they possess, and those not possessed by them. This seems to be an extremely complicated premise. It is not easy to comprehend the crux of fundamental truth. Despite that, if an individual has an enriched, righteous perspective, the entities with which they interact during day-to-day life can

---

1 *je aigam jārnhiye se savvam jārnhiye, je savvam jārnhiye se aigam jārnhiye.*

become the sources of immense learning.

To consider the inanimate, non-sentient entities first – each grain of dirt has an inconceivable number of qualities. It does not have a single shape or color, nor a single taste or natural characteristic. In just a small piece of land made up of dirt, a farmer can grow wheat, or flowers, or sweet sugar cane, hot peppers, or tart lemons, with all of them receiving nutrition from the same piece of land. But their shape, form, color, size, nature, and nutritional value vary drastically. Each of the items draws specific nutrients from the same dirt to flourish and create its own unique set of properties. Understood relationally, one cannot say that dirt has only one set of characteristics from the perspective of each of these different crops. If one understands dirt from not only its own qualities, but also its transformational potential into different crops, one can see that there is no singular entity called "dirt," nor does any single perspective (from the standpoint of each crop) fully encapsulate "dirt." Although at some level a singular perspective could be true from a particular viewpoint of material properties, it might also be false when one considers the doctrine of changing forms.

A non-living entity was considered in the above example. A similar logic applies to living beings. Consider a man who may be a son to one person, an uncle to another, and a father to someone else. Professionally, he could be a businessman, a software engineer, a teacher, or a pupil. A variety of designations can be assigned to a particular individual when one considers relational dynamics. From one particular vantage point, the "father" and "son" attributes of the same person could seem mutually contradictory since the same person cannot be both a son and a father to the same person. These types of perspectival-based contradictions commonly create divisiveness when a person is unable to see any perspective other than their own, and then clings to that perspective as being absolute and universally applicable. But the theory of Anekāntavāda includes all perspectives as relationally inclusive.

Similarly, contradictory designations can be applied to other living or inanimate entities. The inherent or acquired properties, fixed or changing properties, singular or non-singular properties of all entities can be demonstrated to be mutually related and not contradictory. Understanding this reality is the foundation of Anekāntavāda.

Applying the principles of Anekāntavāda while attempting to understand life and fundamental truths can mitigate a wide variety of problems. Many Jain thinkers believe that Anekāntavāda has the potential to eliminate religious clashes, academic disagreements, fighting between cults, and the multitude of general assaults on the soul committed in human culture. It inspires one to adapt a sophisticated perception regarding polemical issues. The practice of Anekāntavāda inspires the human demeanor to become kind, all-embracing, and truthful.

The Jain society has widely adopted Anekāntavāda in the fields of policy, arts, business, family life, etc. It is a general aspiration of those who follow Jain Dharma to see the broader community of philosophers and academicians of the world to widely adopt such a harmonious perspective.

It is hard to understand how can one disregard non-absolutism. In a simple example, a fruit goes through a series of transformations in its life – from unripe to ripe, tart to sweet, fresh to perished state, smooth skin to wrinkly skin, etc. At every moment, one state finishes and gives way to the next. Every state has a multitude of differences from the other, whose magnitude is hard to comprehend. The fruit, while going through these immense transformations, maintains the same designation throughout. Therefore, there is both identity and difference; changelessness occurs in the context of change.

Jain philosophy explains this doctrine of relative manifoldness by affirming that the fundamental identity of an entity – which adopts different characteristics at different times – is the essential form of the entity; it is that object's substance (*dravya*). The changing forms of the entity are its exterior successions (*paryāya*). Each entity has two forms – internal (*antaraṅga*) and external (*bahiraṅga*) – where the internal form is the *dravya*, while the external form is the *paryāya*. An entity's internal form is unique, perpetual, and non-transformational, while the external form is multifaceted, transitory, and transformational.

A substance is a conglomerate of endless and mutually agreeing and disagreeing properties. Whether a living or non-living substance is miniscule, subtle, or large, it has an astounding amalgamation of basic conforming and non-conforming properties. Under these circumstances, it is absurd to evaluate the state of an entity by observing only one or a few of its properties while disregarding all others. It is unrealistic to perfectly prove the state of a substance, or to have such an expectation, when observed from this state of imperfection.

A follower of non-absolutism believes that what is fundamentally true, what is real (*sat*), is never destroyed, and the false existence of non-reality (*asat*) can never be created or imagined. To illustrate – clay can be transformed into a new object (a pitcher or a sculpture), but its fundamental set of properties remains unchanged. This is the state of a dual-typed substance – fundamental properties of clay and the properties of its transformed state. It is impossible to understand clay from a singular perspective that does not account for others. For one to understand an object, it is essential to consider multiple aspects of a substance to derive at its true nature. This need has given rise to the doctrine of Anekāntavāda.

The Doctrine of Qualified Assertion (Syādvāda)

In principle, Syādvāda (qualified or conditional assertion) is the application of Anekāntavāda using the framework provided by Nayavāda. Put differently, one might consider Anekāntavāda as the doctrine and Syādvāda as the methodology that is used to apply the concept of Anekāntavāda using the guidelines of Nayavāda. Once one accepts Anekāntavāda, they also subscribe to the theory of Syādvāda; that is, that each entity is an indivisible conglomerate of innumerable properties, each having its own viewpoint and some of which may appear to be contradictory. No single definition can adequately describe an entity's complexity. This multiplicity of a complex entity needs to be expressed in an appropriately complex framework. This conceptual framework is called Syādvāda, the doctrine of "qualified assertion." The term *syādvāda* is derived from the term *syād* or *syāt*, which means "may be," or "in some respect," which connotes a qualified assertion about any substance or viewpoint.

A language is made up of words and other lexical and syntactical elements. A word may connote multiple meanings with a given combination of time, location, and context. A word formed with only a specific combination of syntactical and lexical elements can represent only one specific signification. Since this is how words occur in sentences, paragraphs, texts, journals, etc., they usually only apply to their specific application and context. But as seen earlier, entities are not just specific; they are general. They are not just stable, but are ephemeral and relative as well. Hence it is essential to represent an entity's entire set of properties, such as what it is and what it is not, in a language that conveys all of these states.

Let us illustrate this concept. If one is looking at a pen and seeks to be irrefutable and comprehensive in its designation and description, one cannot just state, "It is a pen." In this case, the speaker cannot be sure that his perspective is being adequately conveyed and understood by the listener. Also, this statement only addresses "what it is" (i.e., "a pen") without overtly addressing "what it is not." There are innumerable additional apophatic states of the pen, as discussed earlier. The designation "pen" does not encapsulate its transformations, nor its multiple and perhaps seemingly contradictory perspectival possibilities. Beyond that, even "what it is" may imply multiple vantage points and states depending how one views it.

A word configured from and for a specific set of characteristics, situations, and vantage points can represent only one perspective of an entity. However, an entity is made up of innumerable states, qualities, etc. By not looking at all of the complex and comprehensive states of an object, one may fall in the trap of commonly accepted dogmatic views. But employing a verbose onslaught of words does not necessarily convey an entity's complexity. From the pragmatic perspective, such communication would become cumbersome and would likely still remain incomplete at best, or misunderstood at worst. This is why Jain philosophers have designed Syādvāda as a framework of expression that addresses this complex issue. It is based on the use of *syād* or *syāt*, which means "it may be," "it might be," "in some respect," or perhaps even "in this particular respect." This is an acknowledgment that no one simple proposition can fully express the nature of reality, and any given perspective necessarily excludes others. From that perspective, Syādvāda is an attempt to rectify the situation by allowing for other possibilities that may even seem contradictory. Its conditional nature also expresses the reservation of judgment about whether each perspective has truth in it or not, and invites further motivation to examine every possibility rather than outright dismissal.

In addition, Syādvāda seeks to create a comprehensive account that mitigates uncertainty and vagueness. For instance, one could say: "Deva is a father and a son." While this statement may be true, it conveys an inconclusive and unsure message. On the other hand, if one says, "The person Deva is a son because Rāma is his father, and he is a father because Kr̥ṣṇa is his son," then this expression leaves no room for any ambiguity. This is a rudimentary example of Syādvāda where an expression seeks to attenuate uncertainty.

As discussed earlier, an entity is perpetual because it is a substance (*dravya*) and it is constantly changing because it is transitory (*paryāya*). Syādvāda addresses both unilateral and multilateral views to ensure Anekāntavāda, and by Jaiṇ philosophy, there is no single definitive view of reality. The Syādvāda expressions are based on seven-part truth values (*sapta-bhaṅgī*) that define a comprehensive approach to configure any statement.

1. *Syād-asti* ("it may be that or in some respects it is" or "it exists"): Each specific entity (*sva-dravya*) exists (*asti*) when seen from its own state (*sva-bhāva*), and a combination of its own time (*sva-kāla*), location (*sva-kṣetra*), and context.

2. *Syād-nāsti* ("it may be that or in some respects it is not" or "it does not exist"): An entity does not exist when perceived from someone else's state and a combination of time, location, and context.

   To illustrate the above two concepts, one might consider the perception of a pen that is made of plastic as the *syād-asti* (from one perspective it is) perspective. At the same time, the perception of such a plastic pen must recognize that it is not made of gold. This would be the *syād-nāsti* (from one perspective it is not) perspective.

   The next five are derived from the above two.

3. *Syād-asti–nāsti* ("it may be that or in some respects it is and it is not" or "it exists and does not exist"): This expression is a combination of the previous two by clarifying both what an entity is and what it is not. For instance, "The pen is made of plastic (*syād-asti*) and it is not a golden pen (*syād-nāsti*)."

4. *Syād-avaktavyaḥ* ("it may be that or in some respects it is indeterminate" or "indescribable" or "non-assertible"): This may be the most agnostic position in which one cannot determine anything about an object that is being perceived. For example, by looking at the pen, one cannot say

if it is a fountain pen.

5. *Syād-asti-avaktavyaḥ* ("it may be that or in some respects it is" or "it exists and it is indeterminate" or "indescribable" or "non-assertible"): It implies an expression of uncertainty towards the affirmed existence of an object. For example, by just looking at the plastic pen (*syād-asti*), one cannot be sure if it is working or not (*avaktavyaḥ*).
6. *Syād-nāsti-avaktavyaḥ* ("it may be that or in some respects it is not" or "it does not exist" and it is "indeterminate" or "indescribable" or "non-assertible"): This implies an expression of certainty towards an object described apophatically. Continuing with the above example, when one is seeing a pen that is not made of gold (*syād-nāsti*) and is uncertain (*avaktavyaḥ*) if it is working or not.
7. *Syād-asti–nāsti-avaktavyaḥ* ("it may be that or in some respects it is" or "it exists" and "it is not" or "it does not exist" and "it is indeterminate" or "indescribable" or "non-assertible"): This implies an expression of certainty regarding an entity in which both the existence and non-existence of it is affirmed along with an uncertainty about the degree that a proposition can be asserted or determined. Continuing with the above example, it is not known if (*avaktavyaḥ*) the plastic pen (*syād-asti*) that is not made of gold (*syād-nasti*) is working.

Various philosophies may be seen as taking an absolutist perspective regarding only a single aspect of "what it is" against another philosophy that believes only in "what it is not." Even when they want to consider both aspects, by virtue of the fact that no perspective can be entirely complete, they have limited means of understanding and explaining those. By not paying respect to the alternate views and by failing to acknowledge their own limitations, such rhetoric may become the source of conflict.

By presenting the knowledge of the fundamental truth (*tattva*) from the non-absolute (Anekāntavāda) viewpoint, Jain Dharma illustrates the magnitude of its understanding of the nature of things. To supplement that, by offering the doctrines of Anekāntavāda and Syādvāda, it has presented a sound platform to the world to amicably bring different philosophies to a common ground.

Syādvāda is an integral part of, and is embedded in, every aspect of Jain doctrine. In the Jain scripture known as the *Sūtrakṛtāṅga*, Jain monks are directed to use a language that unites people and does not divide them. In other words, they were advised to use Syādvāda. For example, Lord Mahāvīra employed the principles of Syādvāda in his answers to the fourteen questions that were considered "unanswerable" (*avyākṛta*) by the Buddha,[2] and also employed Syādvāda to the highly revealing and thoughtful questions raised in the Hindu Upaniṣads.

The Language Policy (Bhāṣā-Nīti)

METHODOLOGY FOR SYSTEMATIC FORMULATION (NIKṢEPA-VIDHĀNA)

Language (*bhāṣā*) is the main medium of interactions and exchange of knowledge from one person to another. It would be impossible to conduct worldly affairs and exchange ideas or views without a rich language. It is difficult to imagine a life without a wealth of knowledge, culture, and civilization – all made possible with the use of language. It is not just the means of communication, but also a vehicle for thinking. Right from childhood, one uses the richness of language for scholastic development.

Language is built of sentences, and sentences are made up of words. A word can have multiple meanings. A properly deployed word or string of words can convey a number of different expressions based on the context, connotation, place, occasion, and environment. With that in mind, Jain scriptures have

---

[2] These are questions that the Buddha refused to answer according to the Buddhist tradition. They deal with four subjects and the possible answers to these:

Under the first subject (1) if the world is eternal (2) or not, (3) or is both eternal and non-eternal, (4) or is neither eternal nor non-eternal.

Under the second subject (5) the finiteness of the universe, or (6) its non-finiteness, or (7) or its being both finite and non-finite, or (8) neither of these.

Under the third subject (9) whether the self is identical with the body, (10) or if it is different from the body.

Under the fourth subject (11) if the Buddha/Tathāgata exists after death (12) or not, (13) or both exists and does not exist, (14) or not.

Where the Buddha seems agnostic, or perhaps his refusal signifies an epistemological reluctance to approach these with the discursive intellect (*anumāna*), Mahāvīra shows no such reluctance.

outlined specific ways to use proper words for intended expressions. The scriptures on grammar and composition have described the methods to properly use sentiments, symbolism, depth, and expressions carried by words.

Jain philosophers created *nikṣepa vidhāna*, which is a "legislation" or "methodology" (*vidhāna*) for systematic consideration of each word. This helps in expressing appropriate knowledge associated with the intended meaning to be expounded with each word. Lord Mahāvīra stated that many different knowledge-retention schemes could be devised to understand the complete intended meaning of a word. However, a minimum of four are needed, because each word is equipped with at least four types of intended meanings: name (*nāma*), formation (*sthāpanā*), substance (*dravya*), and intent (*bhāva*). From among these four intended meanings, retention by the listener of the message intended by the speaker is the key. The Jain philosophers have delineated four ways that a listener might retain the language used by the speaker:

1. *Nāma-nikṣepa*: This is the contemplation of the name associated with an entity without paying attention to the entity's form or characteristics. Primarily, this is for use in worldly interactions without much consideration to the intrinsic properties of the entity. For instance, parents might name their child "Prince" (Rājā, a common Indian name) at his birth. This child is not related to the king of the country and has no relationship to the literal derivatives of the word.

   The name/word can be of three types:

   i. Genuine name, like "driver" for a person who drives a vehicle (chauffeur).

   ii. Non-genuine, like "rich" for a person who is homeless.

   iii. Denotationally neutral name: like "cough" and "pop music."

2. *Sthāpanā-nikṣepa*: This is the contemplation of an entity with due consideration to its name and form while ignoring its characteristics. It is based on using the name of an entity to convey its physical form or its association with a different entity. For example, addressing the picture of Prince William just by his name, "Prince William," although the picture is not the prince himself.

3. *Dravya-nikṣepa*: This is the contemplation of an entity with due

consideration to its name and form, and at the same time its past and future characteristics, while ignoring its present characteristics. Many a time, one addresses someone by a name that does not convey that person's current disposition but refers to their past or future. For example, one addresses a person as "doctor" even though that person is retired, or has not yet received the final certification of MD degree.

4. *Bhāva-nikṣepa*: This is the contemplation of an entity with due consideration to its name, form, and its current characteristics. This is true when the meaning of a name/word is applicable to the present state defined by its form and qualities. For example, a person who is currently the president of the United States is addressed as "Mr. President."

In summary, *nikṣepa-vidhāna* is the systematic process of formulating a natural, enumerable, and expressible meaning of a word or an entity while rejecting its unnatural, innumerable, and inexpressible definitions. By understanding how this process functions, one can work to eliminate unrepresentative and inapplicable interpretations while speaking and hearing in a way that is proper representation and applicable, thereby facilitating accurate communication. For example, if one starts interpreting the word "Mahāvīra" as a reference to Lord Mahāvīra all the time, it could result in some highly inappropriate interpretations when referring to an ordinary individual with the same name. In order to derive the correct interpretation of the word, one should associate it with the appropriate qualifiers such as time, place, profession, achievement, message, and following. This would remove any ambiguity and mitigate any unfortunate interpretation(s).

Of the above four, *bhāva-nikṣepa* (contemplating an entity with due consideration to its name, form, and characteristics) is the most important because ultimately communication is the process of clearly understanding the intent. By understanding the *nikṣepa-vidhāna* process one can focus on how expression of intent by the speaker or writer, and reception of that intent in an undistorted fashion can be cultivated.

8

Jain Psychology (Manovijñāna)

Senses (Indriya)

In General, most living beings are absorbed in indulgent living when seen from the viewpoint of spirituality. It could be honorable or not-so-honorable living, but it is indulgent living nonetheless. In philosophical terms and without perceiving it in negative context, a living being (*jīva*)[1] can be viewed as a haven (*āyatana*) for the formation and embodiment of impious, selfish desires or cravings (*kāma*); for sensory satisfaction and enjoyments; and for willful pandering to consummate (*bhoga*) those desires while being engrossed in ostensible enjoyments. The senses (*indriya*) – seeing (eyes), hearing (ears), tasting (tongue), touching (skin), and smelling (nose) – play the key roles in the execution of *kāma* and *bhoga*.[2] Desires are tangible (*mūrta*) but formless or shapeless (*arūpī*), whereas enjoyments can be either with form (*rūpī*) or formless. Desires and cravings are found to exist only in living beings, and they define one of the key distinguishing factors between living and non-living entities. As discussed in chapter 11 (Doctrine of Karma), one of the most dreadful *karmas* is the *mohaniya-karma* (deluded action), which can be directly attributed to the act of *kāma* and *bhoga* (desire and enjoyment). Since the living being (*jīva*) is the self-propelled knower, enjoyer, and performer of its own deeds, a spiritual seeker must be extremely vigilant about acts of desires and enjoyments.

There is a twofold classification of *kāma* based on the nature of the object

---

1 The term *jīva* is used for soul as well as for a living being. The term "living being" refers to "soul" unless it is accompanied by a qualifier such as "body of a living being" or simply, "a living body."

2 *Kāma* is impious selfish craving or desire, and *bhoga* is fulfillment and consummation of desires and experiencing (enjoying) the consequences. For brevity, *kāma* and *bhoga* are referred to as desire and enjoyment, respectively.

of desire: the desire for that which has a form (*rūpa*) and the desire for that which has a sound (*śabda*). The yearning for pleasant experiences, pleasing forms or beauty, and melodious or enjoyable sounds define the scope of *kāma*. They are both ephemeral types of matter (*paudgalika*) that continuously transition (*parivartita*) from one to other forms of similar properties. The question arises: how can the ephemeral and material interact with the soul that has neither of these features? As discussed below, the sense perceptions in part allow for this interaction and often impel the agentive *jīva* to pursue the *kāma* that results in *bhoga*. This has great relevance for Jain *karma* theory and the praxis of Jain ethics.

The acts of *kāma* and *bhoga* can occur by means of direct connection or a lack of it, all facilitated by the senses. *Bhoga* (enjoyment) is of three types: aroma, taste, and contact or touch. Enjoyments differ from desires in that enjoyment results from some type of connection with the desired object, whereas desires may or may not. It is not possible to experience enjoyment without such a connection with objects of taste, smell, and touch. On the other hand, *kāma* that originate from perceived sounds or shapes do not necessarily require any connection with those, such as the case of hearing and seeing. Some scholars have classified sound as "enjoyment (*bhoga*)" instead of "desire (*kāma*)" because sounds are not perceptible unless they strike the sensory elements of the ears. However, being subtle, they can be part of desires as well. Separately, from among the five senses, sight is uniquely different. Unlike other senses that depend on some sort of contact, sight can capture an entity's specifics based on light, revelation, and colors without any direct contact.

In Jain philosophy, the enjoyment of desires is of five types, corresponding to the five senses. Other Indian philosophies have different numbers of sense perceptions. For instance, in the Vedic tradition, there are five senses for knowledge acquisition and five for performing acts. Buddhist philosophy accounts for twenty-two senses. Jain scholars have incorporated all of those into five senses. For example, all five means by which one commits acts (voice, hands, feet, joints, and lower parts) are consolidated as the secondary elements of contact or the touch-sense since they all have skin as the underlying key component. The touch-sensitive tissues of skin collect knowledge through contact. Hence there is no need to consider these as separate senses.

The senses, being part of the physical body (*pudgala*), have shapes and forms apart from the soul (*jīva*), which has neither. Being formless and shapeless, one cannot accurately visualize the soul with the senses, although the senses assist the soul to perceive, know, and act, and to be the one who knows (*jñānī*), endures (*bhoktā*), and acts (*kartā*). However, the senses are one means by which one might obtain an approximate apprehension of the soul. For example, one can take a look at a body and ascertain if it is lifeless or living. The soul of a lifeless body has departed but its senses, despite being in operational order, cease to function. In a normal living body, senses are continuously performing their assigned tasks. This ongoing operation by the senses, and their failure to operate in a deceased body, is indicative of the existence of the soul in conjunction with the living body.

The senses are not only a means of discerning the soul's existence; they are the resources for carrying out its actions through a causal interrelation between the physical body and the soul that, among other factors, allows for ethical conduct. Although in principle the soul has endless knowledge and perception (*samyag-jñāna* and *samyag-darśana*) it has been weakened because of kārmic blockages[3] (see chapter 11). That is why it has to depend on the senses and has to use them to acquire and understand information about shape, form, etc., and to facilitate the ethical conduct of the *jīva*. The five sense organs are: ears (*śrotra*) for hearing, eyes (*cakṣu*) for seeing, nose (*ghrāṇa*) for smelling, tongue (*rasanā*) for tasting, and skin (*sparśana*) for touch sensitivity.

Jain scriptures have presented analyses and descriptions of senses in vivid detail. They have eliminated redundancies and have shown that these five senses are distinct and complementary to each other. The scriptures

---

[3] Besides the gross (physical) body, every *jīva* has a subtle body known as *karmaṇa-śarīra*, constituted by the *karma-pudgala* (subtle material particles). It continually changes in form and size depending on the state of *karmas* attached in layers over the soul. However, it remains a necessary and inalienable appendage of physical or worldly (*saṁsārī*) *jīva*. The *karmaṇa-śarīra* accompanies a *jīva* as it discards its current physical body at death and adopts a new one at rebirth. The *karmaṇa-śarīra* is discarded and transcended only when the *jīva* attains the perfect state of ultimate liberation.

unmistakably differentiated the senses from the soul (*jīva*). Each of the five senses has two forms – *dravyendriya* (or *dravya indriya*, a substance or physical form) and *bhāvendriya* (or *bhāva indriya,* a psychical or abstract form). The externally visible form is the substance or physical form, and the internal, intuited form is the psychical form. For instance, the visual experiences result from the contact between *dravya indriya* and the physical object being sensed.

The substance form of the senses (*dravyendriya*) has two components. The first, called *nirvr̥tti,* is related to the senses themselves as the origination (*nirvr̥tti*) of perception. The *nirvr̥tti* component is further divided into external and internal classes, but these details are beyond the scope of the current discussion. The second is called *upakaraṇa* (application) of the senses towards the non-sentient material substances (*pudgala*s) that are perceived by the senses.

The soul's power of sensing and responding to worldly experiences involves internalizing sensory information. The sensing (*labdhi)* is akin to collecting data. Utilizing and analyzing the collected data for worldly interactions is called *upayoga.* Senses usually have blockages caused by kārmic residue, and sensed energy, obtained via *labdhi,* is that which has passed through those blockages. Similarly, *upayoga* is processing the information that came through the blockages.

THE OBJECTS PERCEIVED BY THE SENSES (INDRIYOṄ KE VIṢAYA)

It is important to note that unlike some other Indian systems that may tend towards idealism, skepticism, or even perhaps solipsism (perhaps in part based on the doctrine of *māyā*), Jain metaphysics can be considered more realistic and compatible with science. For the Jain metaphysicists, truth can be perceived in the correspondence between cognitive perceptions and objects of reality – unlike other systems that invoke varying degrees of skepticism towards the ability of the senses and the mind to perceive truth. For the Jains, all the sensed objects carry certain signatures through which they are more or less accurately perceived.

For example, sounds carry the signatures for the hearing senses to perceive through the ears. Such sound is of three types: (1) sounds emitted from living entities (*jīva*s), (2) sounds from inanimate matter (*ajīva*), and

(3) sounds that are mixed (*miśra*). Unlike some other Indian systems of thought which associate sound with space (*ākāśa*), the Jain system explains that sound results from the collision of one aggregation of physical objects (*skandha*) with another *skandha* aggregation. Sound is the agitation set up by this collision. When a speaker says something, the sound of speech spreads in the form of sound waves, traveling at a very high speed. One could surmise that these sound waves traverse the universe through some virtual channels ubiquitously present in all directions of the universe.

Sounds heard by the listener can have two components: (1) the original sounds produced by the speaker or originator, and (2) those produced by interactions between the original sound and other existing and derived ambient sounds. A listener situated at the same virtual channel as the speaker or the originator of the sound may hear only the original sounds. On the other hand, a listener situated at a different virtual channel may hear a combination of both types.

In Jain philosophy, the smallest unit of time is called *samaya*, which is much smaller than the smallest fraction of a second and cannot be further subdivided. A sound produced loses its originality after one *samaya* because by then it has traversed through space. But during this time, it converts to perceivable elements as *pudgala*s. After one *samaya*, the sound that is attributed by the receiver to an originator is actually the derived sound that could be a mixture of the two components discussed above and carried by the sound *pudgala*s. It is believed that the entire universe is filled with the original and derived sounds within a period of four *samaya*s.

Shapes and forms are the objects (*viṣaya*) of the sight organs, the eyes. A shape's color is formed with five basic elements, which are black, blue, yellow, red, and white. All shapes and forms result by mixing these material elements (*prakāra*).

The odor or aroma is the object (*viṣaya*) of the smelling organ, the nose. When the aroma particles of a substance enter the nostrils, they interact with the tiny pores and produce the smell sensation. The sensation is felt and processed by the soul. Although there are many different types of smells, for brevity they are categorized into two broad categories of fragrant and noxious.

Flavor is the object of the taste organ, the tongue. When a material interacts with the tiny components of the tongue, it excites the taste receptors with specific knowledge of taste elements. These are processed by the soul. The flavors are of five types: sweet, bitter, sour, salty, and savory. Correspondingly, the taste sensation is of five types as well.

Contact is the subject of the touch sense. The physical organ for the sense of touch is the skin. There are eight types of touch and corresponding sensations: hard, soft, large, small, cold, hot, fine or thin, and smooth.

It would not be a stretch if, in principle, one were to consider the treatment of senses (*indriya*s) and their functionality in Jain doctrine to be analogous to that in science. The Jain viewpoint, formulated millennia ago, differs in specifics but its concepts would make for an interesting dialog between the science and religious philosophies. This dialogue might be particularly fruitful when considering the tension between religious thought and science in our modern age.

Mind (Mana)

The mind plays one of the most important roles in life. It is the main instigator for the soul's spiritual downfall or the key stimulus for its uplift. That is why many spiritual philosophies emphasize the importance and necessity of control over the mind. At the same time, all of them recognize it to be a very difficult task to achieve. For instance, in the *Bhagavadgītā*, Lord Kr̥ṣṇa states:

> Indeed the wandering of the senses is that which is controlled by the mind, and is that which could steal away one's knowledge like the wind does to a boat on the water.[4]

Similarly, in the Jain scripture *Uttarādhyayanasūtra*, section 23, couplet 58, the great saint Indrabhūti Gautama draws parallels between the mind and an adventurous, dreadful, and wicked horse.

It is true that the uncontrolled mind can be extremely problematic. Even great ascetics may lose their control over it. Although they may strive to forego comforts of worldly life and live in forests to tame their minds, the mind still tricks them into constantly reminding them of the comforts of worldly life.

[4] *indriyāṇāṁ hi caratāṁ yan mano'nuvidhīyate* ।
tad asya harati prajñāṁ vāyur nāvam ivāmbhasi ॥ – *Bhagavadgītā* II.67

Despite rigorous self-control training, their minds may continually beckon them back to luxuries of sensory desires. For instance, it is the mind that regularly awakens one's feelings of animosity, jealousy, and attachments despite the hard work towards the contemplation for love, compassion, peace, and detachments from worldly affairs. The mind carries an extraordinary power of beguilement. Whoever wants to tame it could actually land up being controlled by it with only minor missteps or a minimal amount of carelessness. It then rules the individual in whichever way it wants to. In this manner, the mind continues to dominate individuals in ways that are contrary to even the knowledge that they may hold.

Nonetheless, the mind can be tamed. The highly esteemed Guru Gautama Svāmī assures that the mind is not indomitable in spite of being extremely hard to control. In addition, scriptures have expounded the ability to subdue the mind through worldly renouncements and proper training, penance practices, and meditation. Therefore, it is important to define the entity called "mind" and how it causes many eminent and highly achieved ascetics to lose control after years and years of rigorous penance.

Just like the senses, the mind can also be a resource for the soul's perceptive capacities (*saṁvedana*). By itself, the mind is considered a non-sensing entity. The senses deal with their specific single purviews (seeing, hearing, tasting, touching, and smelling), but the mind is a multifaceted entity that processes all that is sensed by the eyes, ears, tongue, skin, and nose, and can associate with shapeless and/or formless objects. The senses have a limited range, while the mind has no limits on its reach. It can traverse heaven, hell, and the entire universe within a moment. Lord Mahāvīra, while addressing Gautama Svāmī said: "The mind is both lifeless and living. It is with conscious and without it at the same time."

The mind has two forms: a substance (*pudgala*) or *paudgalika* form, called *dravya-mana*, and a conscious or *cetanā-mana* form, called *bhāva-mana*. The substance form is responsible for creating the *pudgala* elements that help in reflecting upon the observations. The conscious form extracts the sentient feelings out of those reflections. In other words, the substance form is a cluster of fine particles (*pudgala*s) carrying emotions or sensory observations, and the conscious form is the soul's strength or weakness to analyze and meditate over the emotions and sensory observations.

The mind's substance and conscious forms collaborate to work on the undertakings of contemplation on different observations and experiences including reflection, pondering, remembrance, strategizing, loving, hating, yearning, meditating, and so on. All of these activities happen with active participation of the mind and under its direction.

Jain scriptures have classified living beings on the basis of their states of mind – partial intellectual capacity (*amanaska* or *asaṁjñī*), or full intellectual capacity (*samanaska* or *saṁjñī*). Living beings with full intellectual capacity are those who have intelligence. They are perceptive and have an inclination to analyze and draw conclusions through investigation and reasoning. They show one or more traits of desires, reasoning, thoughtfulness, worry, care, logic, etc. In the absence of such qualities living beings would be considered *amanaska* with only partial intellectual capacity. They would be the living beings with one to four senses. Among the five-sensed living beings, some possess a full intellectual capacity (*samanaska*) and some do not (*amanaska*).

All living beings possess the conscious form of mind because they all have soul, and consciousness (*cetanā*) is one of the key characteristics of the soul. However, the conscious mind is subdued due to the absence of substance of mind (*dravya-mana*) in *amanaska* living beings (those lacking full intellectual capacity). For instance, one could say that the conscious form (*bhāva-mana*) is like electricity, and the substance form is like an electric bulb. The conscious form does not produce results in the absence of the substance form the way electricity does not produce light without an electric bulb.

These types of classification are important for ethical considerations whereby it is seen to be more problematic (kārmically speaking) to harm beings with greater intellectual and sensory capacities. For example, almost no one would argue that humans are more ethically bound to preserve the life of another human being than they are to preserve the life of a microorganism, although the Jain scriptures strongly caution against carelessness towards any life form.

From all of this, one can see that the mind is the dominant organ of the body. But at the same time, it is the chief counsel of the soul. It can take control of the soul and make it wander towards attachments and other sensory passions. But when brought under control through penance and meditation, it could be the key to creating the focus and concentration for spiritual progress. In this situation, the mind becomes a conduit to attain *mati-jñāna* and *śruta-jñāna*, as discussed in earlier chapters. As stated in the *Uttarādhyayanasūtra*, one needs spiritual and religious training to gain control over the mind. This encompasses the practice and austerity that are also suggested in the *Bhagavadgītā*.

When asked by Gautama Svāmī for the ways to restrain the mind, Lord Mahāvīra Svāmī replied:

> By controlling the mind, all five senses can be fully restrained. This eradicates the obsessions caused by the observation of the objects of the senses. This destroys the inconsistencies and wavering in one's spiritual practice. Spiritual seekers who have tamed their mental activities can achieve the introverted, deep meditation and concentration that they have never seen before.

The Kārmic Stains That Obstruct the Jīva (Leśyās)

Through the ages, sages in pursuit of the fundamental spiritual truth have investigated psychology from multiple perspectives related to one's mental state, thought processes, instincts, fickleness, the ensuing repercussions and results, etc. Jain scholars have made immense contributions to these analyses. These invaluable studies, documented thousands of years ago when the contemporary science of psychology did not even exist, have been extremely interesting and thought-provoking for psychologists and researchers even today. An important component and subject matter of these studies is known as *leśyā* (a kārmic stain), which is an indicator of the level of problematic mental disposition.

As discussed earlier, all activities in thought, physical deeds, and speech result in a metamorphosis of these actions into collections of tiny kārmic particles (*karma-pudgala*s). These kārmic particles accumulate in layers over the soul and obstruct the soul from its inherent characteristics. Every act of mind, body, and speech, or a combination thereof, has a character which is related to the type, intensity, motivation, and other such attributes of these acts. This character-of-the-actions in turn defines the properties such as adhesive intensity, adhesive strength, and coloration of the layers of kārmic particles which collect over the soul. Figuratively speaking, the propensity of the mental disposition determines the coloration of the kārmic layers, and it is called *leśyā*, which is also referred to as the kārmic stains over the soul of a *jīva*.

The study of *leśyā*s addresses: how mental dispositions happen, what their characteristics are, in how many and which classes can the mental thoughts be divided, origination of mental thoughts, and how thoughts inherit their properties. These questions are just a few on a plethora of other related topics.

For instance, a crystal is a bright, colorless, and unblemished material. When a colored object is placed behind it, the crystal starts to appear as a colored and/or blemished object. One's soul is like this pure crystal that acquired its apparent coloration and blemish (*leśyā*) from the association with the mental, physical, and spoken actions of the body connected to the soul.

The mind is continuously engaged in innumerable activities. Sometimes mental acts (thoughts, etc.) may be righteous and positive, and other times they could be dark and negative. Many times, they are a combination. Under the influence of the mind, the thoughts can occasionally lead to spoken or physical acts. In Jain scholarly terms, all of these actions ultimately get mutated into the tiny particles (*pudgala*s) discussed above. Although, in general, the meaning of *leśyā* refers to the tendencies of the mind, its thoughts, and its tribulations, the *ācārya*s have also interpreted *leśyā* as the repercussions of the actions of the mind, body, and speech under the *karma* theory (see chapter 11). Some scholars may consider *leśyā*s to exist as an independent entity (not as a layer attached to the soul), but regardless, it is believed to be made up of the tiny kārmic particles.

The color-signature of certain *leśyā*s illustrate the auspicious or inauspicious repercussions of the corresponding mental acts. Since these could be innumerable, so are the corresponding types of *leśyā*s. However, in order to make it easy to understand, they have been classified into six broad categories. The categories and their brief descriptions are presented below using the language of the sermons from Lord Mahāvīra to his chief disciple, Gautama Svāmī, whom he sometimes called Goyama with affection.

1. *Kr̥ṣṇa Leśyā* (black coloration). Lord Mahāvīra says:

> Hey Goyama, *kr̥ṣṇa leśyā* is the meanest and most wicked form of *leśyā*. An individual with this trait has extremely low, negative, violent,

> fierce, inflexible, and inhumane thoughts. Such a person despises non-violence and performs the inauspicious acts with great intensity. He is a thoughtless, reckless, undignified, selfish, and self-centered individual who is passionately absorbed in lustful acts. He is not the least bit concerned about his current life or of hellish consequences. He is always eager to bring a tsunami of cruelty and misery on this earth.

As an illustration, when some hungry individuals see a tree laden with fruits, the *kṛṣṇa leśyā* person among them would want to cut the tree down so they can have some fruits to satisfy only their own hunger. One may not think cutting down a tree to be a severe act of violence, but when considered as a metaphor where tree represents a living entity, the act's severity becomes apparent.

2. *Nīla Leśyā* (blue coloration). Lord Mahāvīra says:

> Hey Goyama, the individuals with *nīla leśyā* also have negatively intense mental disposition, although it is milder than the *kṛṣṇa leśyā* individuals. Such an individual is a jealous, intolerant, deceitful, shameless, sinful, greedy, thoughtless, evil, and violent living being. He is always looking out for his own interests and pleasures. However, he has the capability of doing some good if he sees some self-interest in that.

Continuing with the above illustration, a *nīla leśyā* person wanting to satisfy the group's hunger would want to cut the major arteries of the tree by severing multiple branches full of fruit, which might be much more than their need.

3. *Kāpota Leśyā* (gray coloration). Lord Mahāvīra says:

> Hey Goyama, the *kāpota leśyā* individual is crooked in thought, speech, and actions. He is always looking to hide his deceitful and false thoughts and sinful acts. He tries to camouflage those with kind words and outwardly decent acts. He is willing to help and protect other humans as well as animals only if it promotes his own self-interest.

Continuing with the above illustration, *kāpota leśyā* person would want to sever the smaller arteries with multiple branches that carry the fruit, still obtaining more than what is needed to satisfy the group's hunger.

4. *Tejo Leśyā* (golden coloration). Lord Mahāvīra says:

> Hey Goyama, the *tejo leśyā* individual is pure, polite, humble, compassionate, and a spiritual seeker. He is careful of committing sins and keeps his senses under control. While satisfying his pleasures, he could be generous towards the others.

In the above illustration, a *tejo leśyā* individual would want to cut only the branches carrying the fruits the group needs, without destroying any major arteries.

5. *Padma Leśyā* (red or lotus coloration). Lord Mahāvīra says:

> Hey Goyama, the mental state of the *padma leśyā* individuals is focused towards spiritual and religious progress, and they continually maintain a positive mental outlook. Such persons bring pleasures to the others just like the aroma of a lotus flower. They are devoted to self-control and strive to minimize acts that result in kārmic accumulation, are amiable individuals who are very soft and pleasantly spoken, and have achieved control over their senses.

In the above illustration, a *padma leśyā* person would want to cut only the individual fruits that the group would need to satisfy their hunger.

6. *Śukla Leśyā* (pure, auspicious, or colorless). Lord Mahāvīra says:

> Hey Goyama, the mental state of the *śukla leśyā* individual is extremely pure. This person has an extremely positive outlook, is a committed meditator, is an unwavering spiritualist, and is internally peaceful. Such persons are accomplished self-controllers who evaluate every step to make sure it does not bring hurt to others, or has unholy, imperfect, or impure consequences. They are far removed from all negativities and are always bringing love, peace, and unattached compassion to others.

Following the above illustration, a *śukla leśyā* person would want to take only the fruits that have been discarded by the tree and are lying on the ground.

Considering the auspicious and inauspicious nature of the thoughts that provoke the corresponding mutations, one should forsake the first three types of *leśyā* and work hard to adopt the last three. Clearly, the first three are sinful, unholy, and unreligious. The last three are their opposite in every sense. The last one, the *śukla leśyā*, definitely opens up the path to the ultimate liberation. When a person's perspective and thinking starts progressing towards increasing auspiciousness, and then finally to the most auspicious types of *leśyā*, they can soon create great benefit for their souls. A person in such a state would be of great help to fostering world peace.

Jain philosophy presents a vivid description of *leśyā* and *kaṣāya* (passions or kārmic bondages, discussed next) in great detail. In simple terms, *leśyā* is related to the mutation of thoughts, actions, and speech into the tiny *pudgala* (material) particles that become attached to the soul, whereas *kaṣāya* (passions) are the causes behind the acts that produce the *pudgala* particles. From *dravya* (substance or physical form) and *bhāva* (intent or abstract form) perspectives, *leśyā* and *kaṣāya* are so intrinsically related that it is hard to describe them separately. In spite of the intricacies, Jain scholars have described them beautifully using appropriate and effective illustrations. The *dravya* form of *leśyā* provokes *kaṣāya*, just like some form of bitterness could trigger anger. *Leśyā*s are responsible for triggering the transmutation of thoughts, consequences, and mental tendencies into the observations of coloration, odor, taste, and touch sensations of the affected individuals.

Lord Mahāvīra elucidated the inner workings of the microcosm of life as impacted by *leśyā* and *kaṣāya*. The lineage of Jain thinkers and *ācārya*s has produced an immense amount of literature to describe the deliberative world of the mind and its actions prompted by *leśyā* and *kaṣāya*. Contemporary science has just begun to scratch the surface of this powerful teaching. Many contemporary scientists and researchers in the field of psychology are using visuals and colors experienced by the mind in meditative states to understand the state of one's mind. One can see that by understanding and applying the concept of *leśyā*, all individuals can progress from inauspicious to auspicious states, and finally to the pure state. This progression is the underlying purpose of the pursuit of right knowledge (*samyag-jñāna*) and its overarching influence on the major tenets of Jain doctrine.

The Passions[5] and Kārmic Bondage (Kaṣāya)

Kaṣāya (passion) is a technical defining term used in Jain philosophy. It is a composite of two words, *kaṣa* which means *karma,* and *āya* which means

---

[5] As noted in an earlier footnote, "passions" are seen as psychological encumbrances in Jain doctrine, and do not have the same positive connotation as may be expressed in English (for example, to "be passionate" about something).

"earning" or "bonding." Therefore, the word *kaṣāya* refers to the collection and bonding of kārmic particles into the layers formed over the soul. This accumulation results in the *jīva*'s entanglement in the cycles of birth and death, and subsequent reincarnation in various life-forms in future births.

In psychological terms, the mental tendencies that afflict the soul and make it divert from its natural state of purity are called *kaṣāya*. The states of excitement and cravings cause these mental tendencies which give rise to *kaṣāya*s. There are various different types of such tendencies but in Jain scriptures, they are divided into four broad categories:

- *Krodha* (anger)
- *Māna* (egoism)
- *Māyā* (deception)
- *Lobha* (greed)

THE PASSION OF ANGER (KRODHA-KAṢĀYA)

Krodha is a mental state of intense emotional turbulence. In this situation, a person's ability to think rationally diminishes significantly under the control of erratic emotions. This emotional state of excitement may induce feelings of enmity resulting in hostility and anguish, which may further lead to aggression or fear. The main difference between the states of anger and fear is that one becomes aggressive when angry and defensive while being fearful. With the onset of anger, the body experiences significant changes – for instance, the stomach is agitated, one's blood pressure rises, the heart rate increases, and the intelligence becomes imbalanced. The individual often becomes incapable of making appropriate decisions. Lord Mahāvīra said:

> Anger is the state that manifests when the deluding *karma* (*mohanīya-karma*[6]) raises its ugly head and destroys one's ability to think rationally and differentiate between right and wrong. It is an incendiary state of the soul and is unnatural to the soul's inherent qualities.

Anger manifests in various forms, but Jain scriptures have classified it in the following ten states which result in excessive aggravation and excitement, making a person ferocious, and inspiring fearfulness among others.

---

[6] *Mohanīya-karma* (deluding *karma*) is described in chapter 11.

1. *Krodha* (anger): A state of excited emotions.
2. *Kopa* (wrath): Unsteady behavior developed while in anger.
3. *Roṣa* (fury): Exposed or visibly fully blown state of anger.
4. *Doṣa* (wickedness): Indicting self and/or accusing others.
5. *Akṣamā* (impatience): Not forgiving a misdeed or crime committed by others.
6. *Sañjvalana* (burning): Repeated sweltering and being impulsive with anger.
7. *Kalaha* (quarreling): Shouting loudly with foul language and creating a brawl.
8. *Cāṇḍikya* (ire): The scheming and wrathful form of anger.
9. *Bhaṇḍana* (hostility): Becoming violent and starting a physical fight.
10. *Vivāda* (argumentativeness): Indulging in scandalous and vicious speech.

THE PASSION OF EGOISM (MĀNA-KAṢĀYA)

Māna is the feeling that results when one feels arrogant due to one's birth in an esteemed family and/or arrogant about one's capabilities such as knowledge, strength, fame, wealth, and intellect. Humans are endowed with a natural sense of self-respect and pride. When it is combined with an aggressive desire to lead, conquer, or rule, one's virtuous qualities are eclipsed, resulting in egoism and arrogance (*māna*). This state has a mix of aggravation and excitement, but it feeds into one's own elevated self-aggrandizement whereby one comes to think of themselves as above everybody else. Lord Mahāvīra defined such *māna* as having twelve states:

1. *Māna* (egoism): False belief in one or more of one's own tendencies.
2. *Mada* (self-importance): Being engrossed in self-elation.
3. *Darpa* (arrogance): An aggressive form of self-elation.
4. *Stambha* (insolence): Being impolite.
5. *Garva* (pridefulness): Being sanctimonious or haughty.
6. *Atyutkrośa* (bombasticness): Thinking oneself to be superior to others.
7. *Para-parivāda* (quarrelsome blame): To ridicule or slander others.

8. *Utkarṣa* (boastfulness): To exhibit one's own fame, fortune, wealth, or supremacy.
9. *Apakarṣa* (being slanderous): To show and highlight the misery and misfortunes of others.
10. *Unnata* (being demeaning): To think others to be worthless, frivolous, or inconsequential.
11. *Unnatanāma* (discourteousness): To not show any respect to a virtuous person.
12. *Durnāma* (disrespectfulness): Failing to extend rightful respect to the deserving.

THE PASSION OF DECEPTION (MĀYĀ-KAṢĀYA)

The accumulation of kārmic bondages due to deceptive or insincere tendencies is defined as *māyā-kaṣāya*. It is further subdivided into fifteen types as listed below:

1. *Māyā* (deception): Fraudulent, delusional, or deceptive tendencies.
2. *Upādhi* (deceit): Planning to approach a gullible person to commit fraud.
3. *Nikṛti* (dishonesty): Extending excessive respect to someone to deceive.
4. *Valaya* (misguidance): Using deceptive language to cheat someone.
5. *Gahana* (pretentiousness): Delivering thoughtful speech with hidden dubious intentions.
6. *Nūma* (wickedness): Committing a highly wicked act to cheat someone.
7. *Kalka* (inducement): Enticing someone to commit violent acts.
8. *Kurūpa* (distortion): Slanderous behavior.
9. *Jihmatā* (dishonesty): Slowing down work with intentions to swindle someone.
10. *Kilviṣika* (ill-willfulness): Having ill-will towards others.
11. *Ādaraṇatā* (speciousness): Taking up an undesirable task with ulterior motives.
12. *Gūhanatā* (concealment): Trying to hide undesired acts or behavior.
13. *Vañcakatā* (fraud): Acts of swindling.

14. *Pratikuñcanatā* (crookedness): To refute someone's straightforward and sincere statements.
15. *Sātiyoga* (covetousness): To mix up an illustrious entity with an inferior one.

THE PASSION OF GREED (LOBHA-KAṢĀYA)

Lobha-kaṣāya is one of the first inauspicious traits of craving and yearning to emerge or strengthen when one experiences the appearance of the effects of deluding *karma* (*mohanīya-karma*) from previous lives. It manifests in the form of an urge to hoard, expand, or enhance wealth, fame, family, lifestyle, worldly items, etc. According to Jain philosophy, greed has sixteen forms:

1. *Lobha* (greed): Inclination to amass things.
2. *Icchā* (desire): Tendency to crave or desire.
3. *Mūrchā* (infatuation): Extreme tendency to accumulate things.
4. *Kāṅkṣā* (hankering): Expectation or aspiration to receive something.
5. *Gṛddhi* (obsession): Tendency to get attached to the received item.
6. *Tṛṣṇā* (avidity): Tendency to collect new items while resisting the distribution of possessions.
7. *Mithyā* (falsehood): To pay attention to qualities which are disconcerting but are disguised attractively.
8. *Abhidhyā* (degradation): To deviate from a rightful decision.
9. *Āśaṁsanā* (craving): To retain the wish to obtain that which is desired.
10. *Prārthanā* (pleading): To plead for wealth and other financial means.
11. *Lālapanatā* (sycophancy): To flatter someone to receive favors in kind or materials.
12. *Kāmāśā* (lustfulness): To expect and crave carnal benefits.
13. *Bhogāśā* (hopeful enjoyment): To expect and crave things for indulgence.
14. *Jīvitāśā* (hoping for longevity): To desire a long life.
15. *Maraṇāśā* (hoping for shortened life): To desire death.
16. *Nandirāga* (attachment to comfort): To develop affection for received property.

Classification of Kārmic Bondage (Bandha)

After understanding various states or forms of the four types of *kaṣāya*, it is important to discuss their classification on the basis of their degrees of intensity (*bandha*). This classification is also relevant for the understanding of psychology. Each of the four passions (anger, ego, deceit, and greed) is classified into four subcategories based on their respective intensity. They are explained by way of examples in Jain scriptures, and are listed below in descending order of intensity.

BONDING DUE TO ANGER (KRODHA-KAṢĀYA BANDHA)

1. *Anantānubandhī krodha* (the anger from the limitless past): This type of anger is without beginning and is the strongest form of the passions that prevents right belief (*samyag-darśana*) and right conduct (*samyag-cāritra*). It is firmly established like the etchings in a stone.
2. *Apratyākhyānāvaraṇī krodha* (the anger of medium-term duration): These obstruct the observance of lay vows (*aṇuvrata*s). This is the secondary, lesser gradation of anger which is a non-permanent form of anger that eventually goes away. It is less recalcitrant, like the streaks left on dried mud at the bottom of a pond that disappear when the pond is filled with water again.
3. *Pratyākhyānāvaraṇa krodha* (the anger of short-term duration): This is a temporary form of anger that obstructs the observance of the mendicant vows (*mahāvrata*s) and disappears after a short while, with changing circumstances. It is like a line drawn in the sand that vanishes with blowing wind.
4. *Sañjvalana krodha* (the anger that is momentary): This is a momentary form of anger that causes brief carelessness in one's observances and then disappears quickly. It is like a wave in water that disappears soon after it is formed.

BONDING DUE TO EGOISM (MĀNA-KAṢĀYA BANDHA)

1. *Anantānubandhī māna* (the egoism from the limitless past): This is a hardened and sturdy form of ego like a column of stone that is unbreakable and impossible to alter.

2. *Apratyākhyānāvaraṇa māna* (the egoism of medium-term duration): This type is not very firm. It is more like the durability of bone when compared to stone.
3. *Pratyākhyānāvaraṇa māna* (the egoism of short-term duration): This is a more brittle form of ego like a piece of wood that can be broken and shaped.
4. *Sañjvalana māna* (momentary egoism that is controlled): It is like a soft bendable stick of wood or soft plastic.

BONDING DUE TO DECEPTION (MĀYĀ-KAṢĀYA BANDHA)

1. *Anantānubandhī māyā* (the deception from the limitless past): This leads to an extremely crooked deceitful nature, like the roots of a bamboo plant.
2. *Apratyākhyānāvaraṇa māyā* (the deception of medium-term duration): This causes a less deceitful and crooked nature that does not seem to be too harmful but can cause damage unexpectedly, likened to the horns of a bull.
3. *Pratyākhyānāvaraṇa māyā* (the deception of short-term duration): This is a form of devious nature that appears to be unpleasant but can be converted to be useful. It is not quite straight, like a bird's flight.
4. *Sañjvalana māyā* (the deception that is momentary): A form of deception that could sting but does not harm and is likened to the skin on bamboo.

BONDING DUE TO GREED (LOBHA-KAṢĀYA BANDHA)

1. *Anantānubandhī lobha* (the greed from the limitless past): This is an extreme form of greed that never ends like the color of the flower madder drug (*Rubia cordifolia*) that stays permanently.
2. *Apratyākhyānāvaraṇa lobha* (the greed of medium-term duration): This is a strong form of acquisitiveness that assists in living like the grease that lubricates the moving parts of a machine.
3. *Pratyākhyānāvaraṇa lobha* (the greed of short-term duration): This is a form of greed that makes someone look bad, like the sludge marks on clothes.
4. *Sañjvalana lobha* (the greed that is momentary): This is a form of

acquisitiveness that does not make one look good in the short-term, like a paste of turmeric on the body.

In general, the *anantānubandhī* (obstructions from the limitless past) class of passions is the most intense. It disables the living beings from getting out of the life-and-death cycles. In the presence of *anantānubandhī*, one cannot achieve an accurate perception of spiritual truths. Such bondages stay permanently through the lifetime of an individual and will certainly take the individual to hell,[7] which is understood to be a place filled with miseries.

The *apratyākhyānāvaraṇa* (obstructions of medium-term duration) class of passions do not destroy the fundamental ability to perceive spiritual truth, but neither do they allow someone's natural character to be fully developed. This form stays with an individual for medium duration, like a year or more. It causes reincarnation into the life of non-human living beings.

The *pratyākhyānāvaraṇa* (obstructions of short-term duration) class of passions are a milder form. They stay with an individual for some duration, like few months. They do not allow a person to elevate to an ascetic's life, but assist in reincarnating into a human life.

The *sañjvalana* (momentary) class of passions are the mildest form. They stay with an individual for a few moments. While they destroy the elements of character that assist the soul in achieving its pure form, they could help a human to elevate to a heavenly life after reincarnation. In future reincarnations, the individual would be able to rebuild the natural character elements and make progress on the path to salvation.

The desire towards place, entity, body type, and possessiveness cause the emergence of passionate elements. When cajoled by the trickeries of the mind, they attract the kārmic particles (*pudgala*s). In doing so, the kārmic particles are transformed and carry the properties of the five colors, two smells, five flavors, and four contact sensations, as discussed earlier.

The world continues to suffer from the evil consequences of kārmic bondages that the living beings experience and earn. They have been

---

7 As has been mentioned previously, according to India's dhārmic traditions "hell" is a temporary place of rebirth just like heavenly or earthly rebirth. It does not carry the same sense of "absolute evil" that it does in the Abrahamic traditions.

responsible for the destruction or diminishing of love, honor, and mutual respect in the world. Lord Mahāvīra tells us:

> Passions and attachments (*rāga*) and malice (*dveṣa*) constitute a poisonous tree. Deceit (*māyā*) and greed (*lobha*) give rise to avarice (*āsakti*) and infatuations, which in turn generate passions and attachments (*rāga*). Similarly, anger (*krodha*) and ego (*māna*) give rise to hatred and detestation (*ghr̥ṇā*), which in turn creates aversion and malice (*dveṣa*). Avarice (*āsakti*) and detestation (*ghr̥ṇā*) have provided the support and abode for selfishness and attachments (*mamatā*).

The entire universe is suffering from the flames of kārmic bondages and passions. The study of unadulterated and wholesome scriptures transcribed from Lord Mahāvīra's sermons, ascetic life, honorable character, penance, meditation, righteous living, and his teachings to acquire knowledge are the only means which are able to extinguish this fire for the entire world. Lord Mahāvīra further states:

> Anger (*krodha*) destroys love (*prīti*), egoism (*māna*) eliminates righteousness (*vinaya*), deception (*māyā*) kills friendships (*mitratā*), and greed (*lobha*) terminates all noble traits (*sadguṇa*). Use peace (*śānti*) and tranquility to win over anger (*krodha*), gentleness (*mr̥dutā*) to conquer egoism (*māna*), honesty (*saralatā*) to end deception (*māyā*), and contentment (*santoṣa*) to defeat greed (*lobha*).

In reality, *kaṣāya*s are the main cause of the soul's derailment from the path of progression towards the eternal liberation. Hence the adage:

> *kaṣāya-muktiḥ, kila muktir eva*

> Liberation (*muktiḥ*) from passions (*kaṣāya*) leads to (*kila*) complete liberation forever (*muktir eva*).

9

Jain Yoga:
Meditation and Union with Divinity[1]

Yoga in Dhārmic Traditions

YOGA has forever been a part of Indian lifestyle. From the ancient Vedic and Purāṇic periods through to the present, as a spiritual practice *yoga* has steadfastly maintained a unique and special place among eminent features of Indian culture. The Vedic tradition has believed that God created the universe and nature with *yoga* as the unifying force. People outside of India have come to associate India with *yoga* practitioners.

From a dhārmic perspective, divinity, nature, and *yoga* are seen as three intertwined elements of spirituality. *Yoga* influences an individual's way of life in many ways; for example, inspiring one to notice divinity in every element of nature. The word *yoga* originated from the root *yuj* which means "to join or merge." Therefore, the means by which a seeker merges with consciousness is called *yoga*. Nowadays, depending on the method and objective behind it, *yoga* practice can have different manifestations, such as spirituality (*ātman-yoga*), knowledge (*jñāna-yoga*), veneration or faith (*bhakti-yoga*), love (*prema-yoga*), action (*karma-yoga*), and physicality (*bhautika-yoga*). Many of India's ascetics have achieved spiritual awakening and physical accomplishments with the help of *yoga*. Lord Śiva, who is believed to be the originator and promoter of *yoga*, considered it to be a comprehensive means for spiritual enlightenment. Although he intended to keep it within the confines of the spiritual community, multiple offshoots of *yoga* forms sprang up over time. Lord Kṛṣṇa connected *yoga* with *karma* for the first time on the battlefield of Mahābhārata war, as elucidated in the revered *Bhagavadgītā*. Upon noticing Arjuna in emotional turmoil when he saw his close relatives on the enemy's

[1] See "Glossary of Terms" for a definition of the term "divinity" in Jain tradition.

side, Lord Kṛṣṇa inspired him towards his destined path of *karma*. Arjuna got rid of his worldly attachments upon witnessing the elaborate and world-encompassing view of his friend and mentor, Lord Kṛṣṇa. Lord Kṛṣṇa had granted Arjuna the powers of *karma-yoga* forever and, at the same time, left this profound teaching for all of humanity via the *Bhagavadgītā*.

THE EVOLUTION OF YOGA PRACTICES

The auspicious stream of *yoga* has been flowing all over the land of India, like the sacred River Gaṅgā. However, with time it deviated from the original form. Individuals such as Yogi Datta, Satyendra Nātha, Gorakhanātha, and others created an association between *yoga* and spiritual powers based on the five basic elements (earth, wind, fire, water, and ether or atmosphere). Followers of Yogi Datta's Rasa sect and the *haṭha-yoga* of Gorakhanātha spread all over India due to their allure. From the ordinary philosophers' perspective, this was an era of exaltation for *yoga*, but the experienced ascetics view it differently. These more accomplished practitioners saw this as the beginning of the unrighteous commercialization of the true virtues of *yoga*. This resulted in the advent of the aforementioned forms such as *ātman-yoga*, *jñāna-yoga*, *bhakti-yoga*, *prema-yoga*, *karma-yoga,* and *bhautika-yoga*. These forms are based on the context and nature of the means of practices and may be viewed as deviations from the original forms of *yoga*.

Notwithstanding the emergence of above-mentioned deviations, the spiritually authentic form of *yoga* continued to flourish as well. The spiritual seekers progressing on the path of profound penance continue with their rigorous practice of authentic *yoga*.

Yoga and Jain Dharma

In Jain and other dhārmic traditions, the common meaning of *yoga* is a state of deep meditation (*samādhi*) in union with one's true nature and the nature of the cosmos. This is contrary to the common belief that *yoga* is just a type of physical exercise regime that is directly or indirectly based on India's spiritual traditions. According to Jain doctrine, for spiritual practitioners deep meditation is the ultimate objective (*sādhya*) of *yoga* and union with the true-self is the means to attain that. In a way, when spiritual practioners unify with their inner nature, they have reached the state of true *yoga*. *Yoga* has also been defined as the cessation (*nirodha*) of the vacillations (*vṛtti*) of the mind (*citta*). Such mental control is essential for deep meditation because it allows the mind to concentrate and achieve unwavering (*susthiratā*), single-pointed (*ekāgratā*) focus, and then to ultimately maintain it. Attainment of this tranquil state is the genuine accomplishment of *yoga* practice.

Jain scriptures have assigned *yoga* with an alternative definition as well, one related to the activities of the mind, body, and speech. For all living beings, mind, body, and speech actively participate in all of the auspicious and inauspicious activities that are routinely undertaken. In essence, speech has much more influence than bodily action, and mind has immensely more idiosyncrasies and powers than speech. The power of the mind propels the content of speech, which is the medium to express inner thoughts, feelings, and the motivations of one's actions. The body is the doer of all the actions. That is why, positively speaking, all of these could be the sources of spiritual growth. To the contrary, from a negative perspective, the three (body, mind, and speech) could become gateways of impurity (*āśrava-dvāra*) that allow for the influx of kārmic particles to adhere to the soul. Since *yoga* is directly linked to the control of mind, body, and speech, Jain scriptures attribute two seemingly contradictory applications to the term *yoga*:

- From a spiritually positive or auspicious perspective, *yoga* can connote the practice of the union of mind, body, and speech with divinity – not just the union of body and mind. When the spiritual practice reaches the state of deep meditation (*samādhi*), *yoga* can result in the separation and detachment of kārmic *pudgala* particles that have accumulated in layers over the soul. The ability to reach that state and the extent to which the soul can be cleansed of the kārmic particles depends on the level of control over the mind, body, and speech activities. From that perspective, these three facilities can be considered as the main participants in the practice of *yoga*.
- The union of mind, body, and speech referred to above is also responsible for the activities in which living beings are involved routinely. Here, *yoga* can be seen as the means for employing the three faculties for material and sensual objectives that cause the collection of *karma*s (kārmic *pudgala*s) due to a living being's indulgence in false beliefs,

unrighteous conduct, and passions (anger, ego, deceit, and greed). From that perspective, *yoga* is one of the causes of the influx of *karma*s to the soul (*āśrava*) – the others being *mithyātva*, *avirati*, *pramāda*, and *kaṣāya*, as explained in chapter 6. In other words, when mind, body, and speech are focused on inauspicious activities, *yoga* can be seen as the cause of undesirable linking of the *jīva* with *karma*.

Characteristics of Yoga Practitioners

Jain scholars and *ācārya*s have presented *yoga* as a methodology for the development of eight qualities known as *mitra* (friendliness), *tārā* (radiance), *bala* (strength), *dīpra* (resplendence), *sthira* (stability), *kāntā* (amicability), *prabhā* (luster), and *parā* (exceptionality). In Jain Dharma, *yoga* and its associated practices are considered the enablers of the appreciation for the fundamental spiritual truth.

To initiate the development of auspicious qualities and to sustain progress in that pursuit, one requires earnest commitment, dedication, and hard work. His Holiness Hemacandrācārya says that knowledge gained with a religious *guru*'s guidance, personal canonical studies, spiritual awakening and experiences must all be present to intensify the determination of the *yoga* practitioners to achieve the final goal. A lack of any one of these could render a practitioner unable to reach that goal.

Right from the beginning, every *yoga* practitioner must keep the above-mentioned qualities and practices in mind. One must remember that realization of miracles or magical accomplishments is not the objective of *yoga*. A living being possesses infinite powers and enjoys a spectacular inner spiritual form. Therefore, one's objective must be to realize the knowledge of one's innate powers and awaken the inner-self. *Yoga* is the means to that end. For sincere and persevering *yoga* practitioners, these innate achievements manifest on their own automatically. Such practitioners steadfastly remain vigilant in their penance, not to be distracted by false pride over their accomplishments. Any distractions may result in their downfall. A story from Jain scriptures narrates the level of excellence of the supreme king, Sanatkumāra. Through his *yoga* penance, he had attained the capability to convert an aged body into an illness-free, handsome, and strong body with a touch of his saliva. Despite his capability, while suffering from horrible ailments during his ascetic life, he endured intense sufferings but never used his own accomplishments for himself. Sincere practitioners never use their own powers for personal benefit.

One of the greatest Jain spiritualists, Śrīmad Rājacandra, divided *yoga* practitioners into three categories depending on their philosophical state, described as follows:

1. The practitioner whose subjective indulgences have been subdued, who is engrossed in spiritual practices in accordance with his *guru*'s guidance, and who has been enriched with traits such as compassion and pleasantness, has achieved the first stage of penance.
2. The practitioner who disregards trepidations of speech and senses (tendencies of words, contact, flavor, aroma, and vision), who can easily block his mental distractions, and whose attention is removed from worldly attractions and is focused on spiritual awakening, that fortunate practitioner is in the middle state.
3. The practitioner who has ended the allure for life and is not afraid of dying, and who has understood the ramifications of life and death, has proven to be the most eminent achiever in the field of *yoga*.[2]

Yoga practitioners must always remember that the practice of *yoga* starts with a clear understanding of the principle of the duality of the *jīva* and matter, which distinguishes soul from the body. *Yoga* practice ends in the perception of the oneness and connectedness between the soul and divinity. *Yoga* cannot be effectively practiced in the absence of this belief of duality.

Yoga of Mind, Body, and Speech

YOGA OF THE MIND (MANA-YOGA)

The mind rules the body and senses. However, just like body and senses, the mind is affected by *karma*. Jain *yoga* is motivated by the effort to prevent

---

[2] *manda viṣaya ne saralatā, saha ājñā suvicāra* ।
karuṇā komalatādi guṇa, prathama bhūmikā dhāra ।।

rokyā śabdādika viṣaya, saṁyama sādhana rāga ।
jagata iṣṭa nahiṅ ātmā thī, madhya pātra mahābhāgya ।।

nahiṅtṛṣṇā līvyātṇī, maraṇa yoga nahiṅ kṣobha ।
mahāpātra te mārganā, parama yoga jita lobha ।।

inauspicious mental activities, and its practice promotes a healthy state of mind. Jain scriptures have classified the mind's functionality in four categories:

1. *Yathārtha* (that which is fixed and real)
2. *Ayathārtha* (that which is not fixed and is unreal)
3. *Ubhaya* (that which is both fixed-real and unfixed-unreal)
4. *Anubhaya* (that which is neither fixed-real nor unfixed-unreal)

In terms of unpleasant mental states, the mind gets overwhelmed by six or more undesirable traits:

1. *Viṣāda* (sadness and dejection)
2. *Nirdayatā-pūrṇa-vicāra* (pitiless and uncompassionate thoughts)
3. *Vyartha kalpanā* (useless and unnecessary web of negativity)
4. *Idhara-udhara mana* (aimless wandering of mind)
5. *Apavitra vicāra* (inauspicious thoughts)
6. *Dveṣa* (malicious, hateful, and despicable contemplations)

To practice Jain *yoga* as a spiritual discipline, one should make an earnest attempt to divert the mind away from these negative traits and focus it towards pure thoughts such as the welfare of the world and spiritual understanding.

YOGA OF THE BODY (KĀYA-YOGA)

Jain scriptures describe the body as an insatiable, gluttonous (*audārika*) entity, which is constantly committing actions and thereby accruing *karma*. Bodily actions can also be classified into auspicious (*praśasta*) and inauspicious (*apraśasta*) actions. In terms of inauspicious actions, the body may commit:

- Hurtful actions
- Sinful acts
- Stealing
- Egotistic demeanor
- Useless actions
- Reckless behavior

One should make an earnest attempt to avoid these inauspicious actions and to maintain actions that are auspicious and do not cause harm, by living a restrained life and engaging in spiritually beneficial practices.

YOGA OF SPEECH (VACANA-YOGA)

Jain scriptures have classified the function of speech into four categories. The four categories for speech are:

1. *Satya* (that which is truthful)
2. *Asatya* (that which is not truthful)
3. *Satya–asatya* (that which is both truthful and non-truthful)
4. *Anubhaya-rūpa* (that which is neither truthful nor completely non-truthful)

The entire spectrum of speech belongs to the above four categories. An individual, when not careful, can easily be entrapped in using inauspicious language which has the following six traits:

1. Untruthful speech (*asatya*)
2. Slander and gossip (*ninda* and *cugalī*)
3. Caustic and abusive language, and giving of curses (*kaṭu–gālī–śāpa*)
4. Self-aggrandizement
5. Inauspicious useless talk
6. Disrespectful and spurious language towards sacred scriptures and other such texts

In the spiritual practice of Jain *yoga*, one should make earnest attempts to use caring, friendly, truthful, pleasant, and kind language for one's self-cultivation.

Types of Yoga

In Jain Dharma, the spiritual discipline of *yoga* is considered to be the state of deep meditation. This is similar to other systems of *yoga* that include *mantra-yoga, laya-yoga, rāja-yoga, haṭha-yoga,* etc. However, Jain Dharma does not define *yoga* as a restrictive discipline only. It is far more comprehensive and is considered to be a contemplation-driven mental and physical exercise as well. The highly distinguished Jain saint, Haribhadra Sūri, stated that the practice of spiritual *yoga* lays the path towards salvation. He proposed five different types of *yoga*. In progressive order, they are:

1. *Adhyātma-yoga* (spiritual *yoga* – contemplation on the self (soul) and the fundamental truth)
2. *Bhāvanā-yoga* (intentional *yoga* – cultivation of a compassionate emotion)
3. *Dhyāna-yoga* (meditation *yoga*)
4. *Samatā-yoga* (equanimity *yoga*)
5. *Vṛtti-saṁkṣaya-yoga* (*yoga* of ending spiritually hindering tendencies)

Of the above-listed types of *yoga*, one could miss the distinctions between *adhyātma-yoga* and *vṛtti-saṁkṣaya-yoga* because they seem to be of similar types. However, in Jain *yoga* doctrine, *adhyātma-yoga* is to contemplate the fundamental truth (*tattva*). This should comprise rightfulness, control over tendencies, study of religious scriptures, friendship, amity, compassion, pleasantness, and rightful expectations. *Vṛtti-saṁkṣaya-yoga* is the complete destruction of deliberate or inadvertent tendencies that create uncertainty about the body-soul relationship (*samyag-darśana*). One should strive to reach a state in which such tendencies never come back.

Of the five types of *yoga* discussed above, *adhyātma-yoga* is of a special significance and is described in more detail as follows.

Spiritual Yoga (Adhyātma-Yoga)

In dhārmic doctrines of India, the soul is the main focus of contemplation, and *adhyātma-yoga* is the form of *yoga* that centers on this contemplation. Philosophically, an individual can be described by four fundamental elements (soul, *karma*, subtle body, and physical body), and several extraneous elements:

- A soul is endowed with an aggregate of characteristics such as wisdom, vigor, tranquility, and bliss. Intrinsically, these characteristics are flawless and a *jīva* starts with a perfect soul with flawless characteristics. When it starts interacting with the external materialistic world, its characteristics start weakening and blemishing.
- *Karma*s define the strength of the soul's bond to worldly affairs that determine the extent to which soul's intrinsic powers are overwhelmed with blemishes – the stronger the bond, the weaker the soul's powers.

- The subtle body is made up of seventeen sub-elements consisting of five knowledge-acquiring senses, five action-oriented senses, five spirits (*prāṇa*), mind, and self-consciousness or pride.
- The physical body is made up of seven natural resources such as bones, flesh, blood, etc.
- The extraneous elements are entities such as wealth, possessions, social prestige, and family. All living beings are continually consumed by the desire to acquire these elements. We succeed sometimes in controlling these desires, and fail at other times.

Every incident in life results in either a good or a bad impression upon our psyche. Ascetics strive to eliminate all of these impressions to purify their souls by discarding its blemishes. That is the key objective of spiritual *yoga*, and progress towards that goal is the key indicator of this effort.

FIVE STATES OF MIND

The cause of life's complexities is neither the soul, nor the body, nor the senses. It is the mind. One feels pleasure and bliss all around when the mind is at ease and in a state of happiness. To the contrary, when the mind is restless and gloomy, we feel misery and agony all throughout. From the viewpoint of *yoga*, the mind is considered to have five states:

1. *Mūḍha* (foolish) state: This is the state of darkness and ignorance where the living being is lethargic and devoid of wisdom. It is mostly found in animals and insects. A step better than the *mūḍha* state is the *avikṣipta* state where the living beings are lethargic and aimless.
2. *Kṣipta* (scattered) state: This state is dominated by passions for love and pleasure that result in several vices. Here, the mind is restless and continuously wanders. A *kṣipta* mind cannot focus on anything, even for a moment.
3. *Vikṣipta* (agitated) state: This is still a state of confusion, but with some positive features that help begin spiritual progression. Both the states of darkness and passions are still present, but they are subdued and controlled by spiritual impulses. The living being is now guided by tendencies of *dharma* (here meaning "righteousness," different from the *dharma-dravya*), non-attachment, and renunciation. However, the state

of passions and pleasure does emerge, but it is subdued by austerities. In this state, one is not able to sustain true *yoga* practices. If one works hard at it, one may make some progress, but then will stumble and lose the way.

4. *Ekāgra* (single-pointed) state: This is the state where one can start focusing on a singular subject or object of meditation. When the effects of darkness and passions have been diminished, the mind stops wandering. Now it can fully concentrate on the chosen topic without wavering around.
5. *Niruddha* (cessation) state: In this state the mind is free of all uncertainties, is in a state of calmness, and is completely focused inward. It does not indulge in any worldly matters and is always preoccupied with its own intrinsic pure nature.

The main purpose of *yoga* penance is to control the mind and move it towards the higher states – whereupon the *niruddha* state is the ultimate desired state. The practice of *adhyātma-yoga* is ideally suited to achieve that goal.

THE FIVE MENTAL ANGUISHES (KLEŚA)

The spiritual practitioners face obstacles and difficulties at every step of their penance. Many times they result from mental trepidations due to worldly distractions, misguided self-contemplations, or some incidents due to misfortunes. Together they all result in mental anguish or *kleśa*s that the practitioner must overcome. The *kleśa*s can be caused by spiritual blockages, wrongful wisdom, and self-action. There are five types of *kleśa*s (anguishes), as discussed below.

1. *Avidyā* (wrongful knowledge): This comes from the misbelief that non-living soulless entities could also have some association with a soul and consciousness. There could be up to four causes behind it: (i) considering something that is temporary and transitory to be eternal or perpetual, (ii) considering something that is impure or inauspicious to be pure, (iii) considering something to be a pleasure when it is actually a misery, and (iv) considering a soulless entity to be one with soul.

2. *Asmitā* (pride): Many times, for a practitioner engrossed in penance, the attainment of glorious achievements such as supernatural powers could lead to egoism. As a result, the practitioner may start extolling his own achievements, lessen his perseverance, and lose the way to spiritual growth. Therefore, one should continue the practice of penance without falling in the trap of intermittent achievements and associated illusory miracles.
3. *Rāga* (passion or attachment): Attachments are triggered by passions. Each of our senses (hearing, taste, sight, smell, and touch) has an auspicious and an inauspicious attribute, for a total of ten elements. Indulgence in any of these ten elements, whether auspicious or inauspicious, creates passions resulting in attachments and arrogance. As long as one has such tendencies, one cannot fully immerse in spiritual *yoga*.
4. *Dveṣa* (malice): This results from the jealousy that occurs when one is unable to fulfill one's desires. When one's pride or passion gets hurt due to someone else's achievements in mind-body-speech, it gives rise to malice. The *Bhagavadgītā* states, "The tendencies of desires and passions result in anger."[3]
5. *Abhiniveśa* (attachment): After one realizes certain capabilities, which result in arrogance and passions, one may feel insecure about losing those capabilities. The state of such worries is called *abhiniveśa*.

In *adhyātma-yoga*, the main subject of contemplation revolves around elimination of the above mental anguishes (*kleśa*s) – the obstacles that continuously corrode our path of spiritual progression.

The Eight Constituents of Jain Yoga (Aṣṭāṅga-Yoga)

The definition of *yoga* in various traditions and religious sects is fairly similar, although the specifics may vary. The *yoga* scholars of Patañjali's tradition describe *yoga* as *yogaś citta-vṛtti-nirodhaḥ* (*yoga* is the obstruction of mental deviation). In other words, considering the unstable nature of the mind, *yoga* helps in achieving mental concentration. Jain scholars describe *yoga* as *yujjate*

---

[3] *kāmāt krodho 'bhijāyate*. – II.62.

iti yogaḥ (*yoga* unites one with divinity), emphasizing the essence of *yoga*. The description of *yoga* by Pātañjala scholars connects the seeker with the essential consciousness, whereas that of Jain scholars aims at purifying the unified actions of mind, body, and speech, and prompting the soul towards its original state of perfection.

The ultimate objective of *yoga* is the purification of the mind and other intellectual faculties of the body. The classical *yoga* practice conceived and formulated by Maharṣi (the great saint) Patañjali consists of eight constituents.[4] Jain *yoga* practice is very similar, and as described in Jain scriptures, it also has eight constituents, as follows:

1. *Mahāvrata* (supreme vows): This is similar to the *yama*s (vows) in Patañjali's system.
2. *Yoga-saṁgraha* (collection of *yoga* principles and rules): This is similar to the *niyama*s (rules) in Patañjali's system.
3. *Kāya-kleśa* (bodily deficiencies): This is similar to *āsana* (seated posture) in Patañjali's system.
4. *Bhāva-prāṇāyāma* (breathing exercise with restrained thoughts): This is similar to *prāṇāyāma* (breathing exercises) in Patañjali's system.
5. *Prati-saṅlīnatā* (withdrawing within): This is similar to *pratyāhāra* (withdrawing the senses) in Patañjali's system.
6. *Dhāraṇā* (firm concentration): This is similar to the *dhāraṇā* (firm concentration) in Patañjali's system.
7. *Dhyāna* (focused contemplation or meditation): This is similar to *dhyāna* (contemplation or meditation) in Patañjali's system.
8. *Samādhi* (deep meditation): This is similar to *samādhi* (deep meditation) in Patañjali's system.

A brief overview of each of these eight constituents is presented below:

---

[4] The eight constituents of the classical Pātañjala *yoga* are: (1) *yama* (vows), (2) *niyama* (rules), (3) *āsana* (seated posture), (4) *prāṇāyāma* (breathing exercise), (5) *pratyāhāra* (withdrawing the senses), (6) *dhāraṇā* (firm concentration), (7) *dhyāna* (contemplation or meditation), and (8) *samādhi* (deep meditation).

THE SUPREME VOWS (MAHĀVRATA)

The five supreme vows are:

1. *Ahiṁsā* (non-violence)
2. *Satya* (truthfulness)
3. *Asteya* (non-stealing)
4. *Brahmacarya* (honorable conduct or celibacy)
5. *Aparigraha* (non-possession or non-attachment)

THE PRINCIPLES OF YOGA (YOGA-SAṀGRAHA)

The *yoga-saṁgraha* is composed of thirty-two principles of Jain *yoga*, as listed here:

1. Critique of sinful acts
2. Not confronting others with criticism
3. Unwavering belief in religion during difficult times
4. Self-driven penance
5. Receiving education and follow teachings in daily life
6. Not celebrating the body or engaging in or accepting self-praise
7. Anonymity in penance without seeking respect or praise
8. Not being greedy
9. Ability to endure difficulty
10. Simplicity or modesty
11. Purity
12. Right perception
13. Practicing deep meditation
14. Adhering to proper behavior
15. Being polite to others
16. Patience
17. Being emotionally sensitive
18. Not being deceitful

19. Forbearance
20. Ability to control actions through self-restraint so as to not collect new *karma*
21. Restraining one's own faults
22. Being free of carnal desires
23. Maintaining of one's own basic virtuous qualities
24. Maintaining of one's own highest virtuous qualities
25. Renunciation (*vyutsarga*)
26. Vigilance or care (*apramādī*)
27. Maintaining meditation (*dhyāna*) and proper conduct (*samācārī*) at every moment
28. Continual meditation (*dhyāna*) and control of actions (*yukta karanā*)
29. Remaining composed even during difficult situations, such as death
30. Abandonment of attachment or desire (*saṅga-tyāga*)
31. Repentance or atonement (*prāyaścitta*)
32. Being prayerful (*ārādhaka*) at time of death

THE BODILY DEFICIENCIES (KĀYA-KLEŚA)

The *kāya-kleśa*s are addressed through postures (*āsana*s), which comprise:

1. *Vīrāsana* (hero's pose)
2. *Kamalāsana* (lotus pose)
3. *Utkaṭikāsana* (chair pose)
4. *Godohāsana* (cow-milking pose)
5. *Sukhāsana* (comfortable seated pose)

These are practiced as a form of religious austerity (*kāyotsarga*).

BREATHING EXERCISE WITH RESTRAINED THOUGHTS (BHĀVA-PRĀṆĀYĀMA)

The breathing exercises of *bhāva-prāṇāyāma* are emphasized in Jain Dharma as a means to increase strength (*bala*), enthusiasm (*utsāha*), resolve (*niścaya*), commitment (*dhairya*), contentment (*santoṣa*), perception of truth (*tattva-*

darśana), renunciation of worldly life (*loka-tyāga*), and stimulation of life-force (*prāṇa-vr̥tti*).

WITHDRAWING WITHIN (PRATI-SAṄLĪNATĀ)

The *prati-saṅlīnatā* is the ability to restrain the senses and to minimize the passions (*kaṣāyas*) and the concomitant accumulation of kārmic *pudgala* while practicing solitary living (*vivikta śayanāsana*) focused on *yoga* practice. *Prati-saṅlīnatā* involves endeavoring towards (*prayāṇa*) commendable behavior (*praśasta*) while leaving behind inappropriate conduct.

FIRM CONCENTRATION (DHĀRAṆĀ)

Dhāraṇā is the ability to maintain a single-pointed focus (*ekāgratā*) on a particular object of meditation. There are five *dhāraṇās*, each involving one of the fundamental forms of matter – earth, fire, wind, water, and the form of the spiritual body. The five *dhāraṇās* are:

1. *Pārthivī-dhāraṇā* (concentration on the terrestrial energy): This specific form of *dhāraṇā* involves resolving to connect with the realms of the physical universe described in the doctrine of Jain cosmology. To practice *pārthivī-dhāraṇā*, one must envision and focus on the pericarp of a virtual golden lotus situated in the middle of the venerated ocean of milk (*kṣīra-sāgara*). Here, the lotus pericarp is symbolic of Sumerū Parvata,[5] a golden lotus is symbolic of Jambūdvīpa,[6] and *kṣīra-sāgara* represents *madhya-loka*.[7] According to Jain cosmology, *madhya-loka*

---

[5] When a *tīrthaṅkara* is born, the gods (*indras*) come to earth, take him to the mountain Sumerū Parvata, and perform his birth ablutions (*abhiṣeka*) there. Jain temples may be surmounted by a tower that symbolizes Mount Meru, the axis mundi of the universe.

[6] According to Jain cosmology, Jambūdvīpa is named after the rose-apple tree (*jambū*) located atop Mount Meru at the center of the island. It comprises seven continents separated by six east–west–oriented mountain ranges. From south to north, these continents are named Bharata-kṣetra, Haimavata, Hari, Mahāvideha (Videha), Ramyaka, Hairaṇyavata, and Airāvata-kṣetra. Of these, Bharata-kṣetra and Airāvata-kṣetra are subject to cycles of time, where living conditions improve and decline. On the others, living conditions remain constant. Some of these are *bhoga-bhūmi* lands, where all of one's needs are satisfied without effort, and others are *karma-bhūmi* lands, where one must labor in order to survive.

[7] The *madhya-loka* (middle realm) is the portion of the occupied universe (*loka ākāśa*)

is the "middle realm" of the universe where humans and animals reside and from where humans can achieve salvation; Jambūdvīpa is a realm likened to an island-continent situated in *madhya-loka*, and Sumerū Parvata is the sacred mountain on Jambūdvīpa. Sumerū Parvata (also called Mount Meru) is regarded as the spiritual center of the universe surrounded by Jambūdvīpa, and by focusing and meditating over it, the seeker is attempting to connect with the spirituality of the universe. After some practice, one establishes a virtual crystal on this pericarp and focuses on that while thinking, "I am peacefully seated to destroy my kārmic particle layers that obstruct my soul's intrinsic nature." Contemplation in this manner is called *pārthivī-dhāraṇā.*

2. *Āgneyī-dhāraṇā* (concentration on the fiery energy): This *dhāraṇā* is the connection with the spiritual energy represented by fire. Having focused on the pericarp of the virtual lotus as described above, the seeker now moves the attention to another virtual lotus situated right behind and underneath the navel. This lotus faces upwards towards the heart and has sixteen white leaves, each with a yellow inscription. Its pericarp has a yellow inscription of the letter *ī*. Next, one imagines a brown lotus with eight leaves, each with a black inscription representing a type of *karma*.[8] One follows this by imagining a virtual fire emanating from the letter *ī* that grows and is destroying each of the eight *karma*s inscribed on the second lotus. This fire is rising towards the head. From the center of the lotus two rays emerge, one touching the left ear and the other touching the right ear. A third ray emerges that connects the

---

located between the upper realm of the heavens (*ūrdhva-loka*) and the lower realm of the hells (*adho-loka*). Within this Jambūdvīpa is surrounded by an ocean. Beyond this, there are innumerable doughnut-shaped concentric island-continents, each surrounded by an ocean. Humans inhabit the innermost three island-continents: Jambūdvīpa, Dhātakīkhaṇḍadvīpa, and the inner half of Puṣkaravaradvīpa, up to a mountain range called Mānuṣottara. Beyond this, only animals live on the other island-continents. The three island-continents inhabited by humans are subdivided into various lands or continents, which are separated by mountain ranges, containing a total of thirty-five continents.

[8] There are eight *karma* types discussed in chapter 11: *darśana-āvaraṇīya, jñāna-āvaraṇīya, antarāya-karma, mohanīya-karma, āyu-karma, nāma-karma, gotra-karma,* and *vedanīya-karma.*

two ears, thus forming a triangular halo illuminated by fire.

At this stage, the seeker thinks of a particular spiritual insignia in conjunction with this triangular halo with the letter *ra* on each ray, a *svastika*[9] on the outside of each corner, and *auṁ arhaṁ* on the inside in each corner. Now envisage that the fire halo is burning all eight *karma*s (represented by eight lotus leaves) inside the triangular halo, and the whole body on the outside. In this manner, the practitioner is visualizing that both the *karma*s and the body are being destroyed. This visualization is a representative of the path that eventually leads to omniscience (kārmic destruction) and ultimate liberation from life–death cycles (body destruction). This is the *āgneyī-dhāraṇā* or the conviction to ignite the subtle spiritual energies to destroy kārmic bondages and ultimately become free from the cycle of birth and death (*saṁsāra*).

3. *Vāyavī-dhāraṇā* (concentration on the wind energy): This is the resolution to connect with the spiritual energy represented by wind. The seeker visualizes a whirlwind airflow around them. This whirlwind has formed an air halo that is blowing away the dust created from the burning of *karma*s and body forms during *āgneyī-dhāraṇā*. In the process, the soul is being cleared of the kārmic dust.

4. *Vāruṇī-dhāraṇā* (concentration on the water energy): This is the determination to connect with the spiritual energy represented by water. The practitioner visualizes the atmosphere being covered by dark clouds and in the midst of lightning. The clouds start thundering, followed

---

[9] The *svastika* is an age-old and commonly used auspicious and important symbol in Jain Dharma as well as other dhārmic traditions of India. Nazis used a variation (a tilted version) of a similar symbol as a logo to symbolize their perverted ideology. Jain Dharma has utilized the *svastika* since antiquity to visually represent the concept of the perpetual nature of the universe. It has four horizontal and vertical arms pointing in clockwise direction, representing the heavenly beings (*deva*s), human beings, hellish beings, and *tiryañca*s (subhumans like flora or fauna) in an ongoing cycle of rebirth. The symbol has three dots at the top, representing the troika of auspicious traits, namely, right perception (*samyag-darśana*), right knowledge (*samyag-jñāna*), and right conduct (*samyag-cāritra*), which are essential for liberation from this cycle of rebirth. Above the three dots is a crescent and a dot centered above the crescent representing the state of the ultimate liberation.

by heavy but calm rain. The rain washes away the dust created during *vāyavī-dhāraṇā* and cleanses the soul.

5. *Tattva-rūpavatī-dhāraṇā* (concentration on the true form of the spiritual body): After cleansing, this discipline involves visualizing the soul in its pure state. One visualizes reaching a bodiless form that is pure and has endless wisdom. The seeker has shed all the accumulated *karma* and has risen to the state that is filled with the divine light.

The *dhāraṇā* techniques described above are utilized for practicing *piṇḍastha-dhyāna* (meditation on intermixture), the first meditation technique for practicing *dharma-dhyāna* as described next under *dhyāna*, the seventh component of *yoga*.

FOCUSED CONTEMPLATION OR MEDITATION (DHYĀNA)

Dhyāna is the state of meditation or focused contemplation that is considered extremely important in Jain Dharma. It is important to note that much like the term *yoga*, the idea of *dhyāna* can involve either positive or negative applications, depending on whether the object of one's contemplation is centered on sensory stimulation and negative emotions and activities, or on virtuous conduct with a meditative discipline that is intended for spiritual progress. As a positive form of concentration, *dhyāna* is defined as the subtle and intense attentiveness that is unwavering like a motionless lamp flame, free of any fluctuation of thoughts. Spiritual power rises proportionally with the firmness and intensity of determination, which in turn is dependent on whether the mental state (*mānasika*) is harmonious (*sāmañjasya*) or unrestrained (*aniyantrita*). When these tendencies are restrained to focus on a single spiritual objective, the contemplation process quickly progresses towards the goal of calmness. In Jain philosophy, *dhyāna* is defined as the unified and controlled flow of thoughts towards the singular goal of mental tranquility.

One's mental powers (*mānasika śakti*) are enriched when one is engrossed (*avalambana*) in *dhyāna*, and the soul experiences its extraordinary capacity (*adbhuta sāmarthya*), which is why *dhyāna* is critically important for deep meditation. This manifested potential becomes the impetus for the destruction of the kārmic particles during the progress of attaining the pure state of the soul. An individual's psychological inclinations have four interconnected options, namely, sorrow (*ārta*), anger or cruelty (*raudra*), virtue (*dharma*), and impeccable purity (*śukla*). The practitioner's choices among these options defines the progress they make in their pursuit of spiritual growth. The corresponding states of meditation (*dhyāna*) are *ārta-dhyāna*, *raudra-dhyāna*, *dharma-dhyāna*, and *śukla-dhyāna*. The first two (*ārta-dhyāna* and *raudra-dhyāna*) are not conducive to spiritual salvation, while the latter two are, as described below.

1. *Ārta-dhyāna* (meditation in a sorrowful state): This is the type of concentration that fixates on the flow of predispositions triggered by feelings of pain, sorrow, worries, fear, etc. Such fixations arise from the delusional demeanor of an individual who has diverted from the righteous way and involve a penchant for comfort and pleasure and avoidance of physical discomfort perceivably associated with honorable living. There are four main reasons, each corresponding to a specific type of *ārta-dhyāna*, for such feelings to take control of the practitioner's mental state:
    i. Craving to obtain an undesirable object, getting emotionally attached to it, and then after getting it, feeling worrisome about the thought of being separated from it.
    ii. After obtaining a desired object, having anxiety about losing it, and then after losing it, having intense cravings to get it back.
    iii. Worrying about the ability to discard the misery and pain caused by an illness.
    iv. Worrying about the ability to fulfill the dreams of worldly comforts and riches.
2. *Raudra-dhyāna* (meditation in angry or cruel state): *Raudra* means ruthless intentions, and *raudra-dhyāna* is concentrating on the instincts generated by such intentions. It is a state of contemplation while engrossed in ill-feelings such as anger, hatred, malice, and violence. This state could lead to evil designs and enjoyment in immoral activities that one must avoid if one has to make progress on the spiritual path. There are four main reasons for this mental state:

i. *Hiṁsānubandhī* (thirst for violence): Being motivated by instincts to cause hurt, feeling delight in developing violent skills and in committing violence against other living beings.

ii. *Mṛṣānubandhī* (thirst for deception): Creating and using language that is deceptive and untruthful for self-pleasure, and deceiving gullible people. It also involves suppressing the truth through denial (*apalāpa*), causing hurt and violence.

iii. *Cauryānubandhī* (thirst for defrauding): Planning by using deceptive means to commit theft or acquire articles such as property that is not granted, or other similar sinful fraudulent acts. It also entails inspiring and training others to do the same.

iv. *Saṁrakṣaṇānubandhī* (thirst for preservation): Psychological tendencies and thoughts obsessed with attaining and protecting one's possessions of enjoyment.

3. *Dharma-dhyāna* (meditation in a virtuous state): A state of mind when one dissociates from *ārta-dhyāna* and *raudra-dhyāna*, and yearns to perceive and unify with the unblemished soul. This involves focusing one's mind on religious and spiritual acts. There are four main reasons for this mental state of *dharma-dhyāna*, and, correspondingly, four subtypes of this meditation form as listed below:

i. *Ājñā-vicaya* (concentrating on auspicious teachings): This is the developing of mental focus to appropriately contemplate on and understand the fundamental principles taught by the *tīrthaṅkara*s, while maintaining unwavering belief in those principles.

ii. *Apāya-vicaya* (concentrating on the eradication of inauspicious thoughts): This refers to contemplating the eradication of passionate thoughts and tendencies of attachment, malice, hatred, etc., towards others, and other similar blemishes. This includes compassionate behavior to encourage and help others towards the same tendencies.

iii. *Vipāka-vicaya* (concentrating on relinquishing expectations): This is the process of relinquishing attachment to feelings of elation during pleasure and happiness, and the corollary of gloominess and dejection experienced during hard and unpleasant times. This type of meditation is meant to cultivate mental equanimity.

iv. *Saṁsthāna-vicaya* (concentrating on universal equanimity): This meditation involves contemplating the vastness and magnitude of the universe and pondering over the characteristics and forms of all that is contained therein.

The practice of *dharma-dhyāna* comprises four progressive meditative techniques with which impure mental impulses can be transformed to facilitate the realization of the state of pure consciousness.

i. *Piṇḍastha-dhyāna* (meditation on body-soul association): This involves focusing on the soul as it is in association with the physical body. There are five *dhāraṇā*s included under *piṇḍastha-dhyāna* (as described above, under the *dhāraṇā* section), each involving one of the fundamental forms of matter which affect the body – earth, fire, wind, water, and the form of the spiritual body.

ii. *Padastha-dhyāna* (meditation on the benevolent *mantra*): This is the process of focusing on the five couplets of the *namaskāra* or *namokāra mahāmantra*.[10] It involves visualizing the five stages of spiritual growth: *arihanta, siddha, āyariya, uvajjhāya,* and *sāhu*, as described below:

- *Arihanta* (victor): This is the state of a divine soul (*jīva*) with a living body who has achieved infinite wisdom and has eliminated all of the *karma*s that can be destroyed with penance and austerities. Here, the divine *jīva* has discarded *darśana-āvaraṇīya-karma, jñāna-āvaraṇīya-karma, antarāya-karma, mohanīya-karma,* and *vedanīya-karma,* but still has outstanding

---

[10] *Namokāra* (*namaskāra*) *mahāmantra*:

ṇamo arihaṅtāṇaṁ	:	Obeisance to the victors (*arihanta*)
ṇamo siddhāṇaṁ	:	Obeisance to the liberated souls (*siddha*)
ṇamo āyariyāṇaṁ	:	Obeisance to the preceptors (*āyariya*)
ṇamo uvajjhāyāṇaṁ	:	Obeisance to the teachers (*uvajjhāya*)
ṇamo loe savvasāhuṇaṁ	:	Obeisance to the monks (*sāhu*)
eso pañca-ṇamokkāro	:	This fivefold obeisance
savvapāpappaṇāsaṇo	:	Ends all sins and bondages
maṁglāṇaṁ ca savvesiṁ	:	This is the most auspicious bliss
paḍhamaṁ havae maṁgalaṁ	:	In the entire universe.

āyu-karma, nāma-karma, and *gotra-karma* (all of these will be described in chapter 11).

- *Siddha* (liberated soul): The state of one who has achieved omniscience and has left their body to attain the ultimate liberation. Here, the divine *jīva* has discarded all eight *karma*s.
- *Ācārya*; *āyariya* in Ardhamāgadhī (preceptors): These are the leaders of the spiritual community.
- *Upādhyāya*; *uvajjhāya* in Ardhamāgadhī (teachers): These are teachers of spiritual knowledge.
- *Sādhu*; *sāhu* in Ardhamāgadhī (monks): These are all male and female ascetics and mendicants.

In one sense, the *namaskāra mahāmantra* represents a progression towards the freedom from the cycles of birth and death by way of progressively shedding *karma* until one has moved beyond the ascetic life to complete liberation. The meditation on this *mantra* directs one's attention to the process of fulfilling one's aspirations for similar spiritual progress. The important thing to note is that the *mantra* does not refer to any individual names but addresses all the *jīva*s in those categories, irrespective of whether they belong to the Jain tradition or not.

iii. *Rūpastha-dhyāna* (meditation on enlightened *jīva*s in bodily form): This form of meditation involves concentrating on one who has attained the *arihanta* state. This is the state when one has achieved omniscience with complete unbounded wisdom, has the clearest perception, and is perfect in conduct. By now all *karma*s except age (*āyuṣ*), name (*nāma*), and lineage (*gotra*) have been destroyed and the soul has reached perfection. This state is different and spiritually elevated from *padastha-dhyāna* because here the seeker is focusing only on the *jīva* who has achieved divinity, whereas *padastha-dhyāna* involved *Arhant*, *Ācārya*, *Upādhyāya*, and Sādhu as well, albeit all in body form. By visualizing this state, the meditator is unifying with the spiritual objective and enjoying the vision of meditative experiences.

iv. *Rūpātīta-dhyāna* (meditation on liberated enlightened *jīva*s): In this form, the meditator is focusing on the *siddha* state, which is achieved after the *arihanta* state. This is the state after there has been the elimination of age, name, and lineage *karma*s that had still been present in the *arihanta* state. By visualizing this state, the meditator is connecting with the final objective of eternal liberation while receiving the energy of inspiration.

4. *Śukla-dhyāna* (deep meditation in a blissful state): *Śukla-dhyāna* is the stage of meditation that the aspiring *jīva* attains after progressing through all four stages of *dharma-dhyāna* in its quest to reach the final, perfected stage. During the *dharma-dhyāna* stages, the *jīva* makes significant spiritual progress but is not able to completely eliminate all the passions (*kaṣāya*s) that cause the accumulation of kārmic particles. However, while progressing from *piṇḍastha-dhyāna* to *padastha-dhyāna* to *rūpastha-dhyāna* and finally to *rūpātīta-dhyāna*, the practitioner achieves the control that they had been aspiring for, and enters the last stage. During the final stage of meditation, *śukla-dhyāna*, the practitioner achieves the elimination of the mind's fickleness, wandering, inauspicious thoughts, and impurities that cloud the soul. This is the fourth stage of *dhyāna*, and it is the same as *samādhi* (deep meditation), which is described below.

DEEP MEDITATION (SAMĀDHI)

In the Jain *yoga* system, the eighth component, *samādhi*, is the same as *śukla-dhyāna*, the fourth type of *dhyāna* (above). This is the purest and most spiritually advanced mental state, where the *jīva* connects with its soul in its purest form. By practicing this form of meditation, all the passions (*kaṣāya*s) are weakened and they become ineffective in their ability to cause the accumulation of kārmic particles. At this level of meditation, the kārmic layers over the soul are incapacitated and ultimately detached. This is the highest level of deep meditation leading to the supreme state. This form of meditation also involves a harmonious order, and thus involves four stages or subcategories (*pr̥thaktva vitarka savicāra, ekatva vitarka avicāra, sūkṣma kriyā apratipatti*, and *vyuparata kriyā nirvr̥tti*), as elaborated in what follows:

1. *Pr̥thaktva vitarka savicāra* (concurrent but separated focus on

sounds and thoughts): In this initial stage of *samādhi*, the focus of meditation involves concurrently ongoing but separated dual-channel contemplations. One channel involves connections between certain sounds or revelations and the mind of the practitioner, and the second channel involves internal thoughts and the mind. Here *pṛthaktva* means the "state of separateness," *vitarka* refers to "sounds" or "revelations," and *savicāra* refers to "transitory but concurrent considerations." This state maintains a degree of separation between the mind and pure spirituality, involves meditating upon the meditative gnosis and incorporating that into one's own ongoing thoughts. This combination may be a dynamic process changing with time; it nevertheless leads to a very peaceful state of concentration. The intention is to bring calmness and peacefulness into the process of meditation.

2. *Ekatva vitarka avicāra* (state of unification of vocal revelations and thoughts): As the spiritual seeker makes progress, meditation becomes more stable and mature. In this stage, the amalgamated flow of entities, their revelations, and the meditator's thoughts cease to exist separately. Here *ekatva* refers to the state of "oneness," *avicāra* means being "beyond discursive consideration" of the "revelations or sounds" (*vitarka*) derived from worldly entities. The object of meditation is revealed in the seeker's mind, unmitigated by the epiphenomenal features of the practitioner's psychology and objects around them, and the subject of meditation is perceived as a singular entity.
3. *Sūkṣma kriyā apratipatti* (state of internalized concentration): The state of *samādhi* intensifies after the unwieldy flow of the activities of mind, body, and speech, and revelations from external objects have been calmed. At this stage, *samādhi* involves only inhaling and exhaling breath. Here all subtle (*sūkṣma*) acts (*kriyā*s) become non-performing (*apratipatti*). Everything else has disappeared now and the practitioner can calmly hear and virtually watch the incoming and outgoing breaths.
4. *Vyuparata kriyā nirvṛtti* (state of exalted oblivion): Finally, after all the subtle activities have been entirely stopped, the practitioner reaches this spectacularly radiant and ecstatic stage. This involves cessation (*nirvṛtti*) of all actions (*kriyā*s) that have persisted (*vyuparata*), and

all body parts and spiritual organs reach mystical calmness, just like Sumerū Parvata.[11] Influenced by this state of deep meditation, one can experience the benefits of complete liberation without actually being there. This is the highest form of deep meditation. It is free of any and all uncertainties.

Samādhi is the deep meditation that is the apex of the eight stages of the *dhyāna-yoga* meditative process that culminates with *śukla-dhyāna*, the final stage of the practice. It is hard to fully explain the state of deep meditation in words since it can only be truly known through experience.

The Practice of Yogic Meditation (Dhyāna-Yoga Sādhanā)

Meditation is that state of consciousness where all experiences and perceptions come together and merge into one. In this state, all contemplations are harmonized, and all differentiations between wisdom and seeker are eliminated. Meditation is one of the intrinsic abilities of the soul and it is an abstract state that evolves from the concentration of mind. Here all mental inclinations, which are normally wandering, become focused on a single object chosen by the seeker. Therefore, all dhārmic philosophies of India have emphasized the importance of meditation.

The practice of meditation has some extraordinary powers associated with it. There are some energy centers in the human body associated with different levels of consciousness. When the mind is oriented on the lower-body energy centers, it is consumed by derogatory thoughts such as anger, passions, and fear. The body becomes unhealthy and the mind becomes restless. The individual starts losing interest in honorable thoughts and auspicious traits. Such negative tendencies manifest into immoral behavioral patterns and demeaning actions.

The situation reverses when one ascends from the lower-body energy centers and starts focusing on those in the upper body. Now, the individual starts uniting with the subtle, worthy, and powerful elements of nature. The person starts detaching from malicious tendencies and begins experiencing

---

[11] Sumerū Parvata, also known as Merū Parvata, is a five-peaked mountain (*parvata*) in Jain, Buddhist, and Hindu cosmology. It is considered to be the center of universe from spiritual, physical, and metaphysical perspectives.

worthy tendencies such as fearlessness and love for others. In this state, they feel the oneness of noble thoughts and behavior, and are impelled by honorable principles.

A human being starts attaining peace and spiritual strength only when his or her mind starts focusing inward. A mind preoccupied with distracted thoughts and adulterated mental tendencies is not capable of receiving thoughts of a spiritual nature. The only way out of this vicious cycle is to bring the mind and senses under control through the rigorous practice of meditation.

The tradition of meditation practice seeks to keep the practitioner calm and quiet, and apart from the chaos of daily life. Meditation is the method by which a soul can enlighten itself. It is a divine art to search for the real self within. It is an ancient gift of extreme importance, and meditation is the essence of spiritual *yoga*.

Jain Yoga and Haṭha-Yoga

There are a lot of similarities between the practice of Jain *yoga* and *haṭha-yoga* commonly practiced in India. For example, there are similar emphases on *prāṇa* currents of the subtle body (*nāḍī*s) such as the *iḍā* and *piṅgalā* currents that form the conscious basis of the body. When in a deep meditation state, the practitioner merges these with the central *suṣumṇā* current and goes beyond the superficial awareness of the physical body.[12]

Another common practice between the two *yoga* systems is called *trāṭaka*, where the practitioner stands under the sun and firmly fixes the eyes on one tiny black object on the ground, like the top of one's shadow. Then slowly the meditator closes the eyelids and fixates the internal vision on the glowing point between the eyes. While doing this, they move the glowing point away from the focus point and experience the combination of subtle sound and light. These are early stages of experiencing the pure form of the soul. In addition, Jain *yoga* also teaches methods of deep meditation by standing still in a vertical posture and concentrating on the ground.

Yoga, Meditation, and Penance: Three Connected Spiritual Practices

The practice of spiritual immersion in India's dhārmic traditions has three

[12] *Nāḍī* is to the subtle body what nerves are to the physical, and *iḍā*, *piṅgalā*, and *suṣumṇā* are the major arteries of the subtle body.

key components: *yoga*, meditation (*dhyāna*), and penance (*tapas*). These are three wonderful and essential components of spiritual practices.

- *Yoga*: In general, *yoga* is considered the foundation of *vaidika* (Vedic) doctrine by numerous ascetics since the period when the Upaniṣads were created. The ascetics immersed themselves in rigorous *yoga* practices in forests away from the cities and developed extensive systems for *yoga* practices even for others who are householders. The aphorisms of *yoga* presented in the Upaniṣads were compiled in a single system by the great ascetic Patañjali, who created the *Yogasūtra* with a great rigor.
- *Meditation*: The essence of Buddhist doctrine (*piṭaka-gata*) is meditation practice. Lord Buddha considered meditation as the center of his perseverance, and the practice has continued for centuries among Buddhists. Lord Buddha experimented with, and practiced, multiple types of meditation during his life. The same practices were followed by his disciples, and continue to be practiced by Buddhist ascetics today. The extent to which the description of meditation, its analysis, and its different forms are provided in Buddhist philosophy are not found in any other philosophy. *Vipaśyanā* (*vipassanā* in Pāli) meditation is well known throughout the world. The greatest perseverance by Lord Buddha was the practice of meditation, and that was the means of his discovery of the fundamental truth.
- *Penance*: Jain doctrine considers penance as the foundation of spiritual perseverance, although *yoga* and meditation are highly emphasized and considered critical for spiritual progression. From Lord Ṛṣabhadeva to Lord Mahāvīra, the twenty-four *tīrthaṅkara*s attained their clairvoyance and wisdom through the rigorous practice of penance. Lord Mahāvīra attained an extreme level of penance, not achieved by any other revered ascetic. He was immersed in the fervor of intense penance for almost twelve and a half years, which is an extrordinary feat only Lord Mahāvīra could accomplish. The level of his intensity in twelve types of penance practices remains unmatched. These twelve penance practices have remained prevalent in Jain traditions through the centuries, and penance has always been the foundation of Jain

doctrine.

In summary, *yoga* is a solemn spiritual practice involving control and navigation of the mind, body, and speech to connect oneself with divinity. The most important constituents of *yoga* practice involve focusing the mind on divinity, invigorating the body to stimulate the mind to reach the state of union with nature, and controlling speech to help remove all disturbances. Physical exercise, which is mistakenly equated to *yoga* these days, is only a small factor. *Yoga* is strongly emphasized in Jain, Vedāntic, and Buddhist doctrines. The objectives are similar, but its practices vary from one doctrine to the other. For Jains *yoga* is considered a critical vehicle in the journey towards ultimate liberation. *Yoga* practice helps accelerate the shedding of kārmic particles (*nirjara*) while opening doors for spiritual progression. That is why *dhāraṇā* and *dhyāna* are considered very important for meditation. The practice of *dhyāna* takes the seeker to the state of *samādhi*, the gateway to salvation. *Yoga* is thus an important contributor to the pursuit of salvation.

10

Spiritual Progression (Ādhyātmika Utkrānti)

Fourteen Virtuous Stages

We know that according to Jain doctrine, there are innumerable souls in this world and each has its own independent existence. None of the souls is an appendage (*aṁśa*) of any superior entity.[1] While all of the souls (*jīva*s) have identical fundamental characteristics (*guṇa*s) of vigor (*vīrya*), consciousness (*cetanā*), and bliss (*sukha*), they also maintain their own separate identities. In spite of their common fundamental characteristics, their apparent distinctions are a result (*pariṇāma*) of the unique paths they traverse while encaged in their respective bodily forms that continuously change (*paryāya*), acquiring new modes (i.e., at birth) while discarding old ones (i.e., at death). All souls have been bound by *karma* since beginningless time due to their personal set of actions over innumerable lifespans they have gone through. As a result of their unique behavior and thoughts, along with other activities of the mind, body, and speech, every soul develops its own customized pattern of kārmic accumulation. The accumulated *karma*s form layers of kārmic residue (*karma-pudgala*s) over the soul, and their strength, duration, attachment, detachment, depth, etc., determine the state of the individual soul and its characteristics, such as its state of delusion, knowledge, and its associated bodily form. The individuals who have awakened and have grasped the principles of right perception while going through these changes work hard for the spiritual progression, called *ādhyātmika utkrānti*. These spiritual aspirants are on an ascending trajectory towards the ultimate liberation.

The uniqueness in the state of a soul occurs at two levels. First, at any

---

[1] For example, certain theistic schools of Vedānta see the soul as having only qualified individuality, but it is in reality merely an appendage (*aṁśa*) of God.

given time, the actions of the body associated with one soul are different from the actions of those of the other souls. Second, one specific soul has one body in one life and a different one in another life. Correspondingly, the actions of the body associated with the soul in one life are different from the actions of the body associated with the same soul in another life. These actions from life to life result in the spiritual uplift or decline of the soul from one life to the other. At the same time, all other souls are going through similar ups and downs of their own. These individual, yet comparative, changes in the state of a soul, when accumulated over the multiple lives, account for the uniqueness in its state.

The stages of progression in the spiritual attainment of the soul have been classified in different ways by different doctrines and scholars. One system classifies all souls into three spiritual categories:

1. *Bahirātmā* (alienated from one's true nature of soul): In this state a bonded soul is engaged in false beliefs (*mithyā-darśī*).
2. *Antarātmā* (internalized towards one's true nature of the soul): Here a soul is on its journey of spiritual progress with truthful beliefs and perceptions (*samyag-darśī*).
3. *Paramātmā* (the soul at its true and highest state): This refers to an eternally liberated soul after attaining omniscient perception, supreme conduct, and boundless spiritual wisdom (*sarva-darśī*).

Jain philosophy goes further and divides the above three categories into a total of fourteen classes, called *guṇa-sthāna*s, which can be translated to and understood as "characteristic stages" or "virtuous stages" of a soul's spiritual travails (*bhūmika*). The term is unique to Jain Dharma, and all states and characteristics of the soul are incorporated within these fourteen virtuous stages. Within their own realm, one can assess one's spiritual status and their upward or downward progression. Of the fourteen stages, the first three belong to *bahirātmā*, the fourth to twelfth belong to *antarātmā,* and the last two stages belong to *paramātmā*.

The term *guṇa* has previously been used to refer to the qualities or characteristics of a soul. There are five basic dispositions of a soul, depending on its characteristics or natural tendencies (*guṇa*s). They are:

1. *Audāyika* (resulting from fruition of *karmas*): The disposition of the soul created by the natural or involuntary emergence of previously accumulated *karmas*.
2. *Kṣāyika* (resulting from destruction of *karmas*): The disposition of the soul created by the destruction of previously accumulated *karmas* (or the discarding of accumulated *karma-pudgalas*). This happens through the process of *nirjara*, comprising natural fruition and the wearing away of the *karmas*, or through resolute spiritual efforts.
3. *Aupaśamika* (resulting from the ceasing of *karma* accumulation): The disposition of the soul created by the mitigation of the passions (*kaṣāyas* – anger, ego, deceit, and greed) which cause the influx of kārmic particles upon the soul and their attachment in layers over it. The *aupaśamika* state represents the impediment of kārmic accumulation (*saṁvara*).
4. *Kṣayopaśamika* (calming or *upaśamika* and diminution of *kṣayas*): The disposition of the soul created by destroying or suppressing previously accumulated *karmas* through self-efforts.
5. *Pāriṇāmika* (intrinsic state): The disposition of the soul that is its natural state. The *jīva* is no more in a depraved form created by the rise of previously accumulated *karmas*.

The progression of a soul is eternal, and in reality, its precise classification is virtually impossible on the basis of the above five characteristics alone. The actual specificity of each individual soul may necessitate a much broader rubric since nuance could be lost in these general categories. This is why Jain scholars have divided the path into fourteen virtuous stages as compared to the above-listed five, so as to understand the state of a soul with greater nuance. The fourteen *guṇa-sthānas*[2] (virtuous stages) are listed below and their descriptions follow:

1. *Mithyātva guṇa-sthāna* (the stage of falsehood or delusions)
2. *Sāsvādana guṇa-sthāna* (the stage of tasting of right belief)

---

[2] In general, the word *guṇa* refers to "good qualities," but here, *guṇa* is used for "quality" in a generic sense that connotes both sensible (auspicious) and reckless (inauspicious) aspects of one's character.

3. *Miśra guṇa-sthāna* (the stage of mixed perceptions)
4. *Avirata-samyag-dṛṣṭi guṇa-sthāna* (the stage of right vision [*samyag-dṛṣṭi*] but devoid of vows and restraint [*avirata*])
5. *Deśa-virati guṇa-sthāna* (the stage of partial vows and initial restraint)
6. *Pramatta guṇa-sthāna* (the stage of total control with somewhat imperfect vows [*pramatta*])
7. *Apramatta guṇa-sthāna* (the stage of complete self-control without carelessness)
8. *Apūrva-karaṇa guṇa-sthāna* (the stage of unprecedented undertakings and accomplishments)
9. *Anivṛtti-karaṇa guṇa-sthāna* (the stage of not turning back)
10. *Sūkṣma-samparāya guṇa-sthāna* (the stage of conquering subtle delusions and passions)
11. *Upaśānta-moha guṇa-sthāna* (the stage of pacified delusions)
12. *Kṣīṇa-moha guṇa-sthāna* (the stage of destroyed delusions)
13. *Sayogī-kevalī guṇa-sthāna* (the stage of the omniscient spiritual conqueror in bodily form)
14. *Ayogī-kevalī guṇa-sthāna* (the stage of the omniscient spiritual conqueror with ultimate liberation)

STAGES OF ALIENATION FROM ONE'S SOUL (BAHIRĀTMĀ)

1. *Mithyātva guṇa-sthāna* (the stage of falsehood or delusions): This lower state is characterized by spurious or delusional perception regarding the state of one's soul with respect to the above-mentioned five characteristics (*audāyika, kṣāyika, aupaśamika, kṣayopaśamika,* and *pāriṇāmika*). The *jīva* is not yet awakened to the righteous (Jain) doctrine and its state is such that hypocrisy is present rather than a genuine understanding and unpretentious faith. This results in attachment to narrow, one-sided misperceptions, and the incorporation of inauspicious traits such as belief in false doctrines. An individual in this state considers that which is the actual fundamental truth to

be untrue, sees moral acts as wicked acts, and welfare as destructive. In terms of spiritual penance, such an individual misses the path by ignoring or not understanding the differences between responsible and irresponsible actions. Such an individual is deeply involved in worldly attachments and is guided by malicious acts of anger, ego, deceit, and greed (*kaṣāyas*). This is a reckless movement of the soul in the direction that is opposite to spiritual advancement.

Most of the souls are in *mithyātva guṇa-sthāna*. This is the first stage of progression, which is before or at the beginning of one's spiritual journey of austerity and penance. Here the individual is consumed by delusional (*mithyā*) perception (*darśana* or *dṛṣṭi*) and is regularly engaged in adverse activities. It is from here that the soul must learn to recognize falsehood and then destroy and/or quash it to make initial progress towards the higher virtuous stages. One must remember that the soul that progresses by destroying falsehood never falls back to this depraved level. On the other hand, the soul that progresses by simply suppressing and not destroying the falsehood tendencies is sure to fall back to this level.

2. *Sāsvādana guṇa-sthāna* (the stage of tasting right belief): This is a state where a *jīva* falls from a higher stage due to emergence of delusional perception resulting from inauspicious *karmas*. When the soul progresses towards righteousness by merely suppressing false beliefs without destroying them, it eventually reverts to the original status of *mithyātva guṇa-sthāna* (first virtuous stage). The *sāsvādana guṇa-sthāna* stage is a transitional state where the *jīva* resides for a very short duration when it is falling from a higher stage but has not fully reverted to *mithyā-dṛṣṭi* or the falsehood state. During the very short period of this state, the soul begins to somewhat enjoy the benefits of the higher spiritual consciousness together with a high risk of regression.

3. *Miśra guṇa-sthāna* (the stage of mixed perceptions): Like the other *bahirātmā* states (the first two virtuous stages), this state is characterized by the bonded soul being engaged in false beliefs (*mithyā-darśī*) although it has attained some righteousness (*samyag-darśī*). Thus, at this third level, the *jīva* is engaged in a "mixture" (*miśra*) of activities consisting of undertakings that are driven by both truthful and false

perceptions. Although this stage is higher than *mithyātva guṇa-sthāna* (first virtuous stage), the soul continues to waver due to the lack of purely noble traits. This stage is also of a very short duration like the second virtuous state (*sāsvādana guṇa-sthāna*), and a soul passes through this stage when going from the first to the fourth stage, or vice versa.

INTERNALIZED STAGES TOWARDS ONE'S SOUL (ANTARĀTMĀ)

4. *Avirata-samyag-dr̥ṣṭi guṇa-sthāna* (the stage of right perception [*samyag-dr̥ṣṭi*] devoid of vows and restraint [*avirata*]): Consider a soul that has achieved pure perception by destroying and/or suppressing most of the deluding (*mohanīya*) *karma*s (see chapter 11) which obstruct right perception (*samyag-darśana*). However, because it has not yet been able to destroy all of the *mohanīya-karma*s, especially those that obstruct virtuous conduct, this *jīva* is in *avirata-samyag-dr̥ṣṭi guṇa-sthāna*. This is the stage where the *jīva* is not completely controlled and therefore cannot fully adopt all of the supreme spiritual principles.

   Nevertheless, at this stage, the *jīva* has gained at least a partial vision of the right perception (*samyag-darśana*) of fundamental truth, which is the first of the three essential virtues (*ratnatraya* or Three Jewels) to attain salvation, the other two being right knowledge (*samyag-jñāna*) and right conduct (*samyag-cāritra*). *Samyag-darśana* constitutes the first ascetic step to attain eternal salvation, as discussed earlier. The soul with the partial gleaning of supreme perception at the level of *avirata-samyag-dr̥ṣṭi guṇa-sthāna* may not be able to fully embody restraint, but it can attain knowledge at this level. Such a living being is fully empowered with knowledge of the virtues of living and non-living beings and is aware of the spiritually beneficial and non-beneficial traits. Although one has not fully overcome passionate enjoyments, one is not attached to them either, and has developed the ability to control one's thoughts. Such a person becomes compassionate upon witnessing afflicted beings in pain, and her or his objective and undertakings are purified. The individual now has a proper view of right perception (*samyag-darśana*) and is eager to walk on the path of restraint. In some sense, this stage could be considered as the gateway to higher stages of enlightenment, and a soul which achieves this stage will eventually progress towards the ultimate liberation.

5. *Deśa-virati guṇa-sthāna* (the stage of partial vows and initial restraint): This level is achieved after attaining right perception (*samyag-darśana*) in the previous state. By now, the aspirant has partially overcome non-restraint (*avirati*), allowing one to at least partly adhere to the limited vows (*aṇuvratas*) of non-violence (*ahiṁsā*), truthfulness (*satya*), non-stealing (*asteya*), carnal restraint (*brahmacarya*), and non-possession (*aparigraha*). Here, one is starting to live a spiritually healthy householder life without major sin, even if not being able to give up subtle offenses. The conduct of such an individual, *samyag-cāritra*, is described in chapter 12.

6. *Pramatta guṇa-sthāna* (the stage of total control with somewhat imperfect vows [*pramatta*]): This occurs when a living being is excelling at conquering the spiritual defects and becomes a true ascetic. This individual completely abides by the five major vows (*mahāvratas*), which are the same vows as the limited vows (*aṇuvratas*), only they are fully restrictive at this level. Such a soul is now in a state of inattentive or natural control (*pramatta-viratta*), but due to occasional carelessness, there may be inconsistencies in following the major vows. The spiritual seeker is in complete control (*sarva-virati*) at this stage and can become a monk but still cannot fully end the distractions of the passions (*kaṣāyas*), such as laziness, involvement in small sinful acts that result in collecting *karma*, excessive sleep, belief in obtuse stories, and indulgence in carnal passions. Some of the hard-to-control negative traits at this stage are: intoxication due to physical substances (*madya*); indulgences in sensory gratification (*viṣaya*); passions of anger, ego; deceit, greed (*kaṣāya*, as previously discussed); excessive sleep and lethargy (*nidrā*); and unnecessary and provocative talk about women (opposite gender, or gender one is attracted to) and materialistic things like food (*niṣprayojana*). Although non-restraint or incontinence (*avirati*) has been overcome, there is still temptation and inconsistency at this level.

7. *Apramatta guṇa-sthāna* (the stage of complete self-control without carelessness): This virtuous stage (*guṇa-sthāna*) marks the beginning of a serious ascent towards spiritual awakening. At this stage, the spiritual seeker is focused on reaching the summit of liberation and arrives at a

juncture where his inner thoughts are unabatedly pure and radiant. Here the spiritual aspirant is observing the vows without any carelessness, and all passions and other distractions have ended. The practitioner is now carefully engrossed in meditation and inner reflections.

The practitioners in the *apramatta guṇa-sthāna* stage can be divided into two classes: *svasthāna apramatta* and *sātiśaya apramatta*. In the *svasthāna* class, which is established in this virtuous stage itself, the seeker repeatedly rises to the seventh stage of *apramatta*, but falls back to the lower stage (stage six, *pramatta guṇa-sthāna*). To start with, the seeker is completely engrossed in self-awareness and spirituality but when that inclination subsides, they fall back to the previous state. The regression could be due to worries or other negative thoughts, or external activities such as inappropriate speech, consumption of wrong food, and other such actions.

For the practitioners in the *sātiśaya* class, inappropriate acts and intentions diminish and finally disappear. The tendencies, which once again become pure, allow the spiritual seeker to rise to the higher level of the seventh stage of *apramatta*.

The *sātiśaya apramatta* class of practitioners may be further divided into two subclasses. The first subclass is *upaśama śreṇī*, the subclass of suppressed *karma*s, where the seeker ascends by suppressing deluding (*mohanīya*) *karma*s and continues to attain higher stages until the eleventh *guṇa-sthāna*. However, the progress stops there, and such a seeker can fall back when the suppressed *karma*s are awakened again. But in the second subclass, *kṣapaka śreṇī*, the subclass of eliminated *karma*s, the practitioners ascend by eliminating the deluding effects of all infatuations. But instead of rising up to the eleventh *guṇa-sthāna*, such a practitioner may bypass the eleventh virtuous stage and enter into the twelfth or thirteenth *guṇa-sthāna*. With appropriate efforts, they may even reach the beginning of the highest state.

8. *Apūrva-karaṇa guṇa-sthāna* (the stage of unprecedented undertakings and accomplishments): Here the word *apūrva* means unprecedented, and the word *karaṇa* refers to causation but can also mean "undertaking," "resolution," "consequences," or "thoughts." Hence, *apūrva-karaṇa* is

the *guṇa-sthāna* where unprecedented accomplishments and levels of determination appear apart from previous kārmic causation. Having destroyed or suppressed the deluded *karmas* (*mohanīya-karma* – the *karma* that leads to anger, ego, deceit, greed), the aspirant starts experiencing higher tendencies towards spiritual advancement in this state. Here, wonderful signs can be seen in the consequences of these novel actions.

9. *Anivr̥tti-karaṇa guṇa-sthāna* (the stage of not turning back): In this ninth stage, the achievements of the seventh stage become even stronger with purer thoughts and inclinations. The eminent achievements of the *sātiśaya* class of *apramatta* practitioners of stage seven become even better as adverse intentions and other mental trepidations are now eliminated, irrespective of their traits and intensity. The natural flow of thoughts becomes positive, focused, and attuned with nature, and the seeker's innermost, subtle, and hidden carnal desires are eliminated at their very roots.

10. *Sūkṣma-samparāya guṇa-sthāna* (the stage of conquering subtle delusions and passions): In this state only the minutest and subtle delusional *karma* (*mohanīya-karma*) remains. By the time the spiritual seeker reaches this level, that person has eliminated or suppressed most of the *mohanīya-karmas* (anger, ego, deceit, and greed) and has fully ended the conversion of actions (*karmas*) into soul-obstructing kārmic stains (*leśyās*) and passions (*kaṣāyas*) and their attachment to the soul. Only exceedingly subtle (*sūkṣma*) fragments of greed account for the surviving components of the *mohanīya-karma*.

11. *Upaśānta-moha guṇa-sthāna* (the stage of pacified delusions): Here all of the passions (*kaṣāyas*) have been pacified (*upaśānta*), including the subtle ones (*sūkṣma*) that remained at the tenth level. Imagine a soldier who somehow and by some peculiar means finds a way to enter the enemy territory and finds them unconscious as he advances through their ranks. After a while, the enemy regains consciousness and the soldier finds himself completely surrounded. The enemy attacks and the soldier meets his end. Spiritual practioners may find themselves in a similar situation while progressing through different *guṇa-sthāna* stages if they have only suppressed *mohanīya-karmas* without completely

destroying them. Such practioners, like the soldier above, will find their progression reversed when the undestroyed *mohanīya-karmas* are awakened again. At this level of *upaśānta-moha guṇa-sthāna*, although the *mohanīya-karmas* have been entirely suppressed, they have not yet been destroyed. Therefore, the seeker may spend just a little time in this eleventh stage, but may once again revert to one of the lower stages as soon as the dormant *karmas* become active.

12. *Kṣīṇa-moha guṇa-sthāna* (the stage of destroyed delusions): Unlike the previous level where the *mohanīya-karmas* had only been appeased (*upaśānta*), here all delusional *karmas* (anger, ego, deceit, and greed) have been destroyed (*kṣīṇa*). This includes the elimination of the final subtle component of delusions. *Mohanīya-karma* is one of the four destructive (*ghātīya*) *karmas*, and is the basis of all of the other three *karmas*: "knowledge-obscuring" (*jñānāvaraṇīya*) *karmas*, "perception-obscuring" (*darśanāvaraṇīya*) *karmas*, and "generally obstructing" (*antarāya*) *karmas*. After *mohanīya-karma* has been annihilated in this stage, the other three are soon eliminated. Once these have been eliminated, the *jīva* progresses to the last two *paramātmā* stages of the *guṇa-sthāna*.

PARAMĀTMĀ STAGES: THE SOUL AT ITS HIGHEST

13. *Sayogī-kevalī guṇa-sthāna* (the stage of the omniscient spiritual conqueror in bodily form): At this stage, all the passions have been destroyed, and there is unabridged and complete wisdom. The soul has now attained an all-encompassing wisdom (*sarvajña*), unlimited perception (*sarva-darśī*), and ultimate spiritual potency (*ādhyātmika vīrya*). At this stage, all four *ghātika karmas* (hurtful *karmas* – *jñānāvaraṇīya, darśanāvaraṇīya, antarāya,* and *mohanīya* – see chapter 11) have been completely destroyed, and the *jīva* is all set for the final liberation from life-and-death cycles. The word *sayogī* means in "union with divinity" and the use of this term in this stage indicates that the *jīva*'s embodied transactions of mind, body, and speech cease to act. However, the soul remains embodied with activity (*sayoga*) due to the force of lifespan (*āyu* or *āyusya*) *karma*. This is the state of the embodied soul of the *arhat, kevalin, jina,* or *tīrthaṅkara*.

14. *Ayogī-kevalī guṇa-sthāna* (the stage of the omniscient spiritual conqueror with ultimate liberation): This is the final state that can be attained just before the *jīva* discards its body and becomes free of the body and speech on the way to the final liberation. The state of *ayoga-kevalī* has very short duration, roughly equal to the time it takes to recite the vowels of the alphabet at an average speed, and is attained through a meditation called *śukla-dhyāna*. In this state, all transactions of mind, body, and speech are eliminated, all connections with worldly affairs cease, and the soul achieves its natural state where it will remain beyond liberation. Having ended the four hurtful (*ghātika*) *karma*s (*mohanīya, jñānāvaraṇīya, darśanāvaraṇīya,* and *antarāya*), the soul eliminates the remaining four non-destructive (*aghātika*) *karma*s of lifespan (*āyu* or *āyuṣya*), embodiment (*nāma*), status or clan (*gotra*), and physical experiences (*vedanīya*). Now the soul is completely free of all kārmic particles forever.

The culmination of the fourteen virtuous stages (*guṇa-sthāna*s) represents the end of reincarnation where the *jīva* continuously transmigrates through cycles of life and death. After the completion of the final *guṇa-sthāna*, the soul achieves perfection in all respects – perfect perception, unbounded perfect wisdom, and perfect conduct. The *jīva* attains *mokṣa* after discarding all eight *karma*s (see chapter 11). Thereafter, the *jīva* attains *nirvāṇa* – an eternally liberated bodiless form – and settles in this state in *siddha-loka*, considered to be at the top of the universe in Jain cosmology.

By meditating on the *guṇa-sthāna*s, one is infused with the inspiration to engage in the efforts of spiritual progression. Each soul begins from the early stages and moves upwards with emergence of spiritual vigor. By the time the *jīva* reaches the fourth state, its perception becomes truthful. When its perception is purified, it systematically starts moving towards the ultimate salvation. By the time it reaches the twelfth state, it is freed of all the blockages. In the thirteenth state, it becomes an embodied Supreme Being, and in the fourteenth, it loses bodily form as well, and reaches the final destination of perpetual liberation.

This sequence of progression demonstrates that Jain Dharma does not consider any single entity as existing eternally beyond *saṁsāra* as the timeless,

Supreme Being; that is the criterion for God in other doctrines (such as Hindu Dharma). In Jain Dharma, every living being is entitled to reach the supreme state with appropriate spiritual efforts, and none is ever barred from this process.

11

Doctrine of Karma (Karmavāda)

ALL spiritual doctrines of the world have developed and espoused their own specific underlying perspectives about the fundamentals of life. Through these perspectives they have developed theories to conceptualize and explain the origination and existence of life and the astounding variations of different living beings. Like other religious traditions, Jain, Buddhist, and Hindu philosophies also seek to explain such concepts in great detail; and in addition, due to their belief in rebirth, they address the different states and types of life forms that a soul embodies from one life to the other. While they might disagree on the specifics, for these doctrines all living beings are fundamentally spiritually equal despite the differing external, material states of different species.

Certain questions are bound to arise when considering the seemingly paradoxical ontology of various doctrines. For example, how is it that all souls are eternal while at the same time living beings are subjected to death? If an all-encompassing consciousness (*virāṭ cetanā*) is the intrinsic characteristic (*svarūpa*) of a soul, how can it be that most living beings seem insensible (*jaḍatā*) due to their ignorance (*ajñāna*)? How can we expain the illuminating power of consciousness that is inherent to *jīva*s while simultaneously considering the seemingly impenetrable darkness (*gahana andhakāra*) of careless behavior that beings exhibit? One might further ask, if the soul is formless and shapeless then why is it caged within a body?

These types of questions regarding the paradoxes of the living entity (*jīva-virodhī*) cannot be answered without an acceptable explanation regarding the proposed ontology (*sattā*). Various Hindu philosophies explain these issues in different ways. For example, in Vedāntic philosophy, such paradoxes are explained with the ontology of *māyā* (illusion) and *avidyā* (ignorance).

Sāṁkhya philosophy attributes these variations to natural processes (*prakṛti*), while Vaiśeṣika philosophy attributes them to fate (*adṛṣṭa*).

Jain doctrine approaches this differently since it attributes the above-mentioned variations in living beings to their own actions alone. This is explained through the *karma* theory epitomizing the paradoxical nature of embodied existence. Although every dhārmic doctrine has its own version of *karma* theory, Jain philosophy is unique and extensive in its exhaustive presentation of *karma* doctrine and its logical considerations from different perspectives.

As discussed earlier, matter (*pudgala*) occurs in multiple states and classes (*vargaṇas*). It has also been mentioned that kārmic matter is ubiquitously dispersed over the entire universe as subtle particles that attach to form layers over the soul when attracted by the actions of the body. Kārmic particles are not an intrinsic part of the soul. Their presence in layers over the soul distort the soul's capacities, and when overlooked, they tend to control it. The soul becomes consumed by its body's materialistic distractions that are not natural to it. While indulging in such delusional activities under the influence of passions, attachments, jealousy, and malice, living beings may consider some of those activities as pleasant and some others as miserable. The experiences associated with the pleasant and unpleasant subside quickly, but their after-effects could last for a long time. The latent impressions (*saṁskāras*) acquired during these activities come to fruition at an appropriate future time with commensurate intensity.

All traits of living beings result from these *saṁskāras* influenced by the tendencies of desire or attachment (*rāga*) and malice or aversion (*dveṣa*). Each *saṁskāra* leaves behind a trait, which in turn gives rise to another impression. This cycle of action to fructification, to impression, to re-emerging tendency has continued throughout the eons that the soul has been in existence.

There are two major categories of *karma* (aka *karma-vargaṇa*):

1. *Dravya-karma* (substance *karma*): The physical manifestation of actions where *karma* is understood as subtle matter (*pudgala*).
2. *Bhāva-karma* (psychological *karma*): The mental manifestation of *karma* in one's thoughts.

The above two categories have a relation of mutual causation – *dravya-karma* is produced by *bhāva-karma* and vice versa. When previously collected *dravya-karma* produce their undesirable results, living beings experience certain *bhāva-karma* that affect their thoughts, such as passion and malice. Such thoughts, in turn, may inspire new physical acts through actions by body and speech, and the cycle continues as it has since beginningless time. But it is possible to terminate this cycle, and the means for that are in the seeker's own power. As discussed in chapter 6, the production of either *dravya-karma* or *bhāva-karma* can be stopped with appropriate, deliberate efforts.

A *karma*-bound *jīva* tends to divide all other entities of the world into two categories – those aligned with it and the others aligned against it. A *jīva* develops attraction and attachment towards those that are aligned with it and abhors those in opposition, seeking to eliminate them. Such feelings are fertile ground for the creation and growth of attachments and aversions (*rāga–dveṣa*). These tendencies result in the accumulation of kārmic particles which give rise to countless miseries. Therefore, so long as *rāga* and *dveṣa* exist, every action will be converted to kārmic particles that form layers of bondage over the soul and obstruct it from making spiritual progress.

No external forces are needed to trigger kārmic repercussions. The results are as inevitable as the effects of the consumption of alcohol, milk, food, or water which result in intoxication, nourishment, energy, and thirst-quenching respectively. The accumulated *karma*s are lifeless by themselves, but their resulting effects are autonomous and self-propelled (*svatantratā*), which give rise to the consequences. The timing, magnitude, and type of repercussions are determined by an unknowable but judicious and well-defined set of formulae. Living beings have the freedom to execute actions as they desire, but they have no control over the consequences. The laws of *karma* alone control the inevitable consequences of one's actions.

It is a principle of Āyurveda that while consuming food one should refrain from all undesirable and inauspicious predispositions of anger, aggression, etc. When one's mind is dignified and at peace, the consumed food works like an elixir for health. To the contrary, in absence of mental calmness, the same food would have unhealthy and toxic effects. *Karma* acts in a similar way. The quality of the kārmic results depends on: (1) whether the individual's internal thoughts and/or actions are auspicious or inauspicious, and (2) the intensity of such mental acts and/or the ensuing physical actions.

The mind is the main source of kārmic bondage, and one's speech and body assist it. There are innumerable auspicious and inauspicious inclinations of the mind-body-speech complex. In terms of the mind's actions, planning to kill, hurt, imprison, and cheat are some examples of a bad mental disposition, while contemplating on spiritual principles and feeling elated about others' success are some of the good examples. In terms of bodily actions, violence, theft, and sensual gratification produce some of the unfavorable effects, while compassion, service, graciousness, and renunciation produce favorable effects. When it comes to speech, untruthful, disrespectful, and crude language produces unfavorable effects, while truthful, pleasant, and harmonious language is favorable. The creation of auspicious kārmic reactions resulting from positive dealings and inauspicious reactions resulting from negative dealings are both, ultimately, sources of bondage since they both cause *karma* to bind to, and weigh down and cloud the soul. But auspicious *karma* is preferable because it is more likely to further one's spiritual development and ultimately allows one to reach the state of having no kārmic bondage at all. Therefore, it is of substantial value as a means to the highest state of being beyond *karma*.

In addition, the intention behind actions is of paramount importance in determining whether one's *karma* will be auspicious or inauspicious – and to what degree it will be either of these. For example, if a surgeon makes a cut on someone's body to hurt them, that surgeon would be bound with inauspicious *karma* even if the victim survives. On the other hand, if the same surgeon makes a cut with compassion during a surgery, he would earn auspicious *karma* even if the patient loses his life during the surgery. Thus, intention behind an action may be more important than outcome.

As discussed in previous chapters, there are two main causes of kārmic bondage:

1. *Kaṣāya*s: Passions that cause the influx of kārmic particles (*pudgala*s) upon the soul triggered by the individual's actions, and their collection in layers over the soul with "coloration" or "staining" (*leśyā*) that correspond to one's actions.

2. *Yoga*: The voluntary or involuntary engagement in mind-body-speech actions that cause the creation of the influx of kārmic particles towards the soul.[1]

All other causes of kārmic adherence are included within these two categories. Referring to the stages of spiritual progression discussed in chapter 10, up to the tenth *guṇa-sthāna* (virtuous stage) both *kaṣāya* and *yoga* effectively cause kārmic bondage, but after that *yoga* remains as the only cause. Therefore, all the kārmic particles that get bound to the soul due to both *kaṣāya* and *yoga* are called *sāmparāyika* (relating to worldly interactions), and those due to *yoga* alone are called *īryāpathika* (relating to the path of ascending mendicant), since the higher levels of *guṇa-sthāna* are achieved by extremely disciplined ascetics. A highly esteemed spiritual seeker becomes inwardly focused after crossing the boundaries of *kaṣāya* in the tenth *guṇa-sthāna*, and engages in activities appropriate to that stage.

In order to understand the process of kārmic bonding, consider a metaphor whereby the soul is a clean wall, *kaṣāya*s are glue, *yoga* is the wind, and *karma* are the dust particles. The wall (*jīva*) is covered with glue (*kaṣāya*s), and dust particles (*karma*) are being carried by the blowing wind (*yoga*). Under these conditions, dust particles (*karma*) will get stuck to the *jīva*. Their attachment to the wall will be as strong as the *kaṣāya* or the force with which they come to wall (*yoga*). The *karma* will get attached whether they are dark and dirty, or they are white and sparkling with beauty (referring to the specific *leśyā*). If one were to remove the *kaṣāya*, the *karma* would still come but they wouldn't get attached. This is the difference between *sāmparāyika-karma* and *īryāpathika-karma*, mentioned above – *sāmparāyika-karma* is when the soul (wall) covered with *kaṣāya* will continue to build layers of attached *karma* being actuated by wind (*yoga*). *Īryāpathika-karma* is when *kaṣāya* is removed and the soul (wall) does not accumulate new layers, although the *karma* continues to be present because of *yoga* (the blowing of the wind). The flow of *karma* depends on *yoga* while bonding, and its intensity depends on *kaṣāya*.

---

1 *Note*: As discussed previously in chapters 9 and 10, the term *yoga* can mean not only the popular spiritually oriented mind-body exercise, but can also refer to the undesirable bondage of *karma* to the *jīva*. In this section, *yoga* refers to this latter definition.

As discussed in chapter 4, regarding principles of bondage (*bandha*), *kaṣāya* determines the timing of kārmic repercussions (*sthiti-bandha*) and their intensity (*rasa-bandha*). When *kaṣāya* is no longer present, *karmas* neither stay with the soul nor are they felt or experienced. With the presence of *yoga*, *karmas* do come but they do not stay. In fact, *kaṣāya* is the main cause of life–death cycles. As soon as *kaṣāya* ends, the soul attains its purity, and all the hurtful kārmic (*ghātika*) activities are demolished.

Classifications of Karmas

Karmas fall into different categories depending on the actions committed by living beings, their constantly changing mental states, intentions during those actions, and the effects produced by those actions. A *jīva* interacts with innumerable living beings, all the time, and correspondingly, propelled by the actions of mind, body, and speech, it commits acts of *dravya-karma* and *bhāva-karma* towards other beings in numerous ways which could be devious or kind-hearted. The consequences of the actions, although determined by a judicious, just, and not-yet-discovered unknown system,[2] are unfamiliar to the individuals engaged in those activities. Also unknown to the individual are the nature, duration, timing, type, intensity of outcome, and the level of impact of these repercussions. It is ironic that living beings continue to engage in such activities despite knowing that their actions have repercussions.

These factors point to the fact that kārmic acquisition is a multidimensional process, and there are innumerable *karmas* that a *jīva* engages in while in bodily form. Each of these innumerable *karmas* can be placed in one of the eight main types as listed below, followed by their explanations. They are grouped into two broad classes of *ghātika* and *aghātika karmas*, based on their effects.

1. *Ghātika* (hurtful) *karma*: *Ghātika* (also called *ghātīya*) *karmas* are hurtful because they negatively affect the soul by deluding its virtues such as knowledge (*jñāna*) and perception (*darśana*). They can be intensively or marginally destructive depending on their nature. The four *ghātika karmas* are:

---

[2] The system that determines consequences of one's actions is unknown to regular human beings because of their contemplative and wisdom limitations. It might be "knowable" or "known" to those who are the *kevala-jñānīs* – the esteemed souls who have attained perfect wisdom and perception.

i. *Jñānāvaraṇīya* (knowledge-inhibiting *karma*)

ii. *Darśanāvaraṇīya* (perception- or awareness-inhibiting *karma*)

iii. *Antarāya* (hindrance-causing *karma*)

iv. *Mohanīya* (delusion-causing *karma*)

2. *Aghātika* (non-hurtful) *karma*: *Aghātika* (also called *aghātīya*) *karmas* refer to non-destructive *karmas* that occur at a stage when all four *ghātika karmas* start to subside. *Aghātika karmas* present no obstruction to the spiritual progression of the soul. They cease to exist after they complete their natural course, and then detach from the soul so it can achieve the final liberation. The four *aghātika karmas* are:

i. *Vedanīya* (physical-experience-causing *karma*)

ii. *Āyuṣya* (lifespan-affecting *karma*)

iii. *Nāma* (designation of the *jīva*'s body-type *karma*)

iv. *Gotra* (clan of birth *karma*)

KNOWLEDGE-INHIBITING KARMA (JÑĀNĀVARAṆĪYA-KARMA)

These types of *karma* result from the accumulation of kārmic particles that obstruct the soul's intrinsic characteristics of true knowledge (*jñāna*). They hinder one's abilities to gain auspicious knowledge and regress their spiritual awakening. They are analogous to the clouds that cover the environment and block sunlight from reaching earth during daytime. *Jñānāvaraṇīya-karmas* are of five types that correspond to the five types of *jñāna* that have been discussed in chapter 4.[3]

PERCEPTION- OR AWARENESS-INHIBITING KARMA (DARŚANĀVARAṆĪYA-KARMA)

These are the accumulated kārmic particles that obstruct the soul's fundamental characteristics of true perception and awareness, called *darśana*. Their effect is analogous to the experience of an individual who has permission to meet the president but is stopped by the security guards from entering the chambers. That is to say, one may have access to knowledge (*jñāna*), but

---

[3] The five types of *jñāna* are: (1) *mati-jñāna* (empirical knowledge), (2) *śruta-jñāna* (scriptural knowledge), (3) *avadhi-jñāna* (clairvoyant knowledge), (4) *manaḥ-paryāya-jñāna* (mind-reading knowledge), and (5) *kevala-jñāna* (supreme wisdom).

darśanāvaraṇīya-karma prevents one from the necessary pre-condition of perceiving (*darśana*) that *jñāna* which constitutes understanding of one's self. The obstruction of true perception causes blindness that prevents perceiving the fundamental reality. *Darśanāvaraṇīya-karma* is of nine types:

1. *Cakṣu-darśanāvaraṇīya-karma*: This obstructs the eyes from visualizing the virtues in the objects it is seeing.
2. *Acakṣu-darśanāvaraṇīya-karma*: This obstructs the normal ability of the other four senses to observe and comprehend.
3. *Avadhi-darśanāvaraṇīya-karma*: This obstructs and limits the ability to observe and comprehend through means other than the five senses.
4. *Kevala-darśanāvaraṇīya-karma*: This obstructs and limits the ability to achieve complete perception.
5. *Nidrā-sāmānya-karma*: This causes excessive normal sleep (disillusionment) that diminishes the perception of reality.
6. *Nidrā-nidrā-karma*: This causes excessive deep sleep (disillusionment) that hampers perception.
7. *Pracalā-karma*: This causes mild laziness (lack of enthusiasm), like dozing off while sitting, which obstructs the ability to perceive.
8. *Pracalā-pracalā-karma*: This causes intense laziness (lack of enthusiasm); for example, walking around inattentively as if one is sleepwalking, which severely diminishes the ability to perceive.
9. *Satyānagṛddhi-karma*: This is an intense state of sleep, where metaphorically speaking, an individual can perform immensely difficult tasks under the spell of disillusionment, which would be impossible in the state of awareness.

The last five types of *darśanāvaraṇīya-karma* cause different levels of sleep or disillusionment depending on their type and intensity.

HINDRANCE-CAUSING KARMA (ANTARĀYA-KARMA)

The emergence of this *karma* creates obstacles in achieving what the living being is desirous of. It is of five types:

1. *Dānāntarāya karma* (obstacles regarding charitable giving): Giving is one of the most important auspicious acts. With the rise of this *karma*, an

individual may have all the intentions and compassion to donate but for some reason that person is not able to do so. For example, a family wants to donate food for Thanksgiving meals, the day before the event. They have bought the food but are caught in a traffic jam on way to deliver it. By the time they reach their intended destination, the agency is closed, and they cannot make the donation despite all of their intentions and efforts.

2. *Lābhāntarāya karma* (obstacles regarding benefits): Human beings are always looking forward to reaping the benefits of their good deeds. With the rise of this *karma*, an individual is lined up to receive certain kind of benefits, but for some unknown reason(s) it does not happen. For instance, one is in close proximity of a great teacher but does not avail oneself of the opportunity to learn, believing it could be done on a later day. However, when the individual is ready to learn, the teacher comes to the end of his life. Thus, the individual had the benefit of a great opportunity but was not able to benefit from it despite good intentions but an avoidable personal shortcoming of tardiness.
3. *Bhogāntarāya karma* (obstacles regarding enjoyment): In this case, one has the possession of a desired thing but cannot enjoy it. For instance, a predator hunts down its prey. However, as soon as it is ready to eat, a stronger predator shows up and takes over the prey. In this case, the first one worked hard and got its prey but could not consume it despite being very close to it.
4. *Upabhogāntarāya karma* (obstacles regarding repeated consumption): This is the case when *karma* obstructs the consuming and enjoying of goods that have recurring use, such as clothes or home and car. Consider a situation where a family builds a beautiful home on the edge of a hill overlooking a lake. A day before moving in, they discover that the house is built on landfill covering a former chemical disposal. Now the family has a house of their dreams but cannot enjoy it.
5. *Vīryāntarāya karma* (obstacles regarding vigor): This is the case when *karma* comes in the way of using one's own power and energy. They could be physical, psychological, or spiritual powers. Consider some examples:
   - A child has a healthy body and wants to be an athlete. However, an

acute heart condition develops and the child is not able to participate in sports.

- An individual desirous of undertaking penance becomes an ascetic but develops a disease that prevents that person from rigorous penance.
- A householder wants to do all the right things to lead an honorable life but is unable to do so due to reasons not under that person's control. For example, one wants to educate oneself, but marries a person who does not support that in spite of earlier assurances.

DELUSION-CAUSING KARMA (MOHANĪYA-KARMA)

Moha refers to intoxicating delusion that creates intense passions of *krodha* (anger), *māna* (ego or pride), *māyā* (deceitfulness), and *lobha* (greed), as discussed in chapter 8. *Mohanīya-karma* is of two types:

1. *Darśana-mohanīya-karma* (delusion regarding perception): This type of *mohanīya karma* creates obstructions to the acquisition and establishment of right perception in an individual. It has three forms:
   i. *Mithyātva-mohanīya-karma*: To believe in delusional or spurious philosophy and ignore the truthful and authentic doctrine preached by Lord Mahāvīra.
   ii. *Samyag-mithyātva-mohanīya-karma*: To be devoted to mixed delusional or spurious, and correct or truthful, doctrines.
   iii. *Samyaktva-mohanīya-karma*: To add impurities in devotion to one's right perception.
2. *Cāritra-mohanīya-karma* (delusion regarding conduct): This type of *mohanīya-karma* obstructs the attainment of right conduct (*cāritra*). It is caused by *kasāyas* and has two forms: (i) *kaṣāya-cāritra-mohanīya* (delusion regarding passionate conduct), and (ii) *Nau-kaṣāya-cāritra-mohanīya* (delusion regarding subsidiary passions).

   As discussed in chapter 8, there are four *kaṣāyas* (anger, ego, deceit, and greed) causing *kaṣāya-mohanīya-karmas* that affect an individual's conduct (*cāritra*), resulting in *kaṣāya-cāritra-mohanīya-karmas*. Each of these *kaṣāyas* has four levels of bondings (*bandhas*), resulting in a total of sixteen types of *kaṣāya-mohanīya-karma*s bondings. In addition, there are nine subsidiary passions or emotions known as *nau-kaṣāya*s, which also incite *kaṣāya* and the subsequent *karma* bondings. Thus, in total there are twenty-five types of *cāritra-mohanīya-karma*s.

The nine subsidary passions (*nau-kaṣāya*s) are:

i. *Hāsya* (laughing): Acts that incite excessive laughing at someone.
ii. *Rati* (pleasure): Pleasure in sense activity such as the acts that make someone enamored, in passionate love.
iii. *Arati* (displeasure): Displeasure with reference to sense activity, such as the acts that cause someone to become unaffectionate and to create malice.
iv. *Śoka* (grief): Acts that incite sadness and anguish.
v. *Bhaya* (fear): Acts that cause fearful feelings that make an individual afraid of certain things or actions.
vi. *Jugupsā* (repugnance): Acts that lead to hatred towards other beings and things.
vii. *Strīveda* (lust for females): Sexual attraction towards women.
viii. *Puruṣaveda* (lust for males): Sexual attraction towards men.
ix. *Napuṁsakaveda* (gender-less lust): Sexual attraction towards those who are neither men nor women.

All together, *mohanīya-karma* has a total of twenty-eight types consisting of three *darśana-mohanīya-karma*s, sixteen *kaṣāya cāritra-mohanīya-karma*s, and nine *nau-kaṣāya cāritra-mohanīya-karma*s. Collectively, these actions of mind, body, and speech prevent an individual from grasping and adopting true devotional principles. In addition, by inciting various types of inauspicious mental inclinations, *mohanīya-karma*s do not allow for the development of one's spiritual nature. *Mohanīya-karma* is very intense and it is the principal instigator of harmful actions committed by living beings.

KARMA THAT CAUSES PHYSICAL EXPERIENCES (VEDANĪYA-KARMA)

These accumulated kārmic particles result in agony associated with both miserable and pleasant experiences. The miserable experiences carry obvious reasons for agony, but pleasant experiences also result in agony for the soul since one clings to what is pleasant, but that to which one clings is ultimately ephemeral. What brings happiness today will bring despair in the future. From the viewpoint of Jain *karma* theory, both that which is pleasant and that which is unpleasant hinder the ultimate liberation of the soul. Therefore, *vedanīya-karma*s are like honey on the edge of a sword; it tastes good but could result in cutting the tongue. There are two types of *vedanīya-karma*s:

1. *Sātā-vedanīya karma*: This results in pleasant experiences.
2. *Asātā-vedanīya-karma*: This results in misery-causing experiences.

LIFESPAN-AFFECTING KARMA (ĀYU- OR ĀYUṢYA-KARMA)

This *āyuṣya-karma* does not allow one's soul to experience full freedom and rather keeps the soul imprisoned in the body of a human being, hellish or heavenly dweller, animal, or other being until the allocated time period ends. An individual's current living form and its longevity is a result of *āyuṣya-karma,* which is sometimes shortened to *āyu-karma.*

DESIGNATION OF THE JĪVA BODY-TYPE KARMA (NĀMA-KARMA)

This *karma* is responsible for creating and embodying the soul with a body of varying shapes, complexions, sizes, etc. This is similar to a painter creating many different types of paintings with his brush and various colors on his canvas. The astounding variety of species and individuals that are seen in the living universe is due to this *karma.* Jain scriptures have described *nāma-karma* in great detail by subdividing it into many classes and subclasses. Of all the categories, forty-two are the main ones which deal with the *jīva*'s designated species, class, shape, size, weight, appearance, physical and biological capabilities, strength, color, voice, beauty, influence, etc. Their detailed description is beyond the scope of this book.

Basically, *nāma-karma*s are responsible for all aspects of the bodily manifestation of the *jīva*, and its effects start from the formational stages of a new body (soon after conception). Although bodily characteristics can also be influenced by external factors, the main intrinsic qualities are determined by *nāma-karma*. The main forty-two classes of *nāma-karma*s define all aspects of the conditions into which a living being is born, such as its designated state (human, animal, etc.), its eminence or notoriety, the body's characteristics, looks, form, size, and condition, and so on.

CLAN OF BIRTH KARMA (GOTRA-KARMA)

This *karma* influences the birth of a living being in the lineage it adopts. In the case of human beings, birth could be in a prosperous family or a struggling one. This *karma* is of two types: (1) *ucca gotra* (esteemed lineage), and (2) *nīca gotra* (humble lineage).

States of Karma

It is clear that *karmas* play a vast role in one's lifespan and spiritual progression over multiple lives, and Jain philosophy has vividly presented this process in a unique, precise, and cogent manner. For each *jīva*, all of its internal tendencies, thoughts, outlooks, and actions are the result of its *karmas*. Also, one's looks, talk, quality of life, etc., are all related to the manifestations of *karmas*.

After understanding the types or classes of *karma*, it is important to understand their states or conditions. At a high level, there are ten states of *karma*:

1. *Bandha* (influx and attachment): This is the state when *karmas* flow towards the soul and attach to form layers over it. After the attachment, they develop five characteristics consisting of type, duration, strength, impact, and results.
2. *Utkarṣaṇa* (strengthening and extension): This is the state when attached *karmas* are extended in duration or their consequential results are strengthened. This happens when an inauspicious deed is followed with its praise or with continued bad behavior.
3. *Apakarṣaṇa* (weakening and reduction): This state is the opposite of *utkarṣaṇa.* Here the duration is decreased, and/or the consequential results are weakened. This happens when an individual realizes the mistake of committing an inauspicious action and follows that realization with repentance and/or corrective actions.
4. *Sattā* (latent existence): In most cases, the consequences of kārmic attachment do not appear right after their attachment. The consequences emerge (also called kārmic emergence or *karma* shedding) after the allocated duration (called *abādhākāla*). They remain dormant in the layers over the soul from the time of attachment to the time of their

emergence or shedding. Their latent existence from the time of kārmic attachment (*bandha*) to emergence is called *sattā*.

5. *Udaya* (timely shedding): This is the emergence that may result in the shedding of *karma*s. If the *karma*s are eliminated after their emergence, it is called *phalodaya* (emerging fruition). This kārmic shedding happens after penalizing or rewarding the living beings with consequences they have incurred. When the *karma*s shed as a result of penance or other noble acts, without penalizing the living beings with consequences, it called *pradeśodaya* (emergence from determination).
6. *Udīraṇā* (accelerated shedding): This is the shedding of *karma*s before their allocated time. It is like accelerating a fruit's ripening with heat or chemicals. In *karma* theory, this happens through penance and auspicious acts in mind-body-speech that can reduce the duration of *karma* attachment.
7. *Saṅkramaṇa* (transformation): This type of *karma* may have multiple different forms. An acquired *karma* may change its form so long as it retains its type. This transition is known as *saṅkramaṇa.* Within the eight classes of *karma*s discussed earlier, any transition has to stay within its class. A *karma* can change its nature within the same class; for example, one type of *darśanāvaraṇīya-karma* can transition into one of the nine types of *darśanāvaraṇīya-karma*, but cannot suddenly become *jñānāvaraṇīya-karma,* or any of the other eight types of *karma*. In addition, there are two exceptions: (i) it does not apply to lifespan (*āyuṣya-karma*). For instance, once a lifespan as a human being has been allocated, it cannot be transformed to a life in heaven or change its span to a different amount. In addition, (ii) *cāritra-mohanīya-karma* (delusion regarding conduct), a subset of deluding *mohanīya-karma*, cannot be interchanged with any other form of *mohanīya-karma*.
8. *Upaśama* (suppression): This involves suppressing the accumulated *karma*s so that when they emerge, their repercussions are milder than originally assigned. It is like covering a burning charcoal with ashes, so its intensity is reduced. This applies only to *mohanīya-karma*.
9. *Nidhatti* (fixed): In this condition, *karma*s neither emerge (*udaya*) nor

can they be transformed (*saṅkramaṇa*).

10. *Nikācanā* (intense): This is the condition when *karmas* are so intensely attached to the soul that they cannot be transformed (*saṅkramaṇa*), and their attachment duration cannot be changed (*utkarṣaṇa* or *apakarṣaṇa*).

Benefits of Karma Shedding (Karma-kṣaya)

The intrinsic characteristics of soul, i.e., *cetanā* (consciousness), *vīrya* (vigor), and *sukha* (bliss), that are suppressed or obstructed due to the attachment of *karmas* in layers over the soul, are re-established, reinvigorated, or strengthened after the *karmas* have arisen and have been expended. These qualities resurface in a purified condition. Some illustrations are provided below:

- After elimination of *jñānāvaraṇīya-karma* (knowledge-inhibiting *karma*), all obstructions of knowledge acquisition are mitigated, and the living being enjoys the unbounded power of complete knowledge.
- After elimination of *darśanāvaraṇīya-karma* (perception- and awareness-inhibiting *karma*), all obstructions to right perception are mitigated, and the living being enjoys clairvoyance.
- After elimination of *antarāya-karma* (hinderance-causing *karma*), the living being is endowed with the ability to enjoy the benefits of spiritual powers, worldly pleasures, or other such benefits.
- After elimination of *mohanīya-karma* (delusion-causing *karma*), the living being enjoys right virtues and principled conduct.
- After elimination of *vedanīya-karma* (physical-experience-causing *karma*), the living being enjoys life that is free of bodily sickness, distress, and misery.
- After elimination of *āyuṣya-karma* (lifespan-affecting *karma*), the living being achieves immortality and eternal youth.
- After elimination of *nāma-karma* (designation of the *jīva*'s body-type causing *karma*), the living being attains formless qualities. Such a liberated soul is welcomed to the location of the highest spiritual aspirants, which is beyond the universe of living beings.
- After elimination of *gotra-karma* (clan-of-birth-causing *karma*), the

living being forestalls rebirth in any type of superior or inferior lineage.

The process of acquiring and shedding of *karma*s has been discussed earlier in chapter 6: The Discussion of the Fundamental Truth (*Tattva-Carcā*).

The Process of Transmigration (Punarjanma)

As discussed before, the soul, despite being an eternal entity which is free from creation and destruction, is forever going through variations due to its acquired qualities (*pariṇāma*) and modes (*paryāya*) caused by the status of its kārmic collection. Its associated exterior bodily forms morph through cycles of creation and destruction uninterruptedly. As a result, the living beings enjoy the pleasures from their virtuous actions and endure sufferings from their inauspicious actions. Clearly, the most significant change occurs when the soul, after having discarded its previous body, adopts a new one in terms of type (species, etc.), shape, and form. This is the process of transmigration, otherwise known as reincarnation.

One can say that a human being is not a singular entity. It is an aggregate of many, many singularities, both physical and non-physical. It is not steady due to the constant changes a life endures. It is self-driven, but at the same time, it is oblivious. Clearly, all human beings should seek spiritual salvation, and with their self-motivating temperament they can successfully pursue it. However, they are oblivious to the intrinsic characteristics of their souls (consciousness, bliss, and vigor). They must find a way to wake up, regain awareness, and embrace and unite with their intrinsic true-self. A human being is neither complete nor the ultimate form. Human life is a form with a consciousness that can help it modify itself and regenerate. Humans are capable of progressively refining themselves through the process of reincarnation. This process of refinement should be the main objective of all religious and spiritual doctrines.

According to Jain philosophy, a living being stays alive with the rise of *āyuṣya-karma* (lifespan *karma*). At every moment, one is consuming one's allocated kārmic particles (*pudgala*) of *āyuṣya-karma*. The consumed *pudgala*s are continuously separated and discarded. When all of them are depleted, the living being discards the current body and adopts a new one with a new starting account of *āyuṣya-karma pudgala*s, and this cycle continues life after life. According to the principles of nature, a living being receives its allocated duration for the next life just before it completes the current one. The soul gives up the current body just as the current life's allocated duration is completed. Right at that moment, a brand new *āyuṣya-karma* allocation comes into existence. This is how the living being transforms to the new life-form.

The *āyuṣya-karma pudgala*s can be divided into two categories:

1. *Prākṛtika* (natural): This is the process through which *āyuṣya-karma* arises and corresponding *pudgala*s are expended and start detaching from the soul. They are completely exhausted by the time life comes to an end.
2. *Prāyogika* (artificial): In this case, life comes to an end through sudden and unexpected means that are not in line with the natural, *prākṛtika* process. In the case of *prāyogika*, the accumulated *āyuṣya-karma pudgala*s allocated to the current life are expended at an accelerated rate. Here one's lifespan was supposed to follow a normal course, but is halted by one or more artificial means. The rate of acceleration depends on the cause of death. The sudden end of life, known as *akāla-mṛtyu* (untimely death) or *ākasmika-maraṇa* (unexpected or sudden death) could be caused by one or more reasons such as consumption of poison, accident, incurable disease, starvation, murderous attack, suffocation, and so on.

At times, a soul discards its current embodiment at a very high speed after expending its allocated lifespan (known as *samohiyā-maraṇa*), like a bullet leaving the gun barrel after being fired. On other occasions, it happens at a slow speed (*asamohiyā-maraṇa*). At death, after discarding its associated body, the soul must go to its next bodily state as determined by its destination *nāma-karma*, which arises right at that moment of death. The new destination *nāma-karma* arises simultaneously with the expending of the old *nāma-karma*.

According to the Jain theory of *jīva* transmigration, the transition speed of the soul when it moves from the worn-out body to the new body is called *vigraha-gati* (changing form). The soul moves along a network of pathways or channels in metaphysical space, analogous to a network of roads and highways. If the soul gets a straight route, it reaches its destined body in one *samaya*, which is the smallest unit of time in Jain doctrine – much smaller than a nanosecond. If it does not get a straight route, it might have to make a few turns, whereby each turn takes one *samaya*. In almost all cases, the soul reaches its destination in up to three *samaya*s. In rare cases, it could take the fourth *samaya*, but never more than that.

During the transition time of *vigraha-gati* (changing form), the soul does not possess any physical body, but it does have a combination of virtual subtle bodies. The subtle bodies are:

1. The *kārmaṇa* body – relating to *karma*. This is a metaphysical body composed of the layers of *karma*s on the soul based on their types, qualities, bonding, duration, etc.
2. The *taijasa* (splendorous) body. This is the metaphysical body defined by the spiritual state of the soul in terms of its characteristics such as vigor, knowledge, and perception.

Once the *taijasa* body reaches its destined form of re-emergence into a new body, the soul creates its new state of embodied existence. Jain doctrine believes there are six empowering abilities or forces that the soul needs to fulfill as soon as it adopts the new body. These adequacies (*paryāpti*s) are the necessary material-substance particles (*pudgala*s) that allow a *jīva* to adopt a new body with its new form and characteristics based on its state of *karma*s. These *paryāpti*s include:

1. *Āhāra-paryāpti* (adequate nourishment): The ability to collect *pudgala*s essential to building a body in accordance with the new form of embodiment and its assigned characteristics based on its state of *karma*s.
2. *Śarīra-paryāpti* (adequate body): The ability to build a body in accordance with the new *nāma-karma*, the form of embodiment and its assigned characteristics.
3. *Indriya-paryāpti* (adequate senses): The ability to collect *pudgala*s essential to building the senses in accordance with the new form of embodiment and its assigned characteristics.
4. *Śvāsocchvāsa-paryāpti* (adequate respiratory system): The ability to collect *pudgala*s essential to building a respiratory system in accordance with the new form of embodiment and its assigned characteristics.

5. *Bhāṣā-paryāpti* (adequate capacity for speech): The ability to collect *pudgala*s essential to building speech-oriented organs in accordance with the new form of embodiment and its assigned characteristics.
6. *Manaḥ-paryāpti* (adequate mental capacity): The ability to collect *pudgala*s essential to building a mind and emotional system in accordance with the new form of embodiment and its assigned characteristics.

In its new emergent body, the soul first receives its abilities allocated from the above-listed six. The living beings with only a single sense receive four of the above abilities. The beings with only a partial mental capacity and two to five senses (*amanaska,* defined in the section "Mind" in chapter 8) receive five of the above-listed abilities. Those beings that have full mental capacity (*samanaska*) and are considered to be intelligent with the capacity to reason, receive all six abilities.

Using these abilities, a living being begins building its body and senses. For human beings, it takes about three-quarters of an hour to be enriched with these abilities. Then it slowly starts building its body, senses, and other components. The dwellers of heaven and hell have a different process described in scriptures.

The creation of new body, or birthing, is of three types:

1. *Garbha* (womb): This is birth resulting from appropriate mixing of reproductive elements from the parents. This class includes mammals, such as humans, that are covered with a thin film at birth and are active right at birth.
2. *Sammūrchima* (collection of material particles): This type of birth results by the mixing of a collection of *pudgala*s.
3. *Upapāta* (appearance): Beings in heaven or hell are born simply by appearance.

All forms of life, whether they are born in heaven, earth, or hell, follow this scheme and are born in the ways described above. The souls that have ended their kārmic structure become free of this life–death cycle. They are the enlightened ones, known as the "Supreme Souls" (*siddha paramātmās*).

12

Right Conduct and Doctrine of Ethics (Samyag-Cāritra and Nītiśāstra)

Right Conduct (Samyag-Cāritra) and Its Importance

In Jain Dharma, right knowledge (*samyag-jñāna*), right perception (*samyag-darśana*), and right conduct (*samyag-cāritra*) are considered three spiritual jewels (*ratnatraya*), or three braids (*triveṇī*)[1] of a confluent flow of spirituality. Also considered as the three essential righteous characteristics, the combined stream of *samyag-jñāna*, *samyag-darśana*, and *samyag-cāritra* is flowing continuously for the benefit of all spiritual aspirants. The ones who choose to immerse in this stream can propel themselves towards ultimate liberation.

The objective of one's spiritual endeavors is to recognize the path of enlightenment and have complete faith in that path. The rate of progression on this path depends on the extent of one's devotional strength, which in turn is directly related to one's state of personal knowledge (*jñāna*), the level of one's perception (*darśana*), and one's resolve and prowess in defining one's conduct (*cāritra*). Spiritual aspirants who are seeking the pinnacle of enlightenment must stay vigilant and continuously work hard to elevate these three key constituents of spiritual endeavors (knowledge, perception, and conduct) to the level of enlightened attainment. The extent to which they adopt this *ratnatraya* or immerse in this *triveṇī* is determined by the individual's personal capabilities.

Jain scriptures have taught that virtuous character or conduct (*cāritra*) is the essence of religion.[2] In other words, *cāritra* determines one's relationship with religion, ethics, social welfare, or even the universal principle of harmony

[1] The term *triveṇī* commonly refers to the confluence of India's two major rivers, namely, the Gaṅgā and the Yamunā, and the mythical Sarasvatī. This river metaphor can be employed to understand Jain praxis.

[2] *cārittaṁ dhammo*, which means, conduct (*cāritra*) is religion (*dharma*).

– all of which are encapsulated in the term *dharma*.[3] Jain scriptures define *samyag-cāritra* as becoming free of inauspicious actions, and adopting auspicious actions.[4] In reality, virtuous conduct and ethical and moral character are attributes that bring dignity to humans. A life without virtuous conduct is like a flower without any aroma.

The doctrines of *samyag-darśana* and *samyag-jñāna* were presented in chapters 3 and 4, respectively, and that of *samyag-cāritra* is presented here. It is important to note that in the Jain system of ethics, *vrata* (vows), described next, and *nīti* (ethics), described later, are the foundational elements of right conduct.

THE DISCUSSION ON VOWS (VRATA)

When it comes to pursuing spirituality, one individual may be able to advance rapidly, while another might do so only modestly. Even when not being able to commit to rapid advancement, one must stay motivated and continuously move towards the objective of salvation, even if only at a moderate pace. One must focus on the final goal of enlightenment and, to that end, continuously control one's senses, ego, and other mental trepidations. The level of success depends on the extent of one's motivation and commitment to honorable conduct. The doctrine of *samyag-cāritra* provides guidance for such a noble pursuit, whereas *vrata*s serve as the key tactical means. There are five fundamental *vrata*s:

1. *Ahiṁsā-vrata* (vow of non-violence)
2. *Satya-vrata* (vow of truthfulness)
3. *Acaurya-vrata* (vow of non-stealing)
4. *Brahmacarya-vrata* (vow of celibacy and carnal restraint)
5. *Aparigraha-vrata* (vow of non-possession)

The *vrata*s can be seen as the binding channels that bring spiritual effulgence for supreme welfare and benefits to the individuals who observe them. There are significant protocols for austerity, and those who are deeply committed to destroying their personal deficiencies develop a natural affinity

---

[3] Here, the term *dharma* refers to the attributes or qualities of a *jīva*, which is a different usage than the term *dharma* as a *dravya*.

[4] *āsuhādo viṇivittī, suhe pavittī ya jāṇa cārittaṁ.*

for these vows. Just as a canal needs two shores to control and guide its flow, spiritual aspirants need vows to bring discipline and honor into their spiritual life. With a lack of commitment to follow these vows, an individual's spiritual life may become chaotic, just like a canal's flow can become unruly in the absence of properly enforced banks. The vows help one to focus one's inner strengths and direct one's energy in a way that is the most beneficial.

A kite, while flying high in the sky, may ponder over why it needs a string. "This string is binding me and without it I would be free to roam all over the sky." But it is well-known what happens to the kite when the string is broken. Its dream of flying all over the sky is shattered and it comes tumbling down to the ground in minutes. In a similar manner, for humans it is essential to abide by a set of vows in order to maintain a lifestyle that is structured, honorable, and allows one to progress spiritually.

BASIC VICES (DOṢAS)

All living beings have innumerable insufficiencies that can be categorized under five fundamental causes or vices (*doṣa*s) that are considered to be the main perpetrators of all human failures. These fundamental vices are:

1. *Hiṁsā* (violence)
2. *Asatya* (untruthfulness)
3. *Adattādāna* (stealing)
4. *Maithuna* (sexual urges)
5. *Parigraha* (possessiveness)

Of these five vices, *hiṁsā* is the chief perpetrator and most heinous of them all. It is the catalyst for the other four.

The five vices have been tormenting humanity and suppressing the *jīva*'s virtuous qualities since beginningless time. Their presence results in a multitude of malicious traits that prompt individuals to become violent, thievish, dishonorable, greedy, self-centered, deceitful, hypocritical, or to adopt other defective behaviors. By perpetuating passions, malice, and jealousies, these vices harm all living beings from within and are the real enemies of the soul. Such dubious characteristics and traits are developed over multiple lives, are difficult to overcome, and hamper spiritual progression.

Nevertheless, when an aspirant completely conquers them, they can become a great soul (*mahātmā*) or a liberated soul (*parmātmā*) shortly thereafter. What follows are descriptions of these *doṣas*:

1. *Hiṁsā* (violence): Generally, it is perceived as violence. However, in Jain philosophy, *hiṁsā* has a much wider meaning and it needs to be analyzed in minute detail with thoughtful and sensitive contemplation.

   Non-violence is the hallmark of a honorable lifestyle, whereas violence accompanies an intense emotional state caused by passion, malice, and jealousy. An individual's mental state is an irrefutable measure of the degree to which one is embroiled in violence or is immersed in peacefulness. Violence arises out of emotional instability, and physical acts are its outward manifestation. The deliberate act of taking someone's life is an obvious example of *hiṁsā*, while emotional aggravation and scheming to cause harm are subtler examples. The physical act is called substance or physical violence (*dravya hiṁsā*), and the mental deliberation of violence is an example of psychological violence (*bhāva hiṁsā*). Generally, *bhāva hiṁsā* is contemplated or committed in solitude, and *dravya-hiṁsā* is not a solitary act but happens when interacting with others. The substance or physical violence that follows psychological violence is the worst kind since it results from both kinds of violence – at first, it involves mental acts of violence (for example, scheming), which is *bhāva hiṁsā,* and then it is followed by the *dravya hiṁsā* resulting from the scheming.

   In Jain Dharma, an individual is responsible when one is knowingly involved in acts of violence directly or indirectly. Clearly, when one commits violence carelessly and/or is impelled by malice, they should be held liable. However, in a court of law, a person would also be liable if they motivated or encouraged others to commit violence or benefited by such actions by others, even while not directly committing those acts. All such intentions, malicious in either thought or behavior, lead to the collection and adherence of *karma* to the soul via the *kaṣāyas* (anger, ego, deceit, and greed).

   The question arises whether it would be considered an act of violence when a living being is accidentally killed by an individual who is trying to save that being's life. Or one might wonder if, in a situation in which one is very careful not to hurt, but still unknowingly or inadvertently becomes the cause of another's death, the resulting act constitutes violence. Although such acts are violent in nature, they do not constitute willful or deliberate violence. Hence, one cannot be held fully responsible if one's actions are driven by noble thoughts with no intentions of causing harm.

As an illustration, consider a swimming instructor who is extremely careful, methodical, and attentive in teaching a child to swim. However, the child drowns due to an inadvertent accident in the swimming pool. In such a situation the instructor is not responsible for the child's death and does not earn any inauspicious *karma*. On the other hand, consider a situation where the instructor is bribed to cause an accident in the swimming pool. However, the child survives without any injury. In this case, although the student escaped injury, the instructor becomes responsible for the intended act of violence. The instructor would collect the corresponding inauspicious *karma*.

In this manner, in Jain doctrine, violence in thoughts and intentions can be considered much more sinful than actual physical actions in which someone is harmed. The quality of thoughts and emotions is the true test of whether a situation can be considered to be one of violence or non-violence.

2. *Asatya* (untruthfulness): Inaccurate and untruthful speech (*asatya*) is the second vice. By nature, untruthfulness is disingenuous and unethical. To represent something in a way that is false is untruth and is generally considered a lie. However, it is also untruth when words are used to hurt someone, or when there are harmful thoughts behind the spoken or written words – even when the intentions are camouflaged in kind or flattering words. This is considered an undignified untruth. To insult a person for being poor, or to tease a blind person, or to call a weak person pathetic are all words that are hurtful. Such spiteful language, even when it is in some way accurate, is considered to be untruthful.
3. *Adattādāna* (stealing or taking without permission): To take or accept something without the owner's permission constitutes stealing or

adattādāna. Taking something which belongs to another individual, even if it was found lying on the street, comes under the definition of *adattādāna*. Similarly, it is *adattādāna* when one takes something without the owner's knowledge even if the owner has forgotten about it. In fact, it is the worst kind of stealing when one takes something without permission when the owner is not aware. It is equally bad when one steals knowing that no one would ever know. When one gives in to their greedy tendencies, they try to exert ownership of things that do not belong to them. In such a situation, one forgets the distinction between honorable versus dishonorable impulses and tries to take possession of articles that are the object of desire. Such premeditated or spontaneous acts result in the collection of ill-fated *karma*s.

4. *Maithuna* (sexual urges): Sexual urges are dishonorable when they are counter-productive to the soul's virtuous behavior. Although all sins affect the soul negatively, the key fault associated with sexual urges is that their expression could leave kārmic impressions, which last for a long time, especially when they cause harm to others. When seeking relief for one's sexual urges, one might be motivated to commit many other types of sins, such as lying, stealing, aggression, or other forms of harmful behavior. This could obviate the soul's ability to perform virtuous behavior and might even destroy the body's vitality. Impulsive or compulsive subjugation to the whims of one's sexual urges may impel individuals overcome by such feelings to cross society's ethical boundaries. Such acts present substantial obstacles to spiritual progression.

5. *Parigraha* (possessiveness): Possessiveness is when one accepts and/or acquires any article with feelings of attachment to that possession. *Parigraha* also comprises acts where individuals are deliriously infatuated with their belongings and are insatiably seeking to acquire more. Possessiveness and the resultant excessive consumption and materialism are at the root of many of the miseries in the world. Obsession with physical articles diminishes one's principled views, especially when one is willing to commit unethical transgressions to obtain the object of desire. As a result, influenced by passions and

malice, one's soul deviates from its intrinsic characteristics of goodness. The soul gets involved in various wrongdoings and loses its path of spirituality.

The above five *doṣa*s give rise to all the maladies of the world. History is full of instances where due to one or more of these vices, humans have caused immense misery for themselves and for others. If these vices are controlled and destroyed, one can readily achieve eternal peace. An individual can then discover the true source of happiness that is devoid of these faults. The main purpose of spiritual endeavors in Jain Dharma is to liberate the soul from these vices, and the aforementioned *vrata*s were formulated to help spiritual aspirants in controlling and eliminating these vices. When this endeavor reaches its supreme level, the vices are eliminated and the soul becomes entitled to be called a "Supreme Soul" (*paramātma*).

Non-Violence (Ahiṁsā)

THE FOUNDATION OF RIGHT CONDUCT

Since *hiṁsā* is the most atrocious kind of *doṣa* and is considered the perpetrator of other four vices – untruthfulness (*asatya*), stealing (*adattādāna*), sexual urges (*maithuna*), and possessiveness (*parigraha*) – the *vrata* to contain and eliminate *hiṁsā* is the most virtuous one. The main purpose for the adoption of the *vrata*s and devotion to virtuous living is to accept that all living beings have spirituality as their core characteristic.[5] In order to progress on the path of spirituality, one should strive to interact with all beings at soul-to-soul level. This is the essence of non-violence. If one were to liken life to an architectural structure, its upper chambers are stable because of the solid foundation. For spiritual progression, non-violence is the foundation upon which the entire edifice of a meaningful, spiritual life is erected.

Non-violence goes beyond simple adherence to a moral code. It is a universal principle of virtue such that philosophy, culture, and social infrastructure are all emanating from non-violence. It is the medium for human evolution, progress, and spiritual awakening. Non-violence perpetuates universal peace and righteousness. These are the reasons that non-violence is the heart and soul, and the foundation, of Jain Dharma. It is considered a

---

[5] *Sarva-bhūtātma-bhūtatā*. (That all living beings have a soul is the truth.)

standard for spirituality, religion, morality, and virtuous conduct. One practices non-violence as a spiritual virtue to align with the source of goodness in the universe.

Non-violence is the heart and soul of Jain philosophy. It is the nourishment for the soul of all living beings and is life's foremost affirmation. Non-violence is supreme strength and is the basis of spirituality. It is the ultimate religion (*ahiṁsā paramo dharma*[6]) and divinity.[7] As such, non-violence is the truest representation of human virtue beyond the worldly sense of mere ethical conduct. Non-violence and violence are the key distinctions between humans and demonic beings.[8] Non-violence is the creator of all universal bliss and peace – a divine power to protect humanity, the world, and the universe.

Upon attaining complete wisdom and enlightenment after twelve years, five months, and fifteen days of intense penance, the first words of Lord Mahāvīra were:

> Do not kill; do not kill![9]
>
> Do not kill any living being. Do not kill. Do not hurt anyone. Do not hurt.
>
> Do not bring anguish or sorrow to any living being.
>
> If you kill any living being, you will get killed as well. If you hurt anyone, you will get hurt too. If you bring anguish and sorrow to others, you too will receive the same from others.

Lord Mahāvīra preached further:

> All of the enlightened souls (*arihanta*s) who appeared in the past, are currently present, and will appear in future, have only one command, one

---

6 These three words encapsulate the universal, cosmic, and divine scope of non-violence, although their literal translation is "non-violence is the supreme religion." Some consider non-violence to be the highest religious duty. Mahatma Gandhi translates it as "non-violence is the supreme law," but illustrates its status as a divine force by adding that "non-violence, as I understand it, is the most active force in the world."

7 See "Glossary of Terms" for a definition of the term "divinity" in Jain tradition.

8 As noted earlier, in Jain and other Indian dhārmic traditions, the "demonic" status is temporary and does not connote the same degree of absolute evil as in Abrahamic faiths. Rather, it is a malleable condition that the living beings can evolve out of with virtuous conduct.

9 *mā haṇa, mā haṇa*.

> edification – do not cause misery or sorrow to any living being, any hellish being, any heaven dweller, or any other form of life. Practicing this is the pure, ultimate, and perpetual form of *dharma* (virtue).

The learned and wise sages have studied and experienced the true nature of the universe and have understood the true *dharma*. All living beings, from the tiniest ones to the largest ones, dislike miseries. They all enjoy pleasures and happiness, adore life and despise death. If people bring miseries to others for their own pleasures, they will receive grief triggered by someone else's desires, in current or future lives. This is the law of *karma*. In this manner, if all living beings are caught in the vicious cycle of pursuing pleasure by committing violence, everyone will be trapped. The end result will only be intense sorrow and widespread misery. No one will become happy and blissful. Therefore, Jain Dharma firmly ascertains that true and eternally blissful life can only be achieved under the nurturance of that heavenly blessing of the supreme mother called *ahiṁsā*.

Two Kinds of Dharma: Householders and Ascetics

Lord Mahāvīra established the organizational structure for Jain ascetics and the non-ascetic (householders) population, to provide an enduring template by which the Jain community might be structured to ensure its survival. Creating an interdependent organization for both ascetics and householders was important in view of the vital mutualism between their respective communities. The structure of the entire Jain community has four categories:

1. *Sādhu*s (male ascetics or monks)
2. *Sādhvī*s (female ascetics or nuns)
3. *Śrāvaka*s (male householders)
4. *Śrāvikā*s (female householders)

The precepts for monks and nuns are similar, and those for male and female householders are also alike.

Lord Mahāvīra deeply emphasized the importance of *vrata*s while distinguishing the extent of their implementation depending on the roles of the individuals in the society. He expressed this in the following words:

> There are two ways to follow *dharma*, or stated differently, to traverse the

path of salvation: householder practice (*āgāra-dharma*) and ascetic practice (*anāgāra-dharma*).[10]

From that perspective, both householders and ascetics follow the same set of fundamental vows for their spiritual advancement. In theory, all vows are identical for everyone; however, their level of implementation is much stricter for the ascetics than for the householders – forming the basis for *āgāra-dharma* and *anāgāra-dharma*, defined below.

1. *Āgāra-dharma* (householder practice): This is the spiritual path followed by the laity or householders while honoring their duties towards family, society, and country. This is also known as *śrāvaka* (Jain spiritual practitioner) or *gṛhastha* (householder) *dharma*. They follow the same five vows as the ascetics, but in a limited manner, and are thus called "follower of limited vows" (*anuvratī*).
2. *Anāgāra-dharma* (ascetic practice): This is the path followed by an ascetic or monk/nun (*sādhu/sādhvī*) as a distinguished individual who has disavowed householder life in favor of renunciate life. Having forsaken all of the worldly possessions and practices while wandering as mendicants with complete restraint, they must follow the five vows strictly and comprehensively. That is why they are called "supremely avowed" (*mahāvratī*) spiritual seekers.

Both ascetic and householder classes of Jain followers have strong aspirations for enlightenment and are progressively traversing the path of spiritual purification. Both are immersed in a lifestyle of self-restraint and strive to refrain from indulgence in sinful acts. However, they are living under different circumstances, so they have different requirements. The ascetics have vowed to eliminate all types of vices or sinful acts and have completely renounced possessions. The householders, on the other hand, are still involved in family and social activities, and thus cannot completely emulate the renunciations of an ascetic. In view of their different lifestyles, in addition to their specific levels of *vrata* implementation, each of the ascetic and householder classes has its respective sets of supplementary guidelines to help them in governing their lifestyles.

---

[10] *dhamme duvihe paṇṇatte, taṁjahā-āgāra-dhamme ceva, aṇāgāra-dhamme ceva* |
– *Ṭhāṇāṅgasutta, sthā*. 2

The vows for the householders are called *aṇuvratas* and those for the ascetics or mendicants are called *mahāvratas*.[11] The *aṇuvratas* along with the supplementary guidelines are discussed next, and *mahāvratas* for the mendicants, along with their supplementary guidelines, are discussed in the next chapter.

Householder Ethics (Gr̥hastha-Dharma)

In Jain society, the lifestyle and conduct of male and female householders is considered the foundation upon which ascetic life is built. The establishment of a structured ascetic organization is important in itself, but the motivational and respectful provisions to promote a virtuous householder way of life evinces Lord Mahāvīra's visionary acumen. The way he structured the householder community shows his empathy and thoughtfulness in inspiring householders towards the path of spiritual progression. Many people think that the Jain religion is beneficial only for the ascetics committed to strict penance in search of enlightenment, but that is not accurate. While the lifestyle of the ascetic is immensely important in the Jain community, the path shown by Lord Mahāvīra can have profound impact on all individuals irrespective of their spiritual inclinations – whether they are committed to the path of strict austerities, or are more attentive to the needs of sustaining a household.

PRECEPTS OF A JAIN HOUSEHOLDER

Jain Dharma has well-established essential conventions of conduct for householders to follow in daily life. These are conceptually similar to those for monastics who have to strictly follow them to be eligible for acceptance to monastic life. Not every individual can be considered a Jain householder. Only those who adopt and follow these rules earn the right to be considered a Jain Householder.

The Jain scriptures, written centuries ago, include instructions to avoid misdeeds such as consumption of meat, hunting, consumption of alcohol and other intoxicants, extra-marital affairs, stealing, and gambling. The specifics of the provisions and their application may change at times due to various social, political, and cultural changes as well as to scientific and

---

[11] Here, the words *aṇu*, *mahā*, and *vrata* literally mean "minor," "major," and "vow," respectively.

technological evolution. But the essence and underlying reasoning behind the provisions have continued to be of relevance. The key is to interpret and understand their purpose. Anyone who engages in any one or more of the transgressions is liable to get entrapped in other inauspicious traits as well, which could lead to a spiritually downward spiral. A true Jain householder avoids any entanglements in dishonorable activities. To sustain householders on a spiritually progressive path and keep them away from any distractions, the guidelines promote an honorable way of living based on the merits of *ahiṁsā*, *satya*, *asteya*, *aparigraha,* and *brahmacarya*. Different times, places, and cultures may have some influence on the details, but their underlying values and purpose remain valid in all circumstances. Some of the key guidelines are:

1. One must earn a living while staying within the rules of good conduct. Spiritually minded householders are advised to be honest in all financial and work-related dealings while staying within religious bounds by avoiding deceitful, malicious, or dishonorable practices. They should learn to differentiate between right and wrong, and engage in honorable practices that are helpful rather than hurtful to others. No householders should be involved in any activities against religion, faith, society, and nation. They should always be judicious and supportive of justice against injustice, both for themselves and for the society at large.

2. Be righteous, thoughtful, helpful, courteous, and humble. This set of guidelines is designed to steer householders towards a wholesome lifestyle themselves as well as for their interactions with others. They should show respect to acccomplished people and their good behavior, and at the same time be eager to learn from their experiences. They should strive for a similar honorable demeanor that is built on internal vigor and gentleness. They should make sincere efforts to minimize anger and passions, and control the senses while being mentally calm, forgiving, friendly, trustworthy, and peaceful.

   Householders should develop virtuous perception devoid of any internal wickedness by frequently (for example, daily) listening to religious teachings. They should try hard to be modest, to not get excited upon hearing or seeing unpleasant things, and not become negatively malicious. Similarly, they should not be overly joyous on being successful.

Householders should be respectful of the destitute and homeless, of ascetics and monks, and be caring of the elderly (for example, parents) and sick, while at the same time a reliable caretaker of dependents.

Householders should work hard to stay healthy, both physically and mentally, and consume healthy, nourishing, and pious food at proper times.

3. Respect honorable deeds. This set of guidelines helps householders in developing earnest outwardly conduct for dealing and communicating with others. The householders should always use gracious and humble language, and be respectful while being faithful, thankful, and duty bound. They are advised to be flexible and accommodating while promptly recognizing and appreciating the good qualities of others. While being cognizant of the core righteous and spiritual ethics, they should be spiritually progressive and deal with others with the future in mind.
4. Have righteous objectives in life and be willing to work hard to achieve those. This set of guidelines helps develop the right attitude and character. It helps one define personal spiritual goals and stay on course while dealing with worldly distractions. Householders are advised to follow the principle that a righteous individual's life is meant to help others.[12] With personal spiritual growth in mind, they should pay attention to the past and future to learn and improve themselves in the present. They should strive to minimize personal possessions and not be extravagant by spending more than one's earnings. In dealing with other living beings, all householders should be merciful and compassionate, and have a temperament that is not hurtful to others.

By adopting the above and other similarly motivated qualities, one can accomplish and lead an ideal householder's life and become a worthy Jain householder. Jain scriptures have elaborated that being engrossed in auspicious deeds while keeping away from inauspicious deeds is honorable conduct (*cāritra*), and *samyag-cāritra* is true *dharma*. The *aṇuvrata* necessary

[12] *paropakārāya satāṁ vibhūtayaḥ* (Greatness [*vibhūtayaḥ*] is achieved [*satāṁ*] by assisting others [*paropakārāya*]).

to facilitate an honorable lifestyle and moralistic character are described next, followed by the supplementary guidelines.

MINOR VOWS FOR HOUSEHOLDER LIVING (AṆUVRATA)

The lifestyle of Jain householders is governed by *aṇuvrata*s that are derived from standard *vrata*s (fundamental vows) and are also the source of the *mahāvrata*s (major vows) adhered to by ascetics. The difference between *aṇuvrata*s and *mahāvrata*s is primarily in the level of their implementation – householders follow them in a limited way or to lesser extent, whereas the renunciate ascetics follow them rigorously to the full extent. This differentiation is based on the recognition that householders are still engaged in worldly affairs[13] as opposed to the ascetics, who completely dissociate themselves from such activities. The *aṇuvrata*s, described below, guide the householders to follow a righteous way of life:

1. *Ahiṁsā aṇuvrata* (minor vow of non-violence): The first vow is to refrain from unnecessary violence against living beings, and further, to halt all life-ending crimes against other beings. There are two types of living beings. The first kind are those who cannot move, called *sthāvara* (not moving). These include certain microscopic beings that inhabit the soil, water, fire, and air, as well as beings that make up vegetation. They have only one sense, which is contact or touch. The second kind of living beings, known as *trasa* (moving), are those who can change place at their will, depending on their emotions that are related to pleasures or miseries. They are capable of movement and communication, and have two to five senses.

   Ascetics are forbidden from committing any violence against both types of living beings. However, the householders cannot live the same way, so are given some flexibility. If need be, they are allowed limited violence against immoveable living beings who are *sthāvara*s, but they give up all intentional violence against innocent *trasa* beings.

   Jain scriptures describe four types of violence (*hiṁsā*):

---

[13] Here, "worldly affairs" refers to activities like marriage, sex life, and procreation, engaging in commerce and earning an income, social activities, civic duties, etc.

i. *Ārambhī hiṁsā* (violence during mundane undertakings): This refers to unavoidable violence executing that is essential in day-to-day chores in family life. This includes violence that occurs while cooking, washing, and other such activities. Also, as an example, when a house is infected with termites, the owners have no pragmatic choice other than to eliminate them.

ii. *Udyogī hiṁsā* (violence during employment): This refers to the unavoidable violence in one's work engagement to earn living for their family. They might be involved in professions such as agriculture, animal welfare, and medicine, but all of these involve some sort of unavoidable violence even when the intentions are strictly non-violent. However, Jain householders must refrain from enterprises that are driven by or involve avoidable violence, such as slaughterhouses, equipment used to kill, etc.

iii. *Virodhī hiṁsā* (violence defending against attack): This type of violence occurs in the act of protecting oneself from an aggressor. All householders have the right to protect themselves, their families, community, and nation against aggression. Violence is permitted against those who attack unprovoked and commit hurtful violent acts.

iv. *Saṅkalpī hiṁsā* (intentional violence): This is the form of violence that is committed intentionally against an innocent (*niraparādha*) living being (*prāṇī*) that is not causing any harm.

Under the first *aṇuvrata* of *ahiṁsā*, householders are completely forbidden to indulge in intentional violence of the above-mentioned fourth kind (*saṅkalpī hiṁsā*) at all costs. They are encouraged to minimize violence of the other three types but are sanctioned to do so under unavoidable and necessary situations. Even in unavoidable situations, one must find ways to commit the minimum level of violence.

In order to comply with the vow of non-violence (*ahiṁsā*), one should avoid the following potential transgressions:

- Physically hitting or thrashing a living being, killing them, fracturing or breaking their limbs or organs, or deforming them.

- Using hurtful language such as cursing.
- Imprisoning, enslaving, or encaging any living beings. This includes taking human or animal slaves, having bonded labor, putting birds in cage, or even putting a leash on a dog. Such actions inhibit the freedom of the affected living beings and therefore should be avoided.
- Withholding food or drink from dependents, or imposing an unbearable burden on individuals such as workers or animals.
- Consuming or serving food after sunset.

2. *Satya aṇuvrata* (minor vow of truthfulness): The second vow is to altogether stop major forms of mistruth and to be vigilant against minor forms of deception. Although there are no well-defined demarcations between major and minor untruthful characteristics, the following are some examples of major lies:
   - Untruthful language and statements, such as false testimony and other such statements punishable under the law, forged documents or incorrect writings against someone, and other similar acts.
   - Using despicable language which is decried in general, and praising oneself and slandering others.
   - Disclosing someone's secrets, spreading rumors, and talking about someone behind one's back.
   - Deliberately giving someone false or wrong advice or encouraging someone on a wrong path by using half-truths.
3. *Acaurya aṇuvrata* (minor vow of non-stealing): The third vow is to avoid taking others' property without their permission, even in one's thoughts. Stealing or theft is of two types – overt and subtle. As an example, overt stealing would be theft punishable under the law such as pickpocketing, planning or engaging in burglary, and excessively and unduly accusing someone under the pretext of accruing interest. Examples of subtle stealing include picking up and keeping some article found on the road or borrowing something without seeking approval from the owner.

   It may at times be impossible for householders to completely refrain from subtle acts of stealing, but they certainly must give up all overt acts of thievery. The following are some examples of stealing which a householder adhering to this *aṇuvrata* should avoid:

- In business, cheating by not providing the complete amount of product or services that were paid for, or using corrupt practices such as adulteration and falsification.
- Acting against the state, such as not paying the due amount of taxes.
- Accepting something without seeking approval from the owner, to the extent of picking up and keeping some article found on the road.
- Assisting a thief in the act of stealing or purchasing stolen goods.

4. *Brahmacarya aṇuvrata* (minor vow of restraint in sexual activity): The fourth vow is to restrain one's sexual desires in mind-body-speech. From the religious perspective, sexual urges may cause anguish and other mental agitation, and one should refrain from copulation, to preserve mental rigor, bodily health, and spiritual clarity. Also, during the act of copulation an unlimited number of life forms (sperms) are killed or destroyed, causing violence.

   When one cannot practice complete abstinence, they should remember that sexual urges and acts could result in increased passions and potentially jealousy and malice, which are the roots of harmful behavior. Therefore, an individual should exercise control and discipline, and strive to achieve complete abstinence at some point. Some of the acts that an individual who carefully follows this limited vow should avoid are:

   - Extramarital relationships or getting involved with someone to cause marital breakup.
   - A relationship with a prostitute or an inappropriate relationship with an unwed or underage person.
   - Indulgence in unnatural (*aprākṛtika*) sexual acts or pursuing intense sexual desires.

5. *Parigraha parimāṇa annuvrata* (minor vow of limited possessions): The actions taken to excessively acquire and possess objects of consumption can be the worst form of sins. This fifth vow is to restrain such acts. All

of the complex problems across the globe, including the international and ethnic conflicts that the world is facing today, can be related to the desires of excessive possession, consumption, and indulgence. This can also include the desire of certain rulers to expand their territory or the yearnings of certain religious leaders to increase their following, etc. As long as human beings continue to pursue unrestricted greed, cravings, desires, attachments, and acquisitiveness, it will be impossible to achieve long-lasting peace. Therefore, it is of the utmost importance to limit one's consumptive patterns. If people complied with this minor vow, everyone would enjoy heavenly life on earth, and life would be full of pleasure and peace. In order to follow this minor vow, some of the misdeeds that one must refrain from are:

- Hording of assets such as clothes, shoes, cars, boats, gold, silver, diamonds, and other luxury items.
- Increasing ownership of assets (residence, business, goods, etc.) by available dishonorable means.
- Political or territorial expansion, and ethnic or religious expansion.

SUPPLEMENTARY GUIDELINES FOR HOUSEHOLD LIVING

The aforementioned five minor vows (*aṇuvrata*s) are essential, but it could be challenging for some individuals to stay within the confines of these vows without some additional help. With that in mind, a set of supplementary guidelines called the *uttara-vrata*s (supplementary vows) were established to assist and facilitate individuals to stay in compliance with the *aṇuvrata*s, and at the same time, to enjoy their full benefits and enrichments. There are seven supplementary vows that are split between two classes called the "vows of virtues" (*guṇa-vrata*s) and the "vows of learning" (*śikṣā-vrata*s):

Vows of Virtues (*Guṇa-Vrata*s)

1. *Dig-vrata* (vow of geographical limitation): Human beings have boundless yearnings. Human beings not only dream of attaining their endless desires, they want to take pride and feel victorious when they are fulfilled. Hence, greedy humans under the influence of these desires are spreading across the planet for business and other financial motives. This supplementary vow (*uttara-vrata*) is designed to curb these endless

desires that are consuming the planet. By following *dig-vrata*, the householders observe well-defined boundaries that restrict their area of travel. All business and professional dealings are contained within this geographical area and no financial transactions are conducted outside of this area.

2. *Upabhoga* and *paribhoga parimāṇa-vrata* (vow of limited consumption): The substances that can be consumed only once, like food items, are called *upabhoga*. Those that can be used again and again, like clothes, are called *paribhoga*. This vow is the commitment to create and observe limited consumption of both types of articles. This vow has two applications – one in private or personal life, and the other in professional life. By controlling desires for clothes, food, etc., one mitigates greediness in private life. By controlling professional transactions, one minimizes business dealings that result in the acquisition of inauspicious *karma*.
3. *Anartha-daṇḍa-tyāga-vrata* (vow of relinquishing meaningless castigation): Unnecessary, meaningless, and aimless acts of punishment and violence are called *anartha* (meaningless) *daṇḍa* (castigation) and can result in inauspicious kārmic acquisition through the following four types of acts:
   i. *Apadhyāna* (negative thinking): To think poorly and negatively about others or indulge in uncivilized and hurtful conversations.
   ii. *Pramādācarita* (behavior that is intoxicated by wealth and power): To have arrogance due to birth in a rich and powerful family, and to slander others with speech or actions.
   iii. *Hiṁsā-pradāna* (supporting violence): Invention and manufacturing of weapons and arms to supply to others, especially those who do not need them and could indulge in individual or mass killing.
   iv. *Pāpopadeśa* (inciting sinfulness): To give lectures or sermons (*upadeśa*) with dubious motives and incite others to commit acts of violence and other misdeeds (*pāpa*).

The above three vows were vows of virtues (*guṇa-vrata*s). The next four are vows of learning (*śikṣā-vrata*s).

Vows of Learning (*Śikṣā-Vrata*s)

4. *Sāmāyika-vrata* (vow of equanimity): The development of passions, jealousy, and malice are the manifestation of various unfortunate vicissitudes of the mind. One should strive to eliminate such inclinations so that one may develop a neutral and objective stance towards the living beings of the world. This is the main purpose of Jain meditation and penance. One cannot attain lasting peace without developing an ethical attitude of equality towards all living beings. That is why the practice taught by Jain *tīrthaṅkara*s considers equanimity (*sāmāyika*) as the critical objective of the austerity that is the path for salvation. *Sāmāyika-vrata* is the supplementary vow (*uttara-vrata*) that helps in developing, enhancing, and stabilizing mental equanimity. A time period of forty-eight minutes is considered appropriate to practice what is prescribed in this vow. During this period, a householder should relinquish all interests in family life, personal life, and business dealings that result in kārmic acquisition. They should completely focus on meditation and mental acts of spiritual development.
5. *Deśāvakāśika-vrata* (vow of delimited location): This supplementary vow (*uttara-vrata*) entails locational restrictions (*avakāśika deśa*) corresponding to *dig-vrata* (vow of geographical limitation), discussed above. But this one includes a temporal component. The purpose is to minimize the amount of time spent on business travels in conjunction with the geographical bounds of the *dig-vrata*. In addition to the time and distance boundaries, the seekers should forsake all inauspicious activities.
6. *Pauṣadha-vrata* (vow of fasting and spiritual nourishment): This is the practice of fasting while nourishing only the soul's spiritual qualities and religious inclinations. This vow is observed on spiritually auspicious days of the lunar cycle such as eighth and fourteenth days. This involves a one-day fast, complete celibacy, contemplation of the spiritual truths while meditating, self-studies, spiritual remembrance, and freeing oneself from all worldly chores and activities. In addition, one lives the life of a ascetic during this period, including wearing ascetic garb.
7. *Atithi saṁvibhāga-vrata* (vow of guest appreciation): A guest (*atithi*)

is considered an individual whose time of arrival is unknown. Beyond this, the word "guest" often refers to an ascetic visitor. Jain mendicants are supposed to visit the householders for alms without any prior intimation. To offer them food, as defined by and within the bounds of ascetic life, is the vow of guest appreciation (*saṁvibhāga*) and is called *atithi saṁvibhāga-vrata*. This vow is enacted to diminish the tendency to hoard. At the same time, it helps to awaken and strengthen the feelings of renunciation for the householder. Although it mainly refers to ascetics, householders are encouraged to have a kind and generous demeanor and to be amicable hosts for any visitors – especially those who are poor or destitute. This is not restricted only to the ascetics, but applies also to all unannounced visitors to Jain households, who should be welcomed in a respectful manner.

The above five *aṇuvrata*s and seven *guṇa-vrata*s for the householders are constructed to invigorate and motivate individuals towards spiritual progress and rekindle personal happiness and satisfaction. The vows facilitate the bringing of social justice to the entire society. If all householders were to comply with these twelve vows, it would lead to universally widespread brotherhood and love. That would transform the planet Earth into an abode of complete peace.

ŚRĀVAKA AND ŚRĀVIKĀ TYPES OF JAIN HOUSEHOLDER

Pragmatically, all householders may not be able to follow the five prescribed minor vows (*aṇuvrata*s) to their full extent. In addition, they may not be able to implement every vow to the same level – the level of adherence could be different for one vow from that of another one. The great teachers of Jain Dharma recognized these limitations in the capacities of individual householders, and created categories of householders depending on their abilities to comply with the vows. Based on this classification, there are three classes of householders:

1. *Pākṣika* (partly observed): These are the individuals who are able to renounce only some of the vices, such as the violence of householder life. As such, they might fully adhere to only some of the householder vows, or even fractions of all of them, or perhaps only follow a few of them.

2. *Naiṣṭhika* (firmly observed): These are the individuals who are a step ahead of the *pākṣika* observers. They begin complying with the vows with unwavering faith, even if their adherence is not completely perfect.
3. *Sādhaka* (completely observed): This is the final step to becoming a true Jain householder (*śrāvaka* or *śrāvikā*). In this stage, the householders strictly adhere to all of the householder vows and are completely devoted to their values and principles. They are completely engrossed in transforming their individual souls to the original natural forms.

Lord Mahāvīra created the visionary structure described above to motivate and inspire householders to engage in righteous living while pursuing spiritual progress. The system appreciates variations in human capabilities and provides a hierarchical structure, so the householders can live a dignified life according to their capabilities and aspirations. This pragmatic structure is a vitally important gift from Lord Mahāvīra to humanity.

Ethical Living of Householders (Śrāvaka-Śrāvikā Jīvana-Nīti)

Ethical living comprises a lifestyle that is within the prescriptive confines of *aṇuvrata*s for the householders and *mahāvrata*s for ascetics, both derived from the main *vrata*s. With respect to the householders, when they reach full compliance with the five *aṇuvrata*s, with assistance from the seven *guṇa-vrata*s, they start leading their lives with a sense of contentment, knowing that they are advancing in the path of spiritual life. At this stage, their daily life consists of:

- Revering and worshipping *tīrthaṅkara jina*s.
- Devotion to the *guru*.
- Self-studies for spiritual knowledge.
- Restraint in life.
- Penance to the best of their abilities.
- Involvement in appropriate acts of philanthropy, donations, etc.

Such householders dutifully observe these practices and lead a happy and spiritually joyful life. For the householders who are not living such a blissful life, it is important to understand what is preventing them from accomplishing it – or what the key elements are that make it difficult for them to engage in a more ethical lifestyle.

Upon studying the household ethics (*gṛhastha-dharma*) presented in previous pages, one can surmise that possessiveness (*parigraha*) is the main enticement for a householder's indulgent life. It is the key cause of the other four *doṣas*, violence, untruthfulness, stealing, and sexual urges (*hiṁsā*, *asatya*, *adattādāna,* and *maithuna*, respectively). Jain scriptures have defined extreme possessiveness, and actions that support it, as the traits that lead to rebirth in a hellish realm.[14] With that in mind, householders should lead a life of simplicity while indulging in only minor forms of possession and other related acts. They should acquire just enough materials to support a satisfactory yet simple lifestyle for their families. This is essential for achieving the highly respected ranks of an ideal Jain householder.

Spiritually inclined Jain householders put limits on the amount of their possessions to curb their desires. To stay within the limits, they reduce the number and quantity of things to be acquired for day-to-day life. In addition, they stop procuring any articles that are not essential to maintain their lifestyle. In this manner, their life becomes simple and spiritually enjoyable, and they abstain from committing any unnecessary misdeeds or sins that a regular, non-ideal householder life might entail.

The individuals whose livelihood is dependent on professions that involve committing violent acts are neglecting their own spiritual advancement. This is harmful for that individual, the community, and the nation. From the Jain perspective, pious householders avoid such professions because it leads to inauspicious kārmic acquisition. An ideal Jain householder only pursues actions that help in shedding kārmic particles and that limit troublesome kārmic acquisition. Some examples of the trades that such a householder stays away from:

- Working to destroy forests, or harm ecology and natural resources.
- Dealing in meat products or other products that involve hurting or

---

[14] As previously noted, "hell" in the Jain and Indian dhārmic traditions is a temporary abode, and therefore does not carry the connotations of "eternal damnation" that is seen in the Abrahamic or other faiths.

killing living beings,[15] and dealings in ivory, leather, silk, etc.

- Employing bonded labor and enslaving people or animals.
- Running a business to produce or trade drugs, alcoholic products, or other illicit and harmful intoxicants.
- Dealings in poison and other life-ending products.
- Producing or trading or dealing in equipment for wars and mass killings.
- Producing instruments and equipment that increase unemployment.
- Conducting or inciting others to indulge in dubious acts for money like tax evasion.
- Any other such inappropriate means of livelihood.

The *Upāsakadaśāṅgasūtra*, a highly revered Jain scripture, presents the characteristic traits of ideal Jain householders. They are to restrict possessions by limiting themselves to whatever properties (land for agriculture, savings, cows, etc.) they had at the time of the vow. It narrates the story of Ānanda Śrāvaka, who had hundreds of thousands of cows, huge lots of land that required hundreds of ploughs for agriculture, and other tremendous assets. He was involved in massive business deals, but limited himself by freezing the growth of his assets upon taking his vows. He continued his agriculture, dairy farms, and other such business but increasingly began committing his profits to philanthropic causes for social welfare.

One may ask, "If you do not want to make profits for yourself, why waste time in business?" The answer is, for ideal householders, business is not for self-indulgence only. It is also a vehicle for social service. Business is conducted to fulfill the needs of the community. Not all articles required by households are widely available. Some items are economically available only at a specific location. Business transactions, for example trading, were originally designed to meet regional supply and demand on the basis of the needs of a particular locality. This was to ensure that articles produced at one location are not wasted while the other location had shortages for the same items. The ideal Jain *śrāvaka-śrāvikā* traders understand this concept and

---

[15] It should be noted here that the modern dairy industry involves killing both the cows and their calves.

run their business practices accordingly. If trading did not exist, communities would suffer from shortages of essential items for living. Ordinary citizens cannot obtain everything needed for their day-to-day living without commerce. They have no means to do so and must depend on the transactions of local businessmen.

Thus, for a businessperson commerce becomes an important mode of social service. While involved in these acts of service, a businessperson saves enough for their family as business profit. For an ideal householder, profits should be just enough to meet the needs of the family. This concept should be reflected in how one prices one's goods. In addition to revenue streams, there is a parallel stream for happy living that is the stream of spirituality for which one does not need any special profits. While enjoying spirituality, the householders continue their business dealings with the spirit of public service.

Jain scriptures provide detailed guidelines on ideal professional life. Such teachings help immensely in developing righteous virtues for joyful living. It is clear that to achieve ethical living, one must start by controlling the urges of possessiveness.

Social Demeanor

Jain Dharma has had its firm roots in India from pre-historic days. All twenty-four *tīrthaṅkara*s were born and raised in India, and their followers have always been an integral part of Indian society and culture. The tradition originated and flourished in the regions that were dominated by Aryans,[16] hence it is believed that all *tīrthaṅkara*s were from the Aryan lineage. All throughout the ages, Jains have been reminiscent of their spiritual heritage and have always been inspired by, and are the followers of, the path of compassion, non-attachment, and non-possessiveness.

Right from the beginning, Jain religion was not a caste-based religion. It was created on the principles of conscious development and the pursuit of eternal liberation. The religion has not strayed from those principles

---

[16] That Jains have Aryan lineage should be considered a belief rather than a historical fact. Many scholars consider Jain Dharma to have existed before Aryan migration into India. Some scholars believe Jain Dharma to be an eternal philosophy because its fundamental principles are so intertwined with the soul, divinity, nature, and the universe.

over the centuries. It has never entertained any individuals with egotistic desires of expansion, or attachment to authority, or entitlements of worldly affairs. Neither has Jain Dharma ever indulged in any activities of that sort. Nonetheless, Jains have made immense contributions to Indian culture and civilization. Yet, they never implanted or forcefully imposed or applied their values, culture, and heritage within India and other parts of the world. Jains have never taken inappropriate steps to expand the tradition's fellowship, even when they were in positions of power and authority. They have left it to individuals to voluntarily adopt the principles and practices of the tradition for their own benefit.

Jains and Jain-inspired people have had traditions based on family and social relations – including marriages – because the religion does not interfere with social traditions. It just provides guidelines for honorable conduct and lifestyle. Jains and the Indian society at large have always been intertwined; hence there are not many fundamental differences in cultural etiquette and tradition between the two. The principles and practices of the Jain doctrine, which have inspired innumerable individuals, have resulted in the proliferation of many of its honorable characteristics in the community at large. The main reason for that has been modesty and humility, the core tenets of Jain philosophy, which are firmly imbedded in the demeanor of Jain practitioners.

Jain Householder Etiquette

As discussed earlier, modesty and contentment are highly emphasized in Jain philosophy. Simplicity, atonement, compassion, and service are the main components of penance. Atonement mitigates the maladies of false pride and arrogance, and eventually ends them. Simplicity strengthens modesty, nobleness, and humility. Jain etiquette is born out of simplicity.

An important form of penance in Jain doctrine consists of the tradition of veneration towards *samyag-jñāna*, *samyag-darśana,* and *samyag-cāritra*, and showing the utmost respect towards practitioners of the tradition. The acts of eschewing undignified, sinful, and malicious tendencies in mind-body-speech, and focusing them towards praiseworthy, virtuous, and useful traits, are considered the acts of great penance.

Jain scriptures have provided detailed guidelines to improve social behavior and interactions with the society. Some of the recommended traits that are considered important are:

- As a disciple, always show obedience towards the learned ones and be respectful when interacting with them.
- Offer charity with humility.
- Show compassion towards all living beings, human and non-human, that are hurting.
- Be aware of the specific circumstances of time and place, and show appropriate respect to the prevailing traditions and cultural norms.
- Interact with everyone with love, respect, and spirituality.

The prime duties of Jain ascetics and householders are to convey heartfelt respect towards mendicants, other householders, *arihanta*s, *siddha*s, deities, religion, and *guru*s – without the slightest hint, internal or external, of disrespect towards any of them.

Jain scriptures have expounded in great detail on the implications of disrespecting religious dignitaries. They describe thirty-two types of disrespect towards the *guru*. This includes standing in front of the *guru*, sitting on his seat, walking in front of the *guru*, and many other such behavioral guidelines.

Similarly, there are prescribed etiquettes for interacting with other dignitaries.

1. *Respect towards tīrthaṅkara, deity, and worldly guru*: When a Jain ascetic or householder goes to an assembly of *tīrthaṅkaras*[17] or to the resting place of a monk, they should follow five protocols, known as *abhigama* (visiting codes):
   i. Remove flowers, garlands, and other such items that once had consciousness.
   ii. It is not necessary to remove items that never had life.
   iii. Do not bring any symbols of superfluous living such as designer clothes, head coverings, and other items such as shoes and turbans.
   iv. Bow with folded hands as soon as the monk sees you or you see

[17] In contemporary times, an assembly of *tīrthaṅkara*s refers to a place where a *tīrthaṅkara* image has been placed, for instance, a temple.

the *tīrthaṅkara*.

v. Stop mental wandering, misgivings, or worrying and concentrate on meditation or on listening to the *guru*.

2. *Devotional recitation*: Show respect and devotion to the *guru* by reciting the following verse (Sāmāyika Pāṭha) from the *Āvaśyakasūtra*:

> Lord, starting from south I go around you three times, bow to you, greet you, and respect you. You are a personification of bliss and welfare. You are like a heavenly being, spiritually awakened and wise. I repeatedly worship you. With bowed head, I greet you.[18]

3. *Behavioral protocols for mutual interactions between householders*: Various illustrations in Jain scriptures show that from ancient times both male and female householders have greeted their older peers first. These scriptures provide detailed protocols for mutual interactions between householders.
4. *Intra-family interactions*: Jain scriptures (for instance, the *Upāsakadaśāṅgasūtra*[19]) have expounded on the relationships within a family (for example, between the siblings, parents, and children, and even husband and wife) and provide protocols for honorable living in a family. The protocols provide inspirations for mutual respect, non-discriminatory treatment of family members while recognizing individual responsibilities, and other similar behavioral traits.
5. *Employer-employee* (*svāmī-sevaka*) *interactions*: Jain scriptures consider a servant or employee as a member of the employer's family (*koṭambīyapuriṣa*). Even a king is supposed to address his workers as *devāṇuppiyā* (god's favorite). One can clearly see the humble connotations of these words. In fact, *devāṇuppiyā* is a common word for addressing each other. It is used between husband and wife, employer and employee, and in all other relations.

The aforementioned behavioral protocols are as relevant, if not more,

---

[18] *tikkhutto āyāhiṇaṁ, payāhiṇaṁ karemi, vaṅdāmi namaṁsāmi, sakkāremi, saṁmāṇemi, kallāṇaṁ maṅgalaṁ devayaṁ ceīyaṁ pujjuvāsāmi, matthaeṇa vaṅdāmi.*

[19] This is a treatise containing the accounts of the lives of ten leading householder followers, or *upāsaka*s, of Lord Mahāvīra.

in today's society as they were millennia ago when they were crafted. The fundamental principles of compassion, peace, and non-violence of Jain Dharma are the foundations of these protocols. One can easily surmise that if humanity had followed these protocols, anti-social activities such as slavery, territorial aggressions, and religious wars would have never materialized. Faithful Jains and other peace-loving individuals continue to live by these principles and have made them part of their celebrations.

13

The Virtues of Jain Mendicants (Nirgrantha Dharma)

Renunciation (Tyāga)

RENUNCIATION (*tyāga*) is the key aspect of ascetic life and it is emphasized in all dhārmic traditions (Jain, Buddhist, Vedic, etc.). However, it has a unique significance in Jain Dharma – the religion of Nirgranthas, the possessionless mendicants. That is why, in the early days, Jain Dharma was frequently referred to as Nirgrantha Dharma.

The characterization, formulation, and structure of renunciation varies from one doctrine to another. For instance, Vedic doctrine divides a lifespan into four stages, where the fourth stage is dedicated to the life of renunciation and asceticism exclusively. However, the reality is that a living being's lifespan is unknown because death is always impending, and life can end at any moment. Thus, it is uncertain that one would even have the necessary duration of life to reach the fourth stage.

Jain Dharma approaches renunciation pragmatically and does not specify any special age for the start and acceptance of the life of renunciation.[1] One cannot assume a well-defined and structured lifespan when, in reality, the duration of life itself is so uncertain. At the same time, Jain philosophy has recognized the ability of an individual to adopt the life of renunciation irrespective of one's age. An individual is ready to be a renunciate when they have:

- Attained the auspicious (*śubha*) vision of the real truth (*tattva-dr̥ṣṭi*).
- Developed a clear understanding of the differences between what is the soul (*ātmā*) and what is not the soul (*anātmā*), and what is one's

[1] In fact, Ācārya Sushil Kumar, whose writings and discourses are the inspiration for this book, started his ascetic life before his eighth birthday.

essential nature (*svarūpa*), and what is not.

- Comprehended the fact that excessive indulgences (*bhoga*) in sensory objects (*indriya-viṣaya*) are poisonous (*viṣākta*) and against the true nature of soul.

When individuals are compelled by austere feelings and tendencies, they are ready to be initiated into the life of asceticism. Thus, they are ready to adopt an ascetic lifestyle after preparing to be free from all worldly attachments, including their own bodies, and they are completely absorbed in spiritual penance.

A human being could be the income provider for the family, a community organizer and activist, or a warrior and a soldier for the country. But ultimately, while all of these may be necessary for the current functioning of society, none of these roles is sufficient in itself for the ultimate fulfillment of the purpose of life. One has to go alone beyond these worldly responsibilities to traverse the ultimate spiritual path. An ascetic who sets out to walk this arduous path earns the right to be named a renunciate or mendicant or, in Jain terms, a *śramaṇa*.[2]

In order to reach the esteemed platform of a Jain mendicant, one has to relinquish home, family life, all properties, money, and other such worldly possessions. But that is not enough. A true mendicant is one who:

- While fully engrossed in ascetic life conquers internal deficiencies.
- Is unaffected by the respect or insults, reverence or slander, accorded to them.
- Is unattached to one's own life and death.

All of these factors become equivalent in every mendicant's eyes.

Jain mendicants consider receiving even rudeness and rejection to be a blessing and are able to accept harsh treatment directed towards them. They never undertake hurtful physical or spoken actions, or disparage anyone. They remain unattached and non-possessive, yet consider the entire planet as their own, treating all living beings with compassion and friendship. They

[2] The term *śramaṇa* refers to both male and female ascetics, also referred to as mendicants or renunciates. The term *sādhus* is used for male ascetics and *sādhvīs* for female ascetics or nuns.

become a wandering source of education, spreading spiritual teachings to enlighten the entire world with kindness.

True Jain mendicants develop a persona that is free of artificial boundaries. That is why they do not support a national identity. To them, the entitlements such as national or international reputation are unnatural and, hence, meaningless. Rather, Jain mendicants are dedicated to the experiencing of life in its entirety, and are not to be fragmented by excessive fixation on color, creed, etc.

Jain mendicants never separate themselves from the welfare of others and they do not desire any benefits for themselves personally. They consider their own pain to be a blessing and accept it with an unbiased, equipoised mind. However, the pain of other beings is unbearable for Jain ascetics. It is true that their predominant focus is on their own spiritual progression, but social welfare is actually the means for that progression. An individual involved in social welfare with the objective of self-improvement and personal spiritual growth does not get any egotistical pride out of it. Jain mendicants maintain that principle and thereby protect their spiritual practice from the blemish of ego. True mendicants, while primarily focused on their own spiritual progression, facilitate the same for all those around them.

Lord Mahāvīra preached to his mendicant disciples thus:

> For possessionless Jain monks (*śramaṇa nirgranthīs*), the dignified way of leading life is to live with minimum resources, stay disinterested in worldly affairs, have no unnecessary feelings or desires, allow no unintentional deviations, maintain self-discipline, observe calmness without any anger, have no arrogance, have no deceit, and be without greed.

With this type of penance, the practitioners can end their cycles of birth and death and receive the ultimate joy of enlightenment by achieving the status of a *paramātma* (Supreme Soul). Jain scriptures have provided extensive details on the lifestyle and conduct of Jain mendicants. Many texts have been written by a multitude of scholars to interpret and describe the ascetic lifestyle as prescribed in scriptures. An extremely high-level version is presented below to describe the key aspects of the lifestyle of a Jain mendicant.

THE FIVE SUPREME VOWS FOR ASCETICS (MAHĀVRATAS)

Five supreme vows (*mahāvratas*) are the essential requirement for being a Jain mendicant and all mendicants must strictly adhere to these.

1. *Ahiṁsā mahāvrata* (supreme vow of non-violence): This *mahāvrata* constitutes vowing:

    - Not to commit any violence in mind-body-speech against any type of stationary or moving living beings.
    - Not to have others commit violence on one's behalf.
    - Not to encourage others in committing violent acts.
    - Not to praise or show reverence to those who commit such violence.

    A Jain mendicant's mind is like a pond of nectar, their speech is like a river of nectar, and their body like a confluence of nectarian streams. A mendicant must always exude a flow of kindness and compassion for all living beings. With this is in mind, a Jain mendicant refrains from all unkind activities and does not encourage or promote them. They maintain supreme vows and have completely renounced killing or hurting any type of stationary or moving living bodies.

2. *Satya mahāvrata* (supreme vow of truthfulness): With this supreme vow, a Jain mendicant commits to:

    - Think truthfully
    - Speak truthfully
    - Conduct truthfully

    In addition, a Jain mendicant must not commit even a subtle untruth under any circumstances. An ascetic devoted to spiritual penance considers truthfulness to be supreme. Jain mendicants never indulge in falsehood in mind-body-speech, even by mistake. They prefer to stay quiet, but when necessary use only truthful, friendly, and blemish-free language limited to basic need. A mendicant never talks without being thoughtful and certainly never uses language to encourage others to indulge in violent acts in mind-body-speech. Such a mendicant avoids laughter and loud talking that could inadvertently provoke untruthful speech.

3. *Acaurya mahāvrata* (supreme vow of non-stealing): Jain mendicants do not accept anything without proper and unreserved permission from the owner. This applies to everything in the world. For instance, this principle is applied when a *guru* accepts someone as a disciple, on the one extreme, and while removing a bit of lifeless grass, on the other, and it applies to everything in between. Jain mendicants do not take even a small thing like a toothpick without permission.
4. *Brahmacarya mahāvrata* (supreme vow of celibacy): Jain mendicants observe complete abstinence from sexual and other lustful activities. To be able to fully comply with this difficult vow, a number of additional rules and guidelines have been established for the mendicants. These rules address how to interact with the opposite gender, avoid food items which stimulate passions that could lead to an aphrodisiac effect, and avoid self-beautification.
5. *Aparigraha mahāvrata* (supreme vow of non-possession): Jain mendicants disown and reject even an interest in having ownership of all types of possessions, in accordance with this vow. They renounce ownership of any material be it home, properties, money, or luxury items. This supreme vow extends to the ownership of non-material and non-tangible entities as well. For instance, when it comes to the *guru*-disciple relationship, neither the disciple nor the *guru* is "possessor" of that relationship. In other words, they have a *guru*-disciple relationship with no ownership rights or other attachments, and either one can terminate the relationship, with no resentments or hard feeling.

   The mendicants adhere to this supreme vow with mind-body-speech at every living moment, whether asleep or awake. They wander from place to place with no worldly attachments to anyone or anything, no interest in any establishment or organization, and no possessions to carry. As inhabitants of the world, they do require some articles for their living. But such articles are limited to the minimum possible possessions, such as one or two pieces of cloth and utensils to collect food when they go out to collect alms. Even these items are reluctantly accepted out of necessity, not because they feel that they own or possess them.

   Carelessness and insensibility are also considered a form of possessiveness for Jain mendicants. Discarding all external or materialistic possessions could lead to the development of disinterest in those. But disinterest could result in careless behavior. So, although Jain mendicants have to be disinterested in objects, they cannot be careless about these things or show disrespect to them.

FIVE BEHAVIORAL CONSTRAINTS (SAMITIS)

It is critical for Jain mendicants to develop an acute mental attentiveness to avoid inadvertently committing any harm to others that would be considered sinful or immoral. To that end, five behavioral constraints, called *samiti*s, were enacted. They are essential constraints observed by the Jain mendicants so that they can comprehensively and irrefutably adhere to the five supreme vows (*mahāvrata*s).

1. *Īryā samiti* (wandering constraint): In order to minimize the inadvertent killing of living beings like insects, worms, or even grass, mendicants are advised to closely scrutinize the area four or more steps ahead of them when they walk. This way, they can carefully track a clear path to walk.
2. *Bhāṣā samiti* (language constraint): Jain mendicants must constrain themselves to always speak in friendly, pleasing, helpful, and truthful language.
3. *Eṣaṇā samiti* (food constraint): Jain mendicants must constrain themselves to only accept pure food which complies with their ascetic lifestyle and vows. Also, they must ensure that taking alms does not hurt anyone in process, such as depriving the givers of food for themselves. The process of cooking by householders is bound to involve some unavoidable violence against some form of life, like airborne insects that might be killed in fire. Jain mendicants accept foods that have a minimum potential of hurting any living beings during harvesting or cooking.
4. *Ādāna-nikṣepaṇa samiti* (moving constraint): A mendicant must always be careful in moving objects from one place to another so that no living beings are hurt or killed in the process.
5. *Paristhāpanikā samiti* (excrement-disposal constraint): A mendicant

must always dispose of excrement in such a way that it does not yield any new life forms due to its fertilizer-like properties. Also, a mendicant must make sure that it does not create difficulty for others, such as pollution.

PROTECTIVE MEASURES FOR THE MIND AND SENSES (GUPTĪ)

It is important to protect the mind and senses from false and potentially harmful inclinations. In order to avoid inadvertently straying into any mental or sensual distractions, the following three types of protective measures, called *guptī*s, were created for Jain mendicants.

1. *Manoguptī* (protection of mind): This protection is intended to focus the mind away from undignified, inauspicious, or despicable thoughts or inclinations.
2. *Vācanaguptī* (protection of speech): This protection is intended to protect against improper use of language. It helps in avoiding words and language that could be untrue, harsh, hurtful, cruel, awkward, or unhelpful.
3. *Kāyaguptī* (protection of body): This protection is to shield one from improper action by one's body. It helps one to stop taking unworthy and improper actions, and diverts the actions of the body towards only auspicious activities. This helps to develop discipline and alertness, so the mendicants can always be watchful, anticipatory, and protective against harmful behaviors during night and day.

PROHIBITIONS (ANĀCĪRṆA)

While engrossed in their life of renunciation, austerities, and meditation, the Jain mendicants regularly interact with householders for sermons, prayers, and other religious activities. In addition, since the mendicants do not carry any money and do not own any means to conduct their daily lives, they need to go to people's homes to collect food; accept clothes, unless they (male mendicants only) have forsaken clothes; accept medicines when they are not well; and other such regular necessities. While interacting with the householders, they may be presented with situations which distract them from their commitment to mendicant lifestyle. These distractions may appear momentarily and may appear insignificant, but they might have significant impact, causing the mendicants to divert from their chosen path. Although the path of renunciation is voluntary and each individual is free to abandon it at one's own will, most of the time mendicants want to continue their journey. The distractions cause them to derail, and it takes significant effort by them to get back on track. Many times, it takes certain stricter austere activities designed for repentance. Therefore, for the sincere ascetic practitioners, it is better to avoid such distractions in the first place. In order to help ascetics avoid such distractions and stay on course to progress efficiently, a number of prohibitive injunctions were enacted.

In Jain scriptures, fifty-two types of actions have been prohibited to help Jain mendicants perform their penance in a streamlined and structured manner. These are activities in which they should never indulge, and involve almost all external endeavors. A detailed description of all the prohibitions is beyond the scope of this text and a summary is presented below to highlight their purpose:

- The primary purpose of food consumption is to satisfy hunger and provide adequate nourishment to the body and not to indulge in serving the sensory palate. With that in mind, mendicants should accept food with only nourishment in mind, not the taste. In addition, the quantity and quality of food consumption should only be to satisfy hunger, not for objectives such as body-building or appearance.

  Furthermore, the food for the mendicants should not cause any burden on the householders, so the mendicants should accept whatever is voluntarily offered by the householders and not ask for any special foods. Old or leftover food may collect insects, etc., so the mendicants should not keep food for later consumption for any reason or accept old food from householders. Also, all Jains, not just the mendicants, are advised to eat before sunset to minimize inadvertent violence, such as insects falling on the food. For the same reason, they should avoid foods which grow underground and have roots because such foods have highest regenerative potential.

- The mendicants refrain from self-indulgence to avoid any unpleasant or distracting interaction with people. They do not use any beauty products such as perfumes, do not pander in self-beautification such as fancy hairstyles or wearing makeup, do not undertake any exercises or products for body-building, do not engage in body massage, or other such actions for self-aggrandization.

- Mendicants minimize their social activities and participate only in spiritual-religious-related or other such events. They do not take part in any games or competitions, and avoid unnecessary interactions with the members of the family they had relinquished, or meet with the opposite gender solitarily, etc. They do not involve themselves in any social talk such as gossiping.

The above summary conveys the essence of these prohibitions. There are other specific and detailed ones designed to motivate austere living with full attention to their penance and dedication to the path of spirituality they have chosen.

The above prohibitions were specified long ago, and as such, some of them refer to the actions that may not be applicable in modern lifestyle. Nevertheless, the underlying message is that it is critical for Jain mendicants to adopt a lifestyle that is conducive to adherence with the *mahāvrata*s of asceticism.

Twelve Reflective Contemplations (Dvādaśa Bhāvanā)

The external demeanor of an individual reflects his or her inner mental predisposition. Therefore, in order to sanctify one's penance, it is absolutely essential to train and control the mind. In this regard, Jain scriptures have prescribed certain subtle and minor, but highly effective, guidelines to reflect upon. These guidelines help in enhancing spiritual devotion by developing and stabilizing feelings that are devoid of affection and attachments. The foremost one, known as *anuprekṣā*s (reflections), is to repeatedly contemplate these guidelines. There are twelve broad guidelines:

1. *Anitya bhāvanā* (contemplation of impermanence): Every inanimate substance (*padārtha*) in this universe, including bodies associated with *jīva*, is destructible, transitory, or unfixed in nature. For instance, social standing, professional prestige, family position, and fame are all momentary. Wealth is not permanent either and disappears quickly like the light of dusk. Life is like a bubble in water that forms and vanishes fleetingly. Youth is like the shade provided by a cloud that soon goes

away. All of these do not take much time to disappear and destruct. It is not wise to be lured by such short-lived attractions and ignore the everlasting joys generated by spiritual cultivation.

2. *Aśaraṇa bhāvanā* (contemplation of self-protection): Nobody can be saved from the dreadful claws of death. At the end, no amount of money, fame, power, or family standing can prevent their inevitable demise. Therefore, it is unwise to take shelter (*śaraṇa*) with ephemeral entities.
3. *Saṁsāra bhāvanā* (contemplation of the universe and cycle of rebirth): This contemplative sentiment is about the real nature of the universe. No king or pauper, rich or poor, is entirely happy and blissful in this universe. Everyone is suffering from some sort of a misery – some self-inflicted, some caused by others, and some caused by nature. All inhabitants on this universe are caught up in the vicious never-ending cycle of life and death. One who is near and dear in this life could become unknown or an enemy in the next one, and vice versa. Therefore, differentiating between beings that one knows or does not know is illusory and immaterial. When considering the vast possibilities for future births and the endless nature of past lives, strictly speaking, no one forever belongs to one person, and neither is anyone permanently one's enemy or completely alien.
4. *Ekatva bhāvanā* (contemplation of solitariness): A living being is born alone and dies alone. Ultimately, one suffers through miseries alone, and enjoys pleasures alone. The company of others is temporary and brief; nobody accompanies you on the voyage to the next life.
5. *Anyatva bhāvanā* (contemplation of soul-body relationship): Every living entity in this universe is endowed with a duality – (a) its unique soul, and (b) its physically observable manifestation (e.g., body). Although the two are associated with each other, the soul is different from the physical manifestation of the entity. This guideline prompts all human beings to contemplate this unique doctrine of soul-body relationship, which elucidates that soul is the real *jīva* and not the body.
6. *Aśuci bhāvanā* (contemplation of the impurity of the body): A living body is impure. It is important to contemplate these realities in order

to minimize and eliminate attachment towards the body, which after all, is ephemeral. This type of contemplation is critical to detaching oneself from worldly affairs.

7. *Āśrava bhāvanā* (contemplation of the influx of *karma*): Despite whatever one may think, the real causes of all miseries are kārmic acquisitions and their attachment in layers over the soul. The reasons for kārmic acquisition are the vices such as passions (anger, ego, deceit, and greed), malice, jealousy, false knowledge, inappropriate beliefs, violence, attachment, non-contentment, untruthfulness, and carelessness. To contemplate these real causes of miseries helps one to progress on the path of spirituality.
8. *Saṁvara bhāvanā* (contemplation of the checking of the influx of *karma*): This constitutes contemplating the ways one can stop the collection and deposition of soul-obstructing *karma*s.
9. *Nirjarā bhāvanā* (contemplation of the destruction of *karma*): This contemplation is about thinking of ways one can start the forceful destruction of *karma*s which have already been acquired and lodged in layers over the soul.
10. *Loka Bhāvanā* (contemplation of the nature of the universe): This is to visualize and contemplate the cosmology of the universe.
11. *Bodhi-durlabha bhāvanā* (contemplation of the rarity of attaining omniscience): The knowledge that enhances the state of the soul and delivers principled knowledge about the entire universe is considered noble knowledge. It helps a living being in progressing towards the ultimate goal of salvation. This contemplation involves pondering why impeccable or supreme wisdom is so elusive and difficult to attain.
12. *Dharma bhāvanā* (contemplation of the teaching of the sacred law or *dharma*): This is to contemplate the real nature of righteousness, its glorious qualities and the benefits.

One can see that although the above twelve guidelines for reflective contemplations are discussed in the context of ascetic lifestyle, they are equally useful and effective for the householder lifestyle as well. The same applies to the four additional contemplations discussed next.

Four Contemplations for Character Building (Cāra Bhāvanā)

In addition to the above twelve guidelines for contemplation (*bhāvanā*s) to reflect on nature, the universe, and divinity, Jain scriptures have prescribed four additional *bhāvanā*s to build character while reflecting on the previous twelve. They are all designed to help progress towards the end goal of ultimate liberation.

1. *Maitrī bhāvanā* (contemplation on friendship): If an ascetic does not develop feelings of friendship towards all living beings, they cannot fully adhere to the principle of non-violence. Friendship involves the cultivation of spiritual feelings for others, and from this affection, creating the desire to not hurt others. Once the feelings of friendship are fully evolved, the ascetic becomes restless upon seeing others in pain or misery. They do everything in their capacity to help rescue others from their suffering. When the ascetic's heart is fully enriched with the feelings of friendship, the auspicious traits of non-violence, truth, etc., are also cultivated. The practitioner's innermost feelings can be expressed in the following words:

   > All living beings on this earth are my friends, irrespective of whether they are human or animals, insects, or plants.[3]
   >
   > I have no enemy because I have developed an everlasting spiritual relationship with all of them.[4]

   With the rise of such feelings of resilient friendship, the mind becomes filled with auspicious tendencies and righteous thoughts. At the same time, passions (anger, ego, deceit, and greed), malice, and jealousy start losing their grip. At the end, the soul reaches a stage where it starts seeing the spiritual nature in every other soul. This leaves no room for violence or any traits that could be harmful to others.

2. *Pramoda bhāvanā* (contemplation on spiritual elation): These are the sentiments when an individual feels spiritual exhilaration upon meeting the learned ones. Generally, human beings have some fundamental weaknesses, for instance, those comprising feelings of jealousy when

---

[3] *metti me savva bhuesu.*

[4] *vairam majjham na kenyee.*

someone is doing better than themselves. Sometimes under the influence of such adverse tendencies one may go to the extent of trying to bring down the person who is seemingly ahead. Until such harmful feelings can be curbed and diminished, it is hard to develop, retain, and enhance auspicious tendencies such as non-violence and truthfulness. Jain scholars created various behavioral provisions, as discussed earlier, to augment the understanding of spiritual elation and to help the spiritual seekers in controlling their adverse feelings such as those of jealousy and malice.

3. *Karuṇa bhāvanā* (contemplation on compassion): These are the sentiments when an individual has heartfelt feelings of empathy (*anukampā*) towards living beings who are in pain and misery, and that individual becomes inspired to help those who are in agony. It is hard to comply with non-violence and other supreme vows when sentiments of compassion are absent or in deficiency. When these sentiments become awakened and solidified in humans, they are no longer inclined to, or are capable of, hurting others by their actions in conduct or thoughts. Furthermore, the spiritual aspirant cannot remain indifferent to one who is being hurt by some other individual.
4. *Madhyastha bhāvanā* (contemplation on neutrality): This refers to the ability whereby one can remain indifferent to the devious actions of others, irrespective of the type and magnitude of such acts. The ability to stay neutral or indifferent may be very helpful under some adverse situations like facing someone's misbehavior or foul language, illogical arguments, unrighteous conduct, or when someone fails to improve and all the attempts to guide and coach them have failed.

   It is very common to see the tendencies of intolerance among human beings. They cannot endure any hostility or antagonism towards themselves or their views, and they easily become intolerant of those opposing them. Disagreements in thoughts and actions usually lead to the termination of personal relationships. This applies to all areas of life – personal or professional. This tendency towards intolerance is a weakness. For its mitigation, it is critical to develop and strengthen the feeling of neutrality. When one has cultivated such equipoise, one does not get agitated or frightened when faced with opposing views or acts. Such a person thereby maintains his virtuous traits and tendencies.

These four motivational contemplations prompt the outflow of a purified stream of joy to inspire the practitioners and all those who surround them. These contemplations manage to calm down the innermost torment and agony of human beings and bring enrichment and magnanimity to all life. They are instrumental in developing and enhancing the spiritual qualities that inspire one to continue on the path of asceticism.

Ten Principles of Dharma (Daśa-Vidhi-Dharma)

Before a soul regains its intrinsically pure and true state through salvation, it continues in the endless vicious cycle of life and death. The redemption to the pure state occurs only in the rarest cases. The attainment of redemption is not linked to the death or destruction of a body – it is the result of intense penance and righteousness, as has been discussed. The point to note is that, of the countless living beings, human beings have the capability to attain salvation. The others (dwellers of heaven, hell, and those in the animal world) neither have it nor are capable of developing the necessary righteousness.

Human beings are always interested in immortality. By seeing patterns of other human lives, they can estimate the future state of their own bodies in a general sense. They know this life's end is certain, and they attempt to deploy various means as if to achieve their own version of immortality before that. However, only a few understand the true meaning of immortality. Some people try to immortalize themselves by attempting to establish the permanence of their own name and fame. Others do so through their lineage of children and grandchildren. Yet others create buildings and memorials to leave behind monuments or memorabilia with their engraved name for posterity. Such acts may be seen as the means to immortality, but none of these can truly satisfy that insatiable hunger. All physical entities are destined to end and to meet their destruction. If one is not immortal oneself, how can one make or motivate others to be everlasting?

All of the above-mentioned actions are related to the physical body and not to the soul. Notwithstanding these extraneous acts in search of immortality, only *dharma* has the power to make someone immortal. Jain scriptures state that ten principles widely called *daśa-vidhi-dharma* or *daśa-dharma* (ten *dharmas*) can lead an individual to immortality. That is why compliance with these principles is considered essential for all Jain mendicants. In some sense, one can consider the ten principles described below as a repackaging of the philosophy discussed hitherto. They provide an alternate, concise way of understanding the crux of Jain philosophy to eliminate the five vices (*doṣas*) discussed earlier (violence, untruthfulness, stealing, sexual urges, and possessiveness – *hiṁsā*, *asatya*, *adattādāna*, *maithuna*, and *parigraha*, respectively).

1. *Kṣamā* (forgiveness): Forgiveness is the foundation of non-violence. *Kṣamā-dharma* entails asking for forgiveness from an individual who has been wronged by one's actions and granting forgiveness to someone who has done wrong. In both cases, it creates intense spiritual feelings when done with true humility.

   There is a profound purpose behind this injunction granted to humanity by the great *tīrthaṅkaras*. The "wrongdoing" referred to above covers all actions by mind-body-speech, including any types of hurt. Irrespective of whether the hurtful act was deliberate or inadvertent, all Jains sincerely ask for forgiveness with an open heart from those who have been wronged by them, and they grant forgiveness in a similar earnest manner. This exchange of forgiveness does not have to be explicit, and as such it is not applicable only to friends or known individuals, but to all living beings including non-human ones.

   Asking for forgiveness, in its truest genuine form, accompanies a sincere effort of repentance and an implied unspoken commitment of not repeating the same or similar acts of offending others. Similarly, granting forgiveness accompanies the elimination of all feelings of anger, malice, revenge, etc., and implies the generation of feelings of love and peace. In some ways, granting forgiveness could be harder than asking for the same because it is not easy to overcome and transform vindictive feelings into neutral or spiritually positive feelings towards the remorseful individual.

   From this, one can easily surmise that asking for and granting forgiveness are highly insightful and effective steps towards non-violence and other virtuous qualities. That is why the tradition of pleading for and granting forgiveness has continued uninterruptedly among Jains for centuries, not only among the ascetics but among the householders as well.

Jain scriptures have provisions for ascetics such that if they have committed an offense against someone, they must leave everything aside and first ask for pardon. Until they have asked for forgiveness, they do not take any meals or water, do not relax, and do not conduct any spiritual self-studies. They do not even swallow their own saliva until they have pleaded for pardon.

The householders too have similar provisions, but they are less rigorous and less strict than those for the mendicants. Similarly, both have prescriptive steps for granting true forgiveness to those who ask for it after having caused any hurt or discomfort to them. The practice of asking for and granting forgiveness is an important part of their spiritual practice – they do so every day, every fortnight, every four months, and every year, at different levels of intensity.

Paryuṣaṇā, the most auspicious Jain festival, is centered around pleading for pardon from others and granting others the same. During this festival, all Jains do this pleading – mendicants, householders, men, women, and children alike. Everyone humbly asks for forgiveness from all living beings whether or not they are known, for all of their misdeeds and sins. The below couplet is frequently recited by Jains, and it summarizes the essence of *kṣamā-dharma.*

> I forgive all living beings, and plead for forgiveness from all living beings.[5] All living beings on this earth are my friends, and I have no enemies.[6]

2. *Mārdava* (humility): To have gentleness of heart and modesty in behavior is the sign of humility. Humility is practiced by way of courtesy and mildness. Courteous behavior is so important in Jain Dharma that sometimes it is known as the religion of courteousness. Jain scriptures state that humility is the root of spirituality. In order

---

5 *khāmemi savve jivā, savve jivā khamantu me.*

6 *metti me savva bhuesu, vairam majjham na kenyee.*

to attain and practice humility, one has to relinquish passions caused by caste, lineage, wealth, fame, position, power, knowledge, spiritual awakening, penance, and all such traits. Having been born in a so-called high caste or famous clan, some individuals show no respect to others. Some, belonging to wealthy families, consider others to be lowly. Ideal ascetics forsake these social designations and are completely immersed in the practice of the supreme religious principle of humility.

3. *Ārjava* (straightforwardness): Sincere and simplistic behavior is the sign of *ārjava*. This principle is practiced when the thoughts, language, and conduct of an individual act in harmony with their sincere intentions. In order to implement straightforwardness in life, it is essential to relinquish cunning and deceptive traits.

   Straightforwardness plays an important role in cultivating right character because the development of mutual trust and confidence with others is essential for that purpose. Right knowledge created with sincerity and openness allows one to grasp the true nature of reality. One who has relinquished deviousness does not indulge in any deceit, hypocrisy, trickery, or other such acts. This person is sincere and simplistic, with a heart and mind that are at peace.

4. *Śauca* (contentment): To get rid of greed is purity. Any amount of greed that blemishes an ascetic's life could become a cause of spiritual ruin. The presence of the slightest amount of greed, even for a miniscule worthless thing, can become a cause for the destruction of all auspicious qualities. Therefore, all householders and ascetics should purify themselves from all forms of greed. The ascetics especially have conquered greediness with respect to obvious things like wealth, property, or other worldly articles, but they also refrain from desirous tendencies such as longing for a disciple or for reputation or prestige.

5. *Satya* (truthfulness): The importance of truthfulness in Jain doctrine is signified by being cited as one of the *daśa-vidhi-dharma*s and, at the same time, being one of the five critical *vrata*s (one of the limited vows for householders, *aṇuvrata*s, and one of the supreme vows for ascetics, *mahāvrata*s). Thus, it is considered a key requirement of spiritual life.

Jain scriptures have explained the importance of truthfulness in great detail. The *Praśna Vyākaraṇa Śāstra* states: "Truth is God."[7] Further, while describing the importance of this virtue, the scriptures state that truthfulness is the only essential entity in this universe; it is more solemn and intense than the great ocean, more steady and stable and firm than the auspicious Mount Meru, more gentle and amiable than the moon's halo and its light, more illustrious and glorious than the sun's halo and its light, more unblemished than the beautiful sky in spring, and grander than the Gandhamādana (a mountain referred to in Jain scriptures). All of these illustrations clearly signify the magnificent status and importance assigned to truthfulness in Jain philosophy.

6. *Saṁyama* (self-restraint): Self-restraint is the restriction of mental turmoil, curbing impure desires occurring in the heart and controlling activities of the senses. The individuals without self-restraint can transgress all boundaries of appropriateness in pursuit of sensory or mental gratification. Their dangerous tendencies, such as the longing for wealth and fame, could become recklessly out of control. Under the influence of such tendencies, many people wrongfully believe that fulfilling their cravings is the main objective of life, and that curbing them is a sign of weakness.

   Everyone in the world confronts the unfortunate consequences of such beliefs on a daily basis as mankind's selfish yearnings continue to escalate. Everyone is increasingly becoming distressed and succumbing to the violent effects of humanity's collective lack of self-control. As a result, the world has become a concourse for struggles and conflicts with no end in sight.

   It is impossible to apprehend the limitations of human greed because, it is said: "Desires are countless as the sky is limitless."[8] Without control over the cravings of the mind and senses it is impossible to bring satisfaction and gratification because multiple new desires emerge even before an existing one is fulfilled. If an individual is not internally at peace, no society, nation, or world can satiate their endless

---

7 *jaṁ saccaṁ taṁ khu bhagavaṁ.*

8 *itchha hu agasa, sama anihantiya.*

desire. Therefore, self-restraint is important and essential to uproot the fundamental causes of many social problems. Societally, the importance of self-restraint is equivalent to the importance of the spiritual progress of the individual practitioner. Lord Mahāvīra tells us:

> If you have achieved victory over your desires, you have achieved victory over your miseries.[9]

7. *Tapas* (austerity): Austerity is extremely important in Jain Dharma. Practicing austerity is an extraordinary and profound bliss that can be instrumental in accomplishing all spiritual tasks. Before Lord Mahāvīra, the Jain ways of austerity had waned, and it was practiced in various forms as ritualistic atonements, such as: (a) lighting a fire and inhaling the smoke, (b) lying on a bed of thorns, (c) standing under the sun, (d) entering a pond in very cold weather, and (e) sacrificing animals. But Mahāvīra inspired people to abandon violence and transformed such ritualistic exercises into benevolent spiritual practices for self-cultivation.

   The Jain practice of *tapas*, preached by Lord Mahāvīra, is neither exhibitionist in nature, nor narrow-minded. According to Jain philosophy, true austerity is that which provides nourishment to soul's intrinsic characteristics. With that in mind, Jain scriptures divide penance into two parts – extroverted and introverted. Extroverted penance consists of activities such as fasting, limited eating, relinquishing tasteful foods, and relinquishing possessions such as clothes and luxury items. Introverted penance consists of acts such as repenting one's own mistakes and sins; asking for forgiveness for offenses against others; respecting, honoring, and serving scholars and *gurus*; spiritual self-study; restricting oneself to some form of spiritual lifestyle; and conducting internal austerities that are not apparent to others.

8. *Tyāga* (renunciation): Renunciation is performed to cease the yearning for items that one does not possess, and to dissociate oneself from the materials that one does possess. True renunciation manifests itself when one finds delight and satisfaction with the minimum number of things. An ever-indulging and desirous person never achieves elevated

---

[9] *kame kamahi kamiyam khu dukham.*

spiritual satisfaction irrespective of all the material goods they might continually collect. According to Jain philosophy, people who practice renunciation do no collect unnecessary items. As a result, others are not deprived of those items, and hence shortages do not occur in the society.

9. *Akiñcanatā* (non-attachment): The signs of non-attachment consist of ceasing the superficial affection towards objects, refraining from considering anything as one's own, and giving up possessions irrespective of their material value. This is one of the most important virtues in Jain Dharma. Affection and attachments are the root causes of all miseries. As long as one is fond of material things or assumes ownership of those, they will feel miserable when those things are lost, taken away, or when they are destroyed. If one does not own anything and does not consider anything as their own, then one will not feel miserable when they experience loss. According to Jain philosophy, the essence of spiritual happiness is contentment and dissociation from material things.

10. *Brahmacarya* (supreme conduct, otherwise known as "celibacy"): Supreme conduct emerges when one avoids perversions that distract one from understanding one's spiritual nature. Celibacy is only one aspect of supreme conduct, and it generally refers to restraint from all sexual interactions. Therefore, all forms of sexual indulgence are prohibited for Jain ascetics, and self-control is recommended for householders. However, the term *brahmacarya* refers to sexual abstinence plus refrainment from all other unrighteous acts of behavior. In its truest sense, *brahmacarya* means "living like *Brahman*, or a noble being."

The ten principles of *dharma* (*daśa-vidhi-dharma*) described above are in essence a summary of how Jain Dharma is observed and practiced in day-to-day life. The extent to which these principles are adopted and exercised signifies the level of an individual's spirituality from being a layman householder to a sincere *mokṣa*-bound enlightened *jīva*. Just by understanding these principles, one can see how Jain Dharma connects individuals with their own true-self and helps create their unification with nature, the universe, and divinity.

Types of Spiritual Mendicants (Nirgranthas)

Living beings are continuously involved in activities that are spiritually unfavorable. As a result, a soul continues to be burdened with its ever-increasing attached *karma*s. This repetition of activities has been going on forever. It is hard to abandon and rise above the age-old practices that are the result of kārmic baggage and result in additional kārmic acquisition.

Jain ascetics have chosen the path of self-improvement by renouncing the worldly life and immersing themselves in a spiritual life of austerities such as penance and meditation. But in spite of their sincere commitment, arduous efforts, repeated attempts, and continuous vigilance, ancient patterns of kārmic behavior manage to reassert themselves continually in their lives. One can thus see how difficult it is to get rid of age-old practices. That is why ascetics must be continuously absorbed and devoted to their own spiritual endeavors. Jain ascetics are also called *nirgrantha*s (spiritual mendicants) because they do not have any possessions and are completely unattached to worldly life. Based on the intensity of their devotion, Jain scriptures have categorized mendicants in various classes. Here, they are grouped into five categories as described below:

1. *Pulāka-nirgrantha* (barely a mendicant): This is the class of mendicants in whom unworthy attributes heavily outweigh their praiseworthy ones. This condition is similar to when wheat plants are harvested: At first, the amount of stalk is excessively greater than the amount of grains that are yielded, or it could yield a bad batch of grain. Here the "stalk" would refer to the unworthy characteristics of the mendicants and "grain" would indicate to the paucity of their worthy characteristics.
2. *Bakuśa-nirgrantha* (trying to be a mendicant): This is the class of mendicants in whom unworthy attributes slightly outweigh their praiseworthy ones. Continuing with the above illustration of the wheat plant, this type of mendicant is analogous to the stalk that has been separated and yet some straw (rather than stalk from the previous example) remains with the grains. Although the weight of these straws is lesser than the stalk of the previous level (*pulāka-nigrantha*), they still outweigh the grains. Here each strand of grass would refer to the unworthy characteristics.

3. *Kuśīla-nirgrantha* (mendicants who succumb): This is the class of mendicants who are trying hard but their unworthy qualities continue to assert themselves. There are two types of such mendicants:
   i. *Kaṣāya-kuśīla-nirgrantha* (mendicants who succumb to passions): In this case, these mendicants observe self-restraint, they are devoted to spiritual studies to enhance their knowledge, and they practice austerities to the best of their abilities. Despite all this, occasionally they succumb to the allure of passions (*kaṣāya*). On such occasions, they get involved in non-meritorious acts that result in collecting more *karma*. They try hard to suppress these non-beneficial traits, but sometimes fail to fully succeed. For instance, they may get angry upon hearing criticism or harsh words. They may feel prideful upon receiving praise. They may even continue to be acquisitive about ordaining new disciples or about enhancing their scriptural knowledge.
   ii. *Pratisevanā-kuśīla-nirgrantha* (mendicants who succumb to enticements): This class of mendicants continues to have various deficiencies. They have not achieved supreme wisdom and are not fully devoted to it. They continue to violate their beliefs in supreme perception as well as supreme conduct. They may still be tormented by their carnal desires, and may try to take short cuts in their austerities.
4. *Nirgrantha* (unfettered mendicant): These are the mendicants who have reached the last stage of their penance. They thoroughly practice all supreme vows (*mahāvrata*s), follow all ten principles of *dharma* (*daśa-vidhi-dharma*), and are deeply immersed in their penance. They are about to achieve supreme wisdom and clairvoyance.
5. *Snātaka-nirgrantha* (eminent mendicant): This is the ultimate class of mendicants who are near the end of their last stage on the path to achieving salvation. Their penance has been completely successful. They have destroyed all internal and external disorders and have become passion-free and attachment-free. They have achieved divinity, have achieved supreme wisdom, and have attained clairvoyance. They have attained the state of freedom from the life-and-death cycle. They are *arihanta*s.

Spiritual Perseverance of a Mendicant (Sādhanā)

THE RIGOR OF SPIRITUAL PERSEVERANCE (SĀDHANĀ KĪ KAṬHORATĀ)

The lifestyle and rules of conduct of a Jain mendicant were drafted to encourage an unwavering commitment to the most rigorous, yet inspiring system of living in pursuit of enlightenment. Some examples of ascetic conduct are:

- Leading a life with no possessions, even for self-caring. As an example, they pull their hair out from the skull by hand using no instruments because the use of devices such as scissors is prohibited since the mendicants do not own any such items. Neither do they want to depend on others to have access to those devices. Also, use of such devices will encourage them to pay attention to their looks, which is also prohibited.
- Lying on the bare floor to take naps or sleep.
- Roaming from one place to the other without any fixed schedule. They should not stay at any one place for more than seven days, except during the rainy season of four months, to avoid formation of any relationships with householders or the development of any form of attachment towards a specific place or community.
- Not carrying any money.
- Staying alert all the time while exercising full control over the mind and senses.
- Not allowing any ill feelings to occur in thought.
- Patiently tolerating, without complaining, all types of discomforts arising from bad health, sickness, cold or hot weather, insect and mosquito bites, etc.
- Not accepting any item by requesting or soliciting from the householders.
- When food or water is not available, not complaining but accepting the situation as a component of penance and renunciation.

The above examples were crafted long ago and may have gone through revisions over time. The underlining objective of the regulations for ascetic lifestyle was and still is to stimulate a renunciate lifestyle with minimum distractions. The original guidelines, formulated centuries ago, have been evolving with time to accommodate changes demanded by time, location, situation, etc. All modifications are considered carefully and analyzed diligently to ensure they comply with and do not compromise the fundamental and basic tenets of Jain Dharma.

THE BASIS FOR RIGOROUS SPIRITUAL PERSEVERANCE (SĀDHANĀ KĀ ĀDHĀRA)

The preceding sections have provided an overview of the lifestyle and daily routines of a Jain mendicant. It leaves the readers with a clear impression that a Jain mendicant is an esteemed exemplar of detachment and renunciation of all materialistic entities, and is one who has complete disengagement with all impious mental inclinations. The reasons behind this rigorous penance have thoroughly been addressed in the Jain scriptures.

In reality, the fundamental objective of all of this spiritual effort is the purification of the soul. In spite of the soul being endowed with unlimited wisdom, unbounded perception, ceaseless tranquility, and consciousness, the living being may continue to be subjected to miseries of the world. No living being can escape these miseries if they continue to collect *karma*s. The only way to break this cycle is to stop collecting *karma*s and to dismantle and discard the *karma* that has already been collected. This can only be achieved with rigorous penance. It must be done by one's own self-motivation and not through any coercion. That is why, inspired by the drive to obtain spiritual bliss, a Jain mendicant makes an independent decision to pursue this lifestyle.

It is not enough to take up an ascetic life based on some capricious whim or emotional thoughts. Such an action would lead to future indecisiveness and uncertainties. In order to dissuade people from making decisions in this manner, Lord Mahāvīra stated:

> Let your life be styled with the resolve and devotion with which you are leaving home to take up the ascetic life until your last breath.

It is not easy to maintain the level of devotion and detachment with worldly affairs with which an individual first leaves the household. It is very difficult to sustain it to the end of one's life. In order to achieve that, the ascetic has to stay vigilant at all times and not indulge in any dishonorable activities.

Lord Mahāvīra states in the *Ācārāṅgasūtra*:

> Whoever negligently indulges in dishonorable acts, falls from asceticism. That is why mendicants are always vigilant.[10]

Jain scriptures have provided many remedial steps to help the mendicants remain watchful and stay on course.

Six Obligatory Duties (Āvaśyaka Kriyās)

All individuals – householders who follow limited vows and ascetics who live with supreme vows – regularly need inspiration and invigoration to continually make progress in their spiritual perseverance. This is to ensure that their spiritual devotion does not diminish, slow down, or regress, and that their devoutness stays on its course of advancement. Jain scriptures have included some provisions to provide this motivation to stay committed on an ongoing basis, such as the six essential (*āvaśyaka*) spiritual tasks. These tasks are deemed so important that they have been named obligatory duties (*āvaśyaka kriyās*) in Jain scriptures, and must be done every day by all householders and mendicants.

1. *Sāmāyika* (equanimity): *Sāmāyika* is an effort to isolate oneself from one's mental tendencies, passions (anger, ego, deceit, and greed), malice, and jealousy, while remaining equipoised and adopting an attitude of neutrality towards those inclinations. For householders, it consists of a daily practice for a minimum period of about forty-eight minutes. During this time, one forsakes all adverse and non-meritorious thoughts and actions in mind-body-speech. The practitioners meditate during this period and try to remain in their natural spiritual state of peace and tranquility. For mendicants, *sāmāyika* is a lifelong practice because they permanently live in this state of neutral inclinations.
2. *Stavana* (praising): This refers to the singing in praise of the qualities of *tīrthaṅkaras*. *Tīrthaṅkaras* are great souls with qualities that are supremely virtuous. They have revealed the ultimate form of the soul in its purified state for us to learn from. By singing the songs about their qualities, one is reminded of, and can understand, the natural

---

10 *suta amurni, munino sya jāgranti.*

characteristics of one's own soul. Through such recitations, one's perception gets purified and one becomes inspired to develop similar qualities of their own.

3. *Vandanā* (veneration): *Vandanā* is expressing reverence towards great souls. In Jain society five types of individuals are revered, and together they are called the "five-tiered supreme holiness" (*pāñca-parmeṣṭhī*). They are supreme liberated souls (*siddha*s), omniscient souls who have achieved supreme wisdom and clairvoyance but are still in body form (*arihanta*s), learned male and female mendicants who are the highest-level leaders of the mendicant clan (*ācārya*s), teachers of the mendicant clan (*upādhyāya*s), and monks (*sādhu*s-*sādhvī*s). *Vandanā* is paying respect to the five almighty ones (*pāñca-parmeṣṭhī*) in mind, body, and speech.

4. *Pratikramaṇa* (confession and repentance): The word *pratikramaṇa* implies "confess" or even to "return to oneself." *Pratikramaṇa* is the combination of two words, where *pra* means "return" and *atikramaṇa* means "violation." Literally, it means "returning from violation," implying to "spiritually scrutinize" oneself. This activity is just that, in a spiritual way, since confession entails a significant degree of introspection. Under the influence of various distractions, one may deviate from the honorable determination to do good, and instead may commit harmful acts against others. This happens repeatedly, knowingly or unknowingly, in spite of one's best intentions. *Pratikramaṇa* is an activity for correcting this, where one sits down and meditates over one's past actions. They analyze and evaluate their misdeeds and repent those. The misdeeds may have been leveled against family or friends, or even strangers or adversaries. These violations could also be against other living beings like animals, vegetation, and nature. During *pratikramaṇa*, the practitioner asks for forgiveness from all of these in a remorseful manner. This repenting includes a commitment to not deliberately repeat past transgressions and to make a commitment that the practitioner will remain vigilant against committing wrongful acts and other such violations.

   Pratikramaṇa is a very noble and heartfelt act. Nobody forces anyone else to do it. One must be self-motivated to do *pratikramaṇa* on their own accord without any coercion. When performed like this, it brings immense satisfaction and peace, and can be truly an uplifting experience. *Pratikramaṇa* differs between householders and mendicants because of differences in their lifestyles and spiritual vows. There are five types of *pratikramaṇa*:

i. *Daivasika pratikramaṇa*: This is repenting in the evening for all the misdeeds committed during the daytime.

ii. *Rātrika pratikramaṇa*: This is repenting in the morning for all the misdeeds committed during the evening and nighttime.

iii. *Pākṣika pratikramaṇa*: This is repenting every fifteen days for all the misdeeds committed during the previous fourteen days. It is conducted in the evening on the days of full moon and new moon.

iv. *Cāturmāsika pratikramaṇa*: This is repenting every four months for all the misdeeds committed during the previous four months. It is conducted in the evening of full-moon days in the months of Āṣāḍha (October–November), Kārttika (June–July), and Phālguna (February–March), following the Jain lunisolar calendar.

v. *Sāṁvatsarika pratikramaṇa*: This is repenting every year on the Sāṁvatsari day during Paryuṣaṇa Mahāparva (the supreme festival), for all the misdeeds committed during the previous year. Sāṁvatsari is on the last day of Paryuṣaṇa Mahāparva.

5. *Kāyotsarga* (removing attachment to one's body): Literally, the word means "dismissing (*utsarga*) the body (*kāya*)." *Kāyotsarga* involves eschewing bodily comforts and minimizing body movements. It could be done while sitting or standing. In both positions, the body is held as steady as possible. This practice mitigates one's attention to the body and improves virtuous characteristics by allowing one to focus on the true nature of the soul instead of being fixated on the body.

6. *Pratyākhyāna* (disallowance): *Pratyākhyāna* is the practice of renunciation in mind, body, and speech. There are two types of renunciations:

   i. Taking the oath and practicing to give up materialistic items such as clothes, food, and travel. This is called *dravya pratyākhyāna*.

ii. Resolving to restrain and eliminate passions, malice, jealousy, belief in falsehood, ill-advised knowledge, etc. This is called *bhāva pratyākhyāna*.

Neither of these types is easy to implement in practice, but *bhāva pratyākhyāna* is harder because a firm resolve is much harder to apply to one's mind than giving up materialistic things. *Pratyākhyāna* is done to control and stop desires. It is essential for making any progress in the spiritual journey.

The Art of Dying (Sallekhanā Vrata)

The above spiritual practices are well ingrained in the lives of true Jains. They bring joy, peace, and satisfaction in a manner similar to that which people feel from participating in art. Jains consider spiritual practice to be an art form of the highest order, as articulated in the saying, "The art of religion triumphs over all other art forms."[11] The art of religion or spirituality applies to all parts of life – and even to how one relates to death.

Death is the predestined culmination of a life, with a timing unknown to living beings. All religious doctrines have addressed the process of death in their own ways. Jains have treated death in their own uniquely inspirational manner – it is considered a spiritually pleasant and triumphant event, rather than a sorrowful tragedy. Lord Mahāvīra described death as the second and decisive chapter after one's life. He considered the practice of dying as an essential part of the art of religious practice. Lord Mahāvīra masterfully transformed how everyone considers death, from what would be a terrifying event for spiritually less-advanced individuals into a stepping stone which opens the doors to the fruition of one's lifelong spiritual work. He defined death as a refined form of art that must be mastered by spiritualists if they are to succeed in their perseverance. Lord Mahāvīra preached:

> To be terrified of death is the final obstacle to wisdom. However, death is not a dreadful monster. It is the friend of human beings that represents the worthy culmination of a lifetime of penance and perseverance. Without death's help, how would we achieve the celestial outcome of our worldly

---

[11] *savva kala dhamma kala jinai.*

religious undertakings? Without death, how would we ever enjoy the heavenly life, or for that matter, ultimate salvation?

A guard who releases one from a prison is considered a munificent savior, so why not consider death as a friend as well? Death relieves one from the cage of a worn-out body filled with innumerable afflictions. Thus, nothing can be more obliging than death.

Death can be a blissful transition from a broken and expended shanty to a majestic palace. However, unwise and ill-informed people believe it to be a calamitous termination rather than a highly favorable transformation. Vexed about separation from their families and luxurious livelihoods, they are distressed by the thought of death. On the other hand, a wise individual who is righteous and non-attached stays calm and maintains an equipoised demeanor. Such a virtuous person considers death to be the gold covering over their temple of lifelong perseverance. Such sages peacefully complete their life journey with a deep sense of fulfillment. In this manner, one can rejoice and bring blissfulness to not only one's present but to one's future as well.

Jain Dharma does not believe in running away from life. To the contrary, the doctrine teaches that it is one's duty to respect life. Jain Dharma teaches seekers to be self-controlled and humble while propelling their lives with rigorous penance and adhering to the Jain principles. Such practitioners should enjoy their lives, characterized by nobility and spiritual restraint to the fullest extent. For such seekers, accepting death is not running away from life but acknowledging it as the next natural step. At the end, when death comes, one must learn to welcome it with open arms, marking the completion of lifelong spiritual endeavors. One should diligently acknowledge death as the facilitator to help in realizing the next life's spiritual objectives. For it is death that helps the most fortunate seekers to attain the ultimate salvation when they reach the finality of life–death cycles upon depleting *āyuṣya-karma* of their last life, after rigorous penance and austerities over numerous lives. Therefore, there is no reason to be afraid of death.

For individuals who are fixated on attaining mundane pleasures, human life is thought of as a platform for material enjoyment, the fulfillment of desires and general sensory pleasure. For such individuals, death is considered undesired, dreadful, and dire. That is why the ascetics who cannot relinquish their attachment to life at the time of death, can risk wasting their lifelong perseverance. Such ascetics risk convoluting the outcome of their current endeavors both in the present and in future lives.

While describing the art of death, Lord Mahāvīra delineated it to be of seventeen types:

1. *Āvīci maraṇa* (involuntary death): Life continues to diminish in duration with every moment that one is alive. The individual's life comes to an end at a pre-determined (based on *āyuṣya-karma*) time although one has not accomplished anything worthy. This type of death is when life ends while one is living from moment to moment.
2. *Tad-bhava maraṇa* (one's existence dies): This is the end of the body's existence and passing away into death in sleep under the influence of drugs or anesthetics.
3. *Avadhi maraṇa* (timely death): This is when one dies when one's allocated lifespan is completed.
4. *Ādyanta maraṇa* (similar death in two lives): This is to die from the same cause in two successive lives, which could be due to vices and unfinished desires from one life to the other.
5. *Bāla maraṇa* (untimely death): To die from the consumption of poison or other means such as jumping from a bridge, while being devoid of right knowledge and perception.
6. *Paṇḍita maraṇa* (wise death): After accomplishing spiritual feats such as right perception, right knowledge, and right conduct, this is when one forsakes the body while immersed in deep meditation.
7. *Āsana maraṇa* (seated death): To die while being in a restrained, disciplined state (*saṁyama*).
8. *Bāla paṇḍita maraṇa* (death of worthy householder): This is the worthy death of a householder who dies while observing limited householder vows (*aṇuvratas*).
9. *Saśalya maraṇa* (death with unworthy thoughts): To die while immersed in thoughts of desires of obtaining a good life in one's next birth or with some other unworthy thoughts.

10. *Pramāda maraṇa* (negligent death): Without completing commitments and resolves, one may relinquish life with a sense of carelessness or neglect to one's spiritual potential.
11. *Vaśāt mṛtyu* (death while being controlled by senses): To die when still under the control of senses or *karma*-earning delusional activities.
12. *Vipula maraṇa* (self-inflicted death): To deliberately end life when unable to comply with vows such as contentment.
13. *Gṛddha-pṛṣṭha maraṇa* (death while fighting for the right cause): To get killed on a battlefield in war while protecting family, community, or nation.
14. *Bhaktapāna maraṇa* (death while immersed in devotion): To die while relinquishing food and the consumption of everything else in an intentional manner while taking one's last breaths, as one is spiritually engrossed.
15. *Iṅgita maraṇa* (death with conscientious restrictions): To die while in meditation or in a state of spiritual perseverance. The seeker gradually stops taking food and confines movements within a limited space.
16. *Pādapopagamana maraṇa* (death by stillness): To die in a still posture, abiding only in auspicious thoughts after forsaking food intake.
17. *Kevalī maraṇa* (omniscient death): To relinquish the body after attaining enlightenment with complete impeccable or supreme wisdom, clairvoyance, and perfect conduct.

Of the above, *paṇḍita maraṇa* (6), *bāla paṇḍita maraṇa* (8), *bhaktapāna maraṇa* (14), *iṅgita maraṇa* (15), *pādapopagamana maraṇa* (16), and *kevalī maraṇa* (17) are the types in compliance with Jain Dharma.

Jain Dharma provides training methods for accepting death while in a state of spiritual awareness. The meditative state is known as *sallekhanā* or *saṅthārā*, which can also be called the art of dying. There are two basic types of *saṅthārā*:

- Bounded *saṅthārā* (dying in a state of detatchment): The preparatory practice or training method of bounded *saṅthārā* involves vowing to be unattached towards one's body every night before going to bed.

This has two advantages: first to get accustomed to the idea of dying and letting go of attachment to the body; and second, if suddenly death comes during the night, the individual is not inflicted with the blemish of worldly attachments. Bounded *saṅthārā* is similar to unbounded full-fledged *saṅthārā* (*samādhi maraṇa*), except that it can be practiced in this way, bounded by sleep time, or can be practiced at the time of sickness or some other emergency circumstance. During the period of bounded *saṅthārā*, the individual meditates on forsaking all worldly possessions and other attachments.

- Unbounded *saṅthārā* or *samādhi maraṇa* (death in a state of meditation): Among all types of death, dying while in the state of death meditation (*samādhi maraṇa*) is considered the most auspicious way. This extremely righteous way of meeting death is also called *paṇḍita maraṇa* (wise death, mentioned above) or *sakāma maraṇa* (consenting death). The exceptionally courageous act is undertaken when someone is in a life-threatening situation such as a famine or enduring an incurable illness. It is described in great detail in Jain scriptures and is often referred to as celebratory death (*mṛtyu-mahotsava*).

The ascetic who has taken the ultimate vow of voluntary death through *samādhi maraṇa* spends all of their time in spiritual contemplation after relinquishing all interest in possessions and affections. They are advised to stay vigilant against the following five misdeeds or blemishes:

1. *Iha-lokāśaṁsā* (desire for the worldly pleasures)
2. *Paralokāśaṁsā* (desire for pleasures in next life)
3. *Jīvitāśaṁsā* (desire to live longer upon experiencing the prestige and honor being bestowed)
4. *Maraṇāśaṁsā* (desire to die earlier due to lack of food, or after extreme pain caused by disease)
5. *Kāma-bhogāśaṁsā* (desire to indulge in sensual pleasures)

The great soul who has taken the vow of *samādhi maraṇa* must refrain from the above five missteps. He should meditate steadfastly on virtues and enjoy the benefits of this eminent undertaking without bringing any blemish upon it.

This is a very brief description of the art of dying preached by Lord Mahāvīra. All mendicants and Jain householders are taught to revere this great process. Extensive descriptions and commentaries on this subject are available in Jain scriptures and numerous other religious and scriptural texts on Jain doctrine.

This chapter has presented an overview of the lifestyle of Jain mendicants – the rigors of the penance, austerities, and perseverance they undertake. It is an intense exercise requiring ardent commitment and complete dedication, but for those who are engaged in this mission to attain the ultimate liberation, this is an exhilarating experience. Some of the guidelines, preventative measures, and prohibitory regulations may appear to be impractical in contemporary times, but the lifestyle of experienced mendicants automatically molds into these bounds, and they effortlessly adhere to all of the rules and regulations. Many of these guidelines and measures are beneficial to the lifestyle of the spiritually inclined householders as well.

The structure and formulation of the guidelines, and the emphasis on their application in mendicant lifestyle without the use of rigid ground rules, are immaculate examples of the beauty of Jain Dharma. The fact that these regulations are voluntarily adopted by the practitioners demonstrates the forte of Jain Dharma in inspiring all living beings towards the path of purification and ultimate bliss. They serve as the motivation to strive for complete *samyaktva* (enlightenment) with *samyag-darśana* (right perception), *samyag-jñāna* (right knowledge), and *samyag-cāritra* (right conduct) – the auspicious troika of Jain Dharma.

14

The Lineage of Jain Dharma (Jain Dharma kī Paramparā)

Contributions by Jain Ācāryas in the Spiritual Evolution of India

ALTHOUGH no systematic research has been conducted to study the impact of Jain Dharma in India, it can be stated in no uncertain terms that Jain scholars and *ācārya*s have had tremendous influence on the cultural, spiritual, and religious traditions of India. In particular, their esteemed lives, characterized by immense restraint and renunciation, have been exceptionally inspirational. When one notes the great religious personalities of India, they can see the vivid impressions left by many great Jain *ācārya*s on all walks of life and many sectors of the society, all over the country.

Ācārya Bhadrabāhu, who came 170 years after Lord Mahāvīra, was an unforgettable great Jain *ācārya*. He prophesied the coming of a twelve-year famine and alerted Magadha city residents and their king, Candragupta Maurya (the founder of the Maurya dynasty). Influenced by the *ācārya*'s sermons, Candragupta accompanied him and they traveled together throughout South India. Later on, Candragupta became an ascetic and eventually took the vow of dying in the state of meditation (*samādhi maraṇa* or *iṅgita maraṇa* – death by restricted movement), as described in the section "The Art of Dying (Sallekhanā Vrata)" in the previous chapter.

While Ācārya Bhadrabāhu's migration to South India left a permanent impression on the region, it also had an adverse outcome – the Jain community of the Magadha kingdom was divided into two parts, between those who accompanied him and those who stayed behind. The division eventually became permanent and led to the creation of two segments, to be known as the Śvetāmbara (white-clad) and Digambara (sky-clad) sects of Jain followers. A positive outcome of Ācārya Bhadrabāhu's time in South India was the influence of Jain Dharma and non-violence on various kingdoms of the region, which was the result of his presence. In particular, his influence on the kingdoms of Kalabhra, Hoyaśala, Gaṅga, and others became instrumental in creating unity between the Aryan and Dravidian societies of India. Ācārya Bhadrabāhu, a great saint and achiever of supreme wisdom, proved to be the first link in an enduring cultural partnership and unity between South and North Indian communities.

Ārya Mahāgiri and Ārya Guṇasundara (a disciple of Ārya Suhasti), propagated Jain Dharma in various states of India as well as in far-off places such as the countries of Afghanistan, Greece, and Iran. Their widespread campaigns were helped by King Samprati through his endeavors.

Ācārya Umāsvāti, the founder of the Jain scriptural era, and Siddhasena Divākara, India's eminent philosopher of that time, presented Jain logic and the science of reasoning in a structured manner. Ācārya Kundakunda's creation of Jain spiritual and religious scriptural traditions brought a new level of richness to Jain literature. At the same time, the scriptures on the science of reasoning and logic, created by Svāmī Samantabhadra, made the Jain literary tradition one of the most abundant in the world.

Upon examining the literary development in the first millennium, one finds significant contributions from many great Jain scholars, philosophers, and eminent *ācārya*s of the era. Their contributions enriched Jain literature in many different ways in many subject matters. Some of the eminent contributors are Devardhigaṇīkṣamāśramaṇa, Śīlāṅka, Dhaneśvara Sūri, Jinabhadraguṇīkṣamāśramaṇa, Abhayadeva, Haribhadra, Kālikācārya, Jinadāsa Mahattara, among many more. Similarly, in the second millennium, eminent Jain *ācārya*s such as the omniscient Hemacandrācārya, Vādī Deva Sūri, Yaśovijaya, and many others made immense contributions to the nation's progress through their political, philosophical, literary, and spiritual reflections and discussions. Also at that time, there were many scholars and religious luminaries who influenced South and North India with their knowledge. Some of them are Ācārya Guṇadhara, Bhūtavalī, Puṣpadanta, Kundakunda, Pūjyapāda, Pātrakesarī, Akalaṅka, Vidyānandī, Siddhāntacakravartī, Nemicandra, Jinasena, Ānandavīrya, Prabhācandra, along with many others.

Although spiritual work comprises the main contributions from Jain scholars to India's development over the centuries, there have been many examples of social and political contributions as well. In all cases, the impetus has been to spread the message of non-violence and other altruistic, humanitarian acts. Some examples are: initiation or ordainment of Kumārapāla of Gujarat into non-violence, a firm establishment of non-violence in political affairs and government operations on Vijayanagara of South India, and the creation of an atmosphere of non-violence in the states of Bihar and Mathurā.

Jain *ācārya*s all throughout history have had significant influence in the development of collective sentiments in favor of non-violence and compassion towards all living beings, the lifestyle of vegetarianism, and other behavioral ethics. The celebrated examples of non-violence, penance, and renunciation on the part of Jain *ācārya*s and mendicants remain the subject of great pride for India even today.

The predominance of the ethic of non-violence in the Saurāṣṭra region of India can be directly attributed to the inspiration of Jain *ācārya*s. For example, the interpretation of Vedas by Svāmī Dayānanda emphasizes non-violence. In addition, the adoption of a non-violence-based philosophy by Mahatma Gandhi was inspired by the cultural milieu of non-violence in Saurāṣṭra. In fact, a Jain monk, Muni Baichar Swami, asked Mahatma Gandhi to pledge abstinence from meat, alcohol, and women before he left for England. The revered Jain ascetic Śrīmad Rājacandra played a pivotal role in inspiring Mahatma Gandhi to lead a life of complete non-violence in mind, body, and speech.

It is heartening to note that the world continues to see the importance of peace and non-violence. The torch of non-violence that Jains have kept lit uninterruptedly through the centuries is the greatest gift given to India, the world, and the entirety of humanity.

Contributions by Kings and Rulers

Some philosophers and scholars of Indian history believe that parts of the spiritual tradition of India started in India's warrior or ruling class (kṣatriya) and then came to the brāhmin or priestly class. A careful study of India's history vindicates this opinion. All of the Jain *tīrthaṅkara*s, from Lord R̥ṣabhadeva to Lord Mahāvīra, were born and raised in the kṣatriya class.

Table 14.1: Some of the Jain Rulers of Different Dynasties

Ruler	*Dynasty*	*Rule Period*	*Year*	*Capital City*	*Notes*
Bimbasāra	Śiśunāga	543-491 BCE	52	Rājagṛha	Śreṇika was Lord Mahāvīra's maternal uncle
Ajātaśatru	Śiśunāga	491-459 BCE	32	Pāṭaliputra	Kuṇika was a contemporary of Lord Buddha
Udayana	Śiśunāga	459-413 BCE	46	Pāṭaliputra	Alexander came to India
Mahāpadma	Śiśunāga	343-321 BCE	22	Pāṭaliputra	–
Candragupta	Maurya	322-298 BCE	24	Pāṭaliputra	Silyūkasa (Seleucus) came to India
Bindusāra	Maurya	298-273 BCE	25	Pāṭaliputra	–
Aśoka	Maurya	273-232 BCE	41	Pāṭaliputra	Aśoka remained a Jain for four years and then became a Buddhist
Samprati	Maurya	224-215 BCE	9	Pāṭaliputra	Grandson of Aśoka
Khāravela	Cedī	177-152 BCE	25	Kaliṅga	Won Kaliṅga
Kaniṣka	Cedī	from 78 CE	unknown	Peśāvara	Buddhist religion split into two sects
Vikramāditya	Paramāra	from 375 CE	unknown	Ujjain	Chinese traveler Fahiyan came to India
Harṣa	Paramāra	606-47 CE	41	Kannauja	Chinese traveler Huaingsang came to India
Amoghavarṣa	Rāṣṭrakūṭa	from 750 CE	unknown	Malakheḍa	–
Sāhila Devarāya	Tomara	1000-50 CE	50	Śrāvastī	Killed Saiyada Sālāra Masūda in a war
Kumārapāla	Cāḷukya	1142-73 CE	31	Aṇahilapura	–

Many Jain kings ruled during the life of each *tīrthaṅkara*. Several monarchs with extensive kingdoms who lived during the times of the *tīrthaṅkaras* undertook the lifestyle of a Jain ascetic in later stages of their lives. They made significant contributions to the expansion of Jain Dharma and the propagation of its philosophy (Table 14.1). Unfortunately, the historical details of many of them are not available today, although ample details are available about the rulers during the time of Lord Mahāvīra and after him. They achieved their greatness in part by contributing to the propagation of Jain Dharma.

KING CEṬAKA AND OTHER RULERS

King Ceṭaka was Lord Mahāvīra's first householder (non-monk) disciple. He was a highly influential and brave ruler of Vaiśālī and was the head of a federation of eighteen kingdoms. He took a vow that he would marry his daughters to no one other than eligible Jain bachelors. At one time, in order to protect the honor of his beliefs and his subjects, he had to engage in a difficult war with Kuṇika, the king of Magadha.

King Udayana of Sindhu Sauvīra, King Pradyota of Avantī, King Śatānīka of Kauśāmbī, King Dadhivāhana of Campā, and King Śreṇika of Magadha were all sons-in-law of King Ceṭaka and were all staunch followers of Jain Dharma. King Udayana actually adopted an ascetic life as a disciple of Lord Mahāvīra.

KINGS ŚREṆIKA AND KUṆIKA

King Bimbasāra, the historically illustrious king of Magadha, is known as King Śreṇika in Jain literature. His tales are very famous among Jains. Śreṇika's son, King Kuṇika, was also a devout disciple of Lord Mahāvīra. And Kuṇika's son, Udayana, was a Jain follower like his father. Eighteen regional kings and rulers of non-mainstream classes (for instance, rulers of the Licchavī and Mallī clans) celebrated Lord Mahāvīra's *nirvāṇa* with great enthusiasm. This indicates that all those kings were greatly influenced by the Jain philosophy.

EMPEROR CANDRAGUPTA MAURYA

As noted above, Candragupta was a follower of Jain Dharma who became a monk as a disciple of Ācārya Bhadrabāhu in the later part of his life. He accompanied the *ācārya* in travels all over the state of Mysore in South India. He conducted rigorous spiritual penance in the cave of Śrāvaṇa-Beḷagolā in the later part of his life. His chief minister and advisor, Cāṇakya, was born and raised in a Jain household and remained an ardent follower of Jain Dharma throughout his life.

EMPEROR AŚOKA

Aśoka was the grandson of Candragupta. His services to the cause of non-violence are well known. Although a known follower of Buddhism, according to the book *Jainism, or The Early Faith of Aśoka*,[1] the principles of non-violence propagated by Aśoka were more in line with Jain doctrine than with Buddhist philosophy. His proclamations to stop killing animals and birds, to stop the unnecessary destruction of forests, and a complete prohibition of animal killing on auspicious dates and festive occasions paralleled Jain principles.

EMPEROR SAMPRATI

Emperor Samprati was emperor Aśoka's grandson. One time, after winning a war, he very joyously went to his mother. There he was taken aback upon seeing tears in his mother's eyes rather than gleeful smiles. When he asked for the reasons for her sadness, she said:

> A victory gained by unnecessary killing of the human beings is not a true victory. Peace is the true sign of victory, and it can be obtained only through non-violent means.

Upon hearing such words, Samprati instantly adopted Jain Dharma under the auspices of the renowned Jain monk Ārya Suhasti. In order to spread Jain religion in culturally and socially underdeveloped regions of the country, he constructed many Jain religious sites to facilitate the spiritual practices of Jain followers. He undertook many critical projects for the development of the impoverished areas and sent various instructors to spread Jain teachings there. Many historians and scholars believe that several stone inscriptions that are attributed to Aśoka were actually created by Samprati.

KHĀRAVELA, EMPEROR OF KALIṄGA

Emperor Khāravela reigned during second century BCE and became the most influential leader of that era. Under his rule, Jain Dharma flourished immensely. A grand congregation of Jain monks and scholars was held as a result of his efforts, and the Jain community honored him with the titles of Eminently Victorious (*Mahāvijayī*) Khema Emperor, and King of Ascetics (*Bhikṣu-Rājā* or *Dharma-Rājā*). Khāravela's contributions and services to Jain Dharma are invaluable, and he was an exceptionally glorious ruler of India.

KING KALABHRAVAṀŚĪ AND KAḶACURI DYNASTY

The Kaḷacurī dynasty was perhaps the most prominent lineage of rulers in

---

[1] *Jainism, or The Early Faith of Aśoka,* Edward Thomas.

the center of the subcontinent at its time. From Tripurī City as its capital city, the glory of its rule was at its peak in the eighth and ninth centuries CE. All of the Kaḷacurī dynasty kings were staunch followers of Jain Dharma. It is believed that some members of this lineage can still be found in Nagpur and surrounding areas. They go under the name of Jain Kalāra.

KINGS OF HOYAŚALA DYNASTY

Many kings, rulers, ministers, and commanders of the forces of the Hoyaśala dynasty of Karnataka region of South India were the followers of Jain Dharma. His Holiness Sudatta Muni was the spiritual guide to the kingdom. Initially he was a spiritual advisor to Cālukya rulers. In 1116 CE, he presided over the consecration of an independent kingdom.

KINGS OF GAṄGA DYNASTY

In the second century CE, Gaṅga rulers established their kingdom in South India. Until the eleventh century, they ruled over a widespread area. All the Gaṅga kings were devoted Jains. King Mādhava was the first king and was also known as Koṁgaṇī Varmā. He was a disciple of Ācārya Siṁhanandī. Jain Dharma became the official religion of the land during King Mādhava's time. Another king of the dynasty, Mārasiṁha, defeated a number of smaller kingdoms and had an extravagant and indulgent life. However, eventually he relinquished everything and adopted an ascetic lifestyle. He took a vow of *samādhi maraṇa* from Ācārya Ajitasena and departed this world in a highly spiritual state. According to the inscription on his memorial stone, he died in 975 CE. The women of this dynasty were also devoted followers of *tīrthaṅkara*s.

CĀMUṆḌARĀYA

A renowned individual of South India, Cāmuṇḍarāya was an able advisor and minister to King Mārasiṁha the second. Cāmuṇḍarāya continued to be the chief minister to King Mārasiṁha's son, Rājamalla, and eventually became commander of the armed forces. Cāmuṇḍarāya was a staunch Jain follower. His spiritual *guru*, Nemicandra, was a supremely principled ascetic. Cāmuṇḍarāya authored the famous scripture in Kannada language, *Triṣaṣṭhi-Lakṣaṇa*, and led the creation of the world-famous idol of Lord Bāhubalī in Śrāvaṇa-Beḷagolā.[2]

[2] Also known as Gommaṭeśvara Statue, this fifty-seven foot-high monolithic idol of

KING ŚIVAKOṬI

Śivakoṭi was the king of Kāñcī in South India. He became a disciple of the renowned Ācārya Samantabhadra after listening to his inspiring sermons. King Śivakoṭi provided significant support to the propagation of Jain Dharma in South India.

KING ĀMANE

This famous king of Gwalior was ordained in Jain Dharma by renowned Ācārya Bappabhūti, the disciple of Ācārya Siddhasena.

THE SUPREME ARHATA (PARAMĀRHATA) KUMĀRAPĀLA

Kumārapāla was a king of Gujarat and an eminent disciple of the renowned Ācārya Hemacandra, and had sincere lifetime devotion to Jain Dharma. By prohibiting hunting, meat eating, and other such violent acts, he brought non-violence into prominence. His historical contributions are well-known. The integration of Jain philosophy into Gujarat's cultural and social life can be attributed to Ācārya Hemacandra and Kumārapāla. Honoring Kumārapāla with the title of Supreme Arhata (*paramārhata*) is a significant commendation, and is very inspirational and certainly without any impropriety.

RULERS OF THE RĀṢṬRAKŪṬA DYNASTY AND AMOGHAVARṢA

The kings of the Rāṣṭrakūṭa dynasty were also very influential rulers of their time and were highly devoted disciples of Jain Dharma. The religion prospered immensely during their time. Amoghavarṣa is especially noteworthy from among these rulers. He was a disciple of the illustrious Ācārya Jinasena. Jain Dharma flourished during his reign. Amoghavarṣa was a respected scholar and authored the noted scripture *Praśnottara Ratna-Mālikā* (Assembly of Topmost Questions and Answers). The rulers of smaller territories of Aṅga, Baṅga, Magadha, Mālavā, Citrakūṭa, and Beḍi served under his command. He ruled the regions of Gujarat and southern states. Later on, he disowned his kingdom and all luxuries, and became a monk during last few years of his

---

Lord Bāhubalī is located on the hills of Vindhyagiri at Śrāvaṇa-Velagolā (also called Śrāvaṇa-Beḷagolā) in the Indian state of Karnataka. One of the most revered religious idols of Jain Dharma and considered one of the finest spiritual and artistic creations in human history, the idol was built around 983 CE. Carved out of the mountain by chiseling the rocks, this is one of the largest free-standing images in the world.

life. Amoghavarṣa's son, Indra, was also a staunch follower of Jain religion. He too became an ascetic in his last few years.

VANARĀJA CĀVAḌĀ AND KING CĀḶUKYA

Many ruling dynasties in Gujarat state, including Mūlarāja, were followers of Jain Dharma. In addition to the aforementioned rulers, other famous leaders include the Cāvaḍā dynasty's King Vanarāja, who was a disciple of Ācārya Śīlaguṇa Sūri. The rulers of Cāḷukya dynasty, which followed Cāvaḍā dynasty, were also the followers of Jain Dharma.

SIDDHARĀJA JAYASIṀHA

Although King Jayasiṁha did not formally espouse Jain Dharma, he had deep affinity for the religion even without being initiated into it. He was highly influenced by Ācārya Hemacandra. It was at the request of Jayasiṁha that the revered Ācārya Hemacandra created the grammar scripture known as the *Siddha-hema-śabdānuśāsana* (Command over Words according to Hemacandra).

Ministers and Generals

The deftness with which the Jain householders carried out the responsibilities of ministers and generals in various ruling dynasties of India is worth mentioning. There have been so many Jain ministers and generals that it is impossible to provide a definitive count.

Among the ministers, the two brothers Vastupāla and Tejapāla have invaluable and unmatched places in India's ruling class. They were the ministers of King Vīradhavala of the Bāghelā dynasty of Gujarat. While being highly skilled in politics and being the followers of Jain Dharma, they showed the utmost respect and understanding towards all other religions. It is hard to describe in simple words their dexterity, extraordinary compassion and charity, and religious commitment in a few pages.

Bhāmāśāha was the well-known chief minister of the famous Mewar King Pratāpasiṁha. His deeds are well documented in history. Jains held the ministerial positions in Jaipur's kingdom for a long time. King Vijayasiṁha's forces were commanded by Dhanavāra Siṁdhavī. The commander of the forces of King Bhīmadeva of Gujarat's Solaṅkī dynasty was Ābhu Jain.

Jains played critical roles in the establishment and successful running of various kingdoms in the state of Rajasthan as well as other states all over India. They had roles of prominence in governments due to their intelligent, skillful, and impartial political acumen. Also, by virtue of being dedicated and committed Jain householders, they had exemplary and highly honorable conduct. In addition, all of the ministers and generals played important roles in propagating Jain values and establishing Jain Dharma as an influential doctrine in India.

Growth of Jain Religion

The heritage of Jain Dharma has continued from the time of Lord Ṛṣabhadeva to the present without disruption. It has continually served humanity with the message of compassion, peace, and non-violence. Jain philosophy has continued for thousands of years on the merits of its intrinsic value. From time to time, the number of Jain followers has increased or decreased in its natural course, but the philosophical stream is time-tested, and it has never gone dry. This is the religion of the conquerors over the obstruction of the soul, and it appeals to and influences those who have control and command over themselves.

Over the millennia, Jain doctrine has deeply influenced the rulers as well as the populace. During the time of Lord Mahāvīra, Jain Dharma was the religion of the Magadha kingdom. After that, it prominently inspired sixteen of India's major states. Five of the daughters of Lord Mahāvīra's maternal uncle motivated five rulers to adopt Jain ascetic life. The other two remained celibates for their lives. Of the five daughters, Prabhāvatī motivated King Udayana of Sindhu Sauvīra, Śivā motivated King Caṇḍapradyota of Avantī, Celaṇā motivated King Śreṇika of Magadha, Mṛgāvatī motivated King Śatānīka of Vatsa, and Padmāvatī motivated king Dadhivāhana of Aṅga.

Lord Mahāvīra had immense influence on the reigning rulers, princes, and princesses of his time and on others for many centuries to follow. Hundreds of rulers were so inspired by him that they decided to give up their worldly lives and become his ascetic disciples. That was the golden era of Jain Dharma. It enjoyed sound support from the governments and rulers of those times. However, Jain Dharma never took any undue advantage of the opportunity because it has always been the religion of virtuous conduct. Jain spiritual leaders never craved the support of the ruling class or of influential leaders.

They always wanted people to recognize the values promoted by the doctrine and to voluntarily follow its teachings. During Lord Mahāvīra's time, or at many other junctures in history, Jain Dharma could have expanded multifold if its leaders had used the techniques of non-voluntary persuasion and other means such as financial inducements or forcible conversions, which have been pursued by other religious traditions. Time and again, the religion had the political influence to do so, but forceful methods were never considered. The deployment of such methods is against the core principles of *dharma*. It is the religion of self-awakening and not forced adoption. Even without the use of coercive techniques, Jain Dharma expanded because scores of people recognized the values of the teachings of Lord Mahāvīra. The message inspired them to follow the lifestyles of Jain householders or ascetics.

The first setback to Jain Dharma occurred after the war of Vaiśālī, between Ceṭaka and Koṇika. Ceṭaka lost the war and eighteen Jain kings lost their lives in various battles. In spite of his win, Koṇika became a target for slander, and he ultimately adopted Buddhism.

Two centuries later Jain Dharma regained its prominence during the Gupta dynasty. King Samprati, the grandson on King Aśoka, made a tremendous effort in propagating the values of Jain Dharma with the blessings of the Jain *guru* Guṇasundara. However, after Samprati, the efforts to bring the message of Jain teachings to farther regions subsided and its heritage stalled or diminished. It is because of the efforts during Samprati's times that the religion expanded considerably in countries such as Iran, Iraq, Afghanistan, and Greece. It is believed by some that the great scholar Pythagoras[3] of Greece was initiated as an ascetic in Jain Dharma.

Even today Jain Dharma is receiving recognition because of its fundamental principles and doctrine. Many social activists, as well as philosophical and political leaders of the world, have accepted non-violence, compassion, and peace as the supreme and most important principles. In today's world, peace-

---

[3] In many ways, Pythagorean beliefs and doctrines are similar to Jain doctrine. In Digambara scriptures, there are mentions of a monk, Pihitāśrava, who is none other than Pythagoras. It is believed that Pythagoras came to India and was ordained and trained by Jain scholars and ascetics. Thereafter he brought Jain Dharma to Greece and publicized its teachings there. Even now, there are many followers of Pythagoras in Greece and other parts of the world.

loving and non-violence promoters are taking stands against wars and bloodshed, in fulfillment with Lord Mahāvīra's command, "Do not commit violence; do not commit violence!"[4] The doctrine of Anekāntavāda provides the perfect method for bringing the disagreeing and fighting sectarian, ethnic, and national entities to a common platform and exploring solutions to their disagreements.

Jain Dharma has never considered it necessary to alter the regional social practices and interpersonal relations in order to follow its religion and its spiritual teachings. Jain Dharma does not advocate significant transformations in language, customs, or culture. It does not interfere in personal liberties and social customs such as marriage and marital practices. It has never depended on executive or ruling powers for its propagation. It intends to promote self-awakening and restraint over perverse thoughts and actions, and it seeks the spreading of spiritual bliss throughout the world.

All the rulers who followed Jain doctrine, some of whom are aforementioned, were inspired by the philosophy's teachings, and they were motivated to adopt virtuous conduct. They did not indulge in the hurting or killing of innocent beings during their reigns. None of them deployed any coercive means or harsh controls to rule their people. Instead they used thoughtful, compassionate persuasion and progressive means to rule successfully and create prosperity. Under their honorable and just rules, the populace enjoyed contentment while experiencing prosperity, contrary to some misbeliefs that honorable rulers cannot deliver prosperous reigns. People cooperated with each other without any jealousy or malice. They attributed their personal vicissitudes in wealth, prosperity, or social positioning to the fruition of unrighteous *karmas* (sinful and immoral acts of their own current or previous lives). That is why folks lived righteously and avoided wicked acts. The rulers of Jain lineage did not interfere in the social or religious practices of their people. They collected taxes only to pay for defense and social services. They never forced any undue contributions. In South India, Jain rulers such as those belonging to the Gaṅga dynasty ruled for centuries without any difficulties or interruption. Brave men like Cāmuṇḍarāya demonstrated their might through noble practices. Even today, the heirs of ruling dynasties are present in places such as Muḍabadrī.

---

[4] *ma hano, ma hano.*

15

Summary of the Distinct Merits of Jain Dharma

AS SEEN in previous chapters, the concept of fundamental truth (*tattva*) is the foundation of Jain doctrine, and a thorough understanding of its nuances is essential in order to fully comprehend Jain Dharma. The determination to thoroughly understand fundamental truth requires sincere effort and exertion by the seekers. The undertaking is neither simple nor trivial – it begins with complete and unrelenting spiritual commitment by the seeker. Once on this path, the rate and extent of knowledge acquisition depends on one's devotional and spiritual fortitude. For sincere seekers, it eventually becomes a self-reinforcing cycle – increasing levels of effort result in a commensurate growth in knowledge, which, in turn, inspires the seekers to become more committed and better at performing spiritual undertakings.

To comprehend this relationship between the sincerity of spiritual efforts and *tattva* knowledge, one does not have to go too far; a study of the life of Lord Mahāvīra is the finest motivator.[1] His level of penance and commitment was exceptional and unprecedented. Lord Mahāvīra was engrossed in almost twelve and a half years of rigorous asceticism and austerities, which resulted in an extraordinary outcome. He unraveled the Ultimate Truth (*tattva*) at a level that ordinary seekers can only imagine and begin to aspire to. Lord Mahāvīra encapsulated his clairvoyant grasp of the fundamental truth in a set of tenets that became the foundation of the Jain doctrine.

The strength of these tenets has withstood the tests of logic and reasoning over the centuries, and this is the reason that contemporary society, and new revelations and discoveries – for instance, discoveries in ecology and environmentalism – find merits in them even today.

According to Jain philosophy, the universe is an amalgamation of living

---

1 It is worth reiterating here the potential of spiritual growth that Jain Dharma bestows on individual human beings. With sufficient fortitude, devotion, and effort, each soul has the potential to salvage itself and attain enlightenment.

and non-living matter. It is believed to be perpetual and everlasting at a macro level[2] and is constantly transforming at a micro level. As discussed in earlier chapters, due to various reasons and interdependent processes, both living and non-living entities continually undergo changes at differing speeds and time intervals. When non-living matter meets with other matter, both of them can go through transformation. Similarly, a living entity may go through transformation when it comes in contact with a non-living entity. But amidst these ongoing transformations, each entity retains its fundamental characteristics; for instance, the intrinsic nature of *jīva* and its persistent qualities of *cetanā* (consciousness), *vīrya* (vigor), and *sukha* (bliss). From that perspective, spiritually speaking, each living entity (for example, the soul) and non-living entity is eternal and is capable of existing for an immeasurable time. A non-quiescent entity cannot transform itself into a void. Similarly, a quiescent entity cannot be transformed or produced from a void.

While all entities retain their fundamental properties forever,[3] they continuously transition through successive physical states by means of modal transformation processes. For instance, a *jīva* eternally retains its fundamental characteristics (*guṇa*s) of *vīrya*, *cetanā*, and *sukha*, whereas its associated physical body changes its form and shape from one life to the other. The physical body associated with a soul (*jīva*) is formed and destroyed as it goes through birth–death–rebirth cycles, although the *jīva* retains its independent existence. Therefore, the universe is never annihilated or created. The universe is eternal according to Jain doctrine.

As discussed earlier, Jain Dharma considers the earth, vegetation, water,

---

[2] In itself, Jain doctrine is a resounding spiritual philosophy that addresses the fundamentals of life. There is no direct or implied claim of scientific basis for the doctrine, and none is needed to compare it with science. However, from time to time many scientific findings have been found to be consistent with certain aspects of Jain philosophy, while many others continue to be in disagreement. The creation of the universe is one instance where Jain philosophy deviates from the Big Bang theory of science.

[3] Spiritually speaking, as stated earlier the intrinsic characteristics of souls remain unchanged. One could see a similarity in science with regards to chemical elements, which are defined as materials which cannot be broken down or changed from one substance to another using chemical means. This is to cite an example and not to surmise that science and Jain Dharma agree on every point of view.

air, and fire to be immovable living entities because they are all believed to have consciousness, sentience, and even a soul, hence the various categories of *jīva*s that we have explored in this book. For millennia, Jain theoreticians have been sensitive to the needs of the biodiversity of the life-forms surrounding us, and have been sympathetic even to plants as life-forms that are deserving of our compassion and respect. These are attitudes towards nature and other living beings that modern thinkers in the environmental movement have only begun to articulate.

According to Jain Dharma, each soul has a boundless capacity for knowledge. However, so long as it is blanketed by the acquired *karma* (*kaṣāya*s), it cannot reveal its true form. As discussed in earlier chapters, when a *jīva* in an associated body manages to reach a state of awakening through the revelation of right perception (*samyag-dṛṣṭi* or *samyag-darśana*), it starts making progress on the path of spirituality through austere means. When empowered by this spiritual growth and unrelenting perseverance, the *jīva* can remove its kārmic coverings and acquire unbounded wisdom. In this state, it starts envisioning the past and future just like the present. Strict penance, deep meditation, and *yoga* are the key components of Jain spiritual perseverance. According to Jain doctrine, through these practices one can attain incredible spiritual powers to achieve revelation of inner hidden strengths.

The objective of genuine philosophical scriptures is to assist in the acquisition of right perception (*samyag-darśana*), right knowledge (*samyag-jñāna*), and right conduct (*samyag-cāritra*). This unadulterated right knowledge is instrumental in realizing freedom from all bondages and worldly shackles. The ultimate aspiration of a human being is to achieve complete liberation from worldly affairs because one cannot attain eternal peace without this liberation. The troika of right perception, right knowledge, and right conduct is the means for attaining liberation.

However, one must remember that knowledge can be a double-edged sword. When born out of and accompanied by modesty, compassion, independent objectivity, sincere and virtuous curiosity, and tolerance it is highly beneficial. With such positive and austere traits, the knowledge acquisition progresses towards and ultimately becomes enlightened. On the other hand, when knowledge is accompanied by defects such as pride, narrow-mindedness, bias, and intolerance, it can become a medium for spiritual downfall. These dishonorable flaws are the symptoms of human weaknesses and can transmute nectar into poison.

The Jain *tīrthaṅkara*s recognized human shortcomings and devised an innovative methodology that can help prevent knowledge from becoming adulterated by such poisonous tendencies. This methodology, based on the concept of open-mindedness, enriches knowledge with truth, greatness, and splendor. This skill, known as "non-absolutism," Anekāntavāda, has been described in earlier chapters. It helps in smoothing out differences between contrarian viewpoints to create a harmonious understanding and establish the complete and universal truth. Through this respectful and thoughtful dialectic one can augment one's knowledge in a way that is rooted in modesty, compassion, and tolerance.

For Jains, non-violence (*ahiṁsā*) is the most important righteous characteristic of one's way of life. We can see that Jain thinkers have extended this ethos to every aspect of their thought and actions – even by devising a rhetorical system based on granting charity and respect to what might otherwise seem like opposing, or even inimical, views (i.e., Anekāntavāda).

For thousands of years, Jains have adopted non-violence in mind, body, and speech with unwavering commitment and intensity. Jain Dharma was the foremost, and earliest doctrine to discourage people from eating meat and sacrificing animals. This was done by educating humanity about the violence it entails. Jain *ācārya*s propounded non-violence with so much fervor and clarity that over a period of time it became the key aspect of all of the dhārmic philosophies of India and eventually outside India as well. Jain Dharma provided the reasoning for the acceptance of non-violence as the basic principle in all other religions. While their philosophies may differ in accepting the range of non-violence, for most of them it has become one of their most important principles.

Generally speaking, when one thinks of non-violence, they do so from the perspective of not eating meat, or finding peaceful solutions to the violent conflicts around the world and in daily life. These are important matters, and without trivializing their value, the fact is that these are only examples of externally observable violence where it is easy to comprehend the application of the doctrine of non-violence. For Jains, curbing the externally observable violence is important, but it is far from being sufficient. Jain philosophy has dealt with non-violence very meticulously in detail. For Jains, physical violence is a behavioral manifestation; the real and much more pernicious form occurs through one's mental contemplations.

If one has to pinpoint the single most important achievement of Jain scholars and preachers, it is the steadfast perseverance and observance of non-violence in their own lives, and their untiring efforts through the centuries to promote it. The result is that non-violence has become well understood to the extent that it is a universally accepted principle. This is the greatest gift of Jains to the world.

Lord Mahāvīra began the crusade for non-violence to stop animal sacrifices, meat eating, and other such practices. His sermons became immensely powerful and effective because he emphasized *ahiṁsā* in thoughts as much as in physical actions. He preached that *ahiṁsā* is intrinsic to mankind, is one of the basic characteristics of *jīva*, and is essential in building an honorable character and acquiring supreme wisdom. Although violence is present everywhere today, thoughtful individuals do not consider it to be just a non-religious, unspiritual, or unethical act. Beyond that, in general violence is considered an inauspicious and sinful practice, although the level of inauspiciousness associated with violent acts varies from one faith to another.

As we have seen, one can consider *ahiṁsā* to be the central teaching and practice of Jain Dharma. If one is to sincerely endeavor to live non-violently, there are a variety of implications of this spiritual ethos when it comes to the cultivation of related virtuous behavior. For example, possessiveness is viewed adversely in almost all of the predominant religious doctrines. India's dhārmic traditions consider possessiveness to be the key reason for a soul's downfall – and no tradition states this with more fervor than the Jain tradition. But even the holy book of Christianity (the Bible) has a well-known saying that it is easier for a camel to pass through the eye of a needle than it is for a rich man to enter through the gates of heaven. Notwithstanding such viewpoints, most doctrines tend to consider possessiveness to be a vice of somewhat lesser significance, much like a malady that should be avoided by spiritually minded people. It is rarely in the forefront of the characteristics that must be forsaken for spiritual advancement.

Jain Dharma is an exception. In Jain philosophy, possessiveness is considered to be one of the five most serious vices (*doṣa*s). Because of the seriousness associated with this vice, a detailed and systematic methodology is provided to help both householders and ascetic practitioners dislodge possessiveness and develop an alternate lifestyle of non-possessiveness. This occurs not only on an ethical level, since consumption can often be considered a form of violence, but in a sense the practice of non-possessiveness is the practical application of *ahiṁsā* in everyday life – and therefore is the very practice of seeing the potential for one's spiritual cultivation in everyday living.

Jain mendicants (*śramaṇa*s) follow a strict mandate to achieve complete non-attachment and non-possessiveness. They do not possess anything other than a limited number of articles to meet their basic needs to live, conduct their penance, and lead a lifestyle of self-restraint. They cannot even keep any food items left over from one day's collection for consumption the next day. They have to forsake all attachments to all living and non-living entities, including all worldly relationships. They have to continually and carefully engage in observance of the supreme vows (*mahāvrata*s) of non-possession (*aparigraha*) and non-attachment (*akiñcanatā*).

Jain householders (*śrāvaka*s), on the other hand, cannot maintain worldly affairs if they observe complete non-possessiveness like the ascetics. Neither are they granted unlimited liberties for acquisitions. In order for one to be considered an ideal Jain householder, one must assess the necessity of one's possessions to control and limit one's tendencies for cravings, greed, and attachments. Regular and ongoing assessment is one of the five fundamental vows (*aṇuvrata*s) of Jain householders. To help observe this vow, they have to undertake two sub-vows: the sub-vow of limited consumption (*bhoga–upabhoga parimāṇa*), and the sub-vow to relinquish meaningless castigations (*anartha-daṇḍa-tyāga*). The householders can properly observe the vow of non-possession only if they limit the articles needed for their daily lives and relinquish their interest in meaningless and unnecessary products. Hence, the two sub-vows are very important for the householders.

It is important to note that the doctrine of non-possession (Aparigrahavāda) is not confined to just physical or tangible objects (wealth, property, etc.). It extends to non-tangible objects as well – such as a father-son relationship, or a *guru-śiṣya* (*guru*-disciple) relationship, or the acquisition of fame or personal knowledge, etc. As discussed in earlier chapters, attachment is also a highly adverse and inauspicious trait, and in some ways it is considered a manifestation of possessiveness. Attachment must also be eliminated to develop and enhance the characteristics of righteousness.

The intent of non-possessiveness is important in life so that, as an example, one's financial inclinations for acquisitiveness do not destroy one's life. One must be careful that becoming rich does not become the only goal in life, that life does not revolve around physical possessions, or that the highest spiritual objectives are not lost in the pursuit of one's attachments. If society were motivated by the intent of non-possessiveness, the problems of society caused by greed for increasing wealth and all sorts of other kinds of ownership would be solved. To solve issues of distribution of wealth, society does not need socialism, communism, or any other new "ism." One just needs to follow the principle of non-possessiveness.

Jain principles of non-attachment and non-possessiveness offer an elegant solution for many prevailing and emerging problems of the world. Hence, it is an important subject for study by scholars of political science and economics. This principle helps the individual to achieve a praiseworthy and higher spiritual state. At the same time, it helps in resolving many of the social problems.

Thus, in a sense, *ahiṁsā* is the spiritual ethos, and *aparigraha* is the practical application of that ethos, while Anekāntavāda teaches how *ahiṁsā* applies to one's speech and verbal interactions with others. If one is to proceed on the path of spiritual cultivation as articulated in Jain Dharma, one has to be constantly vigilant to cultivate these virtues and the plethora of other related virtues, such as *satya* (truthfulness) and *acaurya* (non-stealing) and others that we have discussed in previous chapters. Thus, we can see that there is a relation of equality – even proportionality – between spiritual development and the cultivation of virtues (*guṇa*) in Jain Dharma. For Jains, virtue is spiritual cultivation.

But aside from the cultivation of these virtues for the sake of one's own spiritual development, the implications of spiritual practice in Jain Dharma has social ramifications. Jain teachings advocate the veneration towards individuals based on their qualities – not just because of their caste, place of birth, lineage, color, creed, or attire. From ancient times, worldwide communities have endured divisiveness based on unjust classifications of people when society could be more unified. Advocates of such divisiveness have sought to establish, consolidate, and protect their own political power through such dubious acts. One might justify certain classification schemes based on the individual skills corresponding to certain tasks a community may undertake to maintain a structured society. This helps in achieving optimum development at both the individual and community levels. However, it is inappropriate to impose separations only on the basis of one's birth and lineage. This goes against the implications of *ahiṁsā* on a social level.

A society should not promote a person with acclaim, adoration, accolades, honor, and a high-profile position just because one is born into a particularly "priviledged" ethnic or racial group (for instance, the so-called upper caste in India) in spite of being an illiterate, dubious, dishonest, and ill-mannered character. At the same time, a society should not humiliate and denigrate a person born in a different ethnic or racial group, such as the so-called lower caste in India, in spite of being kind, intelligent, righteous, and wise. In the long run, such a system proves to be hurtful to the society – and is disgraceful. It represents an insult to knowledge, virtuosity, and compassion while showing an appreciation for unfavorable qualities.

Therefore, Jain philosophy believes that an individual should earn respect only on the basis of righteous behavior. Conversely, an individual should not be shown undue respect if they lack appropriate worthy characteristics. This belief is imprinted throughout the various Jain scriptures, and some statements are provided below:[4]

- One does not become an ascetic just by shaving hair off one's head, and one does not become brāhmin just by continuously repeating the *oṁkāra mantra*. Similarly, one does not become a monk just by spending time in a forest or wilderness, and one does not become an adept spiritual seeker by simply performing the act of giving up clothes.

---

[4] From *Uttarādhyayanasūtra*, section 25, chapter 2, part 13, couplets 9-11.

- One becomes an ascetic with auspicious tendencies, a brāhmin by living a celibate and righteous life, a monk by adulating knowledge, or a hermit by being engrossed in austerity. By deeds (*karma*), one becomes a brāhmin, or a kṣatriya (warrior class), or a vaiśya (business class), or a śūdra (lower working class).
- Two humans cannot be distinguished on the basis of their lineage, but their individual qualities of austerity and righteousness can definitely give rise to distinctions.

The above statements demonstrate that Jain doctrine has given importance to one's virtuous qualities to distinguish individuals without paying any attention to their lineage or financial position. That is why the Jain community has treated all individuals equally while disregarding their parental or financial background.

Jain doctrine goes to the extent of not accepting any insurmountable wall between an ordinary soul and a "great soul" (*mahātmā*) or a "liberated soul" (*paramātmā,* a Supreme Soul) or God. According to the Jain doctrine, any soul can conceivably rise to the levels of the "great" or "liberated" ones with the appropriate perseverance. With such a distinguished and sound fundamental belief system, Jain doctrine has left no room for any discriminatory behavior between humans, or between any souls.

The belief that all living beings are capable of freeing themselves from the cycles of reincarnation is one of the key principles of Jain Dharma. All religious doctrines have faced the ever-important question on the ultimate state of a human being. Jains are unique in their belief that every *jīva* (soul) is capable of achieving the ultimate liberation and thereafter continuing in that state forever. As an extension of this principle, Jain Dharma does not believe in a single supreme entity – the Supreme God – as the creator of the universe, who is unique, unconquerable, and separate from the living beings. Jains consider eternally liberated *jīva*s (souls) as supreme beings because of their status of enlightenment achieved through intense penance, austerities, and meditation. They have achieved *samyag-darśana*, *samyag-jñāna,* and *samyag-cāritra* with their perseverance. Each individual living being (*jīva* – soul) is inherently capable of independently achieving the same or similar status with appropriate commitment and dedicated perseverance.

Based on this concept, Jains do not have the notion of incarnation. According to Jain doctrine, the liberated souls continue to exist, but they do not undertake incarnation to appear in the world again. The highest ideals and the pinnacle state are available to all living beings, and for whomever is interested in achieving that state Jain doctrine provides the assurance and guidance to achieve these ideals and the ultimate state. Jain teachings present all the possibilities for boundless growth of the soul. The ability for a human to achieve the ultimate liberation and continued existence in that supreme state is completely non-discriminatory – for instance, a disciple could become the Supreme Guru himself. This is one of the most innate beliefs of Jain Dharma.

At the most fundamental level, the spirit of Jain Dharma can be understood as an elaborate revelation of the spiritual potency of non-violence. Through non-violence, the *jīva* sheds *karma* and realizes its spiritual potential through related practices. These involve cultivating non-violence in one's thoughts and intentions, manifesting non-violent intentions in the cultivation of physical actions, such as non-possession and the other virtues we have discussed, and even extending the cultivation of *ahiṁsā* to one's rhetorical interactions with others (e.g., Anekāntavāda). Through the sincere cultivation of *ahiṁsā* the practitioners purify their own karma, which has continually inflicted harm upon the practitioners since beginningless time.

Therefore, the highest spiritual realization in Jain Dharma can be understood, at least partially, as minimization, and ultimately elimination, of violence. This entails the violence that one commits against others which is minimized through the cultivation of virtues, as well as violence one faces from others which is minimized by releasing the burden of one's own *karma*.

In other words, the concept of non-violence is at the core of Jain Dharma and is its most important gift to the world. It is not hard to imagine what our violent world would look like if a significant portion of the earth's population were to sincerely endeavor to cultivate the teachings of Jain Dharma. And, at least figuratively speaking, one can imagine that the spiritual world would also benefit if more of us *jīvas* were to migrate towards our true, non-violent spiritual abode by honoring the teachings of this great tradition.

Appendix:
Jain Mantras

The Art and Science behind Mantra Formulation

MANTRAS are one of the most effective means for staying connected with the inherent characteristics of the soul. A *mantra* is an assembly of words to awaken, rejuvenate, and connect the practitioner's inner energies with those of the supreme beings. The result is a synchronized vibration between the two energies, creating spiritual exhilaration. A *mantra* is an expression that motivates the practitioners to contemplate the messages or directives coming from their respective souls. In Sanskrit, the purpose of a *mantra* is expressed in *manyate vicāryane ātmādaiṣoa yain seḥ*, meaning a channel which facilitates contemplations on the directives of the soul.

An interpretation of the word *mantra* can be derived from the grammar behind this word. The word *mantra* is formed from two components: *mana* and *tra*. *Mana* refers to "mind" and *tra* means to "protect." The composite word *mantra* refers to the means by which one would protect the *mana* (mind) from apprehensions and control it from wandering around. In another interpretation of the word *mantra*, *mana* refers to the function of the mind – contemplation. The word *tra* is derived from the word *tran*, which means to "discard." In Jain doctrine, the two key sources for enlightenment are (1) understanding the nature of the universe – *samyag-darśana* (right perception), achieved through contemplations – the main activity of the mind, and (2) freedom from the worldly attachments, achieved through discarding our attachments (*tra*). Therefore, *mantra* is an expression that inspires one to develop a true understanding of the universe while motivating one to renunciate all the things that are holding one back.

In India's religious traditions, *mantra*s are utilized in most of the prayers and worship. From that perspective, a *mantra* can also be considered as a way to convey in few letters or words the meaning implied in a longer expression of reverence. The creators of *mantra*s were spiritualists and preceptors with deep insight into the interactions of the mind-body-soul. They configured *mantra*s with words to best express veneration and invoke specific energies which result in optimal resonation of the body's energy centers (*cakra*s). Therefore, it is important to know what a *mantra* represents and comprehend its meaning. At the same time, it is important to use correct pronunciation to properly stress the sounds to invoke the related energy and vibrations. Take the example of the *namokāra* (*namaskāra*) *mahāmantra* (discussed below). Its words are profoundly spiritual, and its recitation delivers an insight into the mind-body-soul connections.

Many times, a specific *mantra* is shortened to fewer letters of Ardhamāgadhī (Prākr̥t) or Sanskrit – the language of the *mantra* – to incorporate it within a different *mantra*. In this case, the letters represent the essence of the full *mantra* and are called the "kernel *mantra*" or "seed *mantra*" (*bījākṣara*). For instance, in the *ṛṣi maṇḍala mantra* presented below, the letters *a*, *si*, *ā*, *u*, and *sā* represent *arihaṁtāṇaṁ, siddhāṇaṁ*, *āyariyāṇaṁ*, *uvajjhāyāṇaṁ*, and *savvasāhuṇaṁ*, respectively, of the *namokāra mahāmantra* (see below for further discussion of this *mantra*).

It is believed that, when recited in the appropriate frame of mind, the vibrations and energy generated by a kernel *mantra* could be much more intense than those generated by the full *mantra*. This is because while reciting the kernel version, the spiritual energy is spread over a short span and hence its intensity is higher. Because of this reason, *mantra* scholars have created many kernel *mantra*s, which in some cases are made up of only one letter.

It is very important to understand that just the recitation of any *mantra* does not result in the expected benefits, unless the recitation is accompanied by the necessary efforts by the practitioner. *Mantra*s help in creating a mental and spiritual state of the highest effectiveness and optimum efficiency such that the practitioner thinks clearly and acts prudently in exerting the efforts. In the end, as seen in previous chapters, one receives the desired results like wealth, fame, education, etc., as determined by the previously accumulated *karma*s and righteousness (or lack thereof) of the efforts in this life. The kārmic results are prompted by one's efforts, and *mantra*s help in optimally configuring the efforts.

Some of the most common *mantras* used in Jain spiritual activities are presented below along with their meanings and explanations.

Namokāra (Namaskāra) Mahāmantra

Namokāra (*namaskāra*) *mahāmantra*, sometimes called *namokāra mantra*, is a *mantra* to invoke spirituality by expressing obeisance to those who have achieved or are on their path to achieve spiritual liberation or ultimate salvation. Here, the word *mantra* is appended with *mahā-* because it is the supreme (*mahā*), most auspicious *mantra* in Jain tradition, and is considered to encompass all other *mantras* within it.

णमो अरिहंताणं
णमो सिद्धाणं
णमो आयरियाणं
णमो उवज्झायाणं
णमो लोए सव्व साहुणं
एसो पंच-णमुक्कारो, सव्व पावप्पणासणो
मंगला णं च सव्वेसिं, पढमं हवइ मंगलं।।

ṇamo arihaṁtāṇaṁ
ṇamo siddhāṇaṁ
ṇamo āyariyāṇaṁ
ṇamo uvajjhāyāṇaṁ
ṇamo loe savva sāhuṇaṁ
eso paṅca-ṇamukkāro, savva pāvappaṇāsaṇo
maṅglā ṇaṁ ca savvesiṁ, paḍhamaṁ havai maṅgalaṁ।।

ṇamo arihaṁtāṇaṁ	Obeisance to the victors (*arihaṁta* or *arihanta*)
ṇamo siddhāṇaṁ	obeisance to the liberated souls (*siddha*)
ṇamo āyariyāṇaṁ	obeisance to the preceptors (*āyariya*)
ṇamo uvajjhāyāṇaṁ	obeisance to the teachers (*uvajjhāya*)
ṇamo loe savva sāhuṇaṁ	obeisance to the monks (*sāhu*)
eso paṅca-ṇamukkāro	this fivefold obeisance
savva pāvappaṇāsaṇo	ends all sins and bondages
maṅglā ṇaṁ ca savvesiṁ	the most auspicious harmony is generated in the entire universe

paḍhamaṁ havai maṅgalaṁ	by the blissful rendition of this *mantra.*

Namokāra mantra involves visualizing the five stages of spiritual growth: *arihaṅta, siddha, āyariya, uvajjhāya*, and *sāhu*, as described below:

1. *Arihaṁta* or *arihanta* or *arihaṁt* (victor): This is the state of a divine soul (*jīva*), which is still associated with a body, although it has achieved infinite wisdom after eliminating all of the *karmas* that can be destroyed with penance and austerities. Here, the divine *jīva* has discarded *darśanāvaraṇīya-karma, jñānāvaraṇīya-karma, antarāya-karma, mohanīya-karma*, and *vedanīya-karma*, but still has outstanding *āyu-karma, nāma-karma*, and *gotra-karma* (refer to chapter 11 for descriptions of the classes of *karmas*).
2. *Siddha* (liberated soul): The state of one who has achieved omniscience and has left their body to attain the ultimate liberation. Here, the divine *jīva* has discarded all eight *karmas*.
3. *Ācārya*; *āyariya* in Ardhamāgadhī (preceptors): These are the leaders of the spiritual community.
4. *Upādhyāya*; *uvajjhāya* in Ardhamāgadhī (teachers): These are teachers of spiritual knowledge.
5. *Sādhu*; *sāhu* in Ardhamāgadhī (monks): These are all male and female mendicants.

In one sense, the *namaskāra mahāmantra* represents a progression towards the freedom from the cycles of birth and death by gradually shedding *karma* until one has moved beyond the ascetic life to complete liberation. The meditation on this *mantra* directs one's attention to the process of fulfilling one's aspirations for similar spiritual progress. The important thing to note is that the *mantra* does not refer to any individual names but addresses all the *jīvas* in those categories, irrespective of whether they belong to Jain tradition or not.

Typically, *namokāra mantra* is recited five times, preferably in the morning. However, other times are fine as well, and the more one can recite, the better the results will be in terms of feelings of peace and calmness. Many times, practitioners recite it over a rosary of beads – a Jain rosary has 108 beads.

Maṅgala-Pāṭha (Cattārī Maṅgalam)

This spiritual recitation is an expression of the recognition of, and gratitude and obeisance towards, the most auspicious entities of the universe. It does not contain any specific names but like *namaskāra mahāmantra* addresses all the auspicious entities whether or not they belong to Jain tradition.

चत्तारी मंगलं, अरिहंता मंगलं, सिद्धा मंगलं।
साहू मंगलं, केवलिपन्नत्तो धम्मो मंगलं।

चत्तारी लोगुत्तमा, अरिहंता लोगुत्तमा।
सिद्धा लोगुत्तमा, साहू लोगुत्तमा।
केवली पन्नत्तो धम्मो लोगुत्तमो।

चत्तारी सरणं पव्वज्जामि, अरिहंते सरणं पव्वज्जामि।
सिद्धे सरणं पव्वज्जामि, साहू सरणं पव्वज्जामि।
केवलिपन्नतं धम्मं सरणं पव्वज्जामि।

cattāri maṅgalaṁ, arihaṅtā maṅgalaṁ, siddhā maṅgalaṁ।
sāhū maṅgalaṁ, kevalipannatto dhammo maṅgalaṁ।

cattāri loguttamā, arihaṅtā loguttamā।
siddhā loguttamā, sāhū loguttamā।
kevalī pannatto dhammo loguttamo।

cattāri saraṇaṁ pavvajjāmi, arihaṅte saraṇaṁ pavvajjāmi।
siddhe saraṇaṁ pavvajjāmi, sāhū saraṇaṁ pavvajjāmi।
kevalipannattaṁ dhammaṁ saraṇaṁ pavvajjāmi।

cattāri maṅgalaṁ	The below four entities are auspicious
arihaṅtā maṅgalaṁ	*arihanta*s are auspicious
siddhā maṅgalaṁ	*siddha*s are auspicious
sāhū maṅgalaṁ	*sādhu*s are auspicious
kevalipannatto dhammo maṅgalaṁ	the *dharma* (doctrine) expounded by the enlightened *jina*s is auspicious
cattāri loguttamā	the below four entities are the greatest
arihaṅtā loguttamā	*arihanta*s are the greatest
siddhā loguttamā	*siddha*s are the greatest
sāhū loguttamā	*sādhu*s are the greatest
kevalī pannatto dhammo loguttamo	the *dharma* (doctrine) expounded by the enlightened *jina*s is the greatest

cattāri saraṇaṁ pavvajjāmi	I seek sanctuary under the below four entities
arihaṅte saraṇaṁ pavvajjāmi	I seek sanctuary under the *arihanta*s
siddhe saraṇaṁ pavvajjāmi	I seek sanctuary under the *siddha*s
sāhū saraṇaṁ pavvajjāmi	I seek sanctuary under the *sādhu*s
kevalipannataṁ dhammaṁ saraṇaṁ pavvajjāmi	I seek sanctuary in the *dharma* (doctrine) expounded by the enlightened *jina*s.

Typically, *maṅgala-pāṭha* is recited one or two times, preferably in the morning. However, it can be recited at other times and as many times as one wants.

Kṣamāpaṇā-Sūtra (Forgiveness Couplet)

This recitation is an expression of seeking and granting forgiveness, and articulating a personal duty of friendship and compassion towards all living beings. It exemplifies one of the most important elements of Jain Dharma – peace and tranquility through non-violence and friendship, and equanimity through modesty – and is an essential component of the *pratikramaṇa* practice.

खामेमि सव्व जीवा, सव्वे जीवा खमंतु मे।
मित्ती मे सव्व भूएसु, वेरं मज्झं न केणइ।।

khāmemi savva jīvā, savve jīvā khamaṅtu me।
mittī me savva bhūesu, veraṁ majjhaṁ na keṇai।।

khāmemi savva jīvā	I forgive all the living beings
savve jīvā khamaṅtu me	I plead for forgiveness from all the living beings
mittī me savva bhūesu	I am in friendship with all the living beings on this earth
veraṁ majjhaṁ na keṇai	I have animosity towards no one.

Ṛṣi-Maṇḍala Mantra

Ṛṣi-maṇḍala mantra is an expression of veneration towards all the spiritually enlightened souls and their glorious characteristics. This *mantra* is composed of kernel or seed *mantra*s (*bījākṣara*s). Each of the seed *mantra*s is just a few letters implying a corresponding longer expression – just like the way abbreviations work. Its recitation in the morning invigorates the body with positive vibrations. This *mantra* is recommended to be recited 108 times in the morning with clean body and mind.

ॐ ह्रां ह्रीं ह्रुँ ह्रूं ह्रें ह्रैं ह्रौं ह्रः
अ सि आ उ सा
सम्यक्ज्ञान दर्शन चारित्रेभ्यो ह्रीं नमः स्वाहाः

oṁ hrāṁ hrīṁ hruṁ hrūṁ hreṁ hraiṁ hroṁ hraḥ
a si ā u sā
samyakjñāna darśana cāritrebhyo hrīṁ namaḥ svāhāḥ ।

oṁ	Seed *mantra* of eternal, omniscient, and omnipresent energy. It generates energy which flows upwards in the body to blend with the divine energy at the *sahasrāra*, which is at the mid-point of the skull
hrāṁ	seed *mantra* of knowledge, wealth, virtue, beauty, fame, victory
hrīṁ	seed *mantra* of the universe, the elements and all the extraordinary powers embedded in the universe
hruṁ	seed *mantra* of divine fire
hrūṁ	seed *mantra* of the power to destroy enmity
hreṁ	seed *mantra* of Sarasvatī, the goddess and purveyor of inspiration for knowledge and speech
hraiṁ	seed *mantra* of the auspicious nectar and the life force
hroṁ	seed *mantra* to purify *suṣumṇā* and contact divine energy
hraḥ	seed *mantra* of the power to destroy obstacles
a	*arihaṁta* for *ṇamo arihaṁtāṇaṁ*
si	*siddhā* for *ṇamo siddhāṇaṁ*
ā	*ācārya* (*āyariya* in Ardhamāgadhī) for *ṇamo āyariyāṇaṁ*
u	*upādhyāya* (*uvajjhāya* in Ardhamāgadhī) for *ṇamo uvajjhāyāṇaṁ*
sā	*sādhu* (*sāhu* in Ardhamāgadhī) for *ṇamo loe savvasāhuṇaṁ*
samyak-jñāna-darśana cāritrebhyo	I pray to be endowed with right knowledge, right perception, and right conduct
hrīṁ namaḥ svāhāḥ	All powers come from *hrīṁ*, and I bow to offer my sincere obeisance.

Ṛṣi-maṇḍala mantra is a short but very impactful *mantra*. It quickly brings calmness while accelerating the onset of the meditative state. It can be recited as many times as one wants, for instance, over a rosary of beads.

Sarasvatī Mahāmantra

Devī Sarasvatī is the goddess and purveyor of inspiration for knowledge and the arts. *Sarasvatī mahāmantra* is an expression of reverence towards the *devī* and gratitude for the inflow of wisdom and consciousness. The *mantra* generates vibrations and energizes the practitioners to eliminate ignorance and misconceptions while preparing them for the infusion of intelligence and clarity. The formulation of the *mantra* is such that while chanting, it generates an inner state of calmness, peace, and tranquility. So it is highly recommended for alleviation of anguish and stress as well.

ओं अर्हन मुख कमलवासिनी, पापात्म क्षयंकरी।
श्रुत ज्ञान ज्वाला सहस्र ज्वलिते सरस्वती।।

मत्पापं हन-हन – दह-दह – क्षां क्षीं क्षूं क्षौं क्षः
क्षीर धवले अमृत सम्भवे, वं वं हुं हुं स्वाहाः।

oṁ arhana mukha kamalavāsinī pāpātma kṣayaṁkarī।
śruta jñāna jvālā sahasra jvalite sarasvatī।।

matpāpaṁ hana-hana — daha-daha — kṣāṁ kṣīṁ kṣūṁ kṣauṁ kṣaḥ
kṣīra dhavale amṛta sambhave, vaṁ vaṁ huṁ huṁ svāhāḥ।

oṁ arhana mukha kamala-vāsinī	I am focused on the eternal, omniscient, and omnipresent energies of the universe, and revering that. O! Goddess, your energies reside in the mouth of *arihanta*s
pāpātma kṣayaṁkarī	you have the power to destroy all sins
śruta jñāna jvālā sahasra jvalite sarasvatī	you are emanating thousands of flames of wisdom which distribute divine knowledge everywhere
matpāpaṁ hana-hana – daha-daha	empower me to burn and destroy my sins and eliminate all my negativities, and grant me
kṣāṁ kṣīṁ kṣūṁ kṣauṁ kṣah	• power for protection and happiness (*kṣāṁ*) • psychological abilities for goodness (*kṣīṁ*) • power to remove sadness and depression (*kṣūṁ*)

	• power to purify *suṣumṇā* and contact divine (*kṣauṁ*) • power for universal acceptance (*kṣaḥ*)
kṣīra dhavale amṛta sambhave,	you are radiating like an ocean of milk and you are eternal like being born from nectar
vaṁ vaṁ huṁ huṁ svāhāḥ	bless me and grant me the abilities to receive your blessings. Grant me wisdom.

Sarasvatī mahāmantra is exceptionally beneficial for the enhancement of the body's learning facilities. Its recitation rejuvenates mental alertness, cognitive powers, and comprehension abilities. It is especially recommended for students and researchers. As stated above, the *mantra* also helps in mitigating distress and in creating a mental state of peace and calmness.

Mahālakṣmī Mantra

Mahālakṣmī mantra is a *mantra* to express reverence to Devī Lakṣmī and a prayer to invoke her blessings. Sometimes Devī Lakṣmī is viewed as the deity who only grants monetary benefits, but learned devotees consider her pious benediction to be much broader. They venerate Devī Lakṣmī in eight different manifestations:

1. *Ādi-Lakṣmī*: The first manifestation of Lakṣmī from ancient times, symbolizing all-encompassing prosperity.
2. *Dhānya-Lakṣmī*: Prosperity in agriculture (crops), in view of the fact that ancient civilizations were predominantly agriculture-dependent.
3. *Dhairya-Lakṣmī*: Wealth of courage, to be prepared to face natural disasters and human-made calamities like wars.
4. *Gaja-Lakṣmī*: Wealth of fertility, rain, and food in conjunction with Dhānya-Lakṣmī, symbolized by an elephant (*gaja*) spraying water (wealth) all around himself.
5. *Santāna-Lakṣmī*: Prosperity of continued family lineage and welfare of children.
6. *Vijaya-Lakṣmī*: Wealth of victories in battlefield and other struggles in the world.
7. *Vidyā-Lakṣmī*: Fortune of education, wisdom, and cultural proficiency.

8. *Dhana-Lakṣmī*: Monetary prosperity.

It is believed that meditating and reciting the following *mahālakṣmī mantra* generates strong vibrations and inner feelings which are extremely beneficial in successfully accomplishing the tasks at hand.

ॐ श्रीं ह्रीं श्रीं कमले कमलालये प्रसीद प्रसीद ओं श्रीं ह्रीं श्रीं महालक्ष्म्यै नमः।

oṁ śrīṁ hrīṁ śrīṁ kamale kamalālaye prasīda prasīda oṁ śrīṁ hrīṁ śrīṁ mahālakṣmyai namaḥ।

oṁ	Seed *mantra* of eternal, omniscient, and omnipresent energy
śrīṁ	respectful prefix to address someone
hrīṁ	seed *mantra* of the universe, the elements and all of its extraordinary powers
śrīṁ	respectful prefix to address someone
kamale kamalālaye	sitting on a lotus in meditative lotus posture
prasīda prasīda	revering versatility, wisdom, and creativity
mahālakṣmyai namaḥ	bowing in obeisance to esteemed and venerated Lakṣmī.

One can surmise that recitation of *mahālakṣmī mantra* is very beneficial for the enhancement of one's abilities to prosper. It creates a state of mental alertness which helps in optimally strategizing and planning one's activities to receive the best possible results for one's efforts.

There is an alternative explanation related to *mahālakṣmī mantra* and *sarasvatī mahāmantra*, based on the *yoga* doctrine. According to the theory, the energies of Mahālakṣmī and Sarasvatī reside in two nerve systems (*nāḍīs*) affecting the mind-body functioning in the matters of knowledge acquisition and cultural education (Sarasvatī) and versatility to accomplish success in worldly endeavors (Mahālakṣmī). When the two *mantras* presented above are recited in meditative state with concentration, these two nerve systems are positively activated to resonate with the auspicious directives from the soul in its natural state. Such directives resonate with the body's *cakras* and inspire the creation of internal energy which guides success in worldly endeavors.

Pratikramaṇasūtra

As discussed in previous chapters, *pratikramaṇa* is a highly recommended spiritual practice in Jain tradition. The practice includes internal introspection and repenting one's deliberate or inadvertent hurtful acts committed against others in mind, body, and thoughts through physical actions and speech. The introspection is followed by asking for forgiveness from all those who might have been affected by such undesired and hurtful actions, whether or not they know it or complain about it. The affected entities may be human or non-human beings.

The practice also includes reflecting upon and reviewing all incidents which might have caused anguish or hurt to the practitioner, and forgiving all those who might have committed such offences against the practitioner.

Pratikramaṇasūtra is an essential part of the Jain spiritual practices. It is the absolution prayer.

जं जं मणेण बद्धं, जं जं वायेण भासियं पावं।
जं जं कायेण कयं, तस्स मिच्छामि दुक्कडं।।

jaṁ jaṁ maṇeṇa baddhaṁ, jaṁ jaṁ vāyeṇa bhāsiyaṁ pāvaṁ।
jaṁ jaṁ kāyeṇa kayaṁ, tassa micchāmi dukkaḍaṁ।।

jaṁ jaṁ maṇeṇa baddhaṁ	For all the misdeeds I have committed in thoughts and contemplations in my mind
jaṁ jaṁ vāyeṇa bhāsiyaṁ pāvaṁ	for all the misdeeds I have committed by the use of language in speech or in writing
jaṁ jaṁ kāyeṇa kayaṁ	for all the misdeeds that I have committed through my physical actions
tassa micchāmi dukkaḍam	I ask for unconditional absolution.

The practitioners conduct *pratikramaṇa*, which includes this *sūtra*, every day and/or fortnightly and/or every four months and/or every year.

Logassasūtra – Caturviṁśit Prayer

Logassasūtra is one of the most recited prayers in Jain tradition. The prayer is composed in veneration of the twenty-four *tīrthaṅkaras* and for that reason, it is also known as Caturviṁśit (twenty-four *jinas*) prayer.

लोगस्स उज्जोयगरे, धम्म तित्थयरे जिणे।
अरिहंते कितइस्सं, चउवो संपि केवली।।

उसभ मजिअं च वन्दे, संभवमभि णंदणंच सुमइं च।
पउमप्पहं सुपासं, जिणं च चंदप्पहं वन्दे।।

सुविहिं च पुप्फदंत, सीअल सिज्जंस-बासुपुज्जं च।
विमल मणंतंच जिणं, धम्मं संति च वंदामि।।

कुंथुं अरं च मल्लिं, वंदे मुणिसुव्वयं नमिजिणं च।
वंदामि रिट्ठनेमिं, पासं तह वद्धमाणं च।।

एवं मए अभित्थुआ, विहुय-रयमला पहीणजरमरणा।
चउवीसंपि जिणवरा, तित्थयरा मे पसीयंतु।।

कित्तिय-वंदिय-महिया, जे ए लोगस्स उत्तमा सिद्धा।
आरूग्ग-बोहि लाभं, सभाहिवर मुत्तमं दिंतु।।

चंदेसु निम्मलयरा, आइच्चेसु अहियं पयासयरा।
सागर-वर गम्भीरा, सिद्धा सिद्धिं मम दिसंतु।।

logassa ujjoyagare, dhamma titthayare jiṇe।
arihaṁte kitaissaṁ, cauo saṁpi kevalī।।

usabha majiaṁ ca vaṁde, saṁbhavamabhi ṇaṁdaṇaṁca sumaiṁ ca।
paumappahaṁ supāsaṁ, jiṇaṁ ca caṁdappahaṁ vaṁde।।

suvihiṁ ca pupphadaṁtaṁ, sīala sijjaṁsa-vāsupujjaṁ ca।
vimala maṇaṁtaṁca jiṇaṁ, dhammaṁ saṁti ca vaṁdāmi।।

kuṁthuṁ araṁ ca malliṁ, vaṁde muṇisuvvayaṁ namijiṇaṁ ca।
vaṁdāmi riṭṭhanemiṁ, pāsaṁ taha vaddhamāṇaṁ ca।।

evaṁ mae abhitthuā, vihuya-rayamalā pahīṇajaramaraṇā।
cauvīsaṁpi jiṇavarā, titthayarā me pasiyaṁtu।।

kittiya-vaṁdiya-mahiyā, je e logassa uttamā siddhā।
ārūgga-bohi lābhaṁ, sabhāhivara muttamaṁ diṁtu।।

caṁdesu mimmalayarā, āiccesu ahiyaṁ payāsayarā।
sāgara-vara gambhirā, siddhā siddhiṁ mama disaṁtu।।

logassa ujjoyagare	Your omni-vision and omniscient unbounded and enlightened wisdom cannot be hidden by any darkness and you have glowingly enlightened the entire universe with your divinity
dhamma titthayare jiṇe	you have established the auspicious *tīrtha* – a religious sanctuary – where *sādhu, sādhvī, śrāvikā,*

	and *śrāvaka* all of them come together in a spiritual communion with the *jina*.
arihante kitaissaṁ	You are an omniscient *jina arhanta* and have destroyed all attachments, and all of your *ghātīya-karma*s
cauvo saṁpi kevalī	I am venerating all twenty-four auspicious *tīrthaṅkara*s who have attained *kevala-jñāna* and who have destroyed all of their *karma*s; I am praying for their heavenly blessings
usabha majiaṁ ca vaṅde	I pray to Lord Ṛṣabhadeva (Usabha) and Lord Ajitanātha (Ajiaṁ)
saṁbhavamabhi ṇaṁdaṇaṁca sumaiṁ ca	I pray to Lord Sambhavanātha (Saṁbhava) and Lord Abhinandanātha (Abhiṇaṁdaṇaṁ), and Lord Sumatinātha (Sumaiṁ)
paumappahaṁ supāsaṁ	I pray to the *jina*s Lord Padmaprabhu (Paumap-pahaṁ), Lord Supārśvanātha (Supāsaṁ), and
jiṇaṁ ca caṅdappahaṁ vaṅde	I pray to Lord Candraprabha (Caṅdappahaṁ)
suvihiṁ ca pupphadaṅtaṁ	I pray to Lord Suvidhinātha (Suvihiṁ who is also revered with the name Pushpadanta or Pupphadaṅtaṁ)
sīala sijjaṁsa-vāsupujjaṁ ca	I pray to Lord Śītalanātha (Sīala), Lord Śreyāṁsanātha (Sijjaṁsa), and Lord Vāsupūjya (Vāsupujjaṁ)
vimala maṇaṁtaṁca jiṇaṁ	I pray to venerated *jina* Lord Vimalanātha (Vimala) and Lord Anantanātha (Aaṇaṁtaṁ)
dhammaṁ saṅti ca vaṅdāmi	I pray to Lord Dharmanātha (Dhammaṁ), and Lord Śāntinātha (Saṅti)
kuṅthuṁ araṁ ca malliṁ	I pray to Lord Kunthunātha (Kuṅthuṁ), Lord Arahanātha (Araṁ), and Lord Mallinātha (Malliṁ)
vaṅde muṇisuvvayaṁ namijiṇaṁ ca	I pray to the *jina*s Lord Munisuvrata (Muṇi-suvvayaṁ), and Lord Naminātha (Nami)
vaṅdāmi riṭṭhanemiṁ	I pray to Lord Ariṣṭanemi, also known as Lord Neminātha (Riṭṭhanemiṁ)
pāsaṁ taha vaddhamāṇaṁ ca	I pray to Lord Pārśvanātha (Pāsaṁ) and Lord Mahāvīra (Vaddhamāṇaṁ)

evaṁ mae abhitthuā vihuya-rayamalā pahiṇa-jaramaraṇā	in this manner I pay my obeisance and honor to all those who have destroyed attachment, malice, and all other impurities, have freed their souls from all the kārmic particles (*pudgala*s), and have ended their birth-and-death cycles
cauvīsaṁpi jiṇavarā	they are the twenty-four most auspicious *jina*s
titthayarā me pasiyaṅtu	who have established *tīrtha*s for their followers
kittiya-vaṅdiya-mahiyā	I courteously bow in obeisance with my complete loyalty
je e logassa uttamā siddhā	to these supremely auspicious souls of the entire universe and plead for
ārūgga-bohi lābhaṁ	their blessings and benediction for misery-free and malady-free good health and mind and contemplative powers so I may acquire right perception and right knowledge
sabhāhivara muttamaṁ diṅtu	I respectfully ask with humility for the ability to enjoy deep meditation (*samādhi*), and in the end, enjoy leaving my body while in meditation
caṅdesu nimmalayarā	Lord, you are purer than the moon with your immaculate soul in its intrinsic state of perfection
āiccesu ahiyaṁ payāsayarā	the radiance of your wisdom is brighter than the sun, and
sāgara-vara gambhirā	you are more serene and solemn than the oceans
siddhā siddhiṁ mama disaṅtu	you have achieved perfection and have become the supreme liberated *jina*s. I beg for your blessings for eternal bliss, vigor, and consciousness.

Guru-Vandanā

In India's dhārmic traditions, the *guru* is considered to be the main source of knowledge and spirituality, and is therefore revered as the most esteemed influencer in one's pursuit of enlightenment. In Jain tradition, the *tīrthaṅkara*s (*arihanta* and *siddha*) are the supreme *guru*s and are the ultimate source of enlightenment. *Ācārya*s, *upādhyāya*s, and *sādhu*s – who are in the bodily form – serve as the purveyors of *tīrthaṅkara*s' wisdom for right perception, right knowledge, and right conduct. They are the source of motivation for householders who are pursuing the auspicious path. Jains revere *guru*s with utmost respect, and *guru-vandanā* is a prayer in veneration of the *guru*.

तिक्खुत्तो, आयाहिणं, पयाहिणं, करेमि,
वंदामि नमंसामि, सक्कारेमि, सम्माणेमि,
कल्लाणं, मंगलं, देवयं, चेइयं,
पज्जुवासामि, मत्थएण वंदामि।

tikkhutto, āyāhiṇaṁ, payāhiṇaṁ karemi,
vaṁdāmi namaṁsāmi, sakkāremi, sammāṇemi,
kallāṇaṁ, maṅgalaṁ, devayaṁ ceiyaṁ,
pajjuvāsāmi, matthaeṇa vaṁdāmi।

tikkhutto āyāhiṇaṁ payā-hiṇaṁ karemi	To show my reverence, I circle around you three times
vaṁdāmi namaṁ sāmi sakkāremi sammā ṇemi	clockwise with my folded hands I worship you and bow in front of you to show my respect. I honor you
kallāṇaṁ maṅgalaṁ devayaṁ ceiyaṁ	you are the remover of obstacles. You are an ocean of knowledge. I am at your service
pajjuvāsāmi matthaeṇa vaṁdāmi	you are divine and worthy of worship. I bow my head to your feet with pure reverence.

Lord Śāntinātha Mantra

Lord Śāntinātha inspires tranquility, and repetition of this *mantra* will bring peace and harmony in life. The *mantra* creates an aura of magnanimity which positively inspires the practitioner as well as others. The *mantra* generates vibrations such that the feelings of animosity held by others do not affect the practitioner.

चइत्ता भारहवासं, चक्कवट्टी महिड्डियो।
संति-संति करे लोए, पत्तो गइ मणुत्तरं।।

caittā bhārahavāsaṁ, cakkavaṭṭī mahiḍḍiyo।
saṁti-saṁti kare loe, patto gai maṇuttaraṁ।।

caittā bhārahavāsaṁ	The creator of great prosperity for his citizens all over his kingdom, and
cakkavaṭṭī mahiḍḍiyo	who was enshrined as the great monarch – the king of kings,
saṁti-saṁti kare loe	Lord Śāntinātha, you established complete peace and harmony in your kingdom, and

patto gai maṇuttaraṁ	you forsake your kingdom and all of the worldly possessions to pursue the austere path of enlightenment and attained *mokṣa* – the ultimate liberation. Thereafter, you cultivated *ahiṁsā* (non-violence) and peace in the entire universe.

Simple Recitations for Meditation

Some of the *mantras*, or parts of them, are extremely effective in creating a mental state of peace, calmness, concentration, and tranquility. When such an auspicious state is established, the practitioner fully enjoys the splendor of meditation. Some of the short-form *mantras* are presented below:

ॐ णमो सिद्धाणं, ॐ णमो सिद्धाणं, ॐ णमो सिद्धाणं, ॐ णमो सिद्धाणं

oṁ ṇamo siddhāṇaṁ, oṁ ṇamo siddhāṇaṁ, oṁ ṇamo siddhāṇaṁ, oṁ ṇamo siddhāṇaṁ।

Calmly chant *oṁ ṇamo siddhāṇaṁ* four times in one breath. It can be done either internally or in a soft voice – individually or in a group. One may chant it as many times as preferred. Within a few minutes the practitioner will start experiencing the onset of mental calmness.

ॐ ह्रीं श्रीं क्लीं अर्हं हंसः, ॐ ह्रीं श्रीं क्लीं अर्हं हंसः

oṁ hrīṁ śrīṁ klīṁ arhaṁ haṁsaḥ, oṁ hrīṁ śrīṁ klīṁ arham haṁsaḥ

Calmly chant *oṁ hrīṁ śrīm klīṁ arham haṁsaḥ* two times in one breath. It can be done either internally or in a soft voice – individually or in a group. One may chant it as many times as preferred. Within a few minutes the practitioner will start experiencing the onset of mental calmness.

ॐ अर्हम्, ॐ अर्हम्, ॐ अर्हम्, ॐ

oṁ arham, oṁ arham, oṁ arham oṁ

Calmly chant *oṁ arham* three times in one breath, ending with elongated *oṁ* chant in each breath. It can be done either internally or in a soft voice – individually or in a group. One may chant it as many times as preferred. Within a few minutes the practitioner will start experiencing the onset of mental calmness.

Glossary of Terms

abhaya: Fearlessness

abhigama: Protocols of respect shown to *tīrthaṅkara*s and other holy and divine souls

abhiṣeka: Birth ablutions

ācārya: Highest level of learned mendicants who have become leaders of a mendicant clan and the spiritual community

adattādāna: A presumed charity which is taken without the donor's permission, or is not granted

adbhuta: Extraordinary

adbhuta sāmarthya: Extraordinary capability or capacity

adhyātma-yoga: Spiritual *yoga* – *yoga* of contemplation on self (soul) and fundamental truth

ādyanta maraṇa: Similar death in two lives

agāra dharma: Honorable practices followed by householders

aghātika-karma: Non-hurtful *karma*s that occur at a stage when all four *ghātika-karma*s (defined later) start to subside. They are: *vedanīya*, *āyu*, *nāma*, and *gotra karma*s

aghātīya-karma: Same as *aghātika-karma*

āgneyī dhāraṇā: Concentration on the fiery energy when engrossed in contemplative meditation

ahiṁsā: Non-violence

ājñā-vicaya: Concentrating on eradication of inauspicious thoughts during meditation

Ajñānavāda: Doctrine which denies the necessity and role of knowledge in attainment of salvation

akaṣāya: Dispassionate state

akiñcanatā: Non-attachment

Akriyavāda: Doctrine which denies existence of the soul (*jīva*) and states everything is of momentary existence

amāvasyā: The day of new moon

amūrta: Non-visible shapeless and formless entity

anāgāra dharma: Honorable practices followed by mendicants *ananta cetanā-ghana*: The state of complete, unlimited consciousness attained by soul (*jīva*)

anantānubandhī: Bondage from limitless past

anartha daṇḍa tyāga: Relinquishing meaningless castigation

anaupakramika: Involuntary or automatic shedding of *karma*s

anekānta: Multiplicity of views

Anekāntavāda: Doctrine of non-absolutism which subscribes to acceptance of relativism and pluralism

antarāya-karma: Hindrance-causing *karma*

anubhāga-bandha: Quality of fruition of *karma*s

anubhaya: That which is neither fixed-real nor unfixed-unreal

anuvrata: Limited vows for householders for honorable living, which are less stringent than those taken by ascetics

anuvratī: Householder follower of limited vows

apadhyāna: Negative thinking

aparigraha: Non-possession or non-attachment and contentment

apavitra vicāra: Inauspicious thoughts

apramāda: Spiritual alertness and staying within a righteous way of living

apratyākhyānāvaraṇī: Bondage of medium-term duration

Ardhamāgadhī: The language used by Lord Mahāvīra, and one of the languages in which most Jain scriptures are written

arhanta: Enlightened soul (*jīva*), worthy of worship, who has attained omniscience (supreme wisdom and clairvoyance), has eliminated all of the *karma*s that can be destroyed with penance and austerities, and is still in bodily form

arihanta: See *arhanta* above

ārjava: Straightforwardness – one of the *dasa* (ten) *dharma*

arūpī: Formless or shapeless entity

arūpī-ajīva: Formless and non-visible non-sentient entity

āsana: Seated posture

āsana-maraṇa: Death while in seated meditative posture

asat: Unreal

asatya: That which is not truthful

āśrava: Influx of *karma* upon the soul

asteya: Non-stealing

asti: Exists. The term is also used to denote *pradeśa* (the smallest part)

astikāya: An aggregate of *pradeśa*s (the smallest particles in Jain philosophy – subtler than atoms). The term *astikāya* is formed of two words: *asti* + *kāya*. Here, *asti* denotes *pradeśa*, and *kāya* denotes *samūha* (group or collection)

ātmā: Soul

ātma-yoga: Spiritual *yoga*, contemplating on the soul

aupakramika: Voluntary or deliberate shedding of *karmas* done with rigorous spiritual activities

avadhi-maraṇa: Timely death

avadhi-jñāna: Clairvoyant knowledge

avalambana: Being engrossed

āvaśyaka: Essential spiritual tasks

āvaśyaka kriyā: Essential or obligatory spiritual tasks and duties

avicāra: Beyond discursive consideration of the revelations or sounds

āvīci-maraṇa: Involuntary death

āyambila: An observance of penance entailing consumption of food without any interest in how it tastes or smells

Āyambila Oli or Navapada Āyambila Oli: A special *āyambila* penance conducted two times a year to eradicate the spiritual maladies accumulated over the previous six months

āyatana: Sanctuary for the formation and embodiment

ayathārtha: That which is not fixed and is unreal

āyu-karma: Lifespan-affecting *karma*

āyuṣya-karma: Same as *āyu-karma* above (lifespan-affecting *karma*)

Bakuṣa-nigrantha: Trying to be a mendicant – class of mendicants in whom unworthy attributes slightly outweigh their praiseworthy ones

bāla-maraṇa: Untimely death or death at an early age

bāla-paṇḍita-maraṇa: Death of worthy householder who dies while observing limited vows

bandha: Bondage

Bhagavadgītā: A holy and venerated book of Hindu tradition describing aspects and characteristics of Hindu doctrine

bhaktapāna-maraṇa: Death while completely immersed in devotion

bhakti-yoga: Veneration or faith *yoga*

bhāṣā: Language

bhāṣā nīti: Policy for language formulation

bhautika-yoga: Physical *yoga*

bhāva hiṁsā: Psychological violence – contemplating and scheming for violent actions

bhāva pratyākhyāna: Resolving to restrain and eliminate passions, malice, jealousy, belief in falsehood, ill-advised knowledge, etc.

bhāva-karma: Psychological *karma* (contemplating actions) – manifestation of *karma* in one's thoughts

bhāva-nikṣepa: Contemplation of an entity with due consideration to its name, form, and its existing characteristics

bhāva-prāṇāyāma: Breathing exercise with restrained thoughts or curtailed contemplation

bhāvanā: Desire, sentiments, emotions, spirit, consideration

bhāvanā-yoga: Intentional yoga with cultivation of compassionate emotions

bhoga: Consummate

brahmacarya: Celibacy and controlled carnal activities. The term is also used for honorable conduct

cāturmāsa: Auspicious period of four months in rainy season, when Jain monks stay at one place

cāturmāsika pratikramaṇa: *Pratikramaṇa* (defined later) conducted every four months for all the misdeeds committed during the previous four months. It is conducted in the evening of full-moon days in the months of Āṣāḍha (October–November), Kārttika (June–July), and Phālguna (February–March), following the Jain calendar

cauryānubandhī: Thirst for defrauding

cetanā: Consciousness

catur-viṁśati-stava: Prayer (*stuti*) adoring the twenty-four *tīrthaṅkara*s who overcame their inner enemies such as anger, ego, greed, deceit; and praising their supreme characteristics while aspiring to become like them

citta: Mind

cugalī: Slander and gossip

daivasika pratikramaṇa: *Pratikramaṇa* (defined later) conducted in the evening for all the misdeeds committed during the daytime

darśana-āvaraṇīya-karma: Perception or awareness inhibiting *karma*

dasa-dharma: Ten key characteristics of Jain Dharma

daśa-lakṣaṇa parva: A ten-day spiritual festival celebrated by the Jain community involving austerity and penance and studying each of the *dasa-dharma* (ten auspicious traits of spirituality) – one every day

daśa-vidhi dharma: Ten characteristics of Jain Dharma

daśalakṣaṇī: Ten traits or characteristics of Jain Dharma

devāṇuppiyā: God's favorite

dhāraṇā: Firm concentration or commitment

dhyāna: Focused contemplation or meditation

dhyāna-yoga: *Yoga* of meditation

dig-vrata: Vow of geographical limitation

divinity: In the Jain tradition, "divinity" refers to the auspicious attributes resulting from the attainment of right perception (*samyag-darśana*), right knowledge (*samyag-jñāna*), and right conduct (*samyag-cāritra*). It refers to the qualities and auspiciousness of the enlightened *jina*s (*tīrthaṅkara*s) who have achieved perfection and have freed themselves from the shackles of rebirth cycles. Since Jain tradition does not believe in God as the creator, there is no single divine figure and all the *jina*s or *tīrthaṅkara*s are considered to be the divine figures

dravya hiṁsā: Physical or substance (material) violence

dravya-karma: Substance *karma* – physical manifestation of actions

dravya pratyākhyāna: Taking the oath and practicing to give up materialistic items such as clothes, food, and travel

dravya-nikṣepa: This is contemplation of an entity with due consideration to its name and form and, at the same time, its past and future characteristics while ignoring its present characteristics

dveṣa: Malice, aversion, despicable

ekāgratā: Single-minded focus

ekatva: State of oneness

evambhūta naya: The viewpoint depicting actuality – the scheme to assign a word which is based on the activity and the object so that it is an accurate descriptor and its meaning is precise

*gaṇadhara*s: Chief disciples of Lord Mahāvīra – lit. "those who uphold virtue"

ghātika-karma: The four destructive *karma*s – *mohanīya*, *jñānāvaraṇīya*, *darśanāvaraṇīya*, and *antarāya karma*s

ghātīya-karma: Same as *ghātika-karma*

godohāsana: Cow-milking pose of *yoga* practice

gotra-karma: Clan of birth *karma*

gr̥ddha-pr̥ṣṭha-maraṇa: Death on a battlefield in war while protecting family, community, or nation

gr̥hastha-dharma: Householder ethics

*guṇa*s: Qualities or characteristics

hiṁsā: Violence

hiṁsā pradāna: Dominated by or in support of violence

hiṁsānubandhī: Thirst for violence

idhara-udhara mana: Aimless wandering of mind

iha-lokāśaṁsā: Desires for the worldly pleasures

indriya: Senses – vision, hearing, odor, taste, and touch. Sense organs: eyes, ears, nose, tongue, and skin to sense.

iṅgita-maraṇa: Death with conscientious restrictions

jina: An enlightened soul (*jīva*) who has attained omniscience, is worthy of worship

jinatva: The state of complete spiritual liberation

jīva: Soul (living being)

jīva dravya: Living substance

jīvitāśaṁsā: Desire to live longer upon experiencing the prestige and honor being bestowed

jñāna: Knowledge

jñāna-yoga: Knowledge *yoga* or wisdom *yoga*

jñānāvaraṇīya-karma: Knowledge-inhibiting *karma*

kāma: Impious selfish desires or cravings

kāma-bhogāśaṁsā: Desire to indulge in sensual pleasures

kamalāsana: Lotus pose

kārmic-śarīra (kārmic-body): A subtle (virtual) body composed of the assemblage of all *karma*s or *pudgala*s associated with the soul (*jīva*)

kaṣāya: Passions (anger, ego, deceit, greed) that cause the influx of kārmic particles (*pudgala*s) towards the soul (kārmic bondages). Kārmic bondage is also called *kaṣāya*

kaṣāya-kuśīla-nirgrantha: Mendicants who succumb to passions

kaṭu-gālī-śāpa: Use of caustic and abusive language, and the giving of curses

kāya: The body, or a group or collection (*samūha*), of *pudgala*

kāya-kleśa: Bodily deficiencies

kāyotsarga: Foregoing all attachments to the body, and connecting with one's own self (soul)

kevala-jñāna: Supreme or perfect or impeccable knowledge (wisdom) – omniscient supreme enlightenment – ubiquitous and unbound knowledge and wisdom

kevalī-maraṇa: Omniscient death

koṭambīyapuriṣa: Member of the family

kriyā: Actions or acts

Kriyāvāda: Doctrine which professes the existence of the soul (*jīva*), its impurities (miseries), and its annihilation through extroverted physical exercises such as *yajña*

krodha: Anger

kṣamā: Forgiveness

kuśīla-nigrantha: Mendicant who succumbs to unworthy traits

leśyā: An indicator of the level of problematic mental disposition. Also defined as coloration or staining of kārmic layers over the soul

lobha: Greed

lokākāśa: Part of the universe that is occupied

mahā: Great, supreme

mahātmā: Great soul

mahāvīra: The honorific title meaning "great hero," and prevalent name of Vardhamāna Jñātr̥putra, who is the twenty-fourth and last of the Jain *tīrthaṅkara*s of the current era, who lived in sixth century BCE (599-527 BCE)

mahāvrata: Supreme vows taken by mendicants

mahāvratī: An ascetic – the individual who is supremely avowed with *mahāvrata*

maithuna: Sexual urges, carnal desires

māna: Egoism

mana: Mind

manaḥ-paryāya-jñāna: Mind-reading knowledge

mānasika: Mental

mānasika śakti: Mental powers

mantra: An assembly of words to awaken, rejuvenate, and connect the practitioner's inner energies with divinity

maraṇāśaṁsā: Desire to die earlier due to lack of food, or after extreme pain caused by disease

mārdava: Modesty or humility (one of the *dasa-dharma*s)

mati-jñāna: Empirical knowledge

māyā: Deceitfulness

mithyātva: Wrong perception

mohanīya-karma: Delusional *karma* which obstructs virtuous qualities

mokṣa: The state which a spiritually enlightened *jīva* (soul) attains upon discarding all eight *karma*s (see chapter 11) subsequent to achieving perfection in all respects – perfect perception, unbounded perfect wisdom, and perfect conduct.

mr̥ṣānubandhī: Thirst for deception

mūrta: Tangible – Shape and form

naigama naya: The theological or commonly developed generic view

nāma-karma: Designation of the *jīva*'s body-type *karma*

nāma nikṣepa: Contemplation of the name associated with an entity without paying attention to the entity's form or characteristics

namokāra or *namaskāra mantra*: The supreme (*mahā*) *mantra* for Jains to invoke spirituality by expressing obeisance to those who have achieved or are on their path to achieve spiritual liberation or ultimate salvation *nāsti*: Does not exist

nikṣepa vidhāna: Legislation or methodology for systematic and proper consideration of each word

ninda: Slander

nirdayatā-pūrṇa-vicāra: Pitiless, cruel, and uncompassionate thoughts

nirgrantha: Spiritual mendicants who do not have any tangible or intangible possessions and are completely unattached to worldly life

nirjarā: Discarding accumulated *karma*s with spiritual efforts – in general, riddance of unwanted substance

nirodha: Cessation

nirvāṇa: The eternally liberated state of an enlightened *jīva* (soul) when it attains bodiless form after achieving *mokṣa*. The *jīva* (soul) now settles in *siddha-loka*, considered to be at the top of the universe in Jain cosmology

niṣedhaka: Restriction

pādapopagamana-maraṇa: Death by stillness

padastha-dhyāna: Focusing on the five couplets of the *namaskāra* or *namokāra mahāmantra*

pākṣika pratikramaṇa: Remorsefully repenting every fifteen days for all the misdeeds committed during the previous fourteen days. It is conducted in the evening on the days of full moon and new moon

pāñca-parmeṣṭhī: In Jain tradition, *pāñca-parmeṣṭhī* is the supreme holiness worthy of worship, comprising of five categories – *arihaṁta*s (enlightened supreme teachers in bodily form), *siddha*s (enlightened supreme teachers with liberated souls), *ācārya*s (mendicant leaders), *upādhyāya*s (mendicant preceptors), and *sādhu*/*sādhvī*s (male and female mendicants)

paṇḍita-maraṇa: Wise death

pāpa: Misdeeds or inauspicious or sinful acts

pāpopadeśa: Inciting sinfulness

paralokāśaṁsā: Desires for pleasures in next life

paramātmā: Liberated soul

parigraha: Possessiveness and attachment to accumulated tangible or intangible goods

pariṇāma: Transformation or change (also, translates to results)

parmahaṁsa-dharma: Saintly behavior or *dharma*

parokṣa: Acquired or intermediary or indirect states

pārthivī: The terrestrial earth

pārthivī-dhāraṇā: Concentration on the terrestrial energy

paryāya: Changes or synonym state

paryuṣaṇā: The most auspicious Jain festival, centered around pleading for pardon from others and granting others the same

Pāvāpurī: City where Lord Mahāvīra attained *nirvāṇa*

piṇḍastha-dhyāna: Focusing on the physical body attached to the soul

pradeśa: The smallest possible form that is indivisible

pradeśa-bandha: Magnitude of fruition

prakṛti-bandha: Nature of bondage

pramāda: Indulgence with carelessness or negligence

pramāda-maraṇa: Negligent death

pramādācarita: Behavior that is intoxicated by wealth and power

prāṇāyāma: Breathing exercise

prati-saṅlīnatā: Withdrawing within

pratikramaṇa: A self-analysis, confession, and remorseful-repentance exercise comprising daily, nightly, fortnightly, quarterly, and yearly spiritual cleansing activity to reflect, review, confess, and repent own unrighteous deeds in thoughts, actions, and speech against all living beings by asking for their forgiveness. It also involves extending friendship to all and granting them forgiveness while reverting to the path of non-violence, truthfulness, non-stealing, celibacy, and non-attachment

pratisevanā-kuśīla-nirgrantha: Mendicants who succumb to enticements

pratyāhāra: Withdrawing the senses

pratyākhyāna: Renouncing certain activities for a duration for self-restraint and discipline by taking vows according to one's own capabilities

pratyākhyānāvarṇa: Short-term duration

pratyakṣa: Direct or innate

prema-yoga: The *yoga* of love

pṛthaktva: State of separateness

pudgala: Non-sentient subtle-matter particle which has a configuration (*mūrta*) of shape, form, taste, smell, and touch sensitivity

pulāka-nigrantha: Barely a mendicant

rāga: Desires or atachments

rasa: Intensity

rātrika pratikramaṇa: Remorsefully repenting in the morning for all the misdeeds committed during the evening and nighttime

ṛjusūtra-naya: The linear or momentary view

rūpastha-dhyāna: Concentrating on one who has attained the *arihanta* state *rūpātīta-dhyāna*: Concentrating or focusing on the *siddha* state

sāmarthya ullāsa: Exhilaration

śabda-naya: The literal or verbal view

sadācāra: Right conduct

sādhanā: Spiritual perseverance and intense penance and austerity including the highest level of meditation, contemplations, control of senses and mind, self-restraint, equanimity, self-efforts and self-initiatives and likes

sādhu (*sāhu* in Ardhamāgadhī): Monks – ascetics (generally refers to male)

sādhvī: Female ascetic or nun

sādhya: Ultimate objective

śakti: Vigor or power

sallekhanā or *samthāra*: Accepting death while in a state of spiritual awareness and in the meditative state

sallekhanā-vrata: Taking the vow to discard the body following the spiritually inspired art of dying

samābhirūḍha-naya: The etymological view

samādhi: State of deep meditation

sāmarthya: Capacity

samatā: Equanimous

samatā-yoga: *Yoga* of equanimity

sāmayika: A form of meditation to facilitate unification with one's own soul and experiencing its purified state. It involves developing a state of undisturbed calmness while engaging in spiritual activities free of passions, desires, likes, and dislikes

saṁgraha: Collection

saṁgraha-naya: The group (class) or collective view

saṁjvalana: Momentary

saṁrakṣaṇānubandhī: Thirst for preservation

saṁsthāna-vicaya: Focusing on the soul attached to the physical

saṁthārā or *sallekhanā*: Accepting death while in a state of spiritual awareness and in the meditative state

samūha: Group or collection

saṁvara: Complete cessation of the influx of *karma* towards the soul

saṁvatsarī-paryuṣaṇā: Last day of Paryuṣaṇā festival

sāṁvatsarika pratikramaṇa: Remorsefully repenting every year on the Saṁvatsari day – the last day during Paryuṣaṇā Mahāparva (the supreme festival), for all the misdeeds committed during the previous year

samyag: Right (also: correct, true, or real)

samyag-cāritra: Right conduct or character

samyag-darśana: Right perception

samyag-dṛṣṭi: Right or enlightened vision

samyag-jñāna: Right knowledge – correct understanding of what is right and what is wrong, what is worth practicing and what is not, for the purification of soul

samyag-mārga: Right or correct (enlightened) path

samyak: Original phonetic permutation (non-*sandhi* form) of *samyag*

samyaktva: Right faith enlightenment

saṁyama: Self-restraint

sarvajña: Omniscient

saśalya-maraṇa: Death with unworthy thoughts

sattā: Undertakings

satya: Truthfulness or that which is truthful

śauca: Contentment (one of the *dasa-dharma*)

savicāra: Transitory considerations involving mind and thoughts

śarīra: Body

śubha-yoga: Auspicious activities

siddha: Supreme liberated soul – the state of one who has achieved omniscience and left their body to attain the ultimate liberation

snātaka-nirgrantha: Eminent mendicant

śrāvaka: Male householder

śrāvikā: Female householder

śruta-pañcamī: A festival celebrating every year to mark the completion of the scripture and also to inspire the householders towards their own studies

śruta-jñāna: Scriptural knowledge

stavana: Praiseful rendition

sthāpanā-nikṣepa: Contemplation of an entity with due consideration to its name and form while ignoring its characteristics

sthāvara jīva: Living beings with a single sense

sthiti bandha: Duration of bondage or predicament of fruition

stuti: Prayer

sukha: Bliss

sukhāsana: Comfortable-seated pose

sūkṣma: Subtle

susthiratā: Unwavering, single-pointed

sva-prakāśya: Self-realization

sūtra: Essence of a scripture

svarūpa: Fundamental or inherent spiritual nature

syād or *syāt*: "May be" or "in some respect"

tapas or tapasyā or tapa: Penance

tattva: The fundamental truth

tattva-rūpavatī dhāraṇā: Concentration on the true form of the spiritual body

tīrtha: A religious sanctuary where *sādhu*, *sādhvī*, *śrāvikā*, and *śrāvaka* all come together in a spiritual communion

tīrthaṅkara: The preceptors, "ford-makers," saviors, and spiritual teachers of the righteous path, who have absolutely and completely conquered all personal deficiencies such as attachment, hatred, anger, ego, deceit, and greed. They are the possessors-purveyors of the ultimate wisdom and are devoid of all attachments

tyāga: Renunciation

ubhaya: That which is both fixed-real and unfixed-unreal

upabhoga/paribhoga parimāṇa: Vow of limited consumption

upadeśa: Lectures or sermons

upādhyāya (*uvajjhāya* in Ardhamāgadhī): Learned mendicants of spiritual knowledg who have become teachers of a mendicant clan

upāsaka daśāṅga: Five deficiencies

upayoga: Usefulness, and in the context of the soul, *upayoga* means "conscientious usefulness" involving the soul's inclination towards knowledge (*jñāna*) and perception (*darśana*)

utkaṭikāsana: Chair pose

utsarga: Dismissing

vandanā: Veneration

vandanaka: Respecting and saluting ascetics (Jain *ācārya*s, *upādhyāya*s, and *sādhu*s) who, in absence of *tīrthaṅkara*s, are the true teachers providing guidance to the path of liberation

vāruṇī dhāraṇā: Concentration on the water energy

vaśāt mṛtyu: Death while being controlled by senses

vāyuvī dhāraṇā: Concentration on the wind energy

vedanīya-karma: Physical-experience-causing *karma*

vijñāna: Science

Vinayavāda: Doctrine which does not accept the scriptures but upholds the supremacy of reverence as a supreme virtue leading to perfection

vipāka-vicaya: Concentration on relinquishing expectations and fruitions

vipula-maraṇa: Self-inflicted death

vīrāsana: Hero's pose

vīrya: Vigor

viṣāda: Sadness and dejection

viśiṣṭa sādhanā: Specific spiritual practices consisting of rigorous penance, austerity, meditation

vitarka: Revelations

viveka: Comprehensive and honorable consideration

vrata: Vow

vr̥tti: Vacillations

vr̥tti-saṁkṣaya-yoga: *Yoga* of ending spiritually hindering tendencies

vyartha kalpanā: Useless and unnecessary web of negativity

vyavahāra-naya: The practical or empirical view

vyuparata: Desisted

yathārtha: That which is fixed and real

yoga-saṁgraha: Collection of *yoga* principles

yogaś-cittā-vr̥tti-nirodhaḥ: *Yoga* is the obstruction of mental deviation

yujjate iti yogaḥ: *Yoga* unites one with divinity

Bibliography

Dundas, Paul. 1992. *The Jains*. New York: Routledge.

Jain, K.C. 2010. *History of Jainism*. 3 vols. New Delhi: D.K. Printworld.

Jaini, S. Padmanabh. 2000. *Collected Papers on Jaina Studies*. Delhi: Motilal Banarsidass.

———, 1979. *The Jaina Path of Purification*. Delhi: Motilal Banarsidass.

Jindal, K.B. 1988. *An Epitome of Jainism*. Delhi: Munshiram Manoharlal.

Lalwani, Kastur Chand. tr. and notes. 1979. *The Kalpasutra*. Delhi: Motilal Banarsidass.

Long, Jeffery D. 2009. *Jainism: An Introduction*. New York: I.B. Tauris.

Mookerjee, Satkari. 1944. *The Jaina Philosophy of Non-Absolutism*. Delhi: Motilal Banarsidass.

Olle Quamstrom, tr. 2002. *The Yogaśāstra of Hemacandra: A Twelfth-Century Handbook on Śvetāmbara Jainism*. Harvard: Harvard University Press.

Roy, Ashim Kumar. 1984. *A History of the Jains*. New Delhi: Gitanjali Publishing House.

Sadhana, Sadhvi. 2005. *The Universe of Acharya Sushil Kumar*. New Delhi: Munshiram Manoharlal.

Sadhvies Kripa-Nidhi. 2006. *Karma Sahiṁtā*. New Delhi: Maitri Charitable Foundation.

Sethia, Tara, ed., 2004. *Ahiṁsā, Anekānta, and Jainism*. Delhi: Motilal Banarsidass.

Sumanta Bhadra, Muni. 1974. *Vishwachetna ke Vishasvi Sant: Muni Sushil Kumar*. New Delhi: Ahiṁsā Prakashan.

Sushil Kumar, Ācārya. 1958. *Jain Dharma*. New Delhi, Vishwa Ahimsa Sangha.

Tatia, Nathmal, tr. 1994. *That Which Is*. San Francisco: The Institute of Jainology and HarperCollins.

Thomas, Edward. 1877. *The Early Faith of Asoka*. London: Trübner and Company.

Wiley, Kristi L. 2009. *The A to Z of Jainism*. Toronto: Scarecrow Press.

Index

About the Author

Parveen Jain, PhD, a resident of San Jose in the Silicon Valley, is a longtime leader in the vibrant Jain and Hindu communities in the San Francisco Bay Area and throughout the United States. He has been deeply involved with the growth of Siddhachalam in New Jersey, the first Jain *tīrtha* outside of India, and was also instrumental in building the Jain Bhawan – the Jain Temple and Community Center of the Jain Center of Northern California, based in the heart of Silicon Valley. As a prolific entrepreneur and as a leader in numerous Silicon Valley tech companies, he has several patents, has published professional reports and papers, and has received awards for his philanthropic and professional endeavors.

After an exciting career in various technology companies as a founder and at executive levels, Parveen retired from the active corporate life in February 2014. And now, he spends time joyously with his grandkids, and in philanthropic activities, self-studies and writing, and mentoring bright entrepreneurs. Some of his writings on day-to-day applications of Jain philosophy are available at www.parveenjain.com/blog.

Parveen is very passionate about his philanthropic work, and has served on multiple non-profit organizations including International Mahavira Jain Mission (IMJM) – Siddhachalam (as Trustee), Jain Center of Northern California (as Chairman and President and other roles), American Foundation for the Blind (as Trustee), Stanford Center for Asian Health Research and Education – Stanford-CARE (as Founding Director), South Asian Heart Center, Sunnyvale Hindu Temple and Community Center (as Founding Director), and other health, education and religious organizations.

Parveen feels immense gratification for the opportunities to serve in founding and leadership capacities at Siddhachalam and Jain Center of Northern California.

Parveen is most passionate about carrying on the initiatives inspired by Ācārya Sushil Kumar in the service of Jain Dharma and promoting the message of non-violence; creating educational platforms for the dissemination of dhārmic doctrines, especially the Jain doctrine; and applying Jain principles and scriptures to everyday practice for the growing global Jain community and beyond, for current and future generations.

Visit: www.parveenjain.com

Scholar Reviews

In the eminently readable summary of Jain thought and practice, Parveen captures the essentials: history, philosophy, and key terminology. The pursuit of nonviolence is the highest of human endeavors: this book explains why life must be protected, and illuminates the ways to accomplish this goal, individually and as a society. For a practicing Jain, this book *[An Introduction to Jain Philosophy]* provides foundational resources for inspiration. For someone new to the tradition, this book provides a highly useful overview.

— **Christopher Key Chapple,** PhD, is Doshi Professor of Indic and Comparative Theology, and Director, Master of Arts in Yoga Studies, Loyola Marymount University, Los Angeles, California.

Parveen Jain, as a seeker and writer, has presented Lord Mahāvira's philosophy to the core in his book, *An Introduction to Jain Philosophy*. It reflects Parveen Jain's dedication to the revered guru, Ācārya Sushil Kumar, and his personal spiritual journey. This clear and thorough compilation on Jain philosophy maintains the essence of its doctrines. It is a laudable effort, which shall prove as a gift for generations. Our wishes and blessings for continued progress on his spiritual journey.

— **Sadhvi Nidhi and Sadhvi Kripa,** are female monks belonging to the Jain Sharman Sangha of India.

For Jain practitioners and other spiritually inclined individuals, Parveen Jain has provided an encyclopedic storehouse of spiritual teachings. I would especially recommend this book to those individuals seeking to further their basic knowledge of Jainism, or to members of the Jain community who would like to know more about specific interpretations of Jain teachings according to the lineage of Ācārya Sushil Kumar.

For scholars, this book provides a treasure chest of fresh data for understanding one particular way that Jainism, as a religious practice, has been translated into contemporary global society.

Scholar-practitioners, as well as those who, at a minimum, are not necessarily Jains by birth but nevertheless continually seek to adopt the Jain way of life, *An Introduction to Jain Philosophy* provides inspiring Jain theological formulations we can turn to as we teach, and earnestly live, Jain principles.

— **Christopher Jain Miller,** PhD, is Bhagwan Mallinath Assistant Professor of Jainism and Yoga Studies, Loyola Marymount University, Los Angeles, California.

Parveen Jain has done a great service to the Jain tradition, and to scholars and students of Jainism, by making the teachings of Ācārya Sushil Kumar, until now accessible mostly to Hindi-speakers, available to the English-speaking world. This book will no doubt serve as an important primary source for scholars for generations to come, as well as a most useful teaching tool for instructors who wish to incorporate a Jain voice into their curriculum.

Jain's *An Introduction to Jain Philosophy*], covers an enormous range of topics, giving the reader a thorough introduction to Jain thought from the perspective of a practitioner of this tradition.

Jain Dharma [the source of *An Introduction to Jain Philosophy*] is a comprehensive overview of Jain philosophy and, with Parveen Jain's translation, it makes the subtlest, most difficult Jain concepts understandable to the average educated reader. I believe this book will become important both for scholars of Jainism and Indian philosophy as a whole, and for laypersons wishing to better understand these teachings.

— **Jeffery D. Long,** PhD, is Professor of Religious and Asian Studies, Elizabethtown College, Elizabethtown, Pennsylvania.

Parveen *Jain's An Introduction to Jain Philosophy* is a magnificent accomplishment for Jain scholarship and those interested in learning about world religions. In a careful and accessible manner, he introduces the core ideas of the Jain Dharma: from ethics and salvation, through epistemology and philosophy of language, to metaphysics. It is both historical and topically comprehensive across the main doctrines of Jain philosophy, such as ahiṃsā, anekāntavāda, nayavāda, and syādvāda. But, importantly, it also discusses Jain psychology and Jain Yoga, two areas that are often not discussed in introductions, which desperately need much more attention. Finally, it includes a summary of Jain Mantras for those that wish to practice. I found the book a pleasure to read both for the fluidity of Parveen's writing as well as the insights the book brings out. I would recommend the book as an introduction to Jain Dharma and think it is suitable as a book, alongside primary texts, for teaching introductory courses on Jainism.

— **Anand Jayprakash Vaidya,** PhD, is Professor of Philosophy, San Jose State University, San Jose, California

My overall impression is that you [Parveen Jain] have written a very valuable book. You strive everywhere to be precise and succinct, focusing on what will be of universal interest for both Jains and non-Jains. ... Particularly noteworthy is your clarity; no specialist knowledge is necessary for understanding what you've written. This is a difficult achievement.

This book has a lot to say to the situation today prevailing throughout much of the world in our internet age, where we are saturated by a great deal of information that is unaccompanied by very much true wisdom.

An Introduction to Jain Philosophy is a splendid achievement, thorough, carefully researched, and well-written. Congratulations!

— **David Pinault, PhD**, is Professor of Religious Studies, Santa Clara University, Santa Clara, California.

Made in the USA
Columbia, SC
29 November 2024

47812955R00211